Management of the Personal Selling Function

Holt, Rinehart and Winston Marketing Series

Paul E. Green, Adviser
Wharton School, University of Pennsylvania

Philip Kotler, Adviser
Northwestern University

James F. Engel, David T. Kollat, Roger D. Blackwell,
All of The Ohio State University
Consumer Behavior
Cases in Consumer Behavior
Research in Consumer Behavior

Ronald R. Gist,
University of Denver
Marketing and Society: A Conceptual Introduction
Readings: Marketing and Society

Charles S. Goodman,
University of Pennsylvania
Management of the Personal Selling Function

Philip Kotler,
Northwestern University
Marketing Decision Making: A Model-Building Approach

John C. Narver, University of Washington
Ronald Savitt, National Economic Research Associates
The Marketing Economy: An Analytical Approach
Conceptual Readings in the Marketing Economy

Thomas R. Wotruba,
San Diego State College
Sales Management: Planning, Accomplishment, and Evaluation

Thomas R. Wotruba, San Diego State College
Robert M. Olsen, California State College, Fullerton
Sales Management: Concepts and Viewpoints

Management of the Personal Selling Function

CHARLES S. GOODMAN
UNIVERSITY OF PENNSYLVANIA
WHARTON SCHOOL OF FINANCE AND COMMERCE

HOLT, RINEHART AND WINSTON, INC.

New York   Chicago   San Francisco   Atlanta
Dallas   Montreal   Toronto   London   Sydney

Editors' Foreword

The Advisory Editors of the Holt, Rinehart and Winston Marketing Series take pleasure in presenting this modern text on managing the personal selling function. Professor Goodman writes with deft and mature knowledge of this field and of the relevance of newer concepts—interactive communication processes, management science models and marketing intelligence techniques—for coping with many of the marketing manager's administrative problems.

All of the principal functions of field sales management—definition of selling task, recruitment and selection, training, compensation, evaluation, sales effort allocation—are covered in a systematic and balanced fashion that reflects the broad experience of the author. The newer management tools are presented as following *from* problem formulation, not as techniques looking for a problem to solve. A particular noteworthy feature of the book is the emphasis placed on the management of marketing information as well as the management of sales personnel. Professor Goodman describes this increasingly important part of the administrative process and what it portends for the role of personal selling in the future.

DECEMBER 1970

—Paul F. Green
—Philip Kotler

Preface

The shift of the American economy from a production to a market orientation, although widely talked about, has, in fact, barely begun. To be sure, many study the consumer carefully to determine his preferences and attitudes. Yet the general tendency is to consider the consumer as a target of the producer's effort rather than as the central director of an economy directed to satisfying his wants.

As the marketing system moves toward becoming a true logistic support and message transmittal system for consumers, many established practices and operating procedures will need to be rethought and reoriented.

The field of sales force management is not immune to these pressures. The role of personal selling in a consumeristic economy is not well defined, let alone understood.

This book focuses on the problems of sales managers, with particular concern for problems likely to be critical in a consumerlstic society. In the treatment of each problem area, the nature of the problems which confront the sales manager is examined. Thereafter the types of tools which may be useful for resolving those problems are reviewed. The emphasis is on questions to which the sales manager must address himself, premises which often underlie sales management practices, and concepts which the sales manager may find useful in thinking about his problems.

This book does not attempt to provide answers to the many problems which the sales manager must resolve in his daily work. In a world of rapid change, both the problems themselves and the environment in which they are set are subject to continuing and often drastic change. As any alert manager knows, simplistic answers can have little meaning in an environment in which new situations and new problems continually occur.

The author hopes that the reader will find new perspectives and insights into the ways in which personal selling can and must serve a consumeristic economy and into an understanding of the means of effective sales management.

Part I deals with the problems of defining the sales task in a particular selling environment. This includes describing personal selling as an interactive process. The next subjects are the managerial jobs of determining the specific roles of salesmen, and the tasks which they should perform. Thereafter, criteria are suggested for allocating effort. Defining territories completes this section.

Part II deals with the problem of securing a sales force and establishing and maintaining its competence to carry out its work.

Following discussion of the problems of recruiting and selecting a sales force, problems of initial training are examined. Then in Chapter 8 a problem likely to increase vastly in import in the 1970s — maintaining the competence of the salesman in a changing world — is examined. The final chapter in this part deals with another problem which is becoming a more significant part of sales-force operations — the development of the sales organization as an intelligence system trained to perceive and evaluate changes and other significant events.

Part III deals with operating problems. First it examines the activities necessary to support the salesman in the field. Then the problems of overall direction — routing, establishing and administering performance standards, and providing a feedback system — are treated. Following this is a discussion of a problem of special concern to the operating manager in the field — the direction and motivation of sales personnel to secure professional growth. The two final chapters in this section deal with the evaluation of individual performance and compensation.

The final chapter suggests the prospective role of the sales force in the future society.

I am indebted to so many of my colleagues that at times I feel more like an editor than an author. Norman Fuss (now with Cresap, McCormick, and Paget) contributed ideas to several of the chapters. He is co-author of Chapter 8. Yoram Wind of the University of Pennsylvania, Frank Eby of Villanova University, and Robert Olsen of California State College at Fullerton each reviewed a number of chapters and made many helpful suggestions. My colleagues, Reavis Cox, F. E. Brown, Scott Armstrong, and Len Lodish, all of the Wharton School, University of Pennsylvania, and my former colleague, James M. Alexander (now with the Lacy Sales Institute), made many valuable suggestions at individual points. Professors Paul E. Green and Philip Kotler, Advisory Editors of the Holt, Rinehart and Winston Marketing Series provided both encouragement and helpful criticism of early drafts.

My wife, Dorothy, and my daughter, Carol Suzanne, contributed to making the manuscript more readable. My secretary Berniece Jordan, Anna Mae Busch and her staff at the Wharton Duplicating Service, and Mrs. Doris Sklaroff deserve credit for their diligence in translating my scrawls into a readable manuscript.

DECEMBER 1970   C. S. G.
PHILADELPHIA, PA.

Contents

Management of the Personal Selling Function

1 The Personal Selling Function and Its Management

The personal selling function is only one of the many elements that make up a firm's "marketing mix." An understanding of the personal selling process within the marketing framework as a whole is a necessary prerequisite to good field sales management. In modern societies an understanding of how the personal selling function fits in with all the other elements which comprise the marketing system gives the manager a valuable perspective. Comprehension of the changing nature of personal selling gives the manager a better grasp of what his salesmen are trying to do, what problems they are likely to encounter, and what tools they will need to perform their jobs effectively. In this chapter we shall examine these areas.

THE MARKETING FUNCTION IN A MARKET-DIRECTED ECONOMY

One popular view of the marketing process, the *product disposal* approach, sees marketing as a system by which producers dispose of their wares. Accordingly, the task of marketing management is to dispose of goods as expeditiously and as cheaply as possible. It is for others to determine what is to be produced; marketing's job is merely to dispose of these goods and services. Consumer wants, tastes, and preferences are assumed to be known by producers and are expected to be unchanging unless manipulated by them. Therefore, the task of marketing management is no more than the application of economic tools (for example, marginal analysis) to allocate means (for example, marketing budgets) in order to achieve the given ends, (for example, profit maximization) most economically.

This view of the marketing and economic processes reflects the posture of "producer sovereignty" which characterized the first century of the industrial revolution. Rather than being conceived of as groups whose ends ought to define and direct the production process, consumers were viewed as markets whose function was to take the output of factories. While allegedly effective in authoritarian economies, the product disposal approach to marketing ceases to be viable when those following it must compete with organizations oriented towards customer needs and desires.[1]

While essentially a nineteenth century view of the marketing and economic processes, the product disposal view of marketing is still prevalent in many firms and is expressed in such ways as "Marketing must grow in importance because we must find ways to sell the increased output of our factories" and "It's up to the sales organization to keep sales up on a year round basis so that we can keep the factory going."

A second view of the marketing process may be termed the *target* approach. It focuses on the consumer, whom it views as a target who must be reached in the most effective manner. Like the product disposal approach, this view of the market is production oriented. Producers or a government elite allegedly know what is best for consumers.[2] The task of marketing is to con them into casting their votes in the market place or the polling place for those things which the producers or government elite have, in their infinite wisdom, determined to be best. The various social disciplines are employed to identify and hit the target most effectively. As in the product disposal approach, consumers are "fair game" for the marketer. Consumers are passive pawns in the system; they do not determine the direction of production or resource use.

Despite lip service paid to consumer orientation approaches,

[1] See Shanti S. Tangri, (ed.), *Command Versus Demand: Systems for Economic Growth* (Boston: D. C. Heath and Company, 1967).

[2] See J. K. Galbraith, *The Affluent Society* (Boston: Houghton Mifflin Company, 1958) for an example of the neo-Tory view that a self-constituted elite should prescribe ends for consumers.

many businessmen, technicians, and officeholders subscribe to the target view of the marketing process. Much effort is expended in order to achive an understanding of the consumer or voter so that the seller or office seeker can identify the best way of reaching and manipulating him.

A more modern view of the marketing function derives from the premise that the role of the economic system is to serve the consumer rather than the reverse. This *consumer support* view holds that the role of marketing is to determine the needs and wants of consumers and to direct economic effort to serve these needs and wants. The consumer is viewed as the central controller in the market place—central not because he is a target but because the economic process is to be end directed (that is, to best serve consumers) rather than input directed (that is, to best serve producers). Because consumers have multiple and frequently changing objectives, such a market system tends to expand the variety of goods from which consumers may choose and the variety of ancillary services which accompany these goods.

In an end-directed economic system profit functions (since it is not a system goal but, rather, a system lubricant) in much the same way as Adam Smith envisaged self-love at the individual entrepreneurial level as providing an invisible hand at the system level. At the level of the firm the drive for profits serves both as an incentive to provide offerings which will better fit the needs of one or more market segments and also as a constraint which restricts the feasible set of alternatives.

In the consumer-support view, the economy is a vast series of consumer support systems. Marketing occupies a central role in determining what is required to satisfy consumer wants and how products and services should be changed in order to better serve the needs of various consumer groups. It is not enough merely to "consider the consumer" or to explain that courses of action chosen for other reasons are really in the consumer interest. The very heart of the consumer-support approach requires that the entire managerial process be consumer oriented.

Even though allegedly a recent discovery by some producers and government officials, the idea of consumer orientation is not new to marketing. Successful retailers have long accepted the idea of consumer sovereignty which was well expressed by one of them when he said that the retailer's job was to "give the lady what she wants"; accordingly retailers base their buying on a determination of what will sell. Similarly, leading manufacturers over the past three decades have increasingly adopted the view that the design of products should be dictated by the job the products are to perform for users; hence products can neither be developed nor improved *until the conditions of use are well defined and understood.* Only then can the engineer have a basis for knowing what attributes are needed in the product he is to design. The high rate of failure of new and so-called "improved" products attests both to the difficulty of determining precisely what is best for a specified need and to the fact that some firms still operate on the premise that they can determine unilaterally what the user *should* want without specific knowledge of the problems the consumer is really trying to solve and his preferences in solving them.

There has been considerably less acceptance of the idea that consumer sovereignty applies to the attributes and quality of the services as well as to the goods provided by the supply system. Indeed, many changes in marketing institutions reflect the failure of established institutions to do what their own managers say they should and thus keep the service mix in tune with changed consumer needs. Downtown department stores in the 1940s and early 1950s in effect tried to force consumers to shop at times and places the merchants found convenient and to choose from stocks selected according to the merchants' ideas as to what constituted "good" assortments. New and more perceptive merchants found important opportunities for growth in a return to the principle that times, locations, and assortments should match the consumers' style of living. Even today, the persistence of merchants oriented around types of goods rather than around the types of situations which bring customers into the market suggests that retailing as a whole faces further change. The rule still holds—retailing, like all marketing, must organize itself as a consumer-support system if it is to flourish, or even to survive.

It must be emphasized that consumer needs and wants cover not merely the physical product itself but the full service of supply that accompanies the physical product. Moreover, in many, perhaps in most, situations, consumers have available to them more effective remedies against deficiencies in a particular supply system's services than they do against deficiencies in its products. This is due to the relative ease of entry into retailing and because modifications of the service mix can be made by individual operators even within a general type of operation. Thus, even when buying products which are themselves fairly standardized (for example, tires, lamps, dairy products) the consumer may choose among suppliers with 1) differing assortments; 2) differing hours of operation; 3) various credit, delivery, or repair arrangements; and 4) different levels of assurance that the product will perform to the buyer's satisfaction, as well as being able to choose personnel with diverse advising capabilities who at the same time display varying attitudes toward customers. Generally, sellers can tailor the service provided to the customer to the individual consumer's wishes more readily than products can be so tailored. The development and growth of many types of small retail businesses at the same time that other retailers in what are essentially the same kinds of business are dropping out attests to the power of the consumer in shaping the service package which he will receive.

It follows that the *sine qua non* of effective marketing management must be the development of full supply-support systems most suitable to the consumers and industries being supported. Marketing, and therefore selling, must start not with, "What do I want to sell and how do I want to sell it?" but with such questions as "What kinds of problems do consumers have?" "How do they proceed to solve them?" "How can I devise and offer to consumers better ways of solving these problems?" and "Are there unrecognized problems?"

A consumer orientation requires more than that the consumer be recognized as the rightful director of the economic process. It also requires full recognition of the fact that consumers are in fact numerous and heterogeneous. "*The* consumer" is a convenient fiction. While the manager may properly group industrial and household consumers into market segments for many purposes, he must not forget that such groupings are essentially convenient clusters of heterogeneous users whose problems, while similar, are not identical. Even a large supermarket is unlikely to have two customers whose weekly food shopping needs are identical in all respects. In fact, it seems quite unlikely that many shoppers will purchase two identical weekly market baskets during their lifetimes.

The marketing system is responsible for matching the diverse heterogeneous needs of users with the tremendous variety of products which a modern economy makes possible. As automation continues to free the production system from the early twentieth century bonds of mass-produced identical products, the practice of adapting products and services to the diverse problems of users will surely grow. In some industries systems are well developed which can produce an almost infinite variety of end products from components that either are standardized or can be altered automatically at little cost. For example, the number of factory options concerning such matters as automotive body colors, models, transmissions, power steering, brakes, windows, and accessories offered to the automobile buyer are so great that Ford or General Motors could go through an entire year's output without producing a duplicate automobile.

But the ability of the productive machine to give each user more nearly optimal solutions to his problems will go for naught unless the communication system—that is, the marketing system—can provide producers with guidance on consumer problems and consumers with information on what is available.

Heterogeneity is not limited to users' wants or problems. It exists also in the information which users need as they search for solutions to their problems and in consumers' ability to perceive needs and integrate information into their patterns of action. The marketing system is largely concerned with the gathering and the dissemination of such information.

Marketing management must establish and operate a firm's part of the marketing system. The growth of heterogeneity is reshaping the role which personal selling must play if marketing management is to do its job well.

THE SALES FORCE AND THE MARKETING MIX

The marketing mix is conventionally considered either as a mix of inputs of different marketing activities or, more commonly, as a mix of dollars spent for various marketing activities.

Marketing mix refers to the amounts and kinds of marketing variables the firm is using at a particular time.[3] The emphasis on a mix of *input* dollars springs from its economic antecedent, the production function, and suggests that by substituting dollars spent on one function for dollars spent on another, the same result may be obtained at lower cost or that a greater result may be attained at the same cost. The various inputs are taken to be interchangeable. That is, although inputs may differ in their effects per unit of input, they all have a common output, usually considered to be sales.

The conventional approach to a marketing mix suggests that the same kind of result is created by inputs of different forms. By thus ignoring the nature of the *outputs* of various elements of the marketing mix (that is, the utilities created) one can phrase marketing-mix questions in relatively simple terms, such as "How much for advertising?", "How much for personal selling?", and "How much for product improvement?" Basically this is a producer's or input view of the marketing process. It lacks the consumer orientation that a supply-support view requires.

A more meaningful perspective can be provided by viewing the marketing mix as a set of outputs, preferably in terms of utilities provided to the prospective buyer who has problems to solve. From such a persepctive, interest can center not on how many dollars are required for the sales force, nor on how many salesmen, nor on how many sales calls are needed, but more cogently on, "How much and what kinds of information should be supplied to the buyer to assist him in his search for better solutions to his problems?" or "How

[3] Philip Kotler, *Marketing Management: Analysis, Planning and Control* (Englewood Cliffs, N.J.: Prentice-Hall, Inc., 1967), p. 266.

closely should this information be tailored to his problems?" The means for providing these outputs can then be considered in terms of their cost and effectiveness. In such a context personal selling and advertising, for example, may not be substituted for one another for the simple reason that they may provide different kinds of utilities to prospective buyers.

The output of personal selling is different in type from the output of nonpersonal communications media. Nonpersonal media must for the most part rely on common elements in the informational needs of the intended receivers. Personal selling on the other hand can concern itself with finding ways in which the objectives of the selling and buying organizations complement each other. Thus the seller can detect and appeal to the particular needs of each prospect. Personal selling and nonpersonal communication thus may perform different functions for the buyer in the same way that product modifications and the furnishing of information perform different functions.

Furthermore, the forte of personal selling is its ability to do what other communications media cannot do—specifically, to provide "a dynamically evolving two-way communicative link between selling and buying systems."[4] Where such relationships are called for, a role for personal selling exists.

What this role will be and how much selling contact is appropriate will depend on the specific nature of the communicative relationship needed. Even in marketing situations where some tasks are best performed by the salesman, other communications tasks can be performed by use of mass media, catalogs, mailings, and so on. The place of personal selling in the mix is thus quite specifically a matter of what needs to be done to create and nurture a mutually beneficial community of interest between a supplier and a user. The salesman is rarely needed for all contacts. Moreover, it is uneconomical to use salesmen to perform communications work that can be performed at less cost by other means. Hence, an important problem in sales management is to determine as precisely as possible those tasks which require the flexibility of the two-way communications system which the sales force provides.

Buyers are likely to find the personal salesman essential where they depend on joint development with suppliers of solutions to their problems. In a world of constant technological change, such interdependence is growing. Buyers are also likely to use the personal salesman to broaden their own search for ways to solve problems. Even if mass media are drawn upon for leads, the salesman may be needed

[4] Patrick J. Robinson and Bent Stidsen, *Personal Selling in a Modern Perspective* (Boston: Allyn and Bacon, Inc., 1967), p. 260.

to transform a general idea into a specific solution—for example, to advise the buyer as to which model or type is best for his application.

From the seller's viewpoint, a need for flexibility in communication that calls for some measure of personal sales activity is likely to arise wherever each buyer's goals and problems are likely to be sufficiently different so as to prevent general solutions optimal to every buyer. Personal selling may also be needed to provide a dis-routinizing influence in situations where buyers are economically, legally, or psycholgically committed to existing solutions to their problems—that is, to traditional methods and patterns as to existing suppliers. Personal selling may serve well where buyers must be induced to extend their search patterns beyond those previously employed.

In summary, it may be observed that the role of the personal salesman in the marketing mix is not so much a question of "How much personal selling should be used?" or of "How much in the way of resources should be devoted to personal selling?" as one of "For what purposes?" Personal selling should rest on a prior understanding of the kinds of relationships which need to be established between buying and supplying organizations. Methods of translating this into plans for sales activity are dealt with more fully in a later chapter.

THE ROLE OF PERSONAL SELLING IN A MARKET DIRECTED ECONOMY

A century ago buyers obtained nearly all the information they had about products and producers from personal contact. Word-of-mouth from family and friends provided the basic notions. Additional information came from shopkeepers, clerks, and salesmen who called upon prospective customers, but these were often concerned only with immediate sales. Thus, the temptation was great to develop and employ a stock "line" without special concern for long-term buyer interest. The public image of the salesman still reflects the role he performed in that era.

Today much information is provided by mass media, which can deliver messages at a small fraction of the cost of doing so through individual human contact. With information and persuasion transmitted in this fashion many transactions can be closed through self-service or automated procedures. Why then the salesman?

The answer to this qestion is complex. The job of the salesman of the nineteenth century has, in fact, largely been taken over by mass media and nonpersonal retailing. The number of hucksters and peddlers reported by the Census of Occupations declined by more than two-thirds between 1900 and 1950. The well-trained salesman with the "canned" sales presentation, upon whom John Patterson built the National Cash Register Company, is largely obsolete.

Yet the number of persons engaged in various types of selling has increased more rapidly than the labor force as a whole. The proportion of the workforce engaged in selling (including retail clerks) increased from 4.5 percent in 1900 to 6.8 percent in 1950. Since 1950, the displacement of retail clerks by self-service has reduced the total proportion of the workforce classified as salesmen. Outside of retail stores, the number of salemen continues to grow. Between 1950 and 1960, while the total experienced civilian labor force increased 14.8 percent, the number of wholesaler salesmen increased 22 percent and the number of manufacturer salesmen increased 42 percent. Perhaps more importantly, the economic and social status of able sales personnel has risen rapidly, as increasing proportions of them devote their efforts to sales to industrial buyers and other businesses. It is evident that personal selling continues to play an important role. The reasons for this importance will become even more evident when the intercommunicative process which we call personal selling is examined in the next chapter.

Although personal selling is pervasive in the economy, its role in the overall marketing process varies from industry to industry and from buying situation to buying situation. These differences spring not so much from differences in the characteristics of the goods being marketed as from differences in the characteristics of the communications problems involved—specifically, in information problems with which buyers and prospective buyers are faced.

Personal Selling as a Communicative Process

The term selling conjures up a vision of persuasive communications. Yet this is perhaps its least significant function in modern markets, because it is precisely in this area that nonpersonal methods are applicable and often less costly. One should not conclude that persuasion plays no part in personal selling; in fact, it plays a very important part. What needs to be pointed out is that persuasion per se, or even persuasion plus the transmittal of information, does not automatically necessitate the use of personal selling. If a unidirectional transmission of information is all that the situation calls for, there is no need to have the drummer of yesteryear deliver the message. In this case, broadcast media (for example, magazines, newspapers, radio, television, outdoor advertising) are almost certain to be more economical per message delivered.

Personal selling becomes relevant when the communication activity can be performed better as a two-way process. In other words, when information can be communicated more effectively if it is subject to modification during the transmission process in response to the development of information about the individual receiver and his needs, personal selling works better than broadcast (that is, one-way) media. The salesman then provides what we may call a responsive instrument for the transmittal of information and persuasion.

Rapid technological change in both using and supplying industries and the increasing complexity and specialization of products tend to increase both the total amount of communication needed and, in turn, the need for bi-directional (personal) communicative activities as well.

Personal Selling as a Tailoring Process

Personal selling also provides the means by which the offerings of sellers can be adjusted to the problems of users. The salesman does this by identifying, clarifying, and pinpointing the often ill-defined problem of the buyer. Then he presents the solution to these problems by recommending the appropriate item from the seller's line of goods.

When complex industrial goods are involved, tailoring may require extensive technical training on the part of the seller's representatives. Narrowing the prospective customer's general problem into a specific one may take several months. It may be necessary to bring in specialists who can propose solutions that will serve the prospect's needs and at the same time provide a profit for the seller.

A good retail sales clerk performs a similar function in helping the customer define his need and suggesting how it may best be met. An able clerk need not limit his suggested solutions to merchandise on hand but may suggest that merchandise be ordered specially, or that some other store or department may have the solution, or even that the customer can solve his problem by purchasing something entirely different than originally intended or perhaps even nothing at all.

The increased variety of goods offered in the marketplace and further variations which automation promises to provide, suggest that tailoring in the future will become an increasingly significant part of the personal selling process. In the advanced economies, if the problem solver has not yet replaced the drummer, he is rapidly doing so.

Personal Selling a Source of Intelligence

Personal selling has another very important but less conspicuous role in directing the productive forces in the economy toward meeting the needs of users. As the group within the marketing organization which has greatest direct contact with the problems and wants of both customers and noncustomers, the sales force usually is a vital part of the seller's system of intelligence about the marketplace.

Despite the growth of formal market research in the past thirty years, most companies depend upon the sales force to tell them much of what they know about the needs and wants of customers or prospects and about many of the environmental factors with which the marketing manager is concerned. For the small firm, the sales force may be the sole source of market information. For other firms when the collection of information by more formal methods is either not feasible or not economical, the sales force may be the only source for some types of information.

THE NATURE OF SALES FORCE MANAGEMENT

Management of the personal selling *function* involves three areas of activity:

defining the sales task,
providing the sales force,
operating the field sales organization.

Each of these activities is carried out in an ever-changing environment. Management must, consequently, always be in the process of adjusting the sales force to ongoing change.

The executive charged with managing the sales force is always responsible for these areas. In addition, he may perform a number of other duties growing out of his relationships to other marketing and nonmarketing activities of the firm. This book examines each of the major areas and the tools by which the sales manager can identify his problems, obtain any information he needs in order to solve them, and achieve his solutions.

The Application of Management Science Methods to Sales Force Problems

It is sometimes said that marketing problems are not subject to treatment by scientific methods because they deal with unpredictable humans rather than with predictable inanimate objects. This argument is emphasized particularly in the area of personal selling, because personal factors affect both sides of the activity—the salesman and the prospective buyer. Scientific method is not, however, a phenomenon that resides in the subject matter under investigation. It is rather a property of the means of investigation themselves. The fact that human behavior is more difficult to understand and predict than that of chemical or physical elements does not completely preclude the application of scientific, as opposed to intuitive, methods of determining causal or associative relationships. It is possible in the social sciences to formulate hypotheses, test their validity by experimental or non-experimental research designs (for example, observation, surveys), and infer results. As there is commonly a very large number of factors affecting an observed result in personal selling, more sophisticated research designs and analytical procedures may be required than in some other fields.[5] However, the very multiplicity of factors makes the need for careful testing of hypotheses more compelling. It also makes the all-too-common practice of theorizing about relationships from hunches or intuitive feelings based on unstructured "experience" so much the more hazardous.

In the chapters which follow the reader will encounter some examples of the application of controlled observation and experimental techniques to detect cause-effect relationships in the areas of selling and sales force management. He should be cautioned at the outset, however, that our study of "hard" knowledge about the personal selling process is only in its infancy. Thus the methods of salesforce management—which should follow from the functions performed by personal selling—are necessarily based on analysis of selling operations as they have existed. As our knowledge of the customer problem-solving process and the sales process grows, it should be possible to apply more objective techniques in evaluating many of the alternatives with which the sales manager is faced.

The Management Process

The management process involves *planning, directing,* and *controlling* the activities of people who are engaged in effort toward achieving group goals. This does not mean that the job of sales management is to somehow employ the carrot and the stick in such a way as to get salesmen to do what management wants them to do. It does mean that management must identify the goals at various organizational levels and provide the conditions which will encourage the people in the organization to direct their efforts towards achieving those goals.

The management process is diagrammed in Figure 1-1.

PLANNING

All managers plan, although sometimes the planning may be informal and intuitive: "I'd better stock up on watermelons; it looks as if a warm weekend lies ahead," or, "The West Coast is booming. We'll need three more men out there." Such seat-of-the pants planning may suffice if the evaluation of what is likely to happen is simple and

---

[5] For a succinct review of commonly applicable experimental and nonexperimental techniques see Paul E. Green and Ronald E. Frank, *A Manager's Guide to Marketing Research* (New York: John Wiley & Sons, Inc., 1967) Chapter 3 or Russell L. Ackoff, *et al., Scientific Method: Optimizing Applied Research Decisions* (New York: John Wiley & Sons, Inc., 1962), Chapter 10.

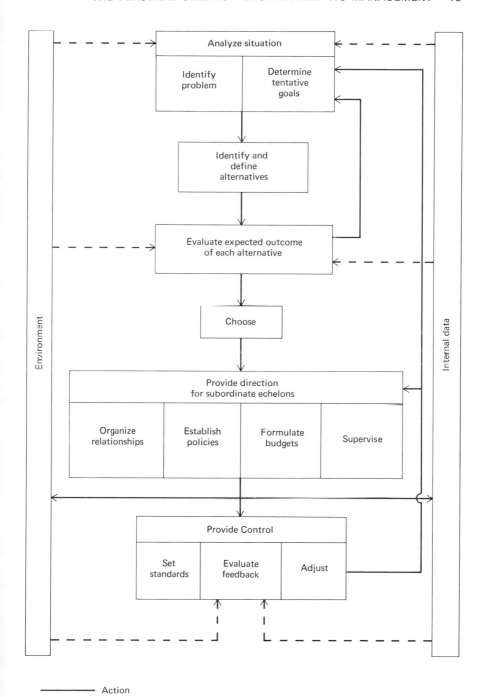

Figure 1-1
THE MANAGEMENT PROCESS

if the alternatives available to the manager are few. Where there are many possible choices or the evaluation of the probable results of any action requires careful analysis, such primitive planning is likely to be quite unsatisfactory.

As business operations become more complex, the analytical, as opposed to the operational, functions of executives become more important.[6] Careful consideration of what should be done becomes relatively more important. On the other hand, the actual carrying out of courses of action which have been decided upon becomes relatively less important, so that it may be routinized or delegated to subordinates.

Planning involves

1. situation analysis,
2. identification and definition of alternatives,
3. evaluation of expected outcomes of each alternative,
4. choice of a course of action.

Because planning is a crucial part of the sales management process, each of these activities will be examined briefly.

Situation Analysis

Situation analysis is essentially a statement of what the problem is for which a solution must be planned. In the context of salesforce management, it may follow from the overall or longer-range plans of the firm, which require the attainment of specified goals by the sales organization. Or it may involve the identification of goals which appear to be feasible in the light of the resources which the manager believes can be made available to him. The situation analysis provides the setting in which plans must be formulated. It establishes provisional goals toward which the planner must point—provisional because goals are not absolute and final. They must be flexible in order to allow for the fact that they are themselves determined by where opportunities lie. The situation analysis also determines the constraints under which plans must operate.

Situation analysis involves more than merely *stating* a problem. The problem must be *defined* with sufficient precision that alternative solutions and the information needed to evaluate them can be identified. For example, the statement "Our salesmen are ineffective," does little more than indicate a broad area in which one or more problems may lie. An operational definition requires clarification of such ques-

[6] Melville C. Branch, "Logical Analysis and Executive Performance," *Journal of the Academy of Management,* April 1961, 27–31.

tions as: "Ineffective in the performance of what activity?" (for example, scheduling calls, presenting products, servicing accounts), "Ineffective by what criteria?" (for example, sales, market share, number of accounts gained) "What kinds of actions are eligible for consideration?" (for example, retraining men, hiring new sales force, elimination of sales force in favor of some other channel, change in compensation, alteration of supervisory relationships).

Unless the problem is carefully defined in operational terms, the analyst has no basis for examining alternative solutions or their possible outcomes.[7]

Identification and Definition of Alternatives

Before the manager can decide anything he must determine what alternatives exist. This requires that all the possibilities be identified and that each alternative be carefully defined so that its scope is clearly understood. A commonly recognized danger is that managements may limit too narrowly the alternatives considered.[8] New ways to accomplish a task may be overlooked, such as contracting out an activity instead of doing it in-house or revising job assignments in the light of changed environmental conditions instead of attempting to train and motivate people to perform better the duties traditionally assigned to them.

Alternatives can be carefully evaluated only if they are clearly defined. A vaguely stated alternative is apt to lead to misunderstandings by those who seek to evaluate its likely results.

Evaluation of Expected Outcomes of Alternatives

The manager has available to him a number of tools for estimating the outcome of a given course of action. These tools provide information about the environment and about cause-effect relationships expected to prevail therein.

Expectations may be derived from analysis of previous performance within the company, observations of the outside world and the activities of others, or from experiments conducted for the purpose. Because the purpose of these tools is to provide the decision maker with information about the state of affairs and relationships, they are referred to here as sensor tools. Some of the more important ones are noted briefly at this point. Illustrations of their application will

---

[7] See Paul E. Green and Donald S. Tull, *Research for Marketing Decisions* (Englewood Cliffs, N.J.: Prentice-Hall, Inc., 1966) pp. 48–52, for the interrelationship between the decision-maker's problem formulation and definition of the analyst's or researcher's problem.

[8] The brainstorming fad of the 1950s was an attempt to deal with this pathological condition sometimes observed in established organizations.

be presented in later chapters when specific management problems are discussed.

Market research is used to obtain information about the environment in which the sales force operates. Two of its more important uses are to identify buyers and buying reasons and to determine the market potential, which provides a basis for applying sales force as well as other marketing efforts.

Informal intelligence about both opportunities and past performance is obtained from customer correspondence, complaints, service reports, trade publications, conventions, and similar sources.

Observations by executives are important to some extent in all firms, but are particularly important where more formal systems for gathering and analyzing data are lacking.

The internal reporting system of a firm tells the manager how previous initiatives have worked out. It can also serve as a means of passing data on the outside world (for example, customers' plans or reported activities by competitors) on to the relevant decision makers. Internal reporting systems in order to be useful must be so designed that the right information is passed through the various filters which exist in any communications system. Both the filtering and digesting processes must be sound. Unless it is carefully designed and operated, an internal reporting system may provide misleading rather than helpful information to the executive.[9]

A marketing audit provides "a systematic, critical, and impartial review and appraisal of the total marketing operation: of the basic objectives and policies of the operation and the assumptions which underlie them as well as of the methods, procedures, personnnel, and organization employed to implement the policies and achieve the objectives."[10] Of particular interest to the sales manager are audit findings which suggest redefining the role of the sales force or reconsidering policies of sales-force management which may no longer be in tune with the larger strategy of the company or changed needs of customer groups.

Sales analyses tell the manager how sales volume is distributed by area, territory, product, and type of customer. They commonly reveal the extent to which sales are concentrated in certain products and in certain accounts or types of accounts. Such findings raise questions about allocations of sales effort.

If allocations of effort have been proportional to potential, a

[9] Donald H. Woods, "Improving Estimates That Involve Uncertainty," *Harvard Business Review,* July–Aug. 1966, 91–98.

[10] Abe Shuchman, "The Marketing Audit, Its Nature, Purposes, and Problems," *Analyzing and Improving Marketing Performance,* A.M.A. Management Report No. 32 (New York: American Management Association, Inc., 1959), 13.

revelation by sales analysis that the results achieved differ from one area to another would suggest that the company's offerings (including the services of its sales personnel) are more acceptable in one segment than another. Such a situation calls for further investigation. Sales analyses also can detect changes in patterns of usage of the company's products and in the growth rates and buying practices of customers. Such developments are likely to call for action on the part of the sales manager.

Profitability analyses go beyond analysis of sales revenue to determine the contribution made to profit (or to overhead and profit) by different territories, customer groups, market segments, or products. By disclosing less-than-optimal application of resources (for example, expenditures for particular customers that are out of line with revenue possibilities), they can help the sales manager make a more effective use of what is under his control. For example, salesmen may be used ineffectively because they make too few calls on some customers and too many on others. Or efforts devoted to a particular group of products may be out of line with its profit potentialities.

Analyses of variances from budgets or other performance standards are among the most important feedback tools available to the sales manager. By observing how inputs and outputs differ from plans or from previously established standards, he can make appropriate adjustments in sales activities or in the plan itself, as circumstances warrant. Variances in either direction may be significant. Whether the results exceed or fall below plans, the analyst will ordinarily want to know why (for example, unexpected changes in the environment, or better results than expected per unit of input). He can then take whatever action seems appropriate.

It must be emphasized that the executive will be interested in examining variances in inputs as well as outputs. Expenditures below plan could, for example, indicate that the firm can achieve its goals with less than expected effort. More often, expenditures below plan may suggest that the company's overall planned sales activity for the period was not in fact carried out.

The information provided by the sensor tools will help the manager find out why things happened as they did. The information will help him make immediate adjustments in sales activities and will also be helpful in formulating future plans. Unfortunately, the hypotheses he derives from such analyses are rarely subjected to rigorous testing—indeed, quick, economical, accurate, and reliable testing may not be possible. Thus, under the best of circumstances the sales manager faces a substantial problem of uncertainty as to what will in fact happen if he chooses to follow a certain course of action.

In addition, the sales manager is likely to be moving on several fronts at about the same time. For example, he may be simultaneously planning a new training program, a change in hiring policy, a new routing plan, and different methods of motivation or supervision. The end effects will thus be the composite result of a combination of all of the things which he does, not the specific consequence of any one of them. Moreover, the operations of the sales force are not conducted *in vacuo.* Other elements of the marketing mix will also be undergoing change, as will virtually all of the elements of the environment, including all the variables which influence demand and the actions of channel members and sellers of competitive products and services.

Despite careful collection and analysis of data, the manager will rarely, if ever, be able to formulate precise hypotheses about causal relationships and about the future state of environmentals. He will not be able to state positively that a particular course of action will necessarily lead to a specific result. Inevitably, in choosing, he must operate in a climate of uncertainties. Although the range of uncertainty will have been reduced by the information which he has gathered and analyzed, his decision rules will still need to take account of what unknowns remain.

Choosing a Course of Action

The classical approach to choice generally assumes that (a) the inputs under any course of action and the results therefrom can both be expressed in dollar amounts, (b) the relations between these money amounts are known precisely, and (c) the objective of the one who makes the choice is in some sense to maximize the profits of the firm for which the choice is being made during the period affected by the choice. Under these conditions one can propose the profit-maximizing rule as: Continue to spend for any activity which brings in more revenue than it costs. Under the conditions of fixed or declining marginal revenue and rising marginal costs (as a consequence of the principle of diminishing returns), such a rule yields the familiar maxim: Add inputs until marginal cost equals marginal revenue. Figure 1-2 is an example of analysis of this sort. An underlying assumption is that no activities for which money can be spent other than those under consideration are taken into account.

In Figure 1-2, *TR* is the revenue-sales curve (total revenue line). In this case a constant unit price is assumed so the slope is the same at all sales volume levels. The curved line *EE* represents the amount of expenditure for a certain type of marketing effort required to attain a given sales volume, all other activities unchanged. In this hypothetical case some sales *(OA)* are obtained without any of this expenditure at all. Small expenditures are seen to produce quite large incre-

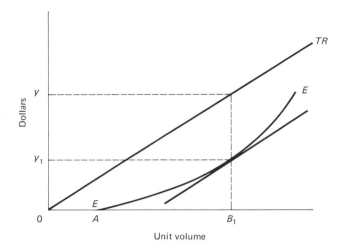

Figure 1-2
REVENUE-COST RELATIONSHIP: CONSTANT
UNIT REVENUE

ments in sales. (That is, the slope of the expenditure-sales curve is low.) As the easiest to reach and most receptive prospects are exhausted, more effort must be undertaken to attain given amounts of sales increases. Thus, the slope of the curve grows steeper. At some point, in this case at an attained volume of B_1 units, the cost required to attain the next unit of sales will just be covered by the revenues obtained therefrom. The slope of the expenditure-sales curve, *EE*, will be the same as (parallel to) the revenue-sales curve. An increase

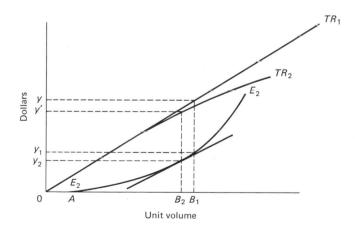

Figure 1-3
REVENUE-COST RELATIONSHIP: DECLINING UNIT
REVENUE

to any volume to the right of this point will require greater expenditure per unit of sales than the revenue that unit of sales will bring in. Hence, this is the point of maximum profit.

In Figure 1-3, the effect of lowering sales prices on larger volumes is taken into account. The lines become parallel at a lesser sales volume *(B₂)*. That is, since marginal revenues are lower than they are in Figure 1-2, revenue is overtaken by the rising costs of securing additional sales at a somewhat earlier point in the sales expansion process.

In both Figures 1-2 and 1-3, the revenue and cost curves tell us that a certain sales volume *will be* attained with a certain expenditure of effort and that this sales volume *will yield* a specific dollar revenue. In short, they assume *perfect knowledge* of the cause-effect relationships represented by the expenditure-sales curve and of the result of all of the marketing and environmental variables which have been used to arrive at the revenue-sales relation. These premises are never literally true. They may, however, be close enough for the manager to act *as if* they were true. More realistically, however, the manager will recognize that these curves are estimates in which he has varying degrees of confidence. He will look at the curves not as sharp lines but as bands. For example, instead of having a single quantity of sales which will be attained at each price, the manager may consider that a particular price would result in sales somewhere within a fairly broad range—for example, that at a price of five dollars, sales will fall between 10,000 and 20,000 units. To further refine the estimate the analyst may assign probabilities to each possible result from 10,000 to 20,000 units. That is, instead of assigning a point value to the expected result from each possible act (such as setting price at five dollars), the analyst may formulate a probability distribution about the results to be expected from a five-dollar price.

It has already been noted that hypotheses about both the environmentals and the cause-effect relationships of marketing actions are clouded with uncertainties under even the most favorable operating conditions. The manager must make his choices in this context. Decision rules premised on perfect knowledge, useful as they are as a starting point, need to be refined to allow for the fact that most of the things which he "knows" and uses as his inputs to his decision system are not hard and precise facts but are, at best, statements with greater or lesser probability of being correct. In most cases the manager has some "feel" for the margin of error in the data and hypotheses which he employs in the course of his daily work. For example, he may believe that 70 percent of a certain class of users are likely to switch to a certain product if such-and-such action is taken, but he is not sure that this will occur and acts with some restraint lest his point estimate be in error.

More formal types of decision theory suggest that the values of unknowns should be treated as random variables, even if the probabilities of occurrence are estimated subjectively by informed executives. In this way, *various* possible outcomes of a specific action can be considered. The probability of occurrence of each can be derived or, more commonly, estimated, and decision rules can be employed which take into account all of the possible outcomes rather than merely the single value which precise knowledge of the act-outcome relationship would have provided. Two of the decision rules which might be employed to choose the best act in the face of uncertainty as to outcomes may be suggested briefly.

EXPECTED MONETARY VALUE CRITERION

The expected monetary value decision rule is the closest approach under conditions of uncertainty to the profit maximization rule. Whereas under certainty the outcome of any act is taken to be a certain result, in the face of uncertainty it is represented as a set of possible results, each having an assessed probability. The expected monetary value criterion, in effect, values the outcome on the basis of a weighted average of the possible outcomes, using the probabilities of occurrence of each as the weighting factor.

EXPECTED UTILITY VALUE CRITERION

The expected monetary value criterion assumes that all units of the payoff are in monetary units and that all increments of such units have the same utility value—that the marginal utility of monetary units is constant for a given decision maker. The utility value criterion permits us to relax these requirements. Consider, for example, a firm making a steady profit of $50,000 per year which has an opportunity that will result, with equal probabilities, in a profit of $1,000,000 *or* a loss of $100,000. It has the alternative of foregoing the opportunity and continuing its present course, which it believes will result in the usual $50,000 profit. It is clear that under the expected monetary value criterion the new opportunity is the preferred choice; it has a EMV of .5($1,000,000) plus .5(-$100,000) or $450,000 which is clearly greater than $50,000. Suppose, however, that a loss of $100,000 would result in bankruptcy or in the bondholders taking over the company. In such a case the owners might well prefer the small but sure profit to the large but speculative one.

The expected utility value criterion permits us to assign to each possible outcome a utility value which is not linearly related to its dollar amount. In the example cited the executive might consider that after contemplating the tax situation of the company and its stockholders, the possible effects of a large profit on labor negotiations and competitive moves and the diminishing marginal utility of money, the difference between zero profit and $1,000,000 profit is worth only eight times the difference between zero profit and a $50,000 profit, even though the dollar amount itself is twenty times as large. At the same time he might consider any loss greater than $60,000—the amount that can be handled without financial disaster—as a very serious matter. Thus his utility scale might look something like the one in Table 1-1.

Table 1-1

Profit	Utility Value
$1,000,000	8
500,000	6
100,000	1.8
50,000	1
25,000	0.6
0	0
−25,000	−0.6
−50,000	−1.3
−100,000	−20
−500,000	−20
−1,000,000	−20

An executive with this scale of values would evaluate the opportunity suggested above as follows:

$$\text{EUV equals} \quad .5(8) \quad \text{plus} \quad .5(-20) \quad \text{or} \quad -6.$$

Because of the factor of *personal risk,* a decision maker may have a scale of utility values that differs from that which applies to the firm for which he is making decisions. That is, assumption (c) on page 18 above may be untrue. Suppose that in the foregoing example, the firm had sufficient financial strength to stand any loss up to $10,000,-000 dollars without seriously impairing its financial stability. The firm's utility scale is thus much closer to expected monetary value than to the utility value table shown. However, the manager believes that if he fails to do at least as well as last year he will be voted out at the next stockholders meeting. *His* utility scale might thus be quite like that in Table 1-1 and he might be expected to behave in such a manner even if this would not produce a decision which is optimal for the firm and its owners as a whole. Such conflicts of interest between decision makers and the firm for which they are making choices are in fact quite common, if not universal.

MULTIPLICITY OF GOALS

The use of the expected utility value criterion provides a means to take into account goals other than, and in addition to, direct profit returns. It does not, however, deal with the broader issue of choosing among the goals themselves.

Every organized behavior system has multiple goals. The most universal of goals is survival. This is expressed in the power principle:

> . . . to prevail in the struggle for survival (an individual or organization) must act in such a way as to promote the power to act.[11]

Application of the power principle requires that the executive make present choices in such a way as to enhance or at least maintain the options which will be open to him in an always uncertain future. This does not mean that the executive will exercise power. Quite the contrary, restraint in the exercise of power may often be the course of action which leaves open the most desirable range of choices for future actions.

In virtually every situation, the manager will have at least the two goals of maximizing return (according to some criterion) and promoting the power to act in the future. More commonly, many divergent, or even conflicting, goals may be involved. In a going business, the issue is frequently not one of how to maximize profit for the next year or from a specific program but one of how to evaluate the relative merit of different corporate goals. This is more than a matter of stating goals and working towards them. A major problem may lie in determining what it is worth to attain various goals.

The merits of attaining subsidiary and short-term goals may be evaluated in terms of their contribution to a major or long-term goal. For example, the value of attaining a goal for opening 50 new outlets or securing 100 new savings accounts might be measured by examining the expected profit to be obtained through those outlets or accounts.

Such quantitative measures are likely to be of little aid in dealing with the formulation of major goals such as those concerning what the business wants to become. How does one measure the value of attaining such goals as being first on the moon, or first in research or sales, or first in public esteem in an industry? Should a business seek to be the most profitable, or to provide the greatest public service at the least cost, or to be the leader in the advancement of social change? Is the principal goal of a university to advance knowledge through research, to train scholars who will go forth to advance

[11] Wroe Alderson, *Marketing Behavior and Executive Action* (Homewood, Ill.: Richard D. Irwin, Inc., 1957).

knowledge, to educate the maximum number of socially disadvan-taged undergraduates, or to provide the best possible education to whatever capable student may knock on its doors? Questions such as these must be resolved by the business planner; commonly he must proceed largely on the basis of his personal evaluation of the merits of the alternatives.

DIRECTING

Plan your work
Work your plan

Selecting a course of action does not, in itself, put the planned action into effect. For this to be accomplished the plan must actually be executed. This execution, in turn, entails planning at subordinate echelons.

Managing, in an organizational context, means finding ways of getting members of the organization to pursue the choices and objec-tives which the planners at peer group or higher echelons have selected.

At any given echelon, the execution of plans requires the day-to-day management of those who use the resources of the organization to make sure that they work towards accomplishing the plans. Much of management at all levels is concerned with this sort of execution—largely with getting things done through people. At the middle and lower echelons, in particular, planning uses comparatively little and execution comparatively much of the managers' time.

Some executives proceed from the premise "If you want it done right, do it yourself." But when they do this they are not managing. They are performing the duties of their subordinates. The sales man-ager who says, "That account is too important to entrust to the sales-man, I'd better handle it myself," is not getting things done through people; he is performing a sales task himself.

As part of their managerial responsibility, sales executives may find it desirable to get into the field to broaden and maintain their own understanding of the situations with which their salesmen must deal. Failure to do so may lead to misperceptions, especially if the manager is a former salesman and tends to place more credence on his own experience than on the reports coming to him from his men.

> A sales manager of an equipment company in travelling with a salesman was shocked by the changes which had taken place since the area had been his territory. He was understandably concerned that other executives might also be operating on obsolete perceptions of the field environment.

In addition, many executives find that they must spend a portion of their time in nonmanagerial activities. It is important to recognize, however, that while such actions may be necessary they should be minimized. The manager's time should be devoted largely, if not exclusively, to the managerial duties of planning, getting things done through others, and controlling.

One view of the managerial process holds that managing consists largely of inducing subordinates to follow prescribed lines. The goals and means to attain them have previously been determined by management, so that execution merely involves directing those in the organization and inducing them to follow desired courses. This is essentially a top-down view of the management process. It may take either "hard" or "soft" forms, depending on the extent to which management at the various echelons in fact enforces compliance with the stated procedures by the subordinates.

An alternative view holds that managers at various organizational levels should merely identify the goals for their areas of responsibility and create conditions which encourage subordinates to direct their own efforts toward achieving the designated goals in ways which they deem appropriate. This approach to management attempts to create an environment in which all of the people on the team are concerned with achieving the team's goals, not only or even primarily because they receive an immediate personal reward, but also because they have been induced to devote their human potential to group goals.

Douglas McGregor, a foremost advocate of the concept of management as a goal-providing force, believes that:

1. The expenditure of physical and mental effort in work is as natural as play or rest.
2. External control and the threat of punishment are not the only means for bringing about effort toward organizational objectives. Man will exercise self-direction and self-control in the service of objectives to which he is committed.
3. Commitment to objectives is a function of the rewards associated with their achievement.
4. The average human being learns, under proper conditions, not only to accept but to seek responsibility.
5. The capacity to exercise a relatively high degree of imagination, ingenuity, and creativity in the solution of organizational problems is widely, not narrowly, distributed in the population.

6. Under the conditions of modern industrial life, the intellectual potentialities of the average human being are only partially utilized.[12]

From these beliefs McGregor concludes that management would do well to forego systems of rewards and punishments that see work merely as a necessary evil men have to accept as the price for enjoying the good things in life. Instead, management should recognize satisfactions from the job itself as the critical means of inducing humans to strive toward organizational goals. In such a context the task of management is primarily to create opportunities, to release latent human potential, to remove obstacles to attainment, to encourage growth, and to provide guidance.

Given a chosen course of action, management must find means of converting its decisions into appropriate actions by people. Among the tools available to managers for this purpose are organizational relationships, policies, budgets and programs, supervision, and directive stimuli. In addition to the specifically directive devices, substantial directive effects may result from several of the sensor tools mentioned earlier.

Organization

The development and maintenance of an effective, viable organization is a key function of the executive at all levels, from the top of a large organization to the newest junior assistant manager.

An effective organization is a system of relationships having its own capability for operating effectively towards group goals. Chester Barnard maintained that it would be illusory to expect any man to control a large organization. In his view, the role of the executive is to develop an organization capable of achieving the goals of the group and to keep that organization tuned up to perform effectively. The job of each manager is conceived as one of inducing subordinates to accept increasing levels of responsibility in coping with the particular problems.[13]

A business is a living, changing, and (hopefully) growing organized behavior system. To be viable it must be organized so that it can adapt, change, and grow. It must be capable of inducing change within itself to meet changes in the opportunities open to it as the environment in which it operates changes. It is not surprising, therefore, to

---

[12] Douglas McGregor, *The Human Side of Enterprise* (New York: McGraw-Hill, Inc. 1960), pp. 47–48.
[13] Chester I. Barnard, *The Functions of the Executive* (Cambridge, Mass.: Harvard University Press, 1938), Chapter XV.

find that organizational planning is a major function of executives at all levels and particularly in the higher echelons.

Good organizational design establishes a system of defined responsibilities and commensurate authorities. Persons in the various parts of the organization are encouraged by the very ways in which responsibilities and relationships are defined to act in order to carry out their responsibilities. Information and instructions flow between various individuals so that the appropriate person makes each decision and undertakes each action. To do this each individual must receive the information he needs, including feedback—that is, information about the results of prior actions.

Good organizational design goes far beyond developing a legible organization chart and the accompanying job descriptions and statements of organizational relationships. It must establish systems that will provide every individual with the information he needs to function effectively. This information not only must have the content he needs, but must be in a form that he can use. If any individual fails to "get the word" on something which affects his own action, the information system is in some way inadequate, and the organization suffers.

The organization planner must take into account not only the formal lines and relationships he can set up on organization charts and in manuals of operating procedures but also the informal or *de facto* organization that will actually operate. It is the latter organization which may in fact determine the lines of effective communication. Stated differently, the manager as an organizational planner must recognize that a "grapevine" will always supplement, modify, and to some extent supplant the prescribed organization of responsiblity, authority and communication. The successful organizer uses the grapevine to support his objectives rather than permitting it to thwart them.

At the same time the manager must correctly read and appropriately control organizational drift. Individuals in any behavioral system tend to modify established practices and routines as time goes on. Such variances range from tendencies for the level of performance to slack off in the absence of adequate control and feedback to the innovative performance of men in the field who are making adaptations to conditions more current or relevant than those envisaged by management. Because of drift an organization, even if it is performing its normal, recognized functions, tends to turn into something else.[14]

[14] See Wroe Alderson, *Marketing Behavior and Executive Action* (Homewood, Ill.: Richard D. Irwin, Inc., 1957), pp. 82–83, 91–97 for a review of drift and other pathological problems of organizations.

The development of *de facto* organizational relationships is one form of organizational drift. Because some of the arrangements which develop in this way represent improvement, the manager will not always want to restrain their development. At the same time, if he is to prevent the organization from gradually turning into something quite different from that intended, and perhaps drifting out of his control, he will find it necessary to monitor these changes. Some may reveal maladjustments or point up ways in which the formal organization ought to be modified. Others he will want to proscribe as adverse to the efficient functioning of the organization.

Policies

Managerial time is in itself a scarce resource. Hence the executive seeks to economize his own time by routinizing activities where feasible. He thus makes more time available for dealing with new or unique problems which require his attention. One way of doing this is to establish *policies.*

A policy is a standing answer to a recurring question.[15] Ideally, policies are formulated to deal with problems before they occur for the first time. In this way there is a greater opportunity to gather and interpret information and to develop a sound solution. Even if this is not always possible, the development of standard answers provides for the application of similar treatments to similar situations arising at different places in the organization or at different points in time. Policies thus serve as rules by which different members of the organization are guided. In addition, policies make possible the practice of management by exception—requiring proposed deviations from policies to be referred to higher echelons in the form of requests for exceptions to policies or modifications of them. Salesmen, for example, may be given authority to close all sales which accord with established policies; those involving special treatment must be referred to an appropriate management level for decision.

The presence of policies provides an important instrument for clarifying intended definitions of authority within an organization. They do this because there must be a careful placement of authority to establish, modify, and grant exceptions to policies. Thus policies are helpful in developing a structure of organizational relationships.

Budgets

A budgetary system is a means through which the top executives of an organization formulate and implement their plans by re-

---

[15] Reavis Cox (unpublished lectures).

quiring subordinates also to formulate and implement programs in support of higher echelon goals and plans. The revenues to be produced by proposed programs and the costs to be incurred to execute them are referred to as revenue budgets and expense budgets respectively. An expense budget is a price tag for carrying out a program.

In a well-developed budgetary system, the top echelon lays out the goals and general plans for the forthcoming planning period. These are furnished to subordinate echelons who now have the responsibility for preparing the plans and programs appropriate to the achievement of their part of the total operation.

In a large organization the staff responsible for each activity prepares programs which it proposes to undertake in the furtherance of its responsibilities. Ideally, each of these programs will have an expense budget attached—that is a statement of the resources required to accomplish it. These budget proposals are forwarded to the reviewing echelon (usually the next higher one) where diverse requests are coordinated and reconciled. Some proposals will be approved; others will be discarded as inappropriate or too costly for the results to be expected; still others will be returned for modifications of one sort or another. When the first reviewing echelon has reconciled all the proposals within its area of responsibility it will itself have a budget proposal—that is, a set of programs of its own. This will be submitted to a still higher echelon where a similar process of review, choosing, and reconciliation will take place. Finally, a corporate or government agency budget will emerge. It will be a statement, in dollars, of the approved plans and programs which the organization and each of its constituent units is to undertake.

In a very real sense the budget-making process is a series of plan-making activities in which subordinate levels are proposing alternatives and higher levels are choosing among them. Yet in its essense, the budget-making process is a directing process. It is the central means through which, in large organizations at least, the top management induces subordinate management levels to develop programs to discharge their responsibilities, determine what is required to implement them, and choose at appropriate places within the organization which programs are to be implemented. At any level, an approved budget stands as a compact between the activity and the level to which it reports. The higher level has agreed to fund a program; the activity has undertaken to carry it out.

Once the budget has been made and placed into effect it places constraints on what may be undertaken. It thus serves to direct the various activities within the organization along the lines which were agreed upon during the budget-making phase.

After the operating period has been completed, comparison of results with budgets provides an important source of feedback information.

Supervision

Supervision is the process through which senior echelons maintain communication with subordinates for the purpose of inducing the subordinates to carry out accepted programs. It is of particular concern in the management of salesforces, and is treated separately in Chapter 12.

CONTROLLING

While planning determines what should be done and directing is concerned in getting it done, there remains the task of determining what has been accomplished, *so that better plans and directions may be taken in the future.* It cannot be too strongly emphasized that the function of control is not to assess performance for its own sake but to assess it in order that, given the outcomes of prior plans, we can formulate both better plans and better schemes for their execution.

Control involves three kinds of activities: setting standards of performance; assessing compliance with these standards (feedback); and taking corrective action.

Setting Standards

Performance standards are an important part of the control activity of any system. A housewife sets the home thermostat at 68 degrees; a production specialist determines that a qualified workman should polish 15 widgets per shift; a wholesaler determines that an order picker should pick 20 lines per hour; a sales-force analyst determines that city salesmen should make 5 calls per working day.

The establishment of relevant and meaningful standards requires an understanding of the nature of the functions performed by an activity and of the means through which they may be accomplished. In sales work, job analyses and time and duty studies generally provide the starting point for work standards while sales potentials may provide a base against which to measure sales accomplishment.

Feedback

Although standards may have some directive value in and of themselves, their value in the control process is dependent upon accurate and timely feedback. The manager must determine whether the planned actions are in fact being carried out and the extent to which the results conform to those which were expected. An important function of some of the sensor tools discussed earlier, especially the internal reporting system and analyses of variances from standards or budgets, is to provide feedback to supervisory and higher echelons. We shall observe the operation of these and other feedback devices in the chapters to follow.

Adjustment

The essence of the control function is not that the manager learns of deviations from planned performance but that he *does* something about them.

This corrective action takes two forms. In the immediate and most obvious sense, steps can be taken to bring performance which does not conform to plans, programs, and directives into line with them. For example, rates of expenditure can be adjusted to bring nonconforming rates into line with those provided for in the budget. Additional efforts can be exerted to overcome the failure of revenues to meet plans. New or revised instructions can be issued to individuals whose performance does not meet the standard.

On the other hand, results may suggest that the plans and standards themselves should be modified. Large deviations in either direction from established standards may suggest that the true response functions are quite different from those envisaged when the standards were set or that the standards are in some way either too difficult or too easy to attain.

For the longer term, feedback provides information on the performance of whole programs and on the execution of plans themselves. It thus provides new information about cause-effect relationships which must, in any viable system, become a part of the information input to any new plans. In this sense we have come full circle: feedback becomes an input to planning.

Introducing Change into the Sales Management Process

Changes bring both stresses and opportunities to a going organization. A major task of sales management is to detect environmental and internal changes of pertinence to the personal sales job and to perceive the significance of these changes. These perceptions become part of the situation analysis. The planning process can then be employed to devise responses which will come as close as possible to the ideal of modification without disruption.

DETECTING AND PERCEIVING THE IMPORT OF CURRENT CHANGES

Of immediate and direct concern to the sales manager is the need to keep the sales force adjusted to an ever-changing current world. The nature and location of opportunity changes. Competitive thrusts create both new problems and new opportunities. The products most suitable to users' needs change with those needs and with new alternatives to meet them. The buying systems with which the salesman is to interact change. Along with those changes may come new perspectives on what particular buyers need or expect to derive from interactions with supplier salesmen.

Successful adaptation to changes in the environment begins with an effective understanding of the changes which are occurring and their significance for the firm. This is not so much a matter of gathering and processing data as of perceiving its significance. Many of the data which suggest that changes are taking place in the outside world exist in the records of the firm and in the files and heads of salesmen and executives. The problem usually lies in developing appropriate data-to-information-to-intelligence transformations so that the significance of the data can be understood. The records of a firm may indicate clearly that certain customer groups have shifted away from certain products or have changed their pattern in the use of optional marketing services or that volume in certain lines is coming from different sources than in those lines a year ago. But this raw data will be of little use as a monitor of change unless the firm's information system can select out from the welter of data those things which tell the decision maker the changes in the outside world which are of significance to him.

For example, the tools discussed earlier can provide measurements of changes in the nature and location of opportunities. For this to be performed effectively, however, the analyst, and often the data source, must know what it is they are supposed to be watching, measuring, or analyzing. Marketing research must ask the right questions about markets. The same may be said of intelligence obtained through salesmen or the observations of executives in the course of their work. A major problem is to develop in all of these individuals a skill in recognizing what could be relevant.

In this context, changes in the geographic *location* of units of opportunity are relatively easy to identify. Changes in the *nature* of opportunity are more difficult to assess. They may require studies of users and prospective users, analyses of changes in sales patterns at company or industry levels and, in some cases, product usage studies. These may show how applications have changed, whether particular products are being used by the same people as heretofore, and, if so, if they are being used for the same purposes and in the same way.

Changes in buying systems and in the ways in which they solve their problems are rarely obvious. Their perception and measurement represent a challenge for salesman and manager alike.

Changes within the firm may also change the situation with

which managers must deal. Corporate reorganization may result in redefinition of the company's goals. New goals may be selected. More likely, the emphasis placed upon conflicting goals within the goal set may be rearranged. The relative importance of such goals as market position, rate of growth, social impact, community image, long term profit, and pleasing the stockholders with an attractive dividend are likely to vary from time to time in any viable organization.

New arrangements with suppliers or customers or attempts to reach new types of markets lead to new strategies and possibly new roles for the sales force. Different types of human resources become available to the sales manager; other types become scarce or unobtainable.

Changes such as these and many others like them must be detected, correctly perceived, and brought into the situation analysis, if even short term plans are to be made in a relevant setting.

DETECTING AND PERCEIVING THE IMPORT OF CHANGES OF LONGER-TERM SIGNIFICANCE

A more difficult but related problem is the detection and valid perception of developments relevant to the firm's longer-term policies and strategies. What changes will occur in the user groups in the next two decades? What will be the role of the salesman twenty or forty years hence? Here perception and interpretation play important roles. Is the observed change the beginning of a trend, or merely a short-term aberration? If a trend, what is its meaning? Is the highly touted new method so glowingly reported in the trade press the forerunner of major change in the industry or an experiment which will in all likelihood fail?

For more than fifty years the trend in nearly all retail lines, and especially in food and related lines has been for open display and arrangements to permit consumers to inspect and handle merchandise.

Flying in the face of this modern trend, Clarence Saunders about 1950 introduced a closed type store, the Keedozall. The physical transfer of goods to the customer was accomplished by the customer going from closed display to closed display inserting a key device into slots for the wanted merchandise and taking the resulting punched tape to a checkout cashier who fed the tape to a register which totalled the amount and delivered the assembled merchandise to the checkout point. The store was launched with maximum publicity as the "store of the future" because of the automated features. Actually the store offered the consumer little or no advantage over ordering by phone and deprived her of the easy inspection and breadth of lines provided by the modern supermarkets. The mechanization conferred a disbenefit to consumers with no corresponding cost benefit to the store. As predicted by this writer, the store soon failed. Yet similar proposals recur from time to time from those who are impressed by mechaical feasibility and give little or no attention to the major services which consumers want from their supply systems.

A major task, then, is to cull from the many events taking place in the outside world those that are likely to have either current or long-term significance and to bring sound perceptions of that significance into the situation analysis at the earliest possible dates.

SUMMARY

The role of marketing is to determine the needs and wants of consumers and other users and to direct economic effort to service those needs and wants. The marketing system must match the diverse, heterogeneous, ever-changing wants of users with the tremendous diversity of products that a modern economy makes possible.

Even more important than the heterogeneity of wants themselves is the heterogeneity in the information which users need as they search for solutions to their problems and in users' abilities to perceive needs and integrate information into their patterns of action. Nonpersonal media must rely for the most part on common elements in the informational needs of the intended receivers. Personal selling, on the other hand, seeks adaptation through interaction. It concerns itself with finding ways in which the objectives of the selling and buying organizations complement each other.

Personal selling becomes relevant when information can be communicated more effectively if it is subject to modification during the transmission process in response to the development of information about the individual receiver and his needs.

Personal selling also provides the means by which the problems of users can be more sharply defined and the offerings of sellers adjusted to better resolve those problems.

In an end-directed economy, personal selling provides producers with an important source of intelligence on how products and services can better meet user needs.

Management of the personal sales function involves three areas of activity: defining the sales task; providing the sales force; and operating the field sales organization. These activities must undergo continual modification because of the ever-changing environment and because feedback provides new and more current information on the effects of actions which have been taken.

The central focus of the management process is planning. Planning starts with analysis of the situation. Alternatives must then be identified. The probable outcomes from the selection of each alternative must be evaluated. The manager then chooses a course of action in accord with some express or implicit decision rule.

Managing in an organizational context means finding ways of getting members of the organization to pursue the choices and objectives which the planners have selected. This is accomplished largely through organizing relationships, establishing policies, formulating budgets and working with others to develop common goals. One result is further planning at other echelons, including planning by the salesman himself to achieve goals of common interest.

Control is largely a process of determining what has been accomplished so that better plans can be formulated. Control involves setting standards, evaluating feedback, and taking steps either to adjust performance or to modify plans.

A major task of sales management is to detect both environmental and internal changes of pertinence to the sales job and to seek continually to modify the organization and its goals and practices. With improved tools of detection, the more challenging problems are in perceiving the current and longer-term import of onrushing changes.

Part I

Defining the Sales Task

2 The Buying and Selling Process

An understanding of the buying process and how it depends on the circumstances in which the buyer finds himself is central to an understanding of the sales process and to the role of the personal salesman. In this chapter the sales process and its correlate, the buying process, are briefly examined in order that the reader may grasp the context in which sales work takes place and in which the problems of the sales manager are posed.

ELEMENTS OF THE PERSONAL SALES SITUATION

We have seen that the role of the marketing system is to match the diverse, heterogeneous needs of users with the tremendous variety of products which a modern economy makes possible. It must both provide producers with guidance on consumers' problems and consumers with information as to (1) what goods and services are or can be made available and (2) what the products' prospective performances and problem-solving capabilities are.

It is useful to visualize marketing firms and the firms, households, and individuals which use products and services as subsystems of the marketing system. Such subsystems operate as organized behavior systems and exhibit properties of systems in themselves.

Take the household, for example. Each member has his own goals, interests, and needs which differ in some ways from those of the other members but which still, in other ways, conform with those of the household group. Each member participates in the pursuit of common goals as well as his own individual ones. Each finds that he has expectations (as to what he will obtain from the survival and activity of the group) and responsibilities towards the group and its other members. As a system, the household has its own internal communications system, internal status arrangements, and internal lines of authority and responsibility. In short, it has the attributes present in firms and other types of organizations. Moreover, like any other ecological behavior system, the household is in a constant state of change both in its internal relationships and in its relationships with the outside world. Like the business firm, it seeks to survive and better its position. In common with other types of organized behavior systems, it is in a continual state of learning how best to solve its problems and meet its needs at the same time that those needs are in themselves undergoing change.[1]

All organized behavior systems interact with their respective environments. These environments not only define their problems and influence their goals, they also provide an important part of the data base for decisions and the actual means by which many goals are achieved.

The interaction of the buying systems of industrial and ultimate consumers with those of sellers is the theatre of marketing. Much of this interaction is nonpersonal. Sellers communicate with consumers through various unidirectional media. They receive information by observing events in the marketplace in terms of their own experience, through the reported experience of others, and as a result of the research of scholars on consumer behavior and human behavior in general. Similarly, consumers obtain information in the marketplace by receiving portions of sellers' messages which are relevant to them, by their own observations and experience, and by the observations and experience of others which are related to them.

Supplying and consuming systems not only receive data about each other, they derive information from this data and utilize it to

---

[1] For a concise examination of the nature of groups, how they form themselves into various types of organized behavior systems, and how such systems operate, see Wroe Alderson, *Marketing Behavior and Executive Action* (Homewood, Ill.: Richard D. Irwin, Inc., 1957), Chapters I, II.

modify their own conduct. Thus, consuming and supplying systems interact, even in the absence of a salesman or other explicit catalyst. These interactions will often lead, in and of themselves, to the establishment of market relationships and to one consequence thereof—individual transactions. From the point of view of operating systems, however, it must be emphasized that the transactions themselves are secondary to the relationships and for the most part follow from them, rather than vice versa. In connection with industrial buyers, this writer has previously noted that "Companies don't make purchases, they establish relationships."[2] This applies to much of consumer behavior in the marketplace as well.

For a transaction to occur, a relationship is necessary. Since the establishment of new relationships generally involves greater information seeking and contactual cost than the maintenance of an existing relationship, buyers as well as sellers prefer the maintenance of an existing relationship to the initiation of a different one.[3] Hence, an understanding of consuming systems (in their market behavior) requires that we grasp clearly the way in which buyers establish and modify their relationships with those who supply them. The growing literature on human behavior and especially that on consumer behavior attests to the increased interest in this field in recent years.[4]

Interaction of buyers and sellers is not limited to that which would result from the impersonal system of unidirectional communication and the indirect media of observation and experience. Often it takes place directly as the result of interpersonal communicative relationships between personnel in the buying and selling systems. Although these relationships may be long or short term and may occur on the initiative of either buying or selling organization, their most common form is that of interaction between the sales personnel of the selling organization and those playing some role in the buying process within the buying system.

[2] Unpublished lecture, quoted in Patrick J. Robinson and Charles W. Faris, *Industrial Buying and Creative Marketing* (Boston: Allyn & Bacon, Inc., 1967), p. 139.

[3] This contrasts with the view in classical economics that ceteris paribus, buyers and sellers are paired off randomly for each transaction, a conclusion which follows from the classical premises that data and its transformation into information are cost- and effort-free to everyone, and that both buyers' wants and units of supply are homogeneous.

[4] For a comprehensive analysis of recent findings on consumer behavior see James F. Engel, David T. Kollat, and Roger D. Blackwell, *Consumer Behavior* (New York: Holt, Rinehart, and Winston, Inc., 1968); Harold H. Kassarjian and Thomas S. Robertson, eds., *Perspectives in Consumer Behavior* (Glenview, Illinois: Scott, Foresman and Company, 1968); and James H. Myers and William H. Reynolds, *Consumer Behavior and Marketing Management* (Boston: Houghton Mifflin Company, 1967).

Personal selling deals with these interpersonal communicative relationships. It is most likely to be useful to buyers where the knowledge needed to understand and resolve their problems is not fully evident or readily obtainable from prior experience or unidirectional information flows.

In a dynamic world, the buyer's state of knowledge is never complete. Today's best way may be supplanted by a better one tomorrow, if only the buyer were to get the word. The problem for the buyer often takes the form of an implicit decision as to whether changes in his problems (needs) or the possibility of uncovering more suitable ways to solve them are worth the effort required to seek out better answers. Persons involved in the buying process have many more demanding uses of their time; even professional buyers routinize many purchases in order to conserve their time for more significant investigations and decisions. In addition, every change of an item or source involves some risk to the buyer. Thus in only a minority of procurements do buyers seek out new sources or new methods of meeting their needs. Hence, the seller must take the initiative.

From the sellers' perspective, it has already been noted that personal selling is likely to be called for where the goals and problems of various buyers differ so that individualized presentations and tailored solutions are indicated. The forte of the personal salesman is the ability to identify the particulars of the buying situation and to deal with them by establishing appropriate systems of interaction with those having the problems.

> *If buyers gain from the interactive process, why should it be necessary for the seller to take the initiative in personal selling activity?*
>
> *If buying organizations are viewed as establishing relationships with sources, rather than making purchases, what does this imply for the role and duties of the salesman? for his training? for supervision and motivation? for compensation? for evaluating salesman performance?*

ALTERNATIVE VIEWS OF THE SALES PROCESS

The traditional view of the sales process conceives of the salesman as the active agent and the buyer either as passive or as a pliable subject towards whom the salesman applies his efforts. Consistent with this view, various sales techniques may be examined in order to determine which are the most effective in "causing" sales. A good deal of the literature of selling and sales management proceeds from this view of the sales process.

One common view of the sales process, for example, considers selling as a four-step process:

A—getting ATTENTION,
I—developing INTEREST,
D—creating DESIRE,
A—securing ACTION.

Sales training then proceeds to develop means through which the salesman can successfully carry out this process and to teach the salesman work habits so that he will do so.

If the buyer is considered in the sales process, he is thought of only in terms of those immediate reactions with which the salesman must deal, such as those which are found in training manuals under the heading "meeting objections." The general context remains one of viewing the salesman as the causal agent in the sale.

Analyses of the effectiveness of sales and of sales management tactics and devices proceed from this same questionable premise. The sales force is the accomplisher; the buyer is the object.

The market-oriented view of the sales process recognizes personal selling as a multidirectional communicative process. It involves the buyer as an active, information-and-service-seeking problem solver. To understand the personal sales process we must examine the nature of the buying unit and understood how it formulates its problems, and at least those parts of its buying process which lead to or involve buyer-salesman interaction.

BUYING AS A COMMUNICATION PROCESS

A buying unit may be an individual, a family, or a business, governmental, social or similar organization. A buying unit embraces the users (consumers) of a product as well as those charged with procuring it. These may or may not be the same individuals. In a household, for example, the housewife may act as buyer for many food, clothing, and household items, while the users will be many members of the family of various ages and occupying various roles in the family. In a business firm, separate individuals or departments may be charged with buying responsibilities.

It does not follow that users and buyers are independent groups, each performing his own role. Rather there is substantial interaction among them. In the household, the housewife's buying is very much influenced by what the users (members of the family) want; their preferences form constraints on what the housewife will buy to meet their needs. In the industrial firm, the user may specify, often in considerable detail, precisely what he wants or what he wishes the desired product to accomplish. In both cases, however, these wants are conditioned by what is available. Within the buying unit, users, buyers, and other influencers interact to reach buying decisions. The roles of each group in different purchasing situations will be examined later. At this point it is sufficient to note that buying and using are distinct activities in both industrial and consumer buying situations but that there is substantial interaction among users and buyers.

Human Behavior as an Ongoing Process

Human behavior is an ongoing process, not a set of discrete events. Individuals' and firms' behavior in their market relationships, although reflected in observable acts, are merely parts of larger patterns of behavior.

All buyer behavior, with the possible exception of that of mentally deranged persons, is rational. The rationale is often not fully known, nor, in some cases, even surmised, by the observer. Hence, observers sometimes attribute irrationality to the behavior of others whose activities are not understood by the observer. Often such statements are little more than confessions that the observer does not understand the behavior of the observed or that the action chosen is not that which the observer in his "superior" wisdom would have chosen. This is not to say that all persons choose wisely, merely that the process of choosing is a rational one—that is, buyers do what they believe at the time "makes sense."

Not all rational behavior is conscious behavior. On the contrary, the rational individual will economize the need for conscious effort by at least routinizing or, better yet, internalizing many courses of action so that they do not require conscious effort. Humans develop habits and routines so as to make unnecessary a conscious deliberation over each motion (for example, each step in walking).

Buyers as Information Processors

The buying process is largely a process of acquiring information (not merely being exposed to data) and using that information to continue, extend, or modify behavior. This information may or may not be consciously sought. Often it is sought only subconsciously in the sense that the receiver is receptive to data which is meaningful to him in terms of his behavior patterns. This is not to say that messages are imposed on buyers. Quite the contrary. *The propensity to receive a message depends on whether or not the data have relevance to the intended receiver in terms of his behavior and rationale.* It should be noted that such propensities are not *themselves* the result of the status of the receiver (for example, income, age, location) or his prior activities (for example, previous user of product type, previous user of specific item, nonuser of product type) although these factors may be important influences and thus more or less crude surrogates for the behavior process.

The individual, whether manager, salesman, or buyer, possesses an information and decision system which, by virtue of the value concepts contained in it, allows him *to develop a certain set of predilections to act in a more or less specific manner in any given situation.* The process of influence required to change such predilections is essentially different from, and more "intensive" than one of information giving.[5]

THE PROCESS OF MUTUAL INFLUENCE

Messages do not, in themselves, cause people to behave differently. They merely provide data which the receiver may convert to information. Whether or not this will occur, what data will be utilized, and how it will be interpreted are internal to the receiver and his frame of reference. Of the vast amount of data to which the individual is exposed, only a small proportion will be conceived of as having *relevance* to the recipient's problems and hence his behavior. Such factors as his perceived problems and his prior experiences and expectations will condition the effect particular data will have on him. Thus the same message may convey different information to different recipients at the same time and to the same recipient at different points in time.

If marketers' messages are to have any effect on prospective buyers they must alter the receivers' behavior in some way favorable to the seller. When or if this occurs is not easily determined because a mere alteration in position does not itself cause a change in behavior. I may, for example, be more favorably disposed toward product X (a new Buick) as a result of some new information, but product X is irrelevant to the behavior associated with my present problem (I must find an apartment, as I already have a new car). Similarly, my new information position, while differing from my former one, does not lead to a change in behavior. (For example, despite new information which I accept and believe, I shall continue to support the candidates of my party.) Even if a change in behavior does occur, it may or may not be observable in terms of measurable (observable) acts. (For example, I become a less ardent advocate of a cause I still support.) Whether or not a receiver's observable acts will be affected by a transmission of data will thus depend on:

1. the receiver's problems, present behavior patterns, perceptions, and predilections, all of which affect whether or not he receives the data and the nature of its transformation into information, if any takes place at all;

[5] Patrick J. Robinson and Bent Stidsen, *Personal Selling in a Modern Perspective* (Boston: Allyn and Bacon, Inc., 1967), p. 93.

2.   whether or not the information alters behavior;
3.   whether or not alterations in behavior lead to changes in observable acts.

Personal selling is essentially interpersonal interaction. If the parties to such a relationship are to have any effective interaction each must understand the behavior of the other. In general, it may be said that the ability of a party to exercise influence on the behavior of the other is directly related to his understanding of the rationale underlying the behavior of the other party. Unfortunately, much of the rationale for an individual's behavior is not observable by someone else. The ability of either party to influence the other is, therefore, sharply constrained by lack of knowledge of the constituents of the other's behavior. Since the process by which salesmen and buyers interact is heavily dependent on their understanding of each other's rationale, the first problem for each is to determine the rationale of the other party and then to attempt to influence that rationale as a step towards influencing behavior.

In the absence of an understanding of the rationale underlying buyer behavior, the transmittal of messages is apt to be fruitless. Because its relevance and/or credibility is not evident to the receiver, the message may not even be perceived.

An originator, not understanding the rationale which links the buyer's information position with his behavior, may succeed in changing the receiver's information position while in no way influencing his behavior simply because the specific kind or item of information has little or no relevance to the particular behavior which the sender wished to affect. For example, if a person's main reason for wanting a car is to have cheap transportation to and from the commuter station, all the information in the world about engine horsepower, acceleration, top speed, and so on will have very little effect on this person's behavior.

Where the sender and receiver lack a common field of experience, data may be perceived and transformed into information in ways vastly different from those intended by the sender. In other words, the interpretation placed on the message is drawn in terms of the receiver's rationale. It may differ from, even be directly opposite to, that intended by the sender. A merchant in a poor neighborhood, for example, may install new fixtures, improved lighting and a new store front intending to convey an image of a better store providing his customers with the same friendly service and low prices as before. But some customers may read the improvements as a message that the merchant has "made too much money" or that prices must have been raised in order to afford these amenities.

THE BUYING PROCESS

Proceeding from the view of buyers as problem solvers, it is appropriate to inquire as to why buyers talk to salesmen and what they hope to attain by so doing. Before examining this issue, however, we must first look at the buying process and at the situations in which buyers find themselves. We shall do this by first examining the steps which are generally involved, either explicitly or implicitly, in the procurement (buying) process. Then we shall examine the extent to which buyers' behavior and behavior-influencing information vary in different buying situations. The examples given here refer primarily to industrial buying situations but the principles apply with only slight modification to consumer goods buying activity.[6] As we shall see later, the buyer's information needs may derive less from the type of product being purchased than from his informational needs in making decisions in the course of the procurement process.

Activities in the Buying Process

The procurement function involves eight more or less distinct types of activities or subfunctions (Figure 2-1). Although they differ in importance in different procurement situations, they appear to be present, at least implicitly, in all types of procurement. They are explained here in the order in which they logically occur in the solution of new procurement problems. In other problems it is by no means necessary or desirable that they be performed in the indicated sequence. For many procurements several of the functions may be concurrent; indeed, some are continuous activities which necessarily proceed concurrently with other subfunctions.

1. *Recognition of the need in general terms* Recognition of a problem may take place in many ways. A few examples suggest the wide breadth of events which might trigger a recognition that a problem exists. The inventory on a shelf may run low. The firm's customers may want attributes which its present products do not afford, leading to attempts to design products with these attributes. Internal engineering or product development groups may generate needs in the same way. Equipment needs may become evident from the unsatisfactory performance, or even breakdown, of existing products. Messages from salesmen or from advertising may induce the users to ask themselves if there may be a better way of performing

---

[6] For models of the consumer buying process, see Engel, Kollat, Blackwell, especially Chapters 3, 16.

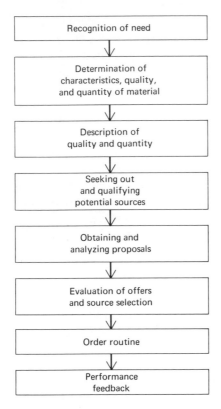

Figure 2-1
THE BUYING PROCESS

some task or if some previously unrecognized problem exists.

Before the recognition of a problem can have any influence on procurement, it must be made explicit to the extent that it must be "uttered" by someone. That is, somebody within the organization having the problem must do something. This may involve no more than "looking into" a situation to see if the prospective problem in fact exists and is worth doing anything about. No doubt, many prospective problems turn out not to be problems at all, or at least not significant enough to warrant attempts to deal with them. Who first recognized the possibility of a problem and how recognition was triggered are significant to an understanding of how purchasing begins. Other considerations are the means by which the originator communicates the problem to others, and the rules by which a decision to communicate is made.

A second element in the recognition of a need involves a perception that the solution to the problem lies in the direction of a particular product or service—for example, a delivery problem calls for more trucks; a load problem suggests new generating capacity; a breakage problem calls for stronger fibre. At this level the problem has been translated into a general solution area.

Recognition of need is almost always an activity of using rather than procurement personnel and departments. An exception is the case of procurement personnel having responsibilities for maintaining inventories in accordance with previously determined replenishment rules.

2. *Determination of characteristics, quality and quantity of material*   Determination of what is necessary to solve the problem is largely an internal step. This involves determining in more specific terms how the problem is to be solved. For technical products the using department may prepare a performance specification of what the proposed product should do or a composition specification of what attributes it should have, cost and procurement considerations aside. For less technical items, this process may involve no more than the determination that a certain product now available on the market will do the job or solve the problem.

The parties primarily interested are within the using department although in some cases procurement or other types of personnel from outside the using department will be consulted. Moreover, this action may be undertaken concurrently with some of the steps below that involve participation by outsiders. Nevertheless, the task of determining the need is of itself internal to the using group.

3. *Description of quality and quantity*   Eventually, an accurate description or specification of what is required must be made available to those outside of the using department. Informational sources outside of the using department and often outside of the firm itself will be drawn upon. As this description becomes the basis for action by those outside the using department, it must be both detailed and explicit.

4. *Seeking out and qualifying potential sources*   The next step is to locate sources of potential supply and to determine which sources are qualified for consideration as

suppliers. For routinely purchased items it may consist of no more than identifying the established preferred source from a reference list or reference person. At the other extreme, consideration of a new item of a type not previously purchased may require both extensive search to find appropriate possible suppliers, and extended consideration of which possible suppliers are in fact qualified.

The emphasis on qualification is directly related to the consequences of nonperformance. The consequences of unsatisfactory performance by a supplier are likely to be greatest where the specification can be defined only loosely (for example in R&D contracts), or where the consequences of failure are grave (for example, where hidden defects can cause substantial losses to the buyer or where long lead times make rejection or late delivery of a component a matter of serious consequence to the buyer).

5. *Obtaining and analyzing proposals* Proposals must then be obtained and analyzed. This activity may involve as little as looking at a price sheet or obtaining a telephone quotation. On the other hand, it may entail months of negotiations with one or more prospective suppliers.

    The analysis may entail involved performance tests or detailed value analysis on the one hand. At the other extreme, it may be no more than a perfunctory matching of a shelf item or catalogue number with the description from step 3.

6. *Evaluation of offers and source selection* Finally, a choice is made among offers. The evaluation of offers may involve several functional activities and several management echelons, each with its own persective. These different perspectives may, on occasion, even lead to reopening decisions which have been made earlier as new criteria are introduced. Finally, however, a choice must be made. If there is a purchasing "decision" as a single event, it is at this point.

7. *Order routine* The order routine involves both (a) external and (b) internal activities. The activities with external aspects include the actual writing and forwarding of the purchase order to the vendor (or counterpart telephone or personal selection activities), and such follow-up activities as expediting, troubleshooting, securing status reports, receiving, inspection, and approval of invoices for payment.

    Two types of internal activities are directly involved

in the order routine. These are internal status reporting—keeping the using department informed of the status of the procurement—and inventory management.

While order routine activities may in a sense be considered post-purchase activities and, hence, of no concern to an understanding of either purchase decisions or marketing, such a position ignores important factors. From the viewpoint of the requiring department, the purchase has not been achieved and its "problems" have not been solved until the material is obtained and ready for use. The effectiveness with which these activities are performed is therefore a matter of no small concern. It is quite conceivable that procurement routine systems are affected, perhaps materially, with reference to these activities. For example, one argument for purchase of certain equipment by using departments directly from equipment manufacturers is concerned with the need for close follow-up relationships.

8. *Performance feedback*   Every procurement involves an accretion to the buyer's learning experience. Performance of the vendor in terms of the supply arrangements—that is, conformance to specifications, delivery times, and so on—provides an important feedback for future qualification of sources.

A more fundamental evaluation occurs after the purchased products are actually in use. This evaluation deals with the question, "How well did the purchased product solve the problem?" Obviously, feedback of this information is necessary if future problems are to be recognized and solved effectively.

Where feedback is not provided for organizationally, it may exist only in the minds of users as they appraise the worth of products that they use in their daily work. Communicated feedback reports may be limited to reports of ineffective performance such as product failures or reports of what the product fails to do. Or feedback may appear only to the extent that shortcomings of a product used by a firm or its customers are made evident as new problems are recognized (step 1). At this point it is necessary only to note that whether purchasing is viewed as a continuing set of relationships with suppliers, or merely as a continuum of discrete events, feedback of performance information (whether explicitly provided for or not) is an integral part of the procurement process.

Multiplicity of Influence on Purchases

The activities enumerated above involve a large number of different persons who make somewhat different contributions to the procurement process. Some of these persons are involved because of their position in the buying firm. Others are called upon to provide relevant information to some portion of the total process. In a major purchase the total number of persons who in some way influence some step is legion. One study found that no one in the organization knew or could even identify the positions of all of those who were participants.

Continuity of the Procurement Process

In the sense that problems are never permanently solved in a going concern, the procurement process, even for a given product, does not "end." The receipt and acceptance of the product is merely an incident in a continuing "learning" flow of supply experience. Although procurement events may themselves be discrete, each event, even a "final" purchase, is but part of the learning experience leading up to the solution of subsequent problems by means of subsequent purchases. A purchase (to the seller, a "sale") transaction is but an event in the process of supply. Even in the relations between particular buyer-seller pairs it may or may not be an important event. This relationship and its maintenance and development are, in most cases, considerably more significant than any individual transaction.

The Creeping Commitment

Earlier we were concerned with the *power principle* asserting that an individual or organization acts so as to promote the power to act. We now consider its converse, the *principle of creeping commitment,* asserting that purchasing and other decisions are not made as moment-of-truth strokes but as a series of incremental choices which reduce alternatives until only one remains.

As we have seen, even in the context of a single procurement a decision doesn't happen between two people at some time and place but rather *develops* as the problem is successively defined in narrower terms. As the problem is studied more closely, different avenues of solution are considered. Some are eliminated; others are pursued more closely. As this process continues, the buyer becomes more and more committed to a smaller and smaller number of possible courses of action. Soon, perhaps, only two or three models or suppliers are left. Some would consider the final choice among them as the "decision." In fact, however, decisions have been made all along which are equally as important in determining the final outcome. The decision to use electric motors rather than gasoline-powered ones on model Z lawnmowers, thus eliminating all gasoline makes, is of as much consequence to a gasoline motor manufacturer as the final choice of brand is to the electric motor manufacturer. When dealing with many complex technical products, the final "decision" may in fact be anticlimactic. The significant decision well may be whether an electric utility will build a nuclear or fossil-fuel plant, for all other decisions are subordinate to it. In most capital equipment cases, a long series of decisions is made, each of which in some way reduces the decision space from which a final choice of a bill of materials or set of specifications will be made. This sequential decision-making process has been referred to by Halbert as the process of *creeping commitment*.

The process of creeping commitment occurs in almost all buying situations, not just those involving capital goods. A family's place of residence, availability of an automobile during the day, and style of living, for example, serve to narrow the choice of places at which the housewife will shop. Her choice of particular goods is constrained by decisions previously made. Thus, specific food item decisions are made within the context of a prior decision as to which store to patronize as well as the food budget. A carpet is chosen with reference to prior decisions on draperies, room decor, and household resources allotted to this use (for example, $500); perhaps both are chosen in the context of a prior decision to reduce both the food and the home furnishings budget in view of expected college expenses of a teen-age daughter.

The widespread operation of the principle of creeping commitment and the continuity of the procurement process should make clear that efforts to identify "*the* buying decision" or "*the* decisive buying influence" are illusory. Buying is, thus, not so much an *act* as a *process*.

THE BUYING SITUATION AS THE BASIS OF CLASSIFYING PURCHASES

The existence of a general buying process, as examined in the previous section, does not mean that all purchases are made in the same way or even that the same item is purchased in the same manner at different times. Marketing authors have attempted to deal with the wide differences in observed purchasing behavior by seeking to identify the buying patterns that apply to particular types of goods. In this way, marketing services could be offered and marketing information could be provided in a manner that would be appropriate to particular buying patterns. Thus we have Copeland's convenience, shopping, and specialty goods, and Aspinwall's red, orange, and yellow goods.[7] The weakness of these approaches is that they focus on the *item being purchased* rather than the *problem being solved.*

For the purpose of understanding the procurement process, and for the marketer who conceives his job as helping his customers solve their problems, the classification of goods on a product basis is largely irrelevant. This applies as well to classifications based on presumed market attributes of products as to classifications based on physical product attributes, chemical composition, or manufacturing processes. Whatever their other merits, such classifications have limited value in studying the procurement process. This is so largely because even a product with well-understood physical and market attributes is likely to be purchased under different circumstances at different times even by the same buyer or by buyers who are differently situated. Thus, while some of the variables surrounding a purchase well may be linked in some way with the type of goods involved (for example, unit cost, degree of technical complexity), others are only remotely related if at all (for example, urgency of need at a particular time, inventory status, user's determinations of quantities required and changes therein). For procurement, the important consideration is not the product type but the *buying situation.*

The Buying Situation and the Procurement Process

A *buying situation* is any problem within an organization for which at least one of the alternative solutions involves the acquisition of a good or service.

[7] Convenience goods are those which customers wish to purchase immediately and with a minimum of effort. Shopping goods are those for which the consumer shops to compare suitability, quality, price, and style. Specialty goods are those for which customers characteristically insist and for which they are willing to make special effort. The basic classification was developed by Melvin T. Copeland (*Principles of Merchandising,* 1924). Holton has pointed out that convenience goods are distinguished by the buyers as those for which the probable gain from searching among alternative suppliers is low relative to search effort required, while for shopping goods the probable gain is large enough to call forth some level of search activity (*Journal of Marketing,* July, 1958).

Rather than assign goods to discrete classes, Aspinwall's characteristics of goods theory sets up a continuous scale using five goods characteristics and defines the criteria by which any product can be assigned a place on the scale. The mean position on the scale then indicates the appropriate distribution system. "Red" goods which call for broadcast distribution have low scores in all five characteristics: average number of days between purchases, gross margin, adjustment services required to meet the exact needs of the consumer, length of time over which the good provides the desired utility, and search time. "Yellow" goods have high scores on these characteristics while

Every buying situation does not lead to a purchase. For example, if a truck is wrecked a buying situation arises because one alternative solution is the purchase of a new truck. But a purchase may not occur because some other solution—working existing trucks longer hours, reducing delivery service, contracting out delivery, or rebuilding the wrecked truck—may be chosen.

Briefly, each buying situation represents a *kind of circumstance* which leads the buying unit to have a procurement problem. Buying situations vary in the amount of activity needed to reach decisions from the initial purchase of a capital good for a new business to the routine re-buy of a common operating supply item for a household. If we are to understand the procurement process we need not a "characteristics-of-goods theory" but a "characteristics-of-buyers'-problems theory."

Kinds of Buying Situations

Three underlying types of buying situations can be distinguished, based on the amount and kinds of information which the buying organization feels it needs in carrying out the buying process: new tasks, re-buys, and modified re-buys.

In the new task or new problem situation, the buying unit finds itself faced with a situation which it has not encountered before. A manufacturer may find that a new production problem suggests the possibility of using a type of machine which he has not previously employed. A merchant ponders whether or not he should consider installing a computer to handle his accounts. A family decides to consider the purchase of an appliance (for example, an electronic garage door opener) which it has not had before. The awareness that a problem exists may develop internally from the operation of existing methods (for example, the wife's complaint that the garage door is hard to lift or her dislike for getting out of the car in bad weather to open the door). More commonly, awareness develops through the efforts of marketers to convince prospective users that there is "a better way" (no need to get out of car in bad weather.)

Regardless of the source of the awareness, the embryonic buyer is a long way from a purchase decision, not so much in time but in terms of *informational distance.* He must satisfy himself on many matters. Because he has little or no background information on the capability of various goods to solve his problem, his information needs

---

goods in the orange range occupy intermediate positions. ("The Marketing Characteristics of Goods," *Cost & Profit Outlook,* September, 1956. Reproduced in *Four Marketing Theories by Leo V. Aspinwall* Commemorative edition. University of Colorado, Bureau of Business Research, 1961.)

are relatively great. This is not to suggest that he must "know all" before he decides but merely that (a) his present information base is small and (b) he recognizes that what he doesn't know *can* hurt him. Hence, he perceives a rather wide information gap to be closed. To do so he draws on various sources: reference persons in his own organization, present users, peers believed to be knowledgeable, salesmen and sellers' catalogues, and advertisements or displays, to suggest a few. Some of these sources lie within the buyer's own organization; others are part of the seller's marketing system; still others are part of neither but nevertheless form a part of the information system upon which the prospective buyer will draw. Moreover, the sources drawn upon will depend on the type of information to be obtained at the various steps in the procurement operation.

In contrast to the new problem situation, many purchases are no more than re-buys. The problem has arisen before and satisfactory solutions have been found. In the fully routinized case, previously established programs provide a solution without action by the buyer. The newsboy brings the paper, the oil company keeps the tank filled, the central computer for a chain notes that the reorder point for item Z in store S has been reached and reorders the item from the warehouse or a previously chosen regular supplier. More commonly, the re-buy is not fully routinized. The general category of goods and specific suppliers used before are accepted as a matter of course, but some details of the purchase itself may be different. Thus, the housewife may routinely undertake her weekly household replenishment each Friday by going to her regular supermarket, although the particular purchases in the market basket will differ from week to week. Her husband may routinely take the car to the same service station although the amount of gasoline put into the tank or the stock number of the lamp (bulb) replaced will not be the same as on the previous trip. In terms of buyer behavior and of information required, these may be treated as routine re-buys.[8] In routine re-buys, the buyer seeks little or no additional information. This is not to say that he is all-knowing but merely that the need for additional information is not perceived as being worth the effort and cost of obtaining it.

Whereas in the new problem situation the buyer believes himself inexperienced or unlearned in terms of what he needs to know, in the routine re-buy he feels no need to learn more. A seller who would break into a routine re-buy arrangement must first convince the buyer of the value to him of looking at alternatives.

[8] The term "routine re-buy" (a process) is not synonymous with "repeat purchase" (an outcome). A routine re-buy need not mean the purchase of an identical item. Moreover, a repeat purchase may occur as the result of an extensive nonroutine investigation and decision process.

In what may be termed modified re-buy situations, the buyer is in a somewhat intermediate position. On the one hand, he has some experience which assists him in understanding his problems and the alternatives available in order to deal with them. Yet for one reason or another, he is not satisfied with a mere routine reordering of what was purchased earlier.

A number of circumstances may lead to modified re-buy situations in home and industry. Someone in the buying organization may feel that a lower price or simply a better value might be obtained by taking another look at buying arrangements. He thus becomes willing to look at possible alternatives. The purpose in doing so is first of all informational. To be sure, he might in the end buy a different item or change suppliers. On the other hand, the new information may serve primarily to confirm his confidence in his present practices.

A second circumstance leading to a modified re-buy situation occurs when the buyer realizes that his need itself has changed in some way so that a different product or service may be more satisfactory than the one purchased heretofore. This realization may come about from activities internal to the buying organization, such as a change in the products it manufactures; developments in its relationships with employees, customers, or governments; or changes in the perspectives of officials. Or it may come about because a prospective supplier has redefined the buyer's situation for him, thereby leading him to consider his practices anew.

Modified re-buy situations also develop from straight re-buys when buyers discover new prospective supply opportunities, perhaps as a result of such efforts of sellers as trade shows, sales calls, or advertising, or because of information obtained from the trade press, general reading or interpersonal communication not directly related to the particular product.

While the foregoing examples of modified re-buy situations develop as dis-routinizing departures from straight re-buy practices, others arise as buyers find it necessary to consider a purchase of an item similar but not necessarily identical to one purchased for the first time. Because of the experience gained in the earlier purchases, much of the ground need not be explored again. Yet the buyer does not believe the solution to be cut and dried and thus appropriate for a straight re-buy solution.

As the learning process unfolds, a given product may be obtained initially as a solution to a new problem, subsequently as a modified re-buy, and eventually, perhaps, as a routine reorder. Consider, for example, a firm purchasing a new type of machine about which it has no knowledge. It needs extensive information and may consider a wide range of alternatives before the initial purchase is finally con-

cluded. Some time later the need recurs. Perhaps an additional machine is needed, or a model with additional features may be sought, or
the machine has worn out. The buyer now starts from a very different
information position than before. In a sense, he is partially informed
about many of the matters of interest to him. He has more knowledge
about technical features than in the earlier procurement. He well may
have made many judgments to eliminate certain suppliers and equipment from consideration in the process of narrowing down possible
solutions to the original problem. Thus, he starts from a substantially
greater information base than in the earlier case. Yet the intended procurement is unlikely to be strictly routine. If the purchase is a major
one, several sources and equipments are likely to be considered in
some way, although not as many as in the earlier case. In short, the
number of alternatives to be considered is likely to be smaller and the
size of the information gaps to be bridged are likely to be narrower
than in the initial procurement. The procurement process has become
simpler but by no means routine. Time passes. With additional purchases, the buyers become increasingly knowledgeable both in terms
of understanding their own needs and understanding the capabilities
of the various possible suppliers and equipments. Eventually they may
feel so knowledgeable that it ceases to be worth the time and effort
to do more than merely order another unit from the regular supplier.

THE BUYING SYSTEM AND THE SALES PROCESS

The situation in which the buyer operates, rather than the type
of merchandise available, plays the central role in determining what
the marketer must do to influence buyer behavior. In particular, it
defines the central role of the salesman in much the same way as it
defines the central role of the purchasing officials.[9]

The Salesman's Role in New Task Procurements

Where the buyer has little or no prior experience either in defining his problem or in evaluating possible solutions to it, the salesman has an extensive and multifold role to play: to open the buyer's
eyes to problems and possible improved solutions, to establish confidence in supplier capability, and to act as a communications link
between the technical personnel in the using and supplying companies.

A key task is to uncover and make explicit problems which
prospective users of his product may have but which they do not

[9] For an explanation of how the role of purchasing department personnel varies
among buying situations, see Patrick J. Robinson and Charles W. Faris, *Industrial Buying and Creative Marketing* (Boston: Allyn and Bacon, Inc., 1967).

recognize. In any firm of size, the original recognition of need is likely to be within the using department or operation; the purchasing department is not likely to even know about it. Thus the salesman must either anticipate buyers' problems and needs before they arise or identify and establish rapport with those individuals within the using firm who are most likely to recognize actual or incipient problems.

The use of some products such as materials and component parts affects the attributes of the customer's own products. In such cases, the salesman's task may focus on obtaining recognition of benefit from the customer's sales department. The salesman may do this by attempting to show customer sales executives that they have resolvable problems. In appropriate circumstances, effort may be directed at customers of customers to encourage them to raise questions or demand attributes which can best be provided by recognizing a problem which the salesman's firm is prepared to solve.

The role of problem definition and resolution in new task selling situations suggests that the salesman must sell performance rather then products. In turn, this demands knowledge of use situations which is at least equal to and preferably superior to that held by the users themselves.

Faced with a new buying situation, the buyer is frequently buying the problem-defining and problem-solving capability of the supplier rather than so many pieces of metal or pounds of equipment. Products can be selected from a catalogue except when they are tailored to order. The salesman is needed to give advice on the best choices to make from available items and on the best specifications to write on those which must be made for the specific application. Particularly in the latter case, it is the capability of the selling firm that the buyer is in fact purchasing. This is evident in the purchase of such services as those of attorneys and architects but applies with almost equal force to many industrial and consumer products which are to be designed and built after the purchase commitment has been made. In situations of this type, the key role of the salesman is often to establish confidence in his firm's capabilities.

The salesman is not the only individual within the supplying organization who provides information to prospective customers. For technical products and especially those which are designed to meet the particular needs of the individual application, the salesman may serve primarily as a discoverer and definer of problems and as a communications link between technical personnel in the designing or using departments of the customer firm on the one hand and their counterparts in the designing and manufacturing sectors of his company. He may, for example, assist a prospect in defining a problem and then ask his own technical personnel to prepare draft proposals. If he is successful in securing interest in such proposals on the part of the prospective customer, this may lead to further interchanges, including meetings between technical personnel at a variety of levels and performing diverse functions. Here the salesman's role is almost literally one of bringing together the right individuals at appropriate times and with appropriate materials.

In many new task and modified re-buy situations, the salesman is faced with the further challenge of inducing engineering personnel to accept risk. While any specifying or purchasing activity entails some risk both to the buying organization and to the individual making or accepting the specification, personal risk is greatest when the individual tries something new. For example, if a "tried and true" part from an established supplier fails, it is likely to be accepted by superiors as a regrettable but normal parts failure. On the other hand, if a new part or new supplier is tried and a failure occurs, the individual responsible may well be held to account for not using known sound products and sources. This is likely to be true even if the new item has a lower probability of failure than the established one. A result of this behavioral phenomenon is to make specifiers highly conservative in the acceptance of new methods, components, and suppliers even if the new alternative offers incontrovertible advantages. One way to overcome this conservatism is for the marketer to make the prospective real gain so great that the risk is worthwhile; small betterments may not be worth the perceived personal risk to the buyer. Another approach is to persuade users of the buyers' products that performance of the end products produced by the buyer will be so improved that the older method will not be accepted by him, a tactic which the reader will recognize as an industrial application of the pull-through-channel marketing strategy. In some cases, engineering conservatism can only be overcome by the vendor accepting much of the risk himself—that is, a credible performance guarantee.

A manufacturer of an air contamination control system based on new principles wished to secure an installation in a major graphic arts plant. To induce the owners to try such a system in place of one based on established principles, the system manufacturer guaranteed not that the equipment furnished as part of the system would be free from defects or that it would conform to the ventilating engineer's specifications but, rather, that it would develop the promised levels of cleanliness. If it failed to do so during a test period and after the seller had the opportunity to attune and adjust the components, the equipment would be removed and the buyer would pay nothing. In short, the seller undertook the risk of proving performance.

The protection of new customers who are induced to risk change may well justify taking unusual pains to insure proper performance of the first shipment or two to a new customer (for example, 100 percent inspection). First shipments are likely to be watched very closely. In any industrial good, it can be expected that every once in a while a bad lot will be shipped out. With established customers this usually does little harm, but if it happens on the first shipment to a new customer it can be devastating. Failure of an initial shipment may bring about an immediate reversion to the old methods, wiping out at one stroke perhaps years of sales effort. At the very least, it gives the new supplier a bad reputation which may take years of above average performance to live down. After some successful experience has been obtained, a bad lot is not nearly so serious. The extra effort and expense necessary to assure that the first shipments to a new customer are good is a form of insurance to protect the new relationship which may have been obtained only after substantial investment of sales effort.

Therefore, in situations such as these the salesman plays a multiple role: (1) securing a clear grasp of the real problem of the buyer not only in a product sense but in the type of assurances which would be meaningful to him; (2) finding an appropriate risk-reducing or risk-absorbing arrangement to overcome the buyers' conservatism; and (3) providing the communications system between personnel with various responsibilities in the buying firm and personnel in his company.

The Salesman's Role in Straight Re-Buys

The role of the salesman in situations which the buyer conceives of as calling for straight re-buys without the consideration of new alternatives will depend upon whether or not he is the present supplier. The "in" salesman's goal is to routinize the buying process as much as possible and thereby cement a favorable current situation. To this end there is likely to be strong emphasis on reliability in the order-filling marketing flows as well as efforts to establish a reputation for capability and performance which acts to reduce the likelihood that buyers will consider alternatives (that is, convert procurement of the items in question to modified re-buys). Sometimes coordinated routines are established—for example, coordinated inventory management, unitized trains. The goal is to pre-empt competitive intrusion.

Where the salesman is calling on retailers or other members of the trade channel, he provides a major part of the internal communications system of that channel. Securing orders from channel members may become relatively unimportant incidents in the effort to make the channel itself a viable competitor in the markets being served by the channel. Here the salesman's role is often to strengthen the performance of the channel members on whom he calls. His activities may include assistance in training of the retailer's sales personnel; ideas for display, layout, or promotion; and assistance in any operating or management problem the solution of which will make the customer a more effective member of the channel. Some of these services to the channel member will be provided by the salesman himself. For others, the salesman may act as liaison with others in his organization.

While the able salesman will establish and maintain favorable relationships with customers, this does not mean that particular items can be maintained as straight re-buys indefinitely. For one thing, buyers, especially experienced industrial and commercial purchasers, are likely to make periodic tests of the desirability of standing relationships by test checks of one sort or another. Builders, for example, obtain quotes on material from diverse sources other than their established suppliers in order to assure themselves that they are not overpaying and to keep the established supplier in line. A large industrial firm reshuffles personnel in the purchasing division from time to time. The management believes that such changes of personnel lead to desirable challenges and tests of established relationships and prevent them from becoming stale.

More importantly in the general case, however, is the fact that buyers' needs and available goods change over time so that the buyer must necessarily review his arrangements—that is, consider some straight re-buys as modified re-buys from time to time. An important function of the salesman is to identify and, if possible, anticipate such situations so that his firm can maintain its preferred or exclusive relationship with the customer. If it were not for the need to perform and act upon these intelligence aspects of the salesman's job, the maintenance of relationships with established accounts could be delegated to a machine or to clerical help.

It is perhaps an oversimplification to say that the job of the "in" salesman in a re-buy situation is "to keep 'em happy" although this is an important task. His more critical function is to anticipate when new situations will develop and maintain a relationship which gives his company the chance to maintain the established arrangements or to participate at least on an equal basis in modifications which will occur.

For the "out" salesman, the situation is almost the reverse. Faced with a buyer following a re-buy routine, his task is to convert it to a modified re-buy by demonstrating that either because the buyer's problem has changed or because improved methods of dealing with it have been developed, at least some of the decisions which led to the original purchase should be reexamined. Success in such an undertaking may be dependent on the salesman's ability to understand the user's product or service needs so well that he can propose improvements sufficiently significant in the buyer's eyes to demand investigation. This has been accomplished for even such commodities as coal (by offering to maintain an inventory at the buyer's plant) and steel (by providing a packaging form which reduced users' difficulties and costs in handling and storing and cut the percentage which ended up as scrap).

Whereas the "in" salesman seeks to keep routine things routine the "out" salesman seeks to show that better ways are desirable.

The Salesman's Role in Modified Re-Buys

Perhaps the greatest challenge to the salesman in the modified re-buy situation is his ability to detect what attributes of the product-service package are significant to buyers. In modified re-buys the buyer already has some, perhaps substantial, information and is likely to have reasonably well-defined evaluation criteria. Hence, the salesman's job often is to determine the areas in which the provision of additional information or guidance is likely to influence the decision-making processes of buyers. Whereas in new tasks, need recognition and problem definition and solution are central, these matters will largely have been resolved in connection with earlier purchases. Buyers' interests are more likely to be concerned with the possibility of better ways, additional sources of supply, new ancillary services, and the like. Depending on the situation which produced the modified re-buy, the salesman will need to identify what is fixed and what is open to change and the kinds of information and interaction with users which are appropriate. If the new task situation requires a technical man, the modified re-buy situation calls for a sales-idea man.

TYPES OF SELLING SITUATIONS FOR INTERPERSONAL INTERACTION

It should be clear at this point that the salesman's job is not, as some have alleged, to "sell people what they don't want." Nor is it merely to "oil the marketing process," although it certainly acts as a lubricant in the course of providing the vehicle for personal interaction. Moreover, the salesman's role in directing one-way messages to buyers continues to decline as unidirectional media become more effective and relatively less costly. The salesman's place rests on the need for bidirectional communications. The survival of personal selling and its importance in the economy will depend on the mutual benefits which such human interactions can provide.

Perhaps we can get a better view of the role of the salesman and the different types of selling situations if we focus not on why the salesman may wish to talk with the buyer but on why the buyer is interested in or even willing to talk to the salesman.

Why Talk to a Salesman?

A number of reasons for seeing salesmen are apparent from our discussion of the buying process. These include:

1. to obtain aid and advice in defining a particular problem;
2. to determine if there is a new or better way of dealing with a problem;
3. to get aid on deciding which of the available goods is best suited;
4. to obtain information on what is available;
5. to determine how or if a good might be tailored to meet a particular need;
6. to determine the capability of possible suppliers to fill a particular need;
7. to find merchandise which the buyer wishes to examine or purchase;
8. to secure aid in the solution of an operating problem.

The reader will note that all of these purposes relate in some way to the information position and information needs of users and buyers as they consider the possibility of changing their present operating methods or purchases.

Types of Salesmen

From the foregoing we may distinguish many types of jobs which seem to fit under the general category "salesman."

1. *Solvers of buyers' unique problems* tailor goods and/or groups of goods into a solution peculiarly appropriate to the customer. Most so-called sales engineers fall into this category. Their function is akin to that of a custom designer or architect.
2. *Discoverers and revealers of buyers' problems* not only deal with buyers' known and expressed problems; they learn to understand the buyer's operations so well that they can discover and reveal problems before the user recognizes that one exists. The truly able salesman in this group anticipates problems before they even arise so that he is prepared to offer the remedy—possibly even as preventive medicine.
3. *Application advisors* suggest to the buyer the best product for use in a particular application. Examples are the store clerk who provides advice as to the best paint for a particular situation and the industrial salesman who recommends the most suitable fastener for an assembly operation.

4. *Educators* present lines which are new to the buyer or which add to his stock of information although not relevant to the buyer's present problems. The salesman hopes that the buyer will discover a problem for which the offering is relevant. If he does and the salesman learns of it, the learning process is reversed. The salesman then takes on another role. In a sense, such salesmen are broadcasters rather than problem solvers; they play a role in personal selling because such work is often part of an inter-educational—problem-discovery—and problem-resolution sequence.

5. *Oral catalogue machines* may best describe many retail clerks and salesmen calling on the trade and industry who largely act as information sources as to what is available. To the buyer, these salesmen provide a reference source as to what is available and on what terms.

6. *Routers* (human signposts) assist buyers in locating merchandise, generally within a store or center.

7. *Operations advisors* assist buyers in the solution of operating problems and efforts to improve operations. Whereas applications advisors assist the buyer in selecting the right product, operations advisors assist him in product use or resale activities. Examples are salesmen who assist customers in store layout, inventory methods, and sales personnel training, and industrial salesmen who work closely with using departments to forestall or resolve problems in the use of the seller's products.

The foregoing classification of salesmen attempts to concern itself with the function of the salesman in terms of the buyer's problem-solving activity.

The tasks listed above are not mutually exclusive. A particular salesman may do many of these things for his customers.

Architects, for example, look to salesmen, and particularly to manufacturers' A-B-C men (Architect and Builder Consultants), who call on them to perform several roles: as information sources to keep them abreast of new products; as application advisors, who can suggest which items are most appropriate for a particular application; and, in some cases, as problem solvers who work with the architect in developing working drawings for custom components and systems. That this job is not always performed to the architect's satisfaction is indicated by such complaints as:

Many salesmen are unable to give us information on in-place costs, performance characteristics, examples of successful use, and other information we must have.

A lot of designing is done with the salesman. But many are not technically equipped for maximum help in specification writing.
Salesmen fail to point out limitations of their products for fear of losing
the business; yet if we knew them, we could design around
them.

Manufacturer and distributor salesmen perform similar combinations of services for contractors; these are of particular value to the
smaller operators who often lack both extensive files and staff expertise.

Nevertheless, a classification of sales tasks in terms of services provided to those upon whom the salesman calls is a useful way of recognizing that a great many different kinds of relationships between buyers and salesmen go under the rubric "salesman."

It should be noted that order takers, check-out counter clerks,
and cashiers are not listed in the above classification. Such persons
are concerned with the order filling rather than the order-getting process and are not involved in the interpersonal communicative relationships relevant to the buying (or selling) process. They are, thus, not
salesmen within the context of this book.

Although they are transaction rather than relationship oriented,
all of the specific sales roles suggested above must be viewed in terms
of the subordinance of the transaction to the relationship. Thus we
find that the salesman's role is not confined to dealing with the buyer's
particular information needs of the moment but rather with establishing relationships so that when relevant needs occur or can be discovered the relationship exists. Much of the day-to-day work of able
salesmen is not "selling" in the sense of presenting goods to buyers
at all. It concerns itself with the longer term aspects of becoming an
accepted supply aide to the user and with the nurturing of such relationships so that the seller's firm is called upon when a problem
arises. In the case of routine purchases, the role of the salesman may
often be to service the account so well that the routine stays routine
or becomes even more rigidly channeled.

SUMMARY

Personal selling deals with interpersonal communicative relationships. It is most likely to be useful to buyers where the knowledge
needed to understand and resolve a problem is not fully evident or
readily obtainable from prior experience or unidirectional information
flows.

To understand the personal sales process we must understand
how the buying unit formulates its problems and at least those parts
of its buying process which lead to or involve buyer-salesman interaction.

Buyers are information processors. Understanding their behavior requires perception of how buyers acquire and use information in solving their problems and, in particular, of how buyers perceive data to which they are exposed and transform selected data into information.

Buying is a process, not an event. The solution space for a buying problem is successively narrowed during the buying process until only a single solution remains. The entire process consists of a series of events which begins with a recognition of a problem or need and, if not aborted, ends when the buyers' experiences with the purchased product become part of his learned experience and thus part of his data bank for the solution of future problems.

The buying process in a particular situation is less a function of the item purchased than of the problem to be solved and the buyer's information situation in regard to possible solutions. In new tasks, buyers recognize that what they don't know can hurt them. That is, there is a wide discrepancy between what a buyer knows and what he believes he needs to know to reduce the risk of an incorrect purchase to an acceptable level. Much information and assurance may be needed at a number of stages in the buying process. In contrast, routinized re-buy procedures are appropriate when the buyer believes that the gain from changing his solution pattern would be too small to warrant the search effort required. In such situations the "in" salesman seeks to extend the scope of the routinization; the "out" salesman seeks to convince buyers that new factors should be considered.

The salesman serves the buyer by assisting him at appropriate stages in the buying process. He serves his employer by establishing and maintaining mutually beneficial buyer-seller relationships. Such transactions as occur are the result of, and to a certain extent incidental to, such relationships.

Salesmen may be classified on the basis of their role in buyer problem-solving activity as (1) solvers of unique problems, (2) discoverers and revealers of buyer problems, (3) application advisors, (4) educators, (5) oral catalogue machines, (6) routers, and (7) operations advisors. A particular salesman may, at times, play many different roles.

In the final analysis it is the buyer, his perceptions, and his information needs which will determine whether interpersonal, or for that matter any, messages will be received and transformed into information which, in turn, might affect behavior.

An understanding of the buying process and how it varies depending upon the circumstances in which the buyer finds himself is thus central to an understanding of the sales process itself and the role of the personal salesman in particular.

SELECTED READINGS

Bearden, James H. (ed.). *Personal Selling: Behavioral Science Readings and Cases.* New York: John Wiley and Sons, Inc., 1967. Part I-C, "Sales as Communication." Four articles dealing with the role of salesmen as communicators. Two of the articles deal with opinion formation and the diffusion of innovation in the medical community; one with communicating agents in technological change in agriculture; one with the salesman as an information source for industrial buyers.

Cox. Donald F. (ed.). *Risk Taking and Information Handling in Consumer Behavior.* Boston: Division of Research, Harvard Business School, 1967. A review of a number of studies on perceived risk and purchasing.

Davis, Kenneth R. and Frederick E. Webster, Jr. (eds.). *Readings in Sales Force Management.* New York: The Ronald Press Company, 1968. Part III, "Analysis of Communication and Buying Patterns—The Basis of Selling Strategy." A series of eight articles on the purchasing process and the role of communications in it.

Engel, James F., David T. Kollat, and Roger D. Blackwell. *Consumer Behavior.* New York: Holt, Rinehart, and Winston, Inc., 1968. Chapters 3, 16–24. A comprehensive analysis of recent findings in consumer behavior.

Evans, Franklin B. "Selling as a Dyadic Relationship—A New Approach." *American Behavioral Scientist,* VI (May, 1963), pp. 76–79. (Also reprinted in Bearden. *Personal Selling* and Davis and Webster, *Readings in Sales Force Management.*) Selling as an under-researched interactive process.

Webster, Frederick E., Jr. "Interpersonal Communication and Salesman Effectiveness." *Journal of Marketing,* XXXII, No. 3 (July, 1968), pp. 7–13. Insights from behavioral sciences which suggest the role of perceptive skills in interactions.

Wind, Yoram and Patrick J. Robinson. "Simulating the Industrial Buying Process." *Marketing and the New Science of Planning.* Edited by Robert L. King. Chicago: American Marketing Association, 1968, (Proceedings Series No. 28), pp. 441–448. Simulation of the industrial buying process using the Robinson-Faris classification of buying situations.

3 Task Determination

Identification of the critical function which the salesman is to perform in dealing with the customer is basic to the role of personal selling in the particular organization. The salesman's critical function (central role) should be derived from the interaction of (1) the firm's conception of the nature of the relationship to be developed with its various customer groups and (2) the firm's corporate and marketing goals.

Both of these elements are unique to the firm at a particular point in its own development. Thus, a new entry in a highly innovative field sets about organizing its sales force with a different set of customer relationships and a different set of objectives than does a firm long in the field or even a company with a solid position in a related field. In particular, the market niche to which it aspires both immediately and over time will have a significant influence on the kinds of relationships which the sales force is likely to have to develop. At the same time, the salesman's role must be laid in the context of the firm's particular goal set—in volume, profit, return on investment, market share, community image, contribution to social goals, or in whatever terms it is posed.

For these reasons, determination of the central function of the salesman is a major responsibility shared by the sales manager and at least the senior marketing executives of the firm. Subsequent task determination problems (Figure 3-1) are primarily the responsibility of the sales-force manager although much information for them may come from activities such as the market research department.

This chapter deals with the determination of what various sales jobs should be. The results should be expressed in comprehensive job descriptions. Chapter 4 will deal with the development of rules for determining *how much* sales effort should be applied in different market situations. Chapter 5 treats the problem of defining market

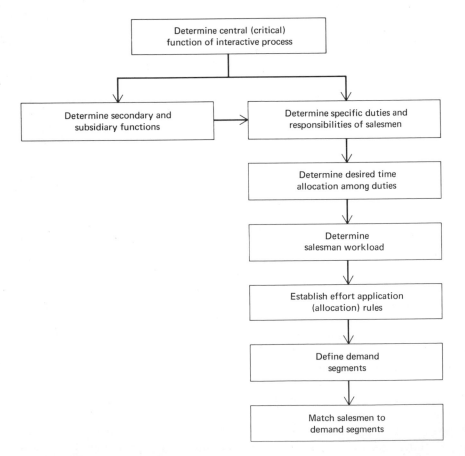

Figure 3-1
TASK DETERMINATION PROBLEMS

segments relevant for personal selling activity and matching (assigning) the salesmen to such demand segments. Part II of this book deals with developing and maintaining the competence necessary for effective and efficient execution of the appropriate salesman duties.

THE NEED FOR COMPREHENSIVE JOB DESCRIPTIONS

Although different companies will have a variety of uses for job descriptions, four types of uses are of particular concern to the sales manager. By understanding how each of these uses will be involved the manager can improve the likelihood that the descriptions developed will provide the information he will need for these purposes.

Managerial Understanding

The paramount managerial need for job descriptions is to contribute to the understanding of the sales job by the sales-force manager. To carry out his own responsibilities, the manager must understand with considerable precision the primary function of his salesmen. This need is not met by simply stating that the salesman's job is to sell or by providing a lengthy list of duties and responsibilities. What is required is clear recognition of the nature of the particular interpersonal relationship with customers and prospects in which the salesman will be the company's representative. What kind of interpersonal communicative relationship is envisaged? How will that relationship differ with different marketing strategies which the company or its customers might be pursuing at different times or in different areas? Within the context of these relationships what is the primary function of the salesman?

In an earlier chapter it was noted that personal selling is a multifaceted process. Nevertheless, in any particular situation, one of these facets or responsibilities is likely to be paramount. Is the salesman primarily an information source for customers? Is he chiefly a problem identifier? Is his central role one of communications broker to bring together appropriate technical staffs of the customer and his company? Is his role chiefly one of keeping customers happy? Or of showing them the disadvantages of their present methods of doing things? Or is the salesman the remainder-man, performing assorted activities which have not been performed by others in the organization?

Because the salesman plays many roles, the set of roles should be clearly defined and decision rules formulated for determining the importance of each role. Not only is it necessary to determine which role is primary at a particular time, but provision must be made for the likelihood that the primary role of the salesman will undergo change with the changing relationships between a firm and its customers. Only after the primary role has been clearly identified and the possibilities of its modification understood, can the lists of salesman's duties which are so easily written into job descriptions have real meaning. Little wonder that when this is not done, we find important disagreement among salesmen, sales management, and customers as to what the salesman's job really is.

Manpower Procurement and Development

Job descriptions play an important role in the development of the man specifications which will be the foundation for hiring and the basis for determining the kinds of training which will be necessary to bring the personnel hired to the competence level set forth in the specification of trained men ready for duty. Job descriptions may also have some bearing on the number of men required. In the more complex selling situation, fewer calls can be made and thus more men are needed for a given amount of coverage.

A meaningful job description is also important in providing job candidates with an understanding of what the job entails and of providing incumbents with a clear picture of what is expected of them. Clarity of goals has been shown to affect motivation favorably. For example,

> . . . job turnover was lower for a group of newly hired life insurance agents who had been given a clear, detailed picture of what to expect on the job (through a descriptive booklet) than for a comparable group not provided with a clear-cut expectation of what the job entailed.[1]

Planning, Measurement, and Control

The job description tells what a man is supposed to do. Thus, it provides direction to the salesman in planning individual calls. It also provides a yardstick for performance measurement. By comparing what a man is supposed to do with what he is actually doing, the salesman himself or his supervisor can foresee trouble spots before they develop into serious situations and quickly take action to clear them up. In discussions with subordinates about their performance on the job, the job description provides a logical and useful starting point.

Salary Administration

The job description is often a major input to the determination of salary levels. The increasing use of the salary form of compensation for salesmen, especially in industrial work, and the increased ten-

---

[1] J. Weitz, "Job Expectation and Survival," *Journal of Applied Psychology,* XL (1956), 245–247.

dency of firms to structure salaries according to meaningful relationships demands job descriptions which are accurate and complete.

Where other forms of incentive compensation are used, the lack of a full understanding of the nature of the job in all of its ramifications can easily lead to the introduction of dysfunctional elements into a compensation plan. Because the job itself is not fully and correctly understood, the firm may provide a reward system which works against the performance of some duties or the discharge of certain responsibilities.

PRINCIPAL PROBLEMS IN TASK DETERMINATION

Determination of *what* the salesman should do entails decisions in five problem areas.

The fundamental problem is the determination of the role of the salesman in the interaction with customers and prospects. Is the sales interview to be aimed primarily at order getting or at establishing broader relationships? What type of relationships is the salesman expected to develop and maintain with his accounts? What is the salesman to offer the user, beyond the goods themselves? Is his role seen as basically diagnostic? prescriptive? informational? What role does he play in the overall marketing strategy of his firm?

The range of possible answers to these types of questions is very broad indeed. At one extreme is the industrial salesman whose charge is to keep a single important account happy so that a favorable, long-standing relationship will be maintained. At the other extreme lies the type of broad responsibility and follow-through expected of salesmen for an acoustical tile contractor in which the salesman not only seeks out business and prepares proposals but is responsible for overall supervision of work to ensure that it is performed satisfactorily for the customer, for final inspection, and even for collection of the account.

Once the salesman's central function has been identified, management can turn to secondary or subsidiary functions which may be appropriately assigned to him provided they do not impair performance of his central function.

What functions in such areas as data collection, account evaluation, credits and collections, and public relations should be part of the salesman's job? What does each entail? Which duties are crucial, which less important? How important is the satisfactory performance of particular duties to the overall performance of the job? What should be the salesman's responsibilities to and relationships with other parts of the organization?

The functions allotted to the personal selling activity and the specific duties and responsibilities assigned to the salesmen will provide the basis for determining the workload which each salesman can be expected to undertake. Management's problem is to translate its understanding of the job and of the human work required to perform it into workload units appropriate for individual men. Excessive workloads can easily lead to the neglect of some duties which management believes to be important parts of the job. A load that is too light imposes excessive costs.

Two types of allocation decisions are required. First, it is necessary to determine how the salesman's time can be allocated most effectively among his diverse responsibilities such as gathering market information, calling on customers, preparing reports, and attending meetings. Second, complete definition of the salesman's job entails selection of the means for carrying out assigned duties. For example:

Should the salesman make more calls per day or devote more time to each call?

Should a formal, written plan be prepared for each call, or would the time thus devoted be used better in some other way?

Are demonstrations or the use of films or other props worth the time they require, or might the time be more profitably devoted to other sales work?

Should the salesman seek to obtain an order on each call or should calls be devoted solely to relationship development, with orders expected to come through the buyer's normal routines?

Some selling is highly routinized with management selecting the best methods; the salesman's discretion may be quite limited.

Some wholesale druggists determine in detail how many calls should be made each day, how much call time should be devoted to promotions, which items should be mentioned in each call, and generally how the salesman should allocate his time.

More commonly, many decisions about how to carry out the sales job are left to the individual salesman, with management providing more or less general guidelines. To some degree, then, such salesmen may be said to be partially defining their own jobs.

DETERMINANTS OF SALES TASK DECISIONS

Solutions to the kinds of sales-management problems raised in the previous section rest heavily on

1. the desired relationships to be established with customers and prospects,

2. the relative effectiveness and efficiency of having various primary and secondary tasks performed by the salesman as contrasted with having particular tasks performed by someone else,
3. the relative payoffs from alternative uses of the salesman's time.

It should be self-evident that definition of the primary role of the salesman must rest on the conceived customer-salesman relationship. Specific salesman's duties must be determined in this context.

Not all duties which might be performed by the salesman should necessarily be performed by him. Some, such as credit evaluation, collections, the determination of quantities needed at a particular time, the transmittal of replenishment orders, follow-up, and status reporting often may be performed more effectively by specialists in the office or in other departments or through the use of routinized systems. In other situations, activities of this sort are most effectively performed by the salesman himself. Nevertheless, *system efficiency* may be improved by having them performed in some other manner when due allowance is made for the opportunity cost value of the salesman's time. For example, the salesman may do the best job, in an absolute sense, of following up service or collecting accounts. Yet it may be more efficient for the firm to have these tasks performed by less costly personnel even if their performance is slightly less effective. Such situations involve a trade-off of effectiveness in the performance of an activity against its *total* cost to the firm.

> An extreme example of disregard for the division of labor between salesmen and other resources is the case of a small wholesaler who used country salesmen to make deliveries of previously ordered merchandise "in order to save parcel post charges."

The most effective use of the salesman's time requires an understanding of the relative payoffs from alternative uses of that time.

> In a study of the practices of wholesale drug salesmen, Davis found that sales were directly correlated with such factors as the proportion of time spent in promotional selling, the number of items mentioned during sales calls and the number of sales arguments given. In that study, the differences between salesmen identified by their supervisors as good salesmen and those considered to be less effective performers were entirely traceable to how they spent their time and what they did rather than how well they made their arguments or, for that matter, the nature of the arguments used.
>
> For example, the routine mention of an item, without a buying reason, resulted in sales one-eighth of the time (12.7 percent for "best" salesmen; 12.4 percent for "other" salesmen). Items mentioned with a

buying reason sold at a 54 percent rate (53.8 percent for "best" men; 54.3 percent for "others"). The differences in total sales achieved were attributed to the fact that the better men introduced buying reasons more frequently (on 29.75 items per day as against 24.3 items). The men identified by their managers as superior salesmen also spent a smaller proportion of their time in general conversation and other nonessential activities.[2]

METHODS OF DEVELOPING JOB DESCRIPTIONS

The traditional method of determining tasks to be performed by salesmen is largely one of following past practices. Management sets forth what it believes the salesman should do and a set of logical arguments is then advanced to support these beliefs. Such an intuitive approach leaves much to be desired.

The need for more objective task-determination decisions requires more objective examination of what the job *should be*. In part, this examination can rest on observational study of the existing job— that is, a descriptive job analysis. However, as the manner in which the present job is conceived and executed is not necessarily the best one, reviews of job concepts, analyses of the results of operations, and, in some cases, experimental studies may provide additional insights for developing descriptions of what the job should be. The conduct of job analyses and other observational and experimental studies is thus an important prerequisite to task-determination decisions.

Responsibility for Job Description Studies

The sales-force manager may be able to draw on the services of an in-house staff of job analysts or the services of an outside consultant or may need to plan and carry out job description studies under his own supervision. The strengths and weaknesses of these alternatives are generally the same that apply when the question of contracting staff services arises in dealing with other activities. The expertise and objectivity of the outsider must be weighed against the greater familiarity of his own people with the operation and its problems and idiosyncracies and the presumably lower out-of-pocket costs involved. The decision is sometimes complicated by the need to recognize the sales manager's own company organizational relationships, possible time or security constraints, or other factors. Even where a firm has an established staff of job analysts in its production divisions, the substantially different character of portions of the sales job may make the conventionally employed analytical tools quite inadequate.

[2] James H. Davis, *Increasing Wholesale Drug Salesmen's Effectiveness* (Columbus: The Ohio State University, 1948), pp. 68, 70, 86.

Whether the sales manager employs an outside firm, a company staff, or his own personnel he is likely to find it necessary to become involved in some measure in determining the kind of studies that will be undertaken. Sound studies must proceed from a clear understanding of the purposes for which the resulting job descriptions will be employed. Moreover, the sales manager who understands what is possible in the way of analyses is more likely to provide the insight in defining and guiding the project which is so important in developing useful results. In addition, effective usage of the results of the studies requires an understanding of the methods employed at least to the extent of recognizing the underlying strengths and weaknesses which derive therefrom. It is appropriate, therefore, to examine briefly some of the techniques which have been found useful in job description studies.

Techniques for Job Description Studies

For an existing sales force, job description studies may start with analysis of the *present job.* Such an analysis is necessarily descriptive rather than prescriptive in that it reveals what the job *is now* rather than what the job *should be* to best fulfill its role. Nevertheless, it provides a useful point of departure in obtaining a clear view of the particular job within a specific firm.

Several approaches are used in attacking the central questions of job analysis. The analyst may observe the performance of salesmen informally or through formal time and duty studies. Such observations will reveal the activities which are being performed but cast only limited and indirect light on the rationale underlying the observed acts. Or the analyst may inquire of salesmen, supervisors or managers, or of customers or others with whom the salesman has communicative relationships, to ascertain their perception of the salesman's job. The conceptions of what the job is or should be sometimes depart rather drastically from the conclusions which might appear most readily from observation through time-and-duty study. The careful analyst may wish to examine both what the salesman is in fact doing and what those to whom he has responsibilities (including customers and the salesman himself) believe his function and responsibilities to be.

In a study of wholesale drug salesmen, Davis found that salesmen, sales executives, and the druggists being called on all agreed overwhelmingly that providing advice and assistance was an important part of the salesman's job. On the average, the executives believed that salesmen should spend about 12 percent of their time in such work. Time study revealed that, in fact, less than 2 percent of the salesman's in-store time was spent in this type of work. Both the salesman and the retailer believed that more time was being spent. A comparison of time actually spent with the perception of retailers and salesmen is shown in Table 3-1.

Table 3-1

TIME SPENT IN ADVICE AND ASSISTANCE TO RETAILERS

Minutes per call	As observed in time study (% of callls)	As perceived by retailer* (% of retailers)	As perceived by salesman* (% of salesmen)
None	77.1%	37.6%	9.8%
0.1–5.0 minutes	19.6	22.3	52.2
5.1–10.0 minutes	2.9	20.2	18.0
10.1 minutes or more	0.4	19.9	18.0
	100.0%	100.0%	100.0%

*Excludes retailers and salesmen not making estimates.

SOURCE: Calculated from data in James H. Davis, *Increasing Wholesale Drug Salesmen's Effectiveness* (Columbus: The Ohio State University, Bureau of Business Research, 1948), pp. 21–23.

TIME-AND-DUTY ANALYSIS

Time-and-duty analysis seeks to describe what the salesman presently does. In employing this observational method, the activities in which salesmen are believed to engage are first listed and classified. For salesmen calling on the retail trade, for example, such a classification might include such activities as checking stock, arranging displays, advising retailers on operations, furnishing new product news, attempting to secure additional shelf space, seeking a trial order, travel time, waiting, general conversation, preparing reports, and attending meetings.

Next, a group of salesmen are selected for observation. In some studies both "good" salesmen and others believed to be below average are included so that differences in the way they spend their time or perform their duties may be noted. A trained observer accompanies each salesman for one or more working days during which he records and classifies the time spent on each activity. Along with the time study, the observer may also note the manner in which duties are performed. Thus the analyst can determine not only the relationships between time spent and results obtained but also whether or not the manner of performing duties has an effect on results. Although time-and-duty studies have many other applications in the management of sales forces (for example, in determining training needs), they are useful in the context of task determination because they reveal what the salesmen are currently doing. Unfortunately, they do not reveal either purpose or motivation. They do not tell us what the salesman is endeavoring to accomplish when he makes certain statements or undertakes certain activities. Thus, they do not provide a full understanding of the job.

Time-and-duty studies may involve substantial problems of obtaining valid and reliable samples of sales work. In those instances where one day is pretty much like the rest (for example, salesmen calling on retail grocers) a one- or two-day observation period is probably sufficient. But for the more complex industrial selling jobs, securing an adequate and representative observation period may pose substantial problems. The industrial salesman typically has few customers, each of whom constitutes a different problem, and, in the strictest sense, a different selling task. He may call on any given customer once a week, once a month, or once every two months, depending on the activity of the customer, his importance to the company, and whether or not the customer in question has any special projects or problems. If the observer travels with the salesman for only a day or two, he may well get a complete misconception of what the job actually entails. For example, if the customers the salesman happens to be calling on during the observation period are primarily established customers of long standing, the observer is likely to come away with the idea that the salesman's job is primarily that of an order taker, information dispenser, or entertainer. A completely different impression of the job would be obtained if the observation period happened to coincide with a period in which the calls were being made primarily on new accounts who were not familiar with the salesman's products and how to use them. In this case the study would probably reveal that the salesman's job is primarily that of an information dispenser, problem solver, and coordinator. Yet a third impression would be obtained if the observation period corresponded with a swing through a recently opened part of the territory. Then the job might appear to be solely that of the missionary salesman. In actuality, most industrial sales jobs combine aspects of all these things. In such circumstances, an observation period sufficiently long to represent adequately the various types of work might well make the time-and-duty study too costly in both time and money.

Another problem with time-and-duty studies is the undetermined effect of the presence of the observer on the behavior of the salesman.[3] To the extent that the salesman believes that his normal pattern is the correct one, if he also feels it agrees with the supervisor's definition, and if he feels there is nothing to be gained by faking

[3] For the effects of an observer or of participation in an experiment, see John H. Madge, *The Tools of Social Science* (Garden City, N.Y.: Doubleday, Anchor, 1965), p. 122ff.

it, the behavior during the observation period well may be typical of the salesman's work. But the analyst has no valid way of determining if this is, in fact, the case.

In some types of sales work, the salesman may believe that the presence of an observer or "shadow" may adversely affect the salesman's relationships with those upon whom he calls. Salesmen seeking to maintain rapport with professional men, for example, may feel that the presence of a "shadow" would not be helpful in furthering the desired relationships. The salesman's fears may or may not be justified; nevertheless, they may exist.

The use of random alarm devices makes it possible to conduct time studies without the use of an observer. The problems of the shadow system are thus avoided. A large number of salesmen can be provided with pocket random alarm devices at substantially lower cost than is possible using observers. Whenever the alarm goes off, the salesman records the activity in which he is engaged at the moment and, if desired, his location.

> In one study using random alarm devices, each man carried the unit for one full week, with instructions to keep it on during all waking hours and to fill out a check-off type card whenever the alarm sounded. About 50 observations of both location and activity were secured per man-week. The preliminary findings revealed that the salesmen spent an average of 58.3 hours per week in work-related activities. Of this time only 7.6 hours per week, or 13 percent of the salesman's working time, was spent in interviews with those with whom the salesman was seeking to establish or maintain relations. Much larger portions of time were spent in travel to call on customers (15.7 hours, exclusive of home-bound travel), and waiting time (14.6 hours). Other activities which consumed two hours per week or more of the salesmen's time were checking store stock (5.6 hours), working with sample cases or promotional materials (3.9 hours), company paper work (3.3 hours), business reading (2.6 hours), and planning (2 hours).

While random alarm devices seem promising for time study, they do not, of course, provide data on the manner in which the salesmen are carrying out the reported activities. The latter require the use either of an observer or of some form of remote monitor.

Time-and-duty analysis and on-the-job observation when applied to more complex selling jobs become more difficult and, thus, less useful. While they work fairly well when the duties are rather routine and the "sales cycle" is relatively short, they become less reliable and more prone to produce misleading results as the sales cycle lengthens and the selling job becomes more complex.

INTERVIEWS AND QUESTIONNAIRE STUDIES

Interviews and questionnaire studies are designed to deal more directly, if less objectively, with the questions for which the job analyst seeks answers. Using these tools, the analyst seeks to determine from each of the key parties what the role and responsibilities of the salesman are conceived to be. Questions may be directed to customers, management, and sales personnel themselves.

Inquiries are directed to customers and noncustomers called upon by the salesmen to determine the function the salesman performs for them, if any.

In the course of a study of the procurement practices of architects, the author found that many architects look to manufacturer salesmen for data on performance characteristics and applications experience. Some hope for assistance in preparing specifications. Commonly the salesmen's competence and performance in these areas is somewhat less than architects would like.

At the same time, information may be sought on the quality of performance of salesmen, and on desirable activities which the salesmen do not perform or do not perform to the full satisfaction of those upon whom they call. Customer groups may also be asked to express their understanding of the salesman's responsiblities and, in some cases, of company policies. Such inquiries may disclose how well company information, practices, and policies have flowed through to the customer groups upon whom the salesman calls.

Inquiries are directed to the sales manager and to intermediate supervisory levels (for example, regional and district managers) to ascertain their understanding of the central function of their salesmen and of the salesmen's duties, responsiblities, and relationships. Inquiries may also be directed to others with whom the salesman interacts or who are dependent on the salesman, such as the marketing research manager or other executives depending on the salesman for intelligence.

Most importantly, inquiries are directed to the salesman himself. Especially in the more complex sales jobs, the salesman may be the only one who has even a reasonably complete grasp of what the job involves. Even for less complex jobs, the salesman may offer insights which an outside observer may not perceive. There is, in addition, an important morale benefit in having the salesmen participate in an activity which will have ramifications on their work and status. Exhibits 3-1 and 3-2 are examples of job descriptions prepared by supervisors and salesmen.

Exhibit 3-1

SUPERVISOR PREPARED POSITION DESCRIPTION

JOB NO. _____

JOB TITLE _____ *Senior Salesman* _____

DIVISION _____ *Industrial Chemicals—East* _____

DEPARTMENT _____ *Sales* _____

LOCATION (PLANT OR OFFICE) _____ *Regional Office* _____

NOTE: Before Answering Questions
Read All Questions Asked.

I. DIRECTIONS RECEIVED FROM _____ *Regional Manager* _____
                                              (Job Title)

II. TO CONDUCT THE ACTIVITIES OF THIS JOB, CERTAIN LATERAL COMMUNICATIONS WITH COMPANY PERSONNEL FROM OTHER DEPARTMENTS AND LOCATIONS ARE NECESSARY. PLEASE LIST YOUR TYPICAL COMPANY ASSOCIATES.	**PLEASE LIST THE REQUIRED BUSINESS CONTACTS OUTSIDE THE COMPANY. DEALINGS WITH SUPPLIERS, CUSTOMERS, TRADE OR TECHNICAL ASSOCIATIONS, AND GOVERNMENT AGENCIES MAY BE TYPICAL EXAMPLES.**

Sales Manager—Organic Chemicals   *Regular calls on all customers and*
Sales Manager—Inorganic Chemicals   *prospects in his territory.*
Product Managers   ←----→ **JOB NO.**   *Trade associations as required.*
Manager of Sales
Technical Service Dept. (use laboratory)
Traffic Dept.

III. DIRECTS THE WORK OF _____
_____
_____
                                    (Job Title(s))

IV. FUNCTION STATEMENT: (Summarize the major activities delegated to you and briefly describe the purpose or objective this job is designed to fulfill.)

Is responsible for sales of both organic and inorganic chemicals to major industrial and municipal accounts. Performs these functions without assistance of his Regional Manager. He also is the individual who represents the Company to each of his customers, and he must conduct himself in such a manner as to present the Company in the best possible light, not only as a dependable supplier of chemicals but as an intelligent, smoothly functioning organization.

He is responsible for a sales volume in excess of $1,500,000 per year.

Must have a college education in Chemistry or Chemical Engineering.

V. DECISIONS: (Your job provides a framework of authority within which you are expected to make decisions and solve problems. State typical examples of decision-making and problem-solving which will highlight the relative importance and difficulty of this job.)

1. Decides on sales objectives and executes strategy for each key account.
2. Since his contacts are on an executive level, he must be so well grounded in Company policy that he can answer almost any questions himself, without reference to his Regional Manager.
3. Decides on allocation of his time, effort and expenses among his customers and prospects.

VI. SPECIFIC EXAMPLES OF DUTIES (Limit to 6): (For each of the 6 duties you describe, explain WHAT is done, briefly HOW it is done, and WHEN it is done.)

1. Makes regular calls on customers and prospects and attempts to obtain maximum sales volume for our products, submitting detailed reports on his calls; analyzes his territory geographically in order to schedule his time so as to obtain optimum return from his sales efforts.
2. Keeps informed of the uses and properties of our products and competitive products, and supply and demand situation; keeps well informed of our Company policies and services.
3. Maintains necessary sales records which provide marketing and competitive data for customer chemical requirements, required call reports, and monthly, yearly and five-year sales forecasts.
4. Keeps his Regional Manager posted on the competitive situation, and on opportunities for new products and new markets for existing products.
5. Handles customer complaints and checks to be sure corrective action is taken. Requests technical service assistance where necessary or desirable.
6. Improves earnings by keeping within his sales budget, by reducing merchandise returns, and requests for adjustments.
7. Negotiates sale contracts, and assists Regional Manager in training new salesmen and as otherwise requested.

VII. EFFECT OF ERRORS: (The consequences of making a mistake, or failure to act properly in respect to funds, confidential data, plans, policies, etc. often determines the impact or importance of this job. Give several examples where errors and faulty management of your delegations could be significant.)

Any errors on the part of the salesman, failure to keep regular contact with customers, or lack of knowledge result in poor customer relations, leading to a loss of confidence in the salesman and the Company. This inevitably leads to a loss of sales and earnings.

(Incumbent) _____   (Supervisor) _G. D. Brogan_____

(Date) _____   (Date) _30 Aug 1965_____

Exhibit 3-2

SALESMAN PREPARED POSITION DESCRIPTION

JOB TITLE _Outside Salesman_

DIVISION _Dental_

DEPARTMENT _Sales_

LOCATION (PLANT OR OFFICE) _Pasadena, California_

*NOTE: Before Answering Questions
Read All Questions Asked.*

I. DIRECTIONS RECEIVED FROM _Mr. Paul O. Morgan, Manager_

(Job Title)

II. TO CONDUCT THE ACTIVITIES OF THIS JOB, CERTAIN LATERAL COMMUNICATIONS WITH COMPANY PERSONNEL FROM OTHER DEPARTMENTS AND LOCATIONS ARE NECESSARY. PLEASE LIST YOUR TYPICAL COMPANY ASSOCIATES.

Purchasing Agent—Pasadena
Equip. Dept.—Los Angeles
Sales Manager—Don Lyon—L.A.
Repair Dept.—Los Angeles
Inside personnel at Pasadena Branch

PLEASE LIST THE REQUIRED BUSINESS CONTACTS OUTSIDE THE COMPANY. DEALINGS WITH SUPPLIERS, CUSTOMERS, TRADE OR TECHNICAL ASSOCIATIONS, AND GOVERNMENT AGENCIES MAY BE TYPICAL EXAMPLES.

*Wholesale representatives of
   manufacturers.*
*Dentists, Technicians, Dental
   Assistants, Hygienists.*
*Purchasing Agents of various
   hospitals and schools.*

III. DIRECTS THE WORK OF _Self-management of territory comprised of approximately 115 accounts._

(Job Title(s))

IV. FUNCTION STATEMENT: (Summarize the major activities delegated to you and briefly describe the purpose or objective this job is designed to fulfill.)

Basically my function is to represent Company in a sales capacity that entails the establishment of rapport in order that I can present our products in a harmonious manner which results in sales.

V. DECISIONS: (Your job provides a framework of authority within which you are expected to make decisions and solve problems. State typical examples of decision-making and problem-solving which will highlight the relative importance and difficulty of this job.)

To clearly have my territory outlined and established to efficiently call upon my accounts providing them with the necessary contact that expedites their office problems of various natures, consisting of sales, deliveries, equipment repairs, bookkeeping, personnel and even personal problems.

VI. SPECIFIC EXAMPLES OF DUTIES (Limit to 6):

(For each of the 6 duties you describe, explain WHAT is done, briefly HOW it is done, and WHEN it is done.)

1. At least weekly personal contact with my accounts, bringing them the best I can in products at a time that is advantageous to them. For example, special campaigns, conventions, new products, technical literature and technical representatives.
2. Put on outside meeting at least once a year for the dentists in my territory, plus, three or four times a year assisting our dental assistants' meetings by having their programs printed and also by helping with the program by either being their speaker or providing them with one.
3. Maintain a public relation image through social contacts, such as luncheons, dinners, sports events, dental golf meetings—in general—taking an active part in their individual offices.
4. Constant communications with the many & varied departments of our business, to inform & to keep informed of product knowledge, thereby providing the most rapid and best service possible in filling the orders or needs of my accounts.
5. Attend sales meetings, conventions, technical meetings whenever they are offered in our area, and in addition, keep myself reading all available literature in order that I may be aware of the very latest in our profession.
6. Be ever on the look-out for new locations and associateship openings in order to provide my accounts with this service whenever there is such a need.

VII. EFFECT OF ERRORS:

(The consequences of making a mistake, or failure to act properly in respect to funds, confidential data, plans, policies, etc. often determines the impact or importance of this job. Give several examples where errors and faulty management of your delegations should be significant.)

Lack of interest or follow-through on the part of the salesman, would lessen customer relationship and failing to be dependable would prove extremely detrimental.
Because we see these people on a weekly basis, the feeling of trust is of the utmost importance. If a good relationship is founded, the customer will go all out for you.
Since we, the salesmen, are symbolic of our company and its policies, a salesman must have the highest ethics and integrity and be beyond reproach in order to establish long-term relationships which prove to be the basis of success.

(Incumbent) _John E. Robonson_

(Date) _December 22, 1966_

(Supervisor) _Paul O. Morgan General Manager_

(Date) _Dec 22-1966_

One problem in questioning salesmen by interview and especially by written questionnaire is their tendency to overlook aspects of the job which are in fact significant but which the respondent wrongly assumes are unimportant to the questioner, outside the area of inquiry, or already known to the inquirer. In fact, errors of omission may be greatest where the salesman has developed work habits so well that he performs duties without consciously recognizing them as specific activities.

These difficulties suggest that steps should be taken through explanations and instructions to encourage full reporting, but even then sole reliance should not be placed on a written questionnaire or on interviews of brief duration. For the small industrial sales force these difficulties may be mitigated through the use of detailed interviews, possibly of the entire sales force. Where sales-force size would make such a procedure prohibitive, a sample of detailed interviews can be used to develop underlying hypotheses about the job which can then be tested through the use of questionnaires.

Interview and questionnaire studies may reveal a substantial consensus on the function of the salesman and on his responsibilities and duties. In that event, the analyst will have a clear picutre of the job *as it is* which he can reduce to a job description for the use of managerial personnel concerned with selection, training, supervising, and evaluating sales work. However, it will not, in and of itself, reveal what the sales job *ought* to be, although ideas along these lines are commonly presented.

Frequently the studies will reveal that there is something less than full agreement among the parties as to the relative importance of various parts of the salesman's job even if there is agreement on its general nature. Thus, the field work, while descriptive to some extent of present practice, is likely to open up rather than resolve the critical question of what the central function of the salesman should be. In fact, an important argument for an interview-type field investigation of those upon whom the salesmen call is that it may provide valuable insights into the customers' side of the salesman-buyer communicative process. This may lead to a more meaningful conception of what the sales job should and should not be in a particular situation.

STUDIES TO DETERMINE CAUSAL RELATIONSHIPS BETWEEN SALESMAN'S DUTIES AND RESULTS

Various types of studies may be useful in identifying the effects of what the salesman does.

Time-and-duty studies can be especially useful in providing data to relate the salesman's work to such obvious results as sales volume, accounts lost, new accounts obtained, and change in customer goodwill. In this way the analyst may be able to postulate some chain of causal relationships between how salesmen spend their time and perform their various activities and the results obtained. Along these same lines, different salesmen's performance of duties can be compared with the results attained by each of them. Information from call reports and other sources can also be used to seek out relationships between task performance and customer relationships.

Of course there is the operational problem in observational studies of securing accurate measures of how the salesman spends his time and the way in which he is performing his duties at any moment. Although the outcomes of many salesman-buyer interactions may rest heavily on *what* the salesman does and says, for others *when* and *how* he does it are important. Moreover, the validity of observational studies as measures of input-output relationships of various sales tasks is limited by the great variety of environmental situations in which sales work takes place.

Task assignments established on the basis of historical or other observationally determined data are subject to the important additional limitation that they do not indicate what might have been had different practices been undertaken.

The use of experiments provides a means of overcoming these objections at least in part. Unfortunately, the possible adverse effects on customer relations and the fact that the experiment must be conducted with live ones has discouraged careful experimentation in this area.

EXPLORATION OF TASK REQUIREMENTS

Another and perhaps more operationally useful alternative to reliance on historical performance is to derive task assignments directly from an understanding of the role to be performed by the salesman. This approach must start with intensive research into the buying process of each account and prospect segment. The first task is the development of an understanding of the problem-solving process which we call buying from the viewpoint of the purchasing organization. Next, the sales task must be defined in terms of the needs of each segment. The central question is: What can the seller best do to assist the buyer in the buying process? Interviews with those upon whom the salesman calls may provide valuable clues as to what the job ought to be in terms which have relevance to these individuals.

ECLECTICISM IS APPROPRIATE

Not one of the methods which have been suggested can, in itself, provide all of the information and perspective which the manager needs to make the many decisions about the sales task which are required.

For an existing sales force, these decisions require (a) a clear grasp of what the present job is, as revealed by time-and-duty studies and interviews; (b) an understanding of the causal relationships between the performance of different duties and resultant effects on buyer-seller relationships, as might be developed from observational or experimental studies; and (c) exploration of the customers' position and ways in which the role of the sales force itself might profitably be revised to better promote mutually beneficial supplier-customer relationships. Several types of analysis are thus appropriate to the full development of job descriptions.

In new sales situations in which there is no sales force in the field to study, the manager's information resources are more limited. In these circumstances he may be tempted to seek a parallel situation in a going operation on which he can model his sales force. Such an approach is almost certain to be in error for the new organization's relationships with prospective customers are necessarily different not only in degree but in kind from those of firms whose sales forces are established in particular customer-supplier relationships. In these situations, the manager may need to rely even more heavily on what he can learn about the users' buying processes and the conditions which would lead them to consider new sources. Interviews and questionnaire studies can be used to a limited extent. Rough forecasts of probable response functions to different activities can be made. In the final analysis, however, the success of the new sales force will depend heavily on how well the needed intercommunicative relationship can be visualized and how well the sales job can be established to develop the appropriate relationships.

Problems in Developing Job Descriptions

While it is clear that a well-defined understanding of the job performed by the salesman must underlie all activities involved in its performance and management, the determination of what a particular sales job *should* be is, in itself, no easy task. Many job descriptions prove to be less than fully satisfactory because they do not provide sufficiently comprehensive information about one or more of the determinant factors which the manager needs to define the job. Commonly, they fail to be sufficiently specific about the relationship and relative importance of the various duties and responsibilities of the job. In turn, these deficiencies often spring from a failure to fully understand the uses to which the job description is to be put; thus the analyses upon which the descriptions will be based is insufficiently probing and excessively general.

Difficulties also occur because most sales jobs involve not one but a whole series of interrelated duties. In addition, problems arise because the sales process itself is adaptive. Particular salesman-customer relationships undergo changes, many of which call for change in the duties and responsibilities of the salesman. But the primary difficulty is much more fundamental. Since selling is basically an individualized intercommunication process, its specific role in particular situations is not subject to blanket prescription. Thus, even if the sales manager or a staff analyst could accurately depict a particular sales job today, it would be suspect if offered as a description of that job tomorrow.

In many of its aspects, analysis of the field sales job is substantially more difficult than in the case of production and routine white collar jobs where the workers' authority and responsibility can be defined quite narrowly and the task itself tends to be standardized and repetitive. The difficulties are compounded because, even in a well-structured organization, jobs are modified by the incumbents who hold them. In particular, administrative and quasi-administrative work is subject to the principle:

> Responsibility gravitates to the shoulders of those demonstrating the willingness and ability to carry it.

Despite the many difficulties and the further hazard that poor job descriptions can create serious problems in sales personnel administration, the need for sound job descriptions based on careful analysis of what the salesman should do is so great that the manager has little choice but to develop them.

REDEFINING THE SALESMAN'S JOB

The job description will describe the salesmen's responsibilities for communication, customer service, and the provision of information for market intelligence. It will be laid in the context of the firm's mix of marketing elements; thus it will indicate the division of responsibilities between the sales force and other marketing elements. Its most critical facet, however, will be its conception of the nature of the relationship which the salesmen must establish and maintain with customers' and prospects' diverse buying systems.

Job descriptions require regular updating. Even if the salesman's job *appears* to remain unchanged in the sense that he is offering the same product line to the same accounts, *customer-supplier relationships may have undergone considerable evolutionary development.* In any living organization provision should be made for monitoring of jobs—perhaps through the same techniques which have been discussed—and for periodic or regular feedback of performance data so that the manager can determine if the conceived job and actual job conform and so that organizational drift can be detected if not forestalled. Such feedback to detect changes in the nature of the job is in addition to and quite independent of the need to obtain performance data for the purpose of evaluating the work of the salesman. A reconciliation of the sales job with other elements of the marketing mix and with broader goals and strategies is required either as part of periodic marketing audits or independently by the sales manager.

Maintaining job descriptions is likely to be particularly difficult where a given individual acts both as a salesman and in some other capacity, so that both jobs and the relative efforts to be devoted to each are subject to change. In a number of sales organizations, individuals bearing such titles as District Manager and Branch Manager may have both managerial and customer-account responsibilities. Changes in both sets of duties must not only be incorporated in job descriptions on a consistent basis but must be translated into the work patterns of the men involved.

> In a packaged products organization, a major responsibility of district and regional managers is to call on important accounts. At one time, as much as 90 percent of the time of many of these "managers" was devoted to the performance of salesman-type responsibilities and only 10 percent to managerial duties. As managerial responsibilities have increased, the jobs have changed. Today, most district managers and many regional managers have become primarily managers generally devoting less than one-third of their efforts to direct relationships with accounts. The jobs of these managers and their relationships with others have had to be redefined.

Major changes often occur in the job itself or in its relationship to other jobs. Corporate reorganizations, mergers, new arrangements with suppliers or customers, or product lines directed to different groups may call for rearrangements within the sales force. Different bases for market segmentation may become appropriate and new bases for territorial breakdown of the total sales task into territorial units may be indicated. These same factors may also lead to changes in the role of personal selling in the marketing mix, in the intelligence needs of decision centers within the firm, or in the kinds of duties which the salesman is to perform for customers.

Regular analysis and review of sales tasks, redefinition of sales jobs, and revisions of job descriptions are required if the sales organization is to remain aligned with its responsibilities to customers and to the firm.

SUMMARY

Comprehensive descriptions of sales jobs are needed so that managers will have the understanding of the job necessary to carry out their own responsibilities. In addition, job descriptions are needed for manpower procurement and development; as necessary inputs to the planning, measurement, and control processes; and for salary administration.

The fundamental problem is the determination of what the role of the salesman should be in the interaction with customers and prospects. Other problems are associated with determining what duties and responsibilities should be assigned to the salesman and how his time should be allocated among his several activities.

The key determinants of what the sales job should be are the kinds of relationships to be established with customers and prospects, the relative effectiveness and efficiency of having particular activities performed by salesmen or other individuals, and the relative payoffs derived from alternative uses of the salesman's time.

Analysis of the present job may provide a useful starting point in developing job descriptions. Both time-and-duty studies and questionnaire and/or interview studies provide useful tools. They need to be supplemented by observational and/or experimental studies to determine causal relationships between duty performance and results and by efforts to explore the buyers' decision processes and the part which the salesman can play in such processes. Many job descriptions are less than fully satisfactory for many uses because they are based on research of inadequate scope and, thus, are not sufficiently comprehensive and detailed.

Job descriptions must be updated regularly because relationships with customers change even if the job appears to remain unchanged. In the more common situation of continually changing product and market relationships, the need for continual analysis, review, and revision is even more urgent.

4 Deployment of Sales Efforts

The previous chapter was concerned with the problems of determining what the sales job should be in a particular setting. The present chapter will examine the quantitative relationships between salesman activity and the market. Whereas Chapter 3 dealt with *what,* this chapter is concerned with *how much.*

TYPES OF DEPLOYMENT DECISIONS REQUIRED

A major deployment decision is the determination of how much total effort should be applied to a particular market. This in turn will determine the most desirable size of the sales force.

More difficult problems are involved in (a) the allocation of sales-force effort among possible buyers, (b) the determination of areas of salesman responsibility (that is, territories) and the amount of effort to be devoted to each, and (c) ascertaining the most desirable way of utilizing the salesman's time, given a particular set of duties and effort allocations (that is, routing and scheduling). The problems of determining the total amount of effort to employ and its allocation among various customers and prospects are examined in this chapter. Territorial assignments are treated separately in Chapter 5; routing and scheduling are covered in Chapter 11.

When personal selling activity is defined as that which is intended to (1) establish, modify, and nurture relationships between the selling firm and buyers and (2) change such relationships in a way beneficial to the seller as well as to the buyer, the salesman's role is to influence the knowledge states and dispositions of customers and prospects so as to favorably affect their actions. The changes which are brought about by the salesman's activities may be termed *responses*. The set of responses which might be evoked by different amounts of sales-effort inputs is called a *response function.*

Different customer and prospect groups can be expected, on the basis of their own goals, problems, predispositions, and states of knowledge at any time, to have different response functions. Moreover, even for an individual buyer, changes in goals or problems over time will result in different responses to the efforts of salesmen.

> Salesmen for a distributor of air-conditioning components call on general and air-conditioning contractors and small manufacturer-assemblers. The response of the latter group is especially sensitive to the efforts of the salesman when components to be used and sources of supply are being determined. Once these decisions have been made, however, manufacturer customers' purchases will be quite insensitive to the amount of salesman activity as long as order-filling and trouble-shooting functions are satisfactorily performed.
>
> Contractors, by way of contrast, are likely to encounter problems unique to each job for which the distributor's assistance may be of help. The smaller contractors, in particular, may have limited technical competence in their own right and may thus require more guidance in choosing components than their larger, more expert counterparts. As a result, such contractors may expect a high frequency of salesman service and may be highly sensitive to its provision. The salesman's time allocations must reflect the response functions which are derived from these needs. One large distributor finds, for example, that a 90 percent:10 percent allocation of salesman time between contractors and manufacturer customers satisfactorily meets the needs of the respective groups. This is not the ratio of either the volume potential involved or of the sales achieved.

DETERMINANTS OF DEPLOYMENT DECISIONS

Deployment decisions rest heavily on the response to sales efforts that the manager expects. They are also affected by the expected effectiveness of the salesman in carrying out assigned duties (that is, his performance), and by territorial characteristics which influence the cost of employing sales inputs in various geographic areas.

Any allocation decision rule or policy requires some expectation of the shape of the various response functions both for individuals and in the aggregate. Hence, the manager must formulate his expectation of response behavior before any rational allocation plan can be devised.

Would the same principles apply to the management of a campaign to influence the behavior of smokers? drug users? polluters? voters?

Often expected response functions are implicit and based entirely on the subjective impressions of the manager or salesman. One of the most widely used allocation rules—effort in proportion to potential—rests on the conception of response functions as being both linear and identical for all parts of the market.

More objective means are, however, often available to provide clearer concepts of probable response functions for particular sales situations. The next section will be devoted to an examination of response functions and means of determining them. Following sections will examine allocation principles for determining the amount of effort to employ and its allocation among various customer and prospect groups.

DETERMINATION OF PURCHASE RESPONSE FUNCTIONS

The first step in securing maximum results from sales calls is to determine how profits are affected by using various levels of selling effort in various ways. To simplify the discussion, sales efforts will initially be expressed in terms of sales calls, although this is at best a primitive measure of efforts. Similarly, immediate purchase response will be used as a proxy variable for the profit effect of personal selling activity.

The immediate consequence of a sales call should be a change in the knowledge state and disposition of the persons called upon. Since knowledge is subject to decay and its relevance is subject to obsolescence, the prospective buyer's knowledge state may be visualized, as Figure 4-1 shows, as a series of increments with each sales call followed by a gradual decay which is then arrested by the next call. It may be noted that some peaks parallel over several calls while others reach new highs.

How might this phenomenon be explained?

Three types of purchase response functions are of interest to the manager or salesman planning field sales activity:

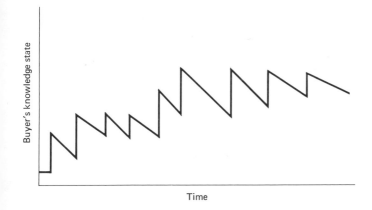

Figure 4-1
STATE OF BUYER'S KNOWLEDGE OVER TIME

1. the response of existing accounts to call levels;
2. the probability of retention versus loss of an account with various call levels;
3. the probability of converting a nonaccount into a customer with various call levels.

These three functions are shown as Figures 4-2, 4-5, and 4-6 respectively. Each of these figures represents the behavior of a single account or prospect or a group of accounts which have a common response function. Differences in prospects' or customers' purchase or use situations can be expected to result in different responses; hence, separate response or probability curves need to be drawn for each such group.

Response functions can be derived or estimated in various ways. The functions themselves will be averages of anticipated outcomes. Actual outcomes will, of course, be affected by chance factors —for example, the coincidence of timing in which the salesman happens to call when a particular environmental condition exists, such as a problem with the existing supplier; an unanticipated problem; a particularly perceptive presentation.

Figure 4-2 represents a short-term idealized response function for an existing customer. The response function for any account is based on the state of the relationship between the selling firm and that account at a particular time. The work of the salesman, the performance of the company in serving the customer, the activities of competitors, and decay of the effects of learning by the customer

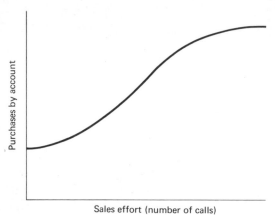

Figure 4-2
IDEALIZED PURCHASE RESPONSE
FUNCTION—EXISTING ACCOUNT

will affect the relationship so that it will be in a different state at the end of any planning period than at the beginning. Hence, a new response function must be projected for each period.

Purchase Response of Existing Accounts

Figure 4-2 describes a case in which the *amount* existing customers will buy is affected by the number of sales calls. The salesman's activity is likely to influence *how much* a customer will buy where the buyer uses fairly standardized goods and has available choices among suppliers, including the possibility of dividing his total purchases among a number of sources. Cleaning and maintenance supplies, office supplies, lamps, printing, industrial components such as resistors, transistors, standard construction material, and many business services are examples of this type of purchasing situation. The salesman's activity is also likely to influence how much the purchaser takes in sales to the trade where the salesman's efforts may have significant influence on the stocking, display, pricing, and promotional activities of his wholesaler or retailer customers.

Particular data to describe the purchase response of existing accounts to call activity can be derived from sales records and call reports. When plotted they typically will reveal that higher numbers of calls are associated with greater sales but will not indicate the direction of causation. Were the greater sales the result of the larger number of sales calls? Or are the numbers of calls greater because of the volumes of the accounts involved?

Since the results of sales calls may reflect type and size of account, it is desirable to develop sales/call experience and to plot sales/call relationships in terms of relevant account characteristics.

Which characteristics are relevant, however, is not always clear. In the Ackoff GE studies, for example, there did not appear to be any relationship between account characteristics, other than purchase volume, and sales per call.[1]

Multiple regression techniques may be useful to identify relationships between such possible causal factors as potential, sales effort, and the effects of other marketing mix elements on the one hand and sales on the other. Both cross-sectional analyses (which compare different territories or control units for a given time period) and time-series analyses, or combinations thereof, are possible. The former is less likely to be affected by unmeasured environmental factors and is thus to be preferred if the number of control units is large enough to permit reliable analysis.

Multiple regression techniques are used to fit each of a set of plausible response functions. The results are compared to determine which function best fits the empirical data. Additional formulations are tried in an effort to improve the fit and thus "explain" a larger proportion of the differences in sales observed among the control units.

In assessing the effect of numbers of salesmen assigned to a district on sales of an undifferentiated institutional consumable—X-ray film—Lambert used multiple regression analysis with the number of salesmen, a product-mix index, a price index, and market potential as independent variables. He was able to "explain" 91 percent of the variance among districts with an estimating equation composed of the first three elements. Market potential was deleted from the estimating equation because its inclusion did not significantly improve it; presumably potential did not operate, in fact, as a factor limiting sales volume in enough of the districts, if any, that consideration of potential would have improved the estimating procedure.[2]

---

[1] Clark Waid, Donald F. Clark, and Russell L. Ackoff, "Allocations of Sales Effort in the Lamp Division of the General Electric Company," *Operations Research*, IV (December 1956), pp. 629–647.

[2] Lambert's best fit was obtained with

$$SV_i = 409220750 \cdot S_i^{.7847286} \cdot PM_i^{1.169518} \cdot P_i^{-2.645349}$$

where:

$SV_i =$ sales volume of medical X-ray film at cost in district i;

$S_i =$ number of salesmen employed by company in district i;

$PM_i =$ percentage of total sales volume of all product lines in district i constituted by medical X-ray film;

$P_i =$ selling price index in district i.

Zarrel V. Lambert, *Setting the Size for the Sales Force* (University Park, Pa.: Pennsylvania State University, 1968).

The Lambert example, in which sales effort is measured in numbers of men, rather than man-hours or number of calls, is one of the few cases of successful measurement of response functions. For the most part, efforts to derive clearly described purchase response functions observationally have not been particularly fruitful. In part, this may be the result of the fact that the sales organization has made responses to sales volume opportunities. Thus, when call frequencies are plotted against sales volume, the results appear to be random, as shown in Figure 4-3, and to suggest that the number of calls had no effect on sales volume.

What Figure 4-3 does not show, and what examination of the records cannot tell us is what the sales results *would have been* had different numbers of calls been made. The analyst has data for only that region of the sales response curve shown in Figure 4-3. Perhaps the entire sales response curve is, unbeknown to the analyst but revealed to the reader, that depicted by Figure 4-4. If the analyst understood the shape of the purchase response curve he well might consider reducing the number of calls on customers in this group to some level such as e_{11}, e_{12}, or e_{13}, the appropriate level depending on the profit and cost consequences of different effort levels and sales volumes. But how can the analyst determine the shape of the purchase response function? One possibility is to utilize historical data to ascertain the effects, if any, of changes in number of calls. Although these additional data may help, in most cases observation is inadequate and it is necessary to conduct experiments to determine the shape of the response function.

Because managements are often hesitant to conduct experiments which involve hazards to relationships with real customers, the analyst may find it prudent to conduct his experiment in two

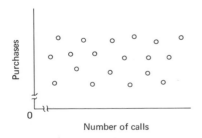

Figure 4-3
**OBSERVED RELATIONSHIP
OF SALES TO NUMBER OF
CALLS ON ESTABLISHED
ACCOUNTS**

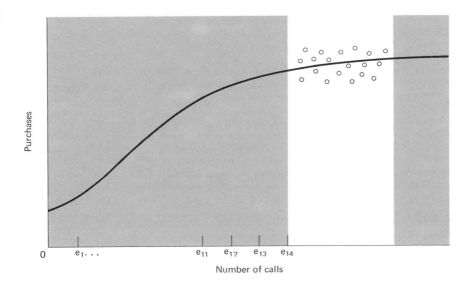

Figure 4-4
TRUE PURCHASE RESPONSE CURVE OF COMPANY WHOSE OBSERVATIONS ARE
SHOWN IN FIGURE 4-3 (SHADED AREA UNKNOWN TO ANALYST BECAUSE OF
ABSENCE OF OBSERVATIONS)

phases. In the first phase, he seeks to test the effect of putting forth
the level of effort which appears to be the minimum for the area in
which no effect appears—that is, at e_{14} or some other point near the
lower limit of the "known" area of Figure 4-4. If an illustration similar
to Figure 4-4, but embodying data for a period of years is available,
the minimum level of effort which has been applied to produce results
indicated can be applied to the test group. If the results of such an
experiment suggest no adverse effect on sales, further experiments
with successively lower call frequencies may then be acceptable to
management. To reduce the possible influence of other variables, it
is preferable to employ a control group as well as a test group in
experiments. Even then, the carry-over effects from prior calls are a
joint cause of any observed results. The "optimal" frequency revealed
by the experiment ignores this element. Moreover, the experiment
measures only the short-run effect; it makes no allowance for the
longer-term effects of current changes in the level of service.

When a study of changes in sales of a lamp manufacturer over a
three-year period revealed no significant variation with the number of
calls, an experiment was conducted during the fourth year by limiting
the number of calls on any account to the lowest number made on that
account in any of the three prior years. When this experiment revealed

no significant sales loss, experiments were continued with lower call frequencies until significant diminution was observed. The company then established call frequency rates at that level.[3]

The procedure used in the lamp example does not in itself take into account the possibility of lag effects—that is, that the lower call frequencies will eventually lead to lower sales.

Another confounding factor is that the effect of sales calls depends on the nature of the buyer-seller relationship, which itself changes. Thus fewer calls while a relationship is being developed might have serious adverse effects, while a similar reduction when the relationship was well established might have little, if any, consequence.

An often underutilized source of information on response functions is the salesman himself. The knowledgeable salesman in the field may be able to provide subjective estimates of the probable consequences of changes in the amount of effort which are at least as good as those derived from historical records.[4]

> Each salesman of a manufacturer of pollutant-control chemicals prepares an estimate, on an account-by-account basis, of the number of calls which he feels is necessary to maintain the desired relationship with that customer. These estimates are reviewed with the district manager. The total planned time must fall within the company's guidelines as to proportion of total time which may be used for account maintenance while retaining sufficient time for developing new accounts. If the salesman's call plans require more time than is available, either the salesman will be counselled (not directed) in his plan revision or, if the district manager believes the plan appropriate, steps will be initiated with the central management for additional manpower or territorial realignment.

The salesman is in an excellent position to formulate the likely response of customers to additional calls because he should be able to describe what he would do in the course of the additional calls and be able to estimate the results which might be expected. A side benefit is that this participation in goal setting is likely to have favorable effects on the salesman's attitudes and efforts towards goal achievement.

Professor Leonard Lodish has developed a computer program for use by salesmen in making their perceptions explicit. As visualized by Lodish, the salesman sitting at a console would indicate the expected results of alternative numbers of calls on an account-by-account basis. The computer would then fit a response curve through

---

[3] Waid, Clark, and Ackoff.
[4] The author knows of no carefully designed experiment to test this hypothesis.

these points and print out the resultant function. The optimal number of calls to make on each account is calculated. The salesman can easily test the consequence of alternative response functions and alternative constraints on his time availability.

Probability of Retention of an Account

In many sales to the trade and in many industrial supply arrangements a supplier may expect either to enjoy the entire volume for the item in question used by the customer or to receive none of it. The influence of the salesman is, thus, not one of influencing *how much* the customer will buy but *whether* he will buy at all. This situation is likely to pertain to the purchase of real estate, plant, and major capital goods items where only a single purchase is involved. There are also many situations involving repeat purchases in which the buyer is best served by a single supplier. Improved quality control, the benefits of routinized ordering, delivery, and inventory management, special services provided by a supplier, and the advantages of simplifying the servicing of equipment in use or sold to customers often suggest real advantages for single-source procurement practices.

Thus a lawn mower manufacturer uses the same make of carburetor and engine in all models to simplify spare parts stocking and customer service. A washing machine manufacturer uses the same brand of control device in as many models as feasible to simplify not only parts stocking and service but the training problems of his own and his dealer's servicemen. Fleet owners prefer to limit the variety of makes for the same reasons. In such circumstances the purpose of sales calls is to increase the probability that the firm will be the supplier when the item is required in the buyer's normal course of business. In this context the measure of the effectiveness of sales work becomes the change in the propensity to select the firm as the source of the item, or in the probability that *the* order will be obtained by the firm rather than by a competitor. We may express the effects of sales work in terms of their effects on these probabilities.

In this situation, two kinds of calls are involved: those to retain present accounts; and those to convert nonaccounts into accounts.

Figure 4-5 shows the relationship between number of calls and the probability of retaining an account through a time period. Its general shape suggests that a fairly large probability for retaining an account exists with few or even no calls and that this probability will increase with additional servicing of the account by the salesman. The curve flattens out at a saturation point which represents the number of calls beyond which there is no betterment of the seller-customer relationship. The dashed line shows the effect of calls this period on

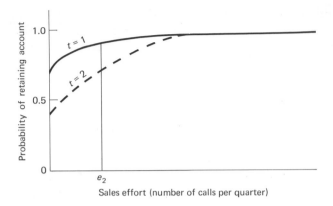

Figure 4-5

IDEALIZED RETENTION-OF-ACCOUNT FUNCTION

retention in the next period. A total lack of calls during the current quarter may reduce the probability of retention only slightly because order routines are likely to persist over short periods and competitors have not had sufficient time to overcome the previously established relationship. However, failure to call this quarter reduces the chance that the routine will be maintained in the next quarter—that is, in time period $t = 2$ in the figure.

Data on the relationship of call frequency to accounts lost is not likely to be readily obtainable from the records of most firms. Thus the development of curves such as Figure 4-5 must be based on the subjective judgment of salesmen and sales executives and on such experiments as management is willing to permit. Both in securing the judgments of executives and in designing experiments, it is probably desirable for the analyst to confine himself to an area of interest in the vicinity of present call frequencies along the lines of experiments suggested in the previous section. The author knows of no reported cases of experiments in this area describing more than one point on the retention probability curve. Brown, Hulswit, and Kettelle experimentally established for a commercial printer that an effort of two hours per month would yield a retention rate of .95 per month, but did not determine other points in the curve.[5]

Response Functions Involving Both Continuance of Relationships and Amounts Purchased

The situations described in the previous sections are not mutually exclusive. For many relationships, both the amount which the

[5] "A Study of Sales Operations," *Operations Research,* Vol. IV (June 1956), pp. 296–308.

customer will purchase and whether or not he will remain a customer are variables which are affected by the work of the salesman. The shape of this function will be generally similar to that shown in Figure 4-2.[6] One type of sales situation in which this condition is likely to exist is that of travelers selling to retailers. Lodish, Montgomery, and Webster have formulated a model which seems most appropriate to this type of situation. The model bases both the probability of securing an order and the amount of the order, if secured, on the potential and past purchasing (or nonpurchasing) history of the account.[7] History of an account's purchases, or its failure to purchase, over an extended series of calls may be an important indicator of the perceived relevance of the seller's offerings to the buyer's needs, and, where purchases have been made, of the buyer's experience with the seller's offerings. In modeling the response function, such experiences may prove a useful proxy for these underlying, but difficult to measure, variables.

Probability of Conversion of Nonaccount

The shape of the conversion curve is likely to be greatly affected by the kind of sales situation. Figure 4-6 shows two types of relationships between number of calls and conversion of nonaccounts into accounts. A salesman with an attractive new offer to the trade may find that his first call is likely to tell the story. His experience

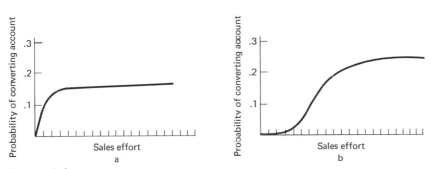

Figure 4-6
TWO IDEALIZED CONVERSION-OF-ACCOUNT FUNCTIONS

[6] The values of purchases in Figure 4-2 are in terms of expected values and thus incorporate the chance that purchases will be zero. The figure does not, however, show whether or not the status of the customer-supplier relationship has changed.

[7] L. M. Lodish, D. B. Montgomery, and F. E. Webster, "A Dynamic Sales Call Policy Model" (Sloan School Working Paper 329–68, Sloan School of Management, M.I.T., 1968). A summary description of the model is available in Philip Kotler, *Marketing Decision Making* (New York: Holt, Rinehart and Winston, Inc., 1971), Chapter 13.

may be that shown in Figure 4-6a. At the other extreme, a salesman attempting to penetrate an account firmly held by a competitor may find that a large number of calls will be necessary until a situation arises which will enable him to secure a footing. Similarly, an industrial salesman may find that he needs to make a number of calls before the buyers will recognize his ability to provide sound advice and service. In part, this is a matter of the cumulative effect of the salesman's interaction with individual buyer personnel. In part, it may also be the result of efforts needed by the salesman to identify and reach the significant buying influences. These latter cases may be depicted by a curve such as that shown in Figure 4-6b in which initial efforts have only limited effect until a threshold of acceptability has been attained after which the effect of additional calls grows rapidly. At some point a maximum is reached beyond which further efforts have no effect on conversion probability. If calls are too frequent, a nuisance effect may be generated and the probability may decline.

Fortunately, both observational and experimental methods are available to determine the shape of the conversion curve. Records can be analyzed to determine the number of calls made on nonaccounts which became accounts and the point in the calling sequence at which this occurred, along with analysis of the numbers of calls made on prospects who never did become accounts.

Figure 4-7 shows the results of one such study. The records, over a two-year period of calls made and accounts obtained, revealed that the probability of making a conversion was .06 on the first call, rose by .08 on the second call and by .10 on the third call (.24 for a three-call pattern); it increased .045 for the fourth call and .025 for the fifth.[8]

The values and even the shape of a conversion-of-account function are particular to the individual sales situation. An equipment manufacturer, for example, found that his curve did not flatten out until after the sixth call. A salesman attempting to substantially alter the prospect's operations, methods or supply arrangements well might find that conversion probability was virtually zero until the fourth call and that fifteen or twenty calls might be necessary to reach the .25 level of conversion probability. Although an average conversion-of-account function can be derived, actual conversions will also be affected by chance factors, for example, the coincidence of timing in which the salesman happens to call when a particular environmental condition exists, such as a problem with the existing supplier; an unanticipated problem; a windfall gain.

[8] Patrick J. Robinson and Bent Stidsen, *Personal Selling in a Modern Perspective* (Boston: Allyn and Bacon, Inc., 1967), p. 50.

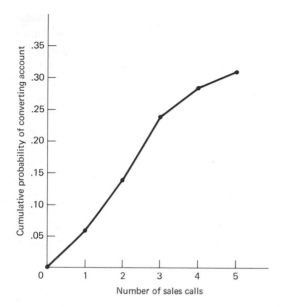

Figure 4-7

**CONVERSION-OF-ACCOUNT FUNCTION—LAMP
MANUFACTURER**

The shape of the conversion curve for a firm sometimes can be estimated from data already at hand. One objection to such observational studies is the inability to measure or to avoid the influence of external factors. Experiments to determine the response propensity of prospects of various types to different levels of sales effort can follow the same approach. While well designed experiments reduce the impact of outside factors, they impose higher costs both in outlay terms and in the time required to carry them out.

In one experiment, Magee studied the effects of modifying a company practice under which missionary sales calls were made on the top 40 percent of retail outlets based on the most recent two month's sales, but no calls were made on the other retailers. For the experiments, all were called upon. The purchases of the bottom 60 percent with calls could then be compared with that of the same group when not called upon. In this way the effect of the calls on the group could be determined.[9] The validity of the experiment could have been improved further by providing a control group during the experiment.

*In what respect does the absence of a control group
raise questions of the validity of the results?*

[9] The essence of the experiment is described in David B. Montgomery and Glenn L. Urban, *Management Science in Marketing* (Englewood Cliffs, N.J.: Prentice-Hall, Inc., 1969), pp. 261–265.

The changing state of a prospect's knowledge and predispositions can be taken into account by analyzing the result of the sales
call through a transition matrix[10] which compares the prospect's state
before and after the call. Observational or experimental means can be
employed to determine transition probabilities. By treating the transition matrix as a Markov chain, the outcome, in probabilistic terms, of
a series of calls can be determined. Such a matrix can be in terms of
the number of calls which had been made on a prospect—that is, the
states can be defined in terms of numbers of calls to which the prospect has been exposed.[11] Especially for developmental work, it may
be more appropriate to express the prospect's state in terms of his
disposition or knowledge-disposition. While conceptually more relevant than historical number of calls, the reader will recognize that
it is much more difficult to measure. The concept is described well
by Thompson and McNeal. Their matrix has four developmental states
in addition to the absorbing states of becoming a customer or being
dropped from the prospect list. These are: no prior call history; low
degree of interest on last call; medium degree of interest on last call;
and high degree of interest on last call.[12] Thus, the matrix consists
of a set of probabilities that a call will move the prospect from one
state to another.

Response to Application Engineering Activity

In modern market economies, the task of demonstrating customer benefit rests with the seller. Much more than sales effort is
often involved. Investigation may be necessary to determine if a problem in fact exists. Thus, sellers offer to investigate the buyer's situation "without cost or obligation" to him. The seller hopes that a
problem will be revealed—that the prospect's insurance program is
inadequate; that the house does have termites; that the accounting
work can be performed more effectively and more cheaply with a new
system employing the seller's machines. Detailed studies of the customer's situation must be undertaken to define his needs and problems
and to determine what attributes are desirable in solutions which
might be proposed.

In its more elementary forms this type of tailoring of product to

[10] The nature of probability transition matrices is explained in the appendix
to this chapter.
[11] Abe Shuchman, "The Planning and Control of Personal Selling Effort
Directed at New Account Acquisition," in Lee Preston (ed.), *New Research
in Marketing* (Berkeley: University of California, 1965), pp. 45–56.
[12] W. W. Thompson and J. U. McNeal, "Sales Planning and Control Using
Absorbing Markov Chains," *Journal of Marketing Research*, IV (February
1967), pp. 62–66.

problem (called application engineering) may be accomplished by the salesman himself or by salesman-support personnel. Examples are the plans prepared for clients by life insurance salesmen, those prepared by some sellers of such decorator items as furniture, carpets and draperies, and the recommendations and bids prepared for clients by trade contractors in the construction trades. In this type of situation, problem diagnosis and solution prescription can generally be prepared in a matter of hours or with few man-days effort at the most.

In many sales situations, however, the problem is more difficult. Commitments of many thousands of dollars may be required to diagnose the customer's problems. Some of this cost is in the form of salesman's time as he interacts with various persons in the buying system. Much of it may involve specialized technical personnel in the selling organization. Additional thousands may be involved in the preparation of proposals. Eventually sales may or may not result. Sellers in such fields, consequently, are faced with decision problems as to the amount of effort which should be devoted to such services in pursuit of sales.

It can be argued that diagnostic services in particular are services for the customer and for which the customer should be expected to pay, without regard to whether he buys a product. In pursuit of such a philosophy, some firms set up consulting subsidiaries or otherwise ask prospective buyers to pay for professional diagnostic services independently of any final purchase activity. They maintain that study of a manufacturer's production system and the recommendation of an improved layout or system are professional activities for which they should be compensated. The situation is especially acute if the buyer, after obtaining the advice, purchases the needed equipment from a competitive supplier who does not offer such application engineering services. A somewhat similar position is taken by those, such as some home decorating organizations, who offer advisory service for a fee, with the fee being cancelled if purchases of a certain amount are made. In this way, it is argued, the seller who provides advisory service avoids losing the business to a nonservice competitor.

Although there are undoubtedly many situations in which it will remain feasible to separate such diagnostic and advisory services and charge for them separately, the facts of modern, competitive, customer-dominated markets mitigate against widespread recompense of diagnostic and prescriptive services through fees. Often buyers do not recognize that a better way to meet their needs is possible. Hence, the burden is on the seller to act as a change agent and demonstrate that this is so.

More generally, market-directed economies operate on the premise of *caveat venditor* not only in the sense of placing responsibility for the *constitution* of the goods on the seller but also in the sense of placing responsibility for *performance* on him. The customer is not buying products, but the performance which they can provide. In a very real sense, all marketing is becoming the marketing of services. A buyer of a data processing system or an automated production system is not interested in what the components *are* but what the system, as a system, will *do.* The same may be said of housing and many other consumer products. So-called "systems selling" and "turnkey" operations are a reflection of this phenomenon. If a seller is to sell performance rather than products, he must play a major role in need diagnosis and solution prescription. He cannot afford inaction or erroneous action in either.

Tailoring, or application engineering, involves three kinds of activities which intimately concern and involve the salesman: interaction, diagnosis, and prescription. Interaction is the forte of the salesman. It is here that he perceives existing or latent problems and discerns sales opportunity. Tailoring raises no new problems here. The areas of diagnosis and prescription do, however, introduce problems. Here the seller organization may be involved in major expenditures. Hopefully, expenditures at each step will be matched by creeping commitments on the buying side so that successive expenditures increase the probability of securing an order. In some situations, however, particular sellers will find the commitment creeping *away* from them. Competitors' diagnoses or offerings appear more attractive to the buyer; or perhaps, the results of studies suggest that the need is not so urgent nor the benefits so great as the salesman had originally believed might be the case. How does the seller know when further efforts are not warranted?

In decision terms, this is largely a matter of weighing the expected value of the prospective profit against the anticipated cost of further efforts. The essence of this problem is to assess the probabilities of success, $p,$ and the profit which success would provide, $V.$ This is largely a subjective process. It may be improved somewhat through periodic status-and-prospect review conferences with the salesman and others involved in the diagnostic and prescriptive process. The essential questions deal with appraising the prospects for success and the cost needed to remain in the game.

Layton suggests that decision tree analysis may be useful in structuring this problem. For each possible course of action at any point in time, a set of conditional probability judgments is made as to each possible outcome of each decision. For example: If a $50,000 survey is made, the probability is .2 that it will show no benefit to the customer, .3 that it will show a modest benefit to the customer, and .5 that it will show a substantial benefit to the customer. Furthermore, subjective estimates are made that the demonstration of a small benefit will yield a sales probability of .1 and of a large benefit a sales probability of .7. With estimates of this type, the decision center can determine whether such a survey is warranted and/or to which prospects available survey resources should be devoted.[13]

GENERAL PRINCIPLES FOR DETERMINING AMOUNT OF EFFORT TO EMPLOY

Planning for the deployment of sales efforts must be formulated in terms of the changes in relationships which might be brought about, the probability of securing those changes, and the sales efforts which would be involved in achieving any given level of probability. The costs of different levels of sales activity can then be appraised in terms of the values derived from prospective changes in relationships.

The Amount of Effort

The *total* amount of sales effort which should be expended can be derived from the economist's principle that profit is maximized by extending efforts to the point at which the cost of additional efforts is just covered by the additional revenues derived. Graphically, this can be shown in Figure 4-8. In the figure, the contribution line, C, is the contribution to profit resulting from alternative amounts of sales effort. It is derived by first describing the response function, S, and

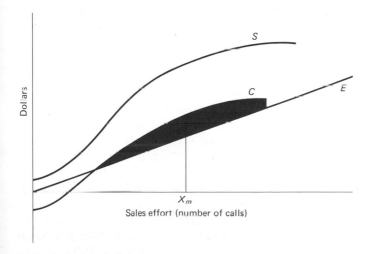

Figure 4-8
EFFECTS OF SALES EFFORTS ON SALES AND CON-TRIBUTION TO PROFIT

[13] For details of the technique as applied to computer sales see Roger A. Layton, "Controlling Risk and Return in the Management of a Sales Team," *Journal of Marketing Research,* V (August 1968), pp. 277–282.

then deducting from sales revenue all costs which vary as a *result* of the sales-effort process. Such costs would include all production and other costs, other than sales force costs, which vary with the sales volume. The sales call effort line, E, represents the cost of calls. In this example, it is a straight line, representing an assumption that the cost per call is the same for all levels of calling activity. The point of maximum profit is the point at which the contribution line, C, and the cost of effort line, E, differ by the greatest vertical distance. At this point the contribution and cost lines will have the same slope. In this example, the maximum profit occurs at X_m .

The actual derivation of curves such as presented here is difficult, chiefly because of the great uncertainties which generally exist about the shape of the response function, but the concept is nevertheless useful. It suggests to the planner that, given any tentative total effort plan, he can address himself to the question of the likely effects of possible changes in either direction from this tentative point. Thus, he might estimate the results to be obtained at the planned level of activity and the differences to be expected at *incremental* levels above and below it.

Response curves of the type shown here are measures of what will happen (either as a certainty or as the product of the probability, p, of a response and V, the value of the response to the seller) in terms of sales and profit effect in a single period. It is a useful measure if the sole significant effect of sales calls is in terms of immediate sales. It becomes somewhat less satisfactory as we view the personal sales effort as one of modifying relationships, the consequences of which will be felt over time. The shape of the relationship will change with a longer period. However, the principles underlying optimal effort allocation remain valid.

Sales efforts have both primary (direct) and secondary (indirect) consequences. The discussion thus far has dealt only with the direct consequence—the cumulative effect of various amounts of sales effort on purchases made by buyers. Such an approach is quite relevant to examination of the conditions which lead to a first purchase by a buyer. But it fails to take into account the consequences of that purchase for subsequent behavior of the buyer.

Consider, as an example, sales efforts designed to secure a trial order or to induce a buyer to change his established purchase or usage pattern. Although the primary effect of these efforts, if successful, will be a trial or initial order, the subsequent reorders may be much more significant. These reorders are in part a result of the buyer's experience with the trial order. Nonetheless, they are an important, if secondary, result of the efforts which secured the initial order. A great deal of personal selling effort to industry, to the trade, and even to consumers is directed beyond the initial purchase to long-term buying and usage patterns. Thus the sales effort to obtain initial purchase may be viewed as development work looking towards profitable sales on the reorder and follow-up business. To take such effects into account it is useful to make the following definition:

$$V = \text{the value of the call effect to the seller.}$$

As has been noted above, this value is measured not by the *absolute* level of what the interviewed members of the buyer unit do (for example, the amount of purchases) but rather by how their action is *changed* as a result of the sales effort (one or more calls). We can thus restate

$$V = \quad \Delta c_1 + \Delta c_2 + \Delta c_3 + \ldots$$

where c_i are the contributions to profit of purchases over successive periods by the buying unit, each discounted to present value and the Δs are increments over what each c would have been in the absence of the effort and

$$p = \text{estimated probability of obtaining the effect } V, \text{ given the}$$
level of effort, E, at intensity level i. Then,

$$pV = \text{the expected value return if } E \text{ is applied, and}$$

$$\frac{pV}{E_i} = \text{return from } i\text{th unit of } E, \text{ and}$$

$$\frac{\Delta(p_i)V}{\Delta E_i} = \text{marginal return at any level of } E.$$

By way of example, a salesman and his district manager are developing plans for the salesman's territory for 1972. In evaluating the effort to be devoted to account A, the salesman notes that the company is presently a fill-in supplier to A, with annual sales of about $2,000, on which a profit of $200 is realized, before deducting the cost of the semiannual sales calls. The salesman believes that this pattern will continue if he maintains his twice-a-year efforts. The salesman is confident, moreover, that if calls are placed on a monthly basis, Company A will buy the bulk of its requirements from him beginning about six months after the more intensive cultivation commences. With a monthly call policy he estimates A's purchases at $10,000 in 1973 and growing at a rate of 10 percent annually with A's business expansion. To hold this business a monthly call pattern would be required through 1974, with some reduction possible thereafter. In response to the manager's inquiry as to what would happen if the salesman concentrated on his other accounts and reduced his efforts on A to an annual reminder call or skipped A completely, the salesman believed that 1972 business would be unaffected because of past relationships but that a competitive firm would take over the fill-in business in a year if no calls were made. A few token orders would be secured with a single call.

Based on these data, the district manager estimated the profit from account A at the amounts shown in Table 4-1. As in this case the salesman is certain of each of the results, $p = 1$. Discounting future profit differences at 12 percent, he calculated the present value of the alternative call patterns. A semiannual call pattern is seen to contribute $305 more over 3 years than no calls, $256 more than one call, and $1901 less than a monthly call policy. The return per effort unit is $49 for the first unit, $256 for the second unit, and $1901/10 or $190 per call if an additional ten calls are made.

Next, the salesman and his manager discussed the prospects for account B. Because the market research department had estimated that B uses $1,000,000 worth of relevant products per year, the salesman has called on B every three months for several years. No orders have been obtained. The manager questioned whether or not the salesman was wasting his time. The salesman believed that if this policy were continued there was perhaps one chance in ten that a small order (say 5 percent of B's requirements) might be obtained in 1972 and similar fill-ins thereafter. There was a substantially smaller chance, perhaps not more than 1 in 100, that the major portion of B's business ($900,000) could be obtained in the next year or two. The salesman pointed out, however, that calls should not be dropped because if a small order was obtained and serviced well, the chances of becoming the major supplier for 1974 would rise to one in five. The salesman believed that doubling the number of calls would only increase chances by about 10 percent.

Based on these estimates, the district manager estimated the profit from account B as shown in Table 4-2. The expected value of the return per call $(\Delta p V / \Delta E)$ is $1258 in moving from a no-call to a quarterly call and $126 per call in doubling the number of calls.[14]

Another important form of secondary effect springs from what can be called a *demonstration effect*. Purchase decisions are not made exclusively as the result of communications between a seller and a

[14] Tables 4-1 and 4-2 overstate the marginal value of 1972 calls by not including the cost of calls in 1973 and 1974, a portion of which will bring benefits beyond 1974. A more conservative set of values can be obtained by multiplying the E column by 3 to include 1973 and 1974 calls. E values will triple and marginal returns per call will be one-third those shown, namely $16, $85, and $63 for the three alternatives for account A respectively, and $419 and $42 respectively for account B. This procedure assumes no post-1974 benefit from calls made during any of the three years. Either of these methods will suffice for allocation decisions, so long as the relationship between short- and long-term benefits is not significantly affected by type of account, because they reveal *relative* returns from present actions under any fixed set of assumptions about future benefits. A more complex formulation can be developed to assign appropriate sets of values to 1973 and 1974 calls in terms of their effects on later years.

Table 4-1

PROFIT RETURN FROM ACCOUNT *A* UNDER ALTERNATIVE 1972 CALL FREQUENCIES (in dollars)

Effort 1972	1972				1973				1974				pV discounted at 12 percent			
													1972 1.00	1973 .88	1974 .774	
E	p	π	pπ	pV	p	π	pπ	pV	p	π	pπ	pV	pV	pV	pV	Σ
0	1	200	200	—	1	30	30	—	1	0	0	—	—	—	—	—
1	1	200	200	0	1	50	50	20	1	40	40	40	0	18	31	49
2	1	200	200	0	1	200	200	150	1	200	200	160	0	132	124	256
12	1	700	700	500	1	1000	1000	800	1	1100	1100	900	500	704	697	1901

Marginal Value of Calls

E	ΔE	ΔpV	ΔpV/ΔE
1	1	49	49
2	1	256	256
12	10	1901	190

Table 4-2

PROFIT RETURN FROM ACCOUNT B UNDER ALTERNATIVE 1972 CALL FREQUENCIES (in dollars)

Effort 1972 E	1972 p	1972 π	1972 pπ	1972 pV	1973 p	1973 π	1973 pπ	1973 pV	1974 p	1974 π	1974 pπ	1974 pV	pV discounted at 12 percent 1972 1.00 pV	1973 .88 pV	1974 .7744 pV	Σ
0	{0 / 0}	{5000 / 90000}	0	0	{0 / 0}	{5000 / 90000}	0	0	{0 / 0}	{5000 / 90000}	0	0				
4	{.10 / .01}	{5000 / 90000}	1400	1400	{.10 / .01}	{5000 / 90000}	1400	1400	{.08 / .03}	{5000 / 90000}	3100	3100	1400	1323	2401	5033
8	{.11 / .011}	{5000 / 90000}	1540	140	{.11 / .011}	{5000 / 90000}	1540	140	{.088 / .033}	{5000 / 90000}	3410	310	140	123	240	503

Marginal Value of Calls

E	ΔE	ΔpV	ΔpV/ΔE
4	4	$5033	1258
8	4	503	126

buying group. They are importantly influenced by the state of know-ledge of those engaged in and influencing buying activity and their perception of the risks entailed in making changes. For these reasons the adoptive processes carry influence in varying degrees from the initial purchasing unit to other buying systems in the economy. In the case of consumer goods, word of mouth and other forms of com-munication (for example, behavior of one's neighbors and peers) are important vehicles of the process through which experience is dif-fused and patterns of change communicated. Thus, purchase of a product by some individuals or groups has its secondary effects in influencing the propensity to buy of other consumers. Their purchases are thus, at least in part, secondary effects of the earlier purchases by influencers.

A similar phenomenon exists in industrial markets. Buyers understandably look to demonstrated proof of performance of equip-ments, materials, components, supplies, or services considered for purchase. They often expect those who advocate change to demon-strate that others have benefited from the proposed change.

In these circumstances, sellers may regard sales efforts to secure initial trials as a form of seed money which, if successful, will establish in numerous prospective users' eyes an image of successful accomplishment. The use of testimonial copy even in media advertis-ing suggests that this need for assurance is widespread. Indeed, an important task of salesmen with innovative products is often to dem-onstrate that other users' experience has validated the claims made for the new product.

A manufacturer of equipment for smoke and odor control was sucessful in having his equipment installed in the spectator areas such as the main arena of the New Madison Square Garden Center. He hoped that its success there would provide the pragmatic test needed to con-vince specifiers of air-handling systems for other densely populated public buildings that the manufacturer's system provided real benefits.

The same manufacturer was successful in having his equipment installed:

1. in a typography shop to prevent the deposit of airborne ink particles on metal surfaces;
2. in a department store to demonstrate that the control of particles in secondary air (air within the room as contrasted with air brought into the room by the ventilating system) would reduce maintenance and redecorating costs;
3. in a telephone exchange to demonstrate the effect of controlled secondary air on the failure rate of points and other equipment requiring maintenance.

In each of these cases, an important consequence of the initial sale was intended to be a demonstration to other prospective users of the validity of the claims made for the equipment.

The approach suggested here for determining the amount of effort to employ is applicable to the treatment of individual accounts, customer groups, market segments, or the market as a whole. The problems of implementing such an approach are substantial. Data on the cumulative effect of a salesman's activities are likely to be limited, although historical data of considerable aid can be accumulated by any company with a moderately sized sales force. Data on secondary effects are more difficult to obtain and estimates about effects on buying organizations other than those interviewed may often be little more than conjectures.

Allowance for secondary effects on persons outside of the buying unit being interviewed suggest that the cs in the foregoing equation be extended to incorporate the changes in behavior of others influenced, as well as in the future buying behavior of the firm or individual directly involved in the buying activity.

The Allocation of Effort

For a given effort level (sales force of a given size) effort should be *allocated* so that the *marginal* return from further effort applied to any market group is equal for all groups, including prospective groups not now being covered. In this condition, no reallocation of effort would increase contribution. If the shapes of the response and derived profit-contribution curves of the various groups are known, the point of optimal allocation can be determined mathematically by determining the marginal contribution response function of each group (the first derivatives of the contribution curve) and solving for the values of E (effort) at which marginal contribution in all territories would be equal.[15]

Given a sales force of a specified size, how should it be assigned for maximum results? It has been suggested that optimal use of sales-force resources will occur where the marginal returns from all efforts will be equal. That is, we can maximize the expression

$$\Sigma_i \ \frac{(pV)_i}{E_i}$$

only if it meets the conditions

[15] The allocation of efforts between existing and prospective accounts is an illustration of this problem in which existing and prospective customers are treated as distinct groups between which an allocation of effort must be made.

$$\frac{\Delta(pV)_1}{\Delta E_1} = \frac{\Delta(pV)_2}{\Delta E_2} = \cdots \frac{\Delta(pV)_n}{\Delta E_n} \qquad (4\text{-}1)$$

and

$$E_1 + E_2 + \cdots + E_n = T \qquad (4\text{-}2)$$

where

T is the total effort inputs,
V is the value of an effect if obtained,
p is the probability of obtaining the effect,
E is the effort input assigned (for example, man-hours).

The approach to allocation suggested above is not limited to situations in which a decision as to the total size of the sales force has already been made. If the optimal size of the sales force is not known, a tentative value can be selected for sales-force size and the allocation made. If the resulting allocation produces an indicated marginal contribution from each territory which is above the opportunity cost of capital, further sales effort would be profitable. Hence, a larger number of sales calls should be planned. Conversely, a marginal return from proposed effort which is below the opportunity cost of capital reveals excessive cultivation of one or more territories and suggests that fewer territories and a smaller number of total calls are required.

The generalized approach suggested above rests on the assumption that the purchase response functions within the various customer groups (including the probabilities of inducing changes in behavior by sales calls) are known or can be estimated with reasonable accuracy. It also assumes that the cost of all sales calls is the same. If calls are of different duration, manpower costs per call will not be equal. However, the approach suggested above can be applied by defining the input effort, E, in man-hours rather than in number of calls.

ALLOCATION OF SALES EFFORT WHERE RESPONSE FUNCTION IS KNOWN

Three types of allocation of effort problems are likely to be of concern to the sales manager:

1. Allocation of manpower over various kinds of assignments or types of markets. Here the question is "How many men to each?"
2. Allocation of the time of the individual salesman among alternative activities and, in particular, among those

designed to retain existing accounts and those seeking to convert nonaccounts.

3. Allocation of men to individual assignment units, called territories, which is essentially a matter of the determination of the optimal work unit and its association with potential demand units. This subject is examined in the next chapter.

The desired pattern should allocate efforts not in terms of total sales to an account but in terms of the amount by which such sales will be affected by the calling process. Ideally, we should like to assign call frequencies in terms of the expected value of the *change* in net profit contribution which will be induced by alternative call frequencies. Unfortunately, such effects are difficult to determine, even experimentally, so that subjective judgments or analyses of historical data are necessarily used as approximations. Despite this weakness, the recognition of the concept of relating effort to expected marginal effect on a customer's purchases, including the risk that a customer will be lost, should produce a more efficient allocation of call efforts than the use of gross sales volume or gross potential.

Allocation of Manpower over Market Segments

Figure 4-9 indicates the response function which might be expected in two regions or market segments among which a manager must allocate any given number of salesmen. The solution for any number of salesmen, T, requires that the slopes of the curves be parallel. Where the slopes are parallel, the marginal returns will be equal.

In Figure 4-9, within each segment the amount added by an additional salesman will be less than that of salesmen already assigned. This example of diminishing returns follows from the premise that if only one man is assigned he will seek out the most lucrative business. A second man thus entails the two of them reaching out for less lucrative accounts, regardless of the way the prospects are divided among them. If, in fact, a second man produced more than the first, he would by definition be the number one salesman in treating any question of whether to retain two men or employ only one. Thus the curves in Figure 4-9 cannot have increasing slopes at any point.

In the figure, segment A is seen to produce an expected profit of $60,000 even if no salesman is assigned. Such a situation could exist, for example, because of previous cultivation, or because information from salesmen was not needed to enable some buyers to reach favorable decisions on the purchase of the firm's products.

The numerals along the curves in Figure 4-9 represent the added profit that would be attained at increasing levels of numbers of salesmen. For example, profits will be $24,000 greater if three men rather than two are employed to reach segment *A* but the employment of a seventh man adds only $16,000 to profits.

In contrast, segment *B* will produce no profits without sales effort. Perhaps *B* is a new market or prospective usage which must be established through some sales activity. As an untapped segment *B* appears to afford great return from the use of one or perhaps two men, but the return from additional manpower declines rapidly.

> *What can Figure 4–9 tell us about how to employ an available supply of seven salesmen? Of ten men? Suppose only one man were available?*

With the slopes clearly marked as in Figure 4-9, it is a simple

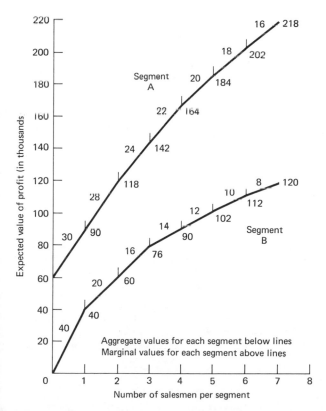

Figure 4-9
PROFIT RESPONSE OF TWO SEGMENTS TO DIF-FERENT NUMBERS OF SALESMEN

matter to assign the men in rank order of the additional contributions which will be made by them. We merely select the assignments which involve the steepest slope—that is, provide the largest return. The optimum allocation, given the response functions, will be that allocation at which the slopes will be equal—that is, parallel. For a large number of alternatives this might be derived mathematically. For a modest number it may be less difficult simply to prepare a grid of marginal contributions directly from estimates of the responses to be derived from the use of different numbers of salesmen. Table 4-3 takes the estimated profit response for different levels of sales effort in several territories (part a) and derives the marginal contribution from it (part b). The optimal allocation of a sales force of a given size can be attained simply by selecting out the largest absolute numbers until the supply of salesmen is exhausted. If desired, a constraint can be added establishing a minimum contribution below which the addition

Table 4-3

DERIVATION OF EXPECTED VALUE OF CONTRIBUTION FROM EXPECTED VALUE OF PROFIT

(a)   Expected Values of Profits Using Alternative Numbers of Salesmen

Segment	Number of Salesmen								
	0	1	2	3	4	5	6	7	8
A	60	90	118	142	164	184	202	218	232
B	0	40	60	76	90	102	112	120	126
C									
D									
.									
.									
.									
n									

(b)   Marginal Contributions to Expected Value of Profit

Segment	Number of Salesmen								
	0	1	2	3	4	5	6	7	8
A	—	30	28	24	22	20	18	16	14
B	—	40	20	16	14	12	10	8	6
C									
D									
.									
.									
.									
n									

of a salesman is not warranted on total return/effort grounds; for example, that no salesman be used where the expected value of the contribution is less than $10,000. This method can thus be used to determine total sales-force size through isolating the point for each segment beyond which marginal cost would exceed marginal revenue.[16]

In the Lambert study mentioned above, the marginal profit consequence of changing the number of salesmen in any territory was obtained by deriving the appropriate gross margin and deducting salesman expenses. Thus, districts which would warrant additional salesmen were identified. In this example, Lambert found that twenty additional salesmen could have been profitably deployed over nine of the twenty-six districts, yielding an additional $295,000 in gross profit on X-ray film. Even if additional salesmen could not be hired, a reassignment of twenty-two men would have yielded $134,000 more gross margin than the pattern used.[17]

Allocation of Sales Time among Existing Accounts and Conversion Activities

The general procedure suggested in the previous section can be applied to the problem of alternative allocations of the time of the individual salesman among retention and conversion activities as well. In this situation, the horizontal axis in Figure 4-9 would be scaled in terms of sales time (for example, man-hours). In terms of our general equations, the Es now are defined in man-hours rather than numbers of salesmen, and the Vs now will represent values of different types of accounts, with different values of p assigned to nonaccounts and present accounts. Different probabilities of success with different account groups can be readily dealt with by defining a new V wherever circumstances suggest it and by assigning an appropriate p.[18]

---

[16] A number of other models which have been suggested for sales-force allocation are noted briefly in the Appendix to Chapter 4.

[17] Lambert, *Setting the Size for the Sales Force,* pp. 86–8. Data for this study covered only a single year. The conditional earnings are based on the variables in the regression only; in effect, the procedure assumed that the variables in the regression analysis were, in fact, causal and that competitive action would not have been different had the men been deployed differently. These assumptions may or may not be warranted when the results of cross-sectional analysis are applied in later time periods.

[18] A simplified procedure for the special case in which all nonaccounts have the same probability of conversion, all accounts the same probability of retention at each effort level, and all accounts have equal profit value was employed by Brown, Hulswit, and Kettelle to determine optimal use of sales time by printing salesmen. ("A Study of Sales Operations," *Operations Research,* IV (1956) pp. 296–308.)

ADJUSTMENT FOR DIFFERENCES IN EFFECTIVENESS

In the foregoing discussion of response to sales effort, responses have been described as functions of the *amount* of effort as expressed in number of salesmen, number of sales calls, or number of hours of salesmen's time. The discussion thus postulates a standard man, call, or hour of effort which will induce the response pattern. It takes no account of what the salesman does or the quality of his work. Only the quantity of his work is considered.

While it may be argued that the differences in effectiveness could be resolved by expressing the inputs as dollar costs, such a procedure is open to serious conceptual objection because the persons called upon do not respond to the costs of inputs but rather to the inputs themselves. It is preferable, therefore, to express inputs in terms of the standard man, call, or hour as employed in Figures 4-1 to 4-9 inclusive. In Figure 4-10, the solid line shows the aggregate response of a market segment to differing numbers of *standard* salesmen. It is an input-result relationship of the same type as those in earlier figures. The slope at any point represents the incremental return from the addition of a standard salesman.

In assigning additional men, the sales manager is not, however,

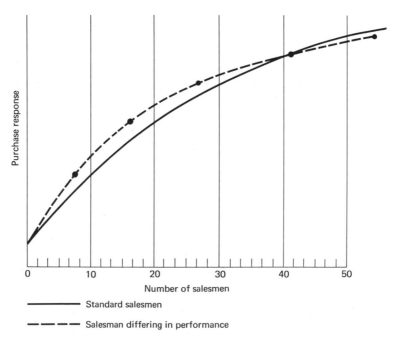

Figure 4-10

AGGREGATE SALES RESPONSE TO NUMBER OF SALESMEN

concerned with the standard salesman but with the marginal one who might be added. How much will this man add to the aggregate purchase response?

The broken line shows the purchase response of the same market segment with allowance made for the different qualities of input efforts. For example, if only the best eight men are employed, results would be somewhat better than those to be expected from eight average or standard men. Successive increments produce marginally smaller returns both (a) because of the declining marginal returns secured from larger application of efforts to the same segment and (b) because decreasingly effective men are employed. In the illustration, the superior performance of the first eight salesmen result in their having the effect on interviewees of ten standard salesmen. Performance declines with increasing numbers of salesmen so that after forty men are assigned it takes fifteen men to accomplish the effects of ten standard salesmen. The slope of this line represents the incremental return at any point from the addition of one more, not necessarily standard, man. Similar scaling techniques can be used to reflect differences in the effect on purchase response of calls made at different times of day, by different men, or using different sales methods.

SOME OPERATIONAL LIMITATIONS

The methods suggested in this chapter for the allocation of effort to activities and accounts depend on two premises that often present real barriers to the analyst and the sales manager.

On the one hand, we have proceeded on the assumption that needed inputs could be obtained or estimated within tolerable limits. Some suggestions for obtaining the required data have been made. But even here the reader must be cautioned that margins of error in estimates and even in so-called hard data often may be substantial. Recorded data are by their very nature backward- rather than forward-looking. Fortunately, the levels of precision needed for results to have managerial utility are often not too demanding. It may be sufficient to know that one should allot efforts between activities in a 60:40 as opposed to an 80:20 manner; there is no need to demand an allocation formula to a fraction of a percent. In addition, results may prove to be insensitive to modest changes in some factors so that measurement variances do not significantly affect them. Nevertheless, the reader should understand that the gap between acceptance of principles such as those offered here and their implementation by the manager is a wide one.

Throughout this chapter, sales-activity inputs have been viewed in terms of calls or time. While such a simplification is useful to explain principles and demonstrate relationships, it takes the nature of the activity as given. It was stressed earlier, however, that personal selling is essentially an intercommunicative process. The salesman is not simply the "actor" in a process in which the buyer is a passive object manipulated by what the salesman does. Alterations in the buyer-seller relationship are complex and sometimes difficult to observe and measure. Even those things embraced in the category "sales call" are varied. Such factors as activities performed, timing of call, and scope and content of intercommunication may, if they could be observed, prove to be at least as important, perhaps more important, than the number of calls made or time spent. The reader should recognize, therefore, that attempts to apply analytical tools and allocative devices will often, for the sake of making the problem manageable, run the risk of oversimplifying it. The need is for manager and analyst to continually seek out those factors which are significant to purchase behavior and to measure and understand them to the end of more precise and knowledgeable management.

Because the perceptive salesman in the field occupies a critical and often superior information position in estimating both the probability of changing buyer behavior and the likely results of success in doing so, the approach suggested here supports the view of the salesman as a manager of his territory who should be given maximum freedom in the execution of his duties. Such a view, of course, requires the salesman to have developed the needed perceptive skills and to possess and be able to use the analytical tools to do the job. Even where the salesman is not in a position to allocate entirely on his own, he can provide critical inputs for the use of others involved in planning.

SUMMARY

Determining the most profitable size of the sales force and how efforts should be allocated among possible buyers is a major managerial responsibility.

Deployment decisions rest heavily on perceptions of response functions.

Different customer and prospect groups can be expected, on the basis of their own goals, problems, predispositions, and states of knowledge at any time to have diverse response functions. Generally, present customers are likely to have response functions quite different from those of noncustomers. Different market segments may differ substantially in their response to particular efforts. The development of reliable estimates of these functions is a difficult, yet critical, task.

A profit-maximizing allocation rule must recognize both the

long-term profit consequence of a sought-after change in relationships and the probability of securing the change.

Both the amounts of effort which should be employed and the allocation of that effort among different segments of the market should rest on the marginal, rather than the total, effect of the sales activity on buyer behavior and its consequent effect on profits. Because of differences in response functions and in the costs involved in applying efforts, allocation of effort in proportion to potential is unlikely to approach an optimal allocation.

Allocation on the basis of expected value of effects requires a greater understanding of response functions of various market segments than is normally available to managers. However, reasonably good estimates of response functions can be derived. Both formal analysis and the salesman in the field have much to contribute in developing and improving such estimates.

APPENDIX TO CHAPTER 4

ADDITIONAL MODELS FOR SALES-FORCE ALLOCATION

Four types of models for sales-force allocation may be distinguished: (1) equal treatment models, (2) allocation in proportion to past sales, (3) allocation proportionate to potential, and (4) allocation to equate marginal returns.

Equal Treatment Model

The equal treatment model applies the same effort to all customers and prospects without regard to the potential business involved or the response functions perceived. A salesman who calls on everyone once is employing this model.

Past Sales Models

Past sales models allocate effort in accordance with either past sales of the company or past sales of the "industry" of which the company is a part. Opportunity (potential) is either ignored or, more commonly, is presumed to be linearly related to past sales. This essentially backward-looking rule tends to keep strong segments strong and undeveloped or weak segments undeveloped or weak.

Allocation Proportionate to Potential

The most widely used formal models for allocation of sales efforts are based on potential. Business practice in many organizations uses estimated potential as a goal both for the allocation of the individual salesman's time and for effort allocations among territories or other market segments. Commonly, accounts are grouped into potential volume categories—for example, *A, B,* and *C* accounts—with the goal of apportioning effort as nearly as is feasible proportionately to potential.

A manufacturer of metal-skin wall schedules sales calls on *A* accounts every two weeks; *B* accounts every four weeks; and *C* accounts every eight weeks.

Models based in potential implicitly assume that all segments of the potential have the same response function and that this function is a straight line. No account is taken either of differences in the ps described in Chapter 4, or in the differences in the costs of applying effort to different segments. Nevertheless, proportional-to-potential models are likely to be superior to the equal treatment model which, in addition to these premises, assumes that all accounts provide the same opportunity (that is, that both all ps and all Vs are identical). They are likely to be more satisfactory than past-sales models where important untapped or underdeveloped opportunities exist and opportunities are a more potent factor in response than are past relationships.

Formal models to apply the proportional-to-potential principle to allocations among territories or other customer groups have been proposed by Heckert and Miner and Semlow.

Heckert and Miner determine the shape of the response function by plotting calls per 1 percent of potential and sales per 1 percent of potential in each territory.[19] With the response function thus identified, the number of calls which will maximize profit is determined. Given the total number of calls to be made and, thus, sales-force size, men are assigned to provide an equal number of calls per 1 percent of potential.

Semlow proposes a similar procedure but uses percentage of national potential per territory rather than calls per 1 percent of territorial potential as the independent variable.[20] Both approaches can be criticized because they attempt to derive territories of equal potential rather than equal work load. These two goals are generally incompatible because of differences in the concentration of potential and differences in the extent of development. In addition to the inequities introduced by establishing territories of equal potential, the methods entail problems of updating. If, in fact, salesmen are assigned and/or calls made in proportion to potential, all future studies should

---

[19] J. B. Heckert and R. B. Miner, *Distribution Costs,* 2nd ed. (New York: Ronald Press Co., 1953), pp. 275–279.
[20] W. J. Semlow, "How Many Salesmen Do You Need?" *Harvard Business Review,* May–June, 1959, pp. 127–131.

reveal that calls per 1 percent of potential are the same everywhere. Thus it can be used but once.

Models Which Seek to Equate Marginal Returns

J. A. Nordin attempts to deal with the allocation problem between two territories under static conditions in terms of equating marginal selling expense.[21] The marginal selling expense curve is represented by

$$Y = A \cdot X^a$$

where Y is the marginal selling expense, X is total unit sales, a is a parameter representing the rate of change of difficulty associated with the marginal selling effort, and A is a parameter derived from a. Unlike the Heckert-Miner and Semlow models, Nordin recognizes the differences in outcome which result from the application of effort to different units of potential. In terms of the notation used in Chapter 4, Nordin recognizes the ps as well as the Vs. The Nordin model has several weaknesses, including those which spring from such static assumptions as that total effort is fixed; that today's sales have no effect on tomorrow's outcomes; and that a remains constant over time. It also suffers from the difficulty of estimating a, the fact that errors in a are compounded by its influence on A, and by concentration on sales rather than profits or some other appropriate objective function.

The Nordin approach does have generality. Thus, although designed for allocation between two territories, it could be applied to allocation between two kinds of accounts, such as customers and prospects, which have different response functions to effort inputs.[22]

Smith has developed an "augmented model" which attempts to refine the Nordin model in order to (a) eliminate the need to take the amount of total effort as given, (b) reflect variable sales expense as well as sales volume, and (c) provide a means for estimating the parameters. His procedure involves three stages: (1) determination of the proportions of effort to be spent on regular customers and prospects, (2) determination of the total amount of effort to employ, and (3) allocation of effort among n territories.[23]

---

[21] J. A. Nordin, "Spatial Allocation of Selling Expense," *Journal of Marketing,* VII (January, 1943), pp. 210–219.

[22] The Nordin model has been extended to more than two territories in John A. Howard, *Marketing Management: Analysis and Planning* (rev. ed.) (Homewood, Ill.: Richard D. Irwin, Inc., 1963), pp. 475–479.

[23] Michael C. Smith, "A Model for Determining Size and Allocation of the Sales Force" (Unpublished MBA thesis, Wharton School, 1968).

NOTE ON MATRICES

A probability transition matrix is a statement in probabilistic form of a subject's change in state between two points in time—for example, before and after a treatment such as a sales call, before and after an exposure to an ad, or even before and after a lapse of time permitting decay to occur. The matrix describes a set of probabilities. For example, in the illustration given in Figure 4-7, the salesmen were successful 6 percent of the time on first calls, 8 percent of the time on second calls, 10 percent of the time on third calls, 4 1/2 percent of the time on fourth calls, and 2 1/2 percent of the time on fifth calls. If we additionally assume that all prospects are dropped after the fifth call, we might state this in matrix form where S_s is the converted state, $S_1, \ldots, S_4$ the condition of having been subject to one to four calls respectively, and S_d the dropped state. In this example, the matrix merely says that of all the persons who have a history of two prior calls (row S_2) 10 percent will become converted on the third call and 90 percent will move to the class "has had three calls." In this example the matrix only reveals the call history.

		s_j ("After" state)						
		S_s	S_0	S_1	S_2	S_3	S_4	S_d
	S_0	.06	0	.94	0	0	0	0
	S_1	.08	0	0	.92	0	0	0
S_i ("Before" state)	S_2	.10	0	0	0	.90	0	0
	S_3	.045	0	0	0	0	.955	0
	S_4	.025	0	0	0	0	0	.975

Consider an example in which the states are conceived in terms of the salesman's appraisal of the situation at the end of each call rather than the number of calls:

S_d Hopelessly negative: There is no chance of a conversion. Such a state could occur because the earlier calls had revealed that the offering was not in fact appropriate to the prospect's problem, or that the prospect was so firmly committed to existing solutions that further calls are not warranted, or even that further calls could not be made because the buyer would not see the salesman.

S_4 Unfavorable: Prospect is willing to see the salesman but is unfavorably disposed towards what he has to offer him.

S_3 Poor: Prospect recognizes some merit in the salesman's offer but for any of a variety of reasons (technical, economic, personal, and so on) does not believe that the establishment of relationships would be in his interest.

S_2 Average: Prospect demonstrates some interest, but is far from convinced that he should become a customer.

S_1 Above average: Prospect favorably disposed.

S_s Prospect converted to customer.

The historical probabilities of prospects changing from one state to another could be expressed in matrix form, thusly:

		S_j ("After" state)					
		S_s	S_1	S_2	S_3	S_4	S_d
	S_s	1	0	0	0	0	0
	S_d	0	0	0	0	0	1
S_i ("Before" state)	S_1	.25	.50	.15	.05	.01	.04
	S_2	.10	.20	.40	.10	.10	.10
	S_3	.07	.10	.20	.30	.08	.25
	S_4	.01	.03	.05	.10	.21	.60

The Probability Transition Matrix tells us that when prospects previously rated "above average" are called upon by the salesman, 25 percent will be converted, 50 percent retained in the above average category, 15 percent downgraded to average, 5 percent dropped to poor, 1 percent considered as unfavorable, and 4 percent dropped as hopeless.

If the transition matrix is applied repeatedly, with the "before" states derived from the "after" states of the previous application, the result is a Markov process. The final outcomes of a repetitive probabilistic process can thus be predicted, given the assumptions made.

SELECTED READINGS

Davis, Kenneth R., and Frederick E. Webster, Jr., *Sales Force Management.* New York: The Ronald Press Company, 1968. Chapter 7. Brief treatment of allocation, territorial and routing problems.

Kotler, Philip, *Marketing Decision Making.* New York: Holt, Rinehart, and Winston, Inc., 1971. Chapter 13. Models of sales force decisions.

Montgomery, David B. and Glenn L. Urban, *Management Science in Marketing.* Englewood Cliffs, N.J.: Prentice-Hall, Inc., 1969. Chapter 6. Review of various management science models dealing with personal selling decisions.

5 Areas of Customer Responsibility

Up to this point we have been concerned with the application of effort to segments of market opportunity without concerning ourselves with the identification of those segments or the grouping of them into manageable work units. We have been concerned with *what* sales effort and *how much.* Now we turn to the question of *where* effort is to be applied and how the various segments of potential should be identified and aggregated for the purpose of assignment to individuals.

A salesman's area of responsibility is called a *territory.* A territory is a group of customers and potential customers used as an assignment unit. Although geography may be one of the dimensions by which a territory is defined, the basic concept is a *group of accounts,* not an area of land. A territory could, for example, consist of all users of a particular type, wherever they might be located. At the other extreme, it could consist of a melange of different types of users whose only common element was their location in the same community.

REASONS FOR AREAS OF RESPONSIBILITY

Areas of responsibility, or territories, are established in order to provide direction to sales activities and to enable control through appropriate feedback procedures.

Territories to Obtain Direction and Economy of Sales Efforts

To the extent that different market segments benefit from different types of information or different types or qualities of selling services, these needs can be met by defining territories so as to recognize and cater to the particular requirements of each segment. Those who differ in the kinds of interpersonal sales activity which might serve their information, diagnostic, or service needs can be recognized as separate segments and can be treated in accordance with their requirements. Thus territorial assignment becomes a means of recognizing operationally the differing marketing inputs needed to reach and serve different market segments.

Even within a recognized market segment, the assignment of specific groups to individual salesmen provides for cultivation of the market along lines desired by management and thus tends to insure coverage of desired accounts and avoidance of overlap. Specific assignments, by providing (hopefully) well-considered work loads and defined responsibility, tend to improve motivation by putting the salesman "on his own" but with known responsibilities. To the extent that the assignment of territories contributes to orderly coverage of the market and improved service of accounts it contributes to customer assurance and stable relationships.

Territories as Control Elements

Territories become the basic control unit for feedback of information about the progress of marketing efforts. Marketing plans and budgets are established with reference to territorial lines. Data about environmentals are structured in territorial terms. Thus, it becomes possible not only to evaluate the performance of the salesman against territorial expectations but also to evaluate the entire marketing operation within a particular area of responsibility.

PRINCIPAL PROBLEMS IN DETERMINING AREAS OF CUSTOMER RESPONSIBILITY

The principal problems in determining areas of customer responsibility are:

1. determination of the dimensions by which territories are to be defined;
2. estimation of market potentials;

3.   determination of the base unit, or control unit;
4.   laying out the territories themselves;
5.   matching salesmen to territories;
6.   identifying needs for changes in territories;
7.   realigning territories and reassigning men.

These problems are examined in this chapter in the context of prior estimates of response functions and workloads. Since determination of territories, workloads, sales-force size, call frequencies, and specific salesman activities are all interdependent, "solutions" in any one of these areas involve changes in any assumptions or inputs concerning the others.

DIMENSIONS FOR TERRITORIAL DEFINITION

Although the concept "territory" suggests a geographic unit, many other groupings are often more relevant to isolating a particular group of customers and prospects as an assignment unit. Indeed, geographic units are often the final basis of subdivision after more critical divisions of accounts have been made.

Territories are work units. They represent segments of supply of marketing activity. Ideally, we should like to match these activity segments with segments of market opportunity (that is, market segments). If we accept the underlying premise of the marketing concept —that supply services should be tailored to customers—our activity segments should be derived from the market segments. But what basis of market segmentation is relevant?

Bases of Market Segmentation for Territorial Definition

Table 5-1 suggests some common bases of market segmentation.

Traditionally, marketers have viewed segmentation largely on the basis of characteristics of the types shown in quadrant (1), a practice which is encouraged by availability of data and ease of measurement. More recently, attempts have been made to segment markets in terms of situation-dependent events such as those shown in quadrant (3).

Quadrant (1) and quadrant (2) criteria are based on who the individuals *are* (the personal characteristics of each possible demand unit). They provide a valid basis for segmenting demand only to the extent that market behavior is *personal-characteristic dependent.* We can thus identify the causal relationship between different personal characteristics and the purchasing process, if any. Quadrant (3) criteria attempt to introduce *situation-dependent* events, such as individual customers' brand loyalty, whether they are heavy or light

Table 5-1

ALTERNATIVE BASES FOR MARKET SEGMENTATION

	Customer Characteristics	
	Enduring Customer Characteristics	**Market-Dependent Customer Characteristics**
Objective Measures	(1) Socioeconomic status, age, stage in life cycle, sex, place of living, industry, size of firm, trade position . . .	(3) Consumption patterns (heavy, medium, light), brand loyalty, kind of use (OEM, replacement), media usage, type of application, . . .
Inferred Measures	(2) Personality traits, values, . . .	(4) Attitudes, perceptions and preferences, stage in product application cycle . . .

SOURCE: Adapted from Yoram Wind and Patrick J. Robinson, "Some Applications of Mathematical Analysis of Perception and Preference in Advertising," (Marketing Science Institute Working paper 45-1), Figure 1.

users, and the kind of use to which the product is put. Although such bases may be situation dependent in the sense that buyers may be grouped in terms of product usage and purchase history, such objective measures are not *problem dependent*—that is, they do not classify or segment customers and prospects in terms of the problems which such buyers seek to resolve in the marketplace. For this purpose we need to classify customers in terms of their attitudes, perceptions, knowledge states, and preferences (quadrant (4)). Our classification scheme must recognize the nature of the customer's information problem, including his perception of the problem for which the product or service is sought. Because of differences in their knowledge state or in the stage in which each customer finds himself in the application life cycle, customers who are similar in terms of the objective measures may have, in fact, quite different relationships to the product and may require quite different types of services. If segments are to be defined in terms of the needs for and effect of marketing services, such customers must necessarily be regarded as within different market segments.

As an example, consider an electronic component appropriate for use in a wide variety of applications. In some applications, its use is well established and may be said to be well along in the product life cycle. For many of the established users for these applications the technology is well known; criteria for source selection are likely to be heavily oriented towards reliability of delivery and conformance to previously established specifications and quality standards. Other users were introduced to these same applications more recently and require some measure of aid and advice from sales or technical personnel. Still other prospective users have yet to adopt and thus may require considerably more information and assistance in the incorporation of the component into their operations.

At the same time, new applications for the component are being uncovered by sales and technical personnel. Although the product itself has been around for a long time, it is a new product insofar as these new applications are concerned and the communications task is largely one of new product prescription and application. It should be clear that the kind of sales task which is involved will differ for each of the foregoing situations. Moreover, the factor which distinguishes the various market segments is neither a property of the personal characteristics of the segment (such as firm size or name of industry in which classified) nor of such objective situation-dependent measures as consumption rates or type of application (for example, use as a rectifier). The critical factor is the position in which the prospective buyer finds himself as a problem-solver. That is, what marketing services, especially information and assurance services, are needed to assist him in his decisions? An ideal segmentation scheme might well classify buyers in terms of such problems.

Selection of Dimensions for Territorial Definition

Operationally, the sales manager is rarely, if ever, able to achieve segmentation by problem situation. Moreover, the need to maintain continuity in relationships between buying and selling personnel sharply limits the extent to which he could employ such a segmentation arrangement in sales-force assignment. For these reasons, he tends to segment on the basis of somewhat more stable characteristics such as those listed below. In doing so, however, the sales manager must recognize that each segment thus defined may embrace important subsegments. Periodic review of such subsegments may suggest a realignment of segments and a consequent shift in the dimensions selected for the definition of territories.

Among the segment dimensions other than geography commonly used to define territorial units are:

industry served (e.g., automobile manufacturers versus utilities),

kind of use (original equipment manufacturers versus replacement buyers),

trade position (wholesalers versus retailers),

type of application (home builders versus commercial builders), dispersion of individual customer (national accounts versus accounts served in one or a few locations),

corporate form of customer (government agencies versus private firms).

The dimensions which should be used to define territories should depend on the kinds of services which the salesman is to provide and the skills, training, capacities, and sales methods which the salesman will employ. Where sales to different customers require different sales methods or capabilities, specialization by customer type is generally indicated as the primary basis of division. This is especially the case where the salesman must become expert in the problems of that particular customer type. At the other extreme, where users and prospective users are all pretty much the same in terms of the problems which they might solve by the purchase of an item and the buying situation in which they find themselves, or where customers are sparsely distributed, cost considerations may dictate exclusive use of geography as a base for defining territories.

In considering whether class of customer should be a major factor, the overriding consideration is the similarity or difference in the salesman-customer interaction itself rather than such obvious and more easily measurable factors as customer size or the industrial classification into which a customer falls. The manager must address himself to the question: How will the sales job itself differ among these various types of accounts and what, if anything, does this mean for the training, knowledge, and skills required to perform it?

The sales job with which the sales manager is concerned is not the *immediate* task which will face the salesman—for example, to secure an opportunity to bid for an initial order—but, rather, the *kind of relationship* which is expected to pertain over some time period. While this may not lead to the most effective immediate assignments, such a course is necessary to recognize that service to an account requires at least a degree of continuity. In fact, in some technical buying situations, the salesman serves largely as a problem identifier and communications focus, bringing in appropriate specialists to obtain sharper problem definition and to develop solutions with counterpart personnel in the buying organization. Thus, the goal of service to the account places constraints on the extent to which division of labor by immediate task can be applied in sales work. Excessive specialization based on immediate task—for example, one man for prospecting, another for securing the first permission to bid, another to service accounts once obtained—tends to violate the concept that the role of the sales organization is the establishment and maintenance of relationships with buyers. Subdivision of sales effort by immediate task is thus appropriate chiefly in situations involving one-time sales relations such as the sale of homes, baby furniture and similar high pressure retail operations, and some "suede-shoe" operations.

An orientation towards customer-supplier relationships as the central role of personal selling works even more strongly against organizing the sales force along product, as opposed to customer, lines.

Geographic Considerations

Geography plays some role in nearly all territorial designs. Salesman assignment always involves a trade-off between giving each customer the maximum specialized knowledge and capabilities on the one hand and securing economical coverage on the other. In input (that is, production) oriented economies and firms where less attention is paid to adaptation to customer problems and needs, geography may play a dominant role. However, as firms move increasingly in the direction of serving customers' needs and solving customers' problems, orientation tends toward customer rather than geographic groupings. This tendency is reinforced by (a) the recognition of the benefits of specialized knowledge in dealing with customers' problems and (b) the relative decline in travel time and costs as compared with the value of salesmen's time.

Nevertheless, a number of geographic factors necessarily influence territorial design. Distances (measured in time) determine to a large extent how much of a salesman's time can be spent with customers. Geographically dispersed territories are more costly to cover in terms of the proportion of travel and other overhead time to productive sales time. Territorial design must reflect such factors as well as the effect of distance on the number of calls which a salesman can make per week. In addition to the travel factors involved, geographical assignments may also be used to recognize differences in customers in different geographical areas. This is particularly evident when different nations are involved but is often true to a lesser degree within many seemingly more homogeneous areas. While less true today than in more provincial times, there is still truth in the adage "you gotta know the territory!"[1]

Administrative Considerations

A number of administrative considerations also affect the design of territories. It is essential that the boundaries of territories

---

[1] Meredith Willson, *The Music Man,* Act 1.

be clearly understood and communicated among the interested par-ties. In addition, if territories are made up of combinations of units for which data on market characteristics are available, planning activ-ities and the analysis of results are simplified. For these reasons geographic boundaries almost invariably follow political boundaries such as states, counties, or municipalities rather than being defined in terms of physical features or familiar landmarks. As data become available for them, zip code sectional and unit boundaries may re-place total reliance on political boundaries. Both political and zip code boundaries have the additional merit of providing a pattern to insure that the set of geographic territories will exhaust the area in which the firm sells—in other words, that every point in the sales area lies in some territory.

In some circumstances, the number of salesmen which can be effectively supervised (the span of control) may also serve to limit the number of territories into which a larger territory is divided. Be-cause the span of control is broader when the jobs being performed by the subordinates are similar, span-of-control factors may tend to make various territories similar if they will fall within the responsi-bility of a single supervisor.

Selecting Dimensions to Reflect the Market

In the entire process of establishing territories, the designer must follow the principle of adjusting the territories to the environ-ment and market characteristics rather than trying to overcome the environment through territorial manipulation. A common example of the latter is the attempt to create territories so that all territories will have equal potential. Establishing territories of equal potential ig-nores several serious considerations. The effort required to properly serve various territories thus established is likely to vary widely. For example, a square mile in Manhattan may have as much potential for the sale of industrial sewing machine accessories as the entire area west of the Alleghenies. Yet the time required to contact each $1000 of potential will be vastly different. Similarly, it is unlikely that an account using $1,000,000 worth of a chemical product per year will require 1000 times the sales time of a firm buying $1000 worth.

Not only are costs-to-service different but the probability of making a sale is unlikely to be the same for all accounts or groups of accounts. Thus $100,000 potential in existing regular customers is quite different from $100,000 potential among customers of leading competitors. In addition, salesmen of superior ability are likely to be more effective so that the probability of a sale per $1000 of potential (and hence the expected monetary return from a sales call) is greater in their assigned areas than in territories assigned to less effective men.

Territorial design should seek to adjust to the existing and prospective environment. Differences in opportunity among various market segments (whether identified in customer type, geography, or in other terms) should be recognized. Territories can then be established and adjusted so as to maximize the sum of the marginal returns from each of the resource units employed (individual salesmen or sales groups).

A (hypothetical) marketer of medical equipment finds that his salesmen must communicate with medical practitioners, with hospitals, and with government and other public bodies which both order equipment for their own facilities and exercise some influence over the equipment used by hospitals and practitioners through their participation either in funding the equipment or in reimbursing patients for services involving its use. Even where the same piece of equipment is being offered to hospitals and to private practitioners, differences in their understanding of the medical applications of the equipment and in their perception of the installation, cost, financing, and business aspects of its purchase and use, result in the salesman facing a substantially different communicative situation in calling on each of these groups.

Private practitioners may be concerned with ease of operation when specialist operators are not employed; with suitability for installation and use in offices where ancillary equipment is not available; and with original cost, financing terms, and tax considerations. Many will have little familiarity with the type of equipment so that an important job of the salesman will be to communicate information about the equipment's capabilities. Calls on practitioners are undertaken to communicate and explain the benefits of the equipment not only to sell equipment to them but also to gain their support in getting equipment into use in hospitals.

Hospitals may be concerned with whether or not the equipment is needed by doctors on its staff, whether or not the need warrants the cost, maintenance problems, cost-to-use over a period of years, and such business matters as whether or not Blue Cross will permit a service charge for use by individual patients, thereby making the machine partially or fully self-supporting to the hospital. Many individuals with diverse perspectives may be involved in decisions of important purchases.

Government purchasing activities may purchase for hospitals, but the applicable criteria may differ from those employed by other hospitals. Most governmental funding systems put emphasis on minimizing original cost rather than cost-to-use over the life of the equipment. Operability by standard-trained government personnel or by skills obtainable at civil service scales may be a consideration. Political factors (for example, preference for suppliers in certain areas) may be significant. Purchasing procedures may require open specifications and competitive bids. Purchasing may take place at locations remote from points of use.

In short, differences in the buying situations in which buyers find themselves, in the amounts and types of information which is significant to them, in the products which they might use, in their needs for credit, installation, and after-service, and in the relationship of purchasing or approving officials to the ultimate users of the equipment, all suggest important differences in what the salesman will need to do in establishing and maintaining relationships with them. In order to develop and maintain the skills required to do so, specialization by type of buyer situation is indicated. The marketer might recognize this by using three dimensions to define his territories. He well may have nine territories in the Middle Atlantic States.

Territory A   All government agencies

Territory B   All hospitals (except government) in the New York metropolitan area

Territory C   All hospitals (except government) except New York metropolitan area

Territories D through I   All physicians and surgeons in geographic areas indicated: *(D)* New York City and Long Island; *(E)* Westchester, Putnam, Orange, and Rockland Counties, New York; *(F)* Remainder of New York State; *(G)* New Jersey; *(H)* Pennsylvania east of the Susquehanna, plus Cumberland County; *(I)* remainder of Pennsylvania.

The reader should note that these territories are mutually exclusive—that is, they do not overlap—and that three dimensions are used in defining them: corporate form of customers (government agencies, even though they are hospitals or government physicians); type of customer (hospitals versus physicians); and geography.

Implications of Product-Use Life Cycle for Account Groupings

Stage in product-use life cycle may be significant in determining relevant account groupings. For the new sales force, the manager may have little choice but to rely on his intuitive judgment and the knowledge of the market which investigations of market opportunity have revealed. Because product uses and users' problems are likely to be only partially understood, specialization along use-application lines may need to be approximated by specializing according to customer types. If the product itself is also new, it may even be necessary to assign salesmen on a product basis because in such cases an important function of the salesman is the identification of applications so that markets can be more precisely identified and targeted. Grouping of prospective customers in this way is, in effect, based on untested hypotheses both as to the uses of the product and as to the buying problems of prospective users. By regarding them as untested hypotheses, the alert manager will seek evidence to verify or modify them as understanding of applications and buying processes develops.

Even if the original grouping of prospects proves to be the one most relevant for initial sales work (a condition more often sought than realized) the changing nature of the buyers' procurement process as relationships become established and, eventually, as the bases of sales change through the product-use life cycle, requires review and realignment.

Figure 5-1 depicts a product life cycle for an industrial product. Four phases are distinguished.

1. *Exploration* · There is little knowledge of product existence by users and even less knowledge of product capabilities. Marketers' knowledge of markets and applications is largely intuitive and hypothetical based on laboratory tests and executive appraisals.

2. *Adoption*   At least some markets have been identified. Initial communicative relationships have been established with some users in each market. Buyers know that the product exists but specific applications to their problems are not well defined. The product is in use in some markets but use is not widespread.

3. *Maturity*   The product and its capabilities in one or more applications are generally known both to marketers and to

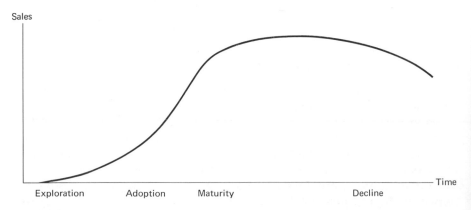

Figure 5-1
PRODUCT LIFE-CYCLE FOR AN INDUSTRIAL PRODUCT

the major sections of the market. The product changes from a specialty to a standard product as substitutes appear. Price, availability, and ancillary services are relatively more important as information needs of both users and marketers have already largely been met.

4. *Decline* The product and capabilities are known in all established markets. Price competition is more intense. The product may approach commodity status or merely may be rendered obsolete by better solutions to users' problems.

The selling task changes throughout this cycle. In the exploratory phase both the salesman and personnel in the buying organization are actively involved in learning. While the interest of buying personnel may lie in improved solutions to their problems, the selling organization seeks to identify applications which represent fruitful opportunities and to define them as sharply as possible.

By the time the adoption stage is reached, at least some markets have been identified and some volume of sales achieved. Feedback on performance provides the basis for improvements in application engineering and in product design. While broadcast (one-way) media are used to create awareness of the product and provide leads, the role of the salesman is likely to shift from explorer to application adviser and product tailor.

Buyers do not need information on the capabilities of mature products although with the acceptance of the product into their own operations they may become increasingly sensitive to such service considerations as reliability of delivery and conformance to specifications and terms. They seek service and low cost. Information needs are likely to revolve around such matters as delivery dates and special services (for example, special packaging to fit user's operation). In this context the salesman takes on the character of a contact man and trouble shooter.

Finally, in the decline stage, need for personal selling is chiefly in maintaining relationships and seeking to insure continuance of established routines.

It should be emphasized that these stages are not clear-cut. A given physical product may be in two or more of these stages at the same time, each in a different market. Particularly in the late stages of the product life cycle, pressures are great to find new applications or otherwise recognize and exploit new markets—in other words, to return to the exploratory phase.

Despite the possibilities of "rejuvenation," the operation of the life cycle has a pronounced influence on how the sales force is organized. Thus, heavy emphasis on product specialization may be important in exploratory market development, but application specialization may become more important once the markets have been identified and initial communications relationships established. Later, as products move toward maturity and uses and applications become more known to buyers and less dependent on personal contacts with suppliers, the changed role of personal selling may call for the abandonment of all criteria other than cost to service. At that point, geographical considerations may become the paramount or sole basis for grouping accounts. Throughout, the need is for classifying potential demand units in terms of their respective buying processes.[2]

Organizing the sales force to recognize the influence of product life-cycle factors is made more difficult by the fact that the seller's offerings commonly will include items at diverse stages of the product life cycle. One consequence is a need for periodic reexamination of sales-force organization.

DETERMINING MARKET POTENTIALS

If efforts are to be allocated on the basis of the expected monetary results of that effort, the manager requires estimates both of the possibility that a marketing input (for example, sales call) will produce a result (for example, change a buyer's behavior), and the effects of that change of behavior on the seller. It was suggested in the previous chapter that the expected value of the return from an effort can be expressed as

$$pV$$

where p is the estimated probability of obtaining an effect with a given effort and V is the value of the effect. This value depends on the possible contribution to profits of changes in purchases resulting from the changed behavior of the interviewee. This change is, in turn, a function of the potential business at risk (untapped potential plus volume which might be lost by not calling). The deployment of sales forces thus requires a determination of the potential business which might be gained by applying efforts to various customer groups.

Market potential is a measure of *market opportunity*. It identifies *the volume* which could be bought by a defined customer group in a defined time period under defined environmental conditions. It should be distinguished from *market demand,* which is a *schedule* of the extent to which potential would be attained at different levels of

---

[2] For a general classification of industrial buying processes, see P. J. Robinson and C. W. Faris, *Industrial Buying and Creative Marketing* (Boston: Allyn & Bacon, Inc., 1967).

effort inputs, and from a *market forecast* which is an estimate of what sales are *expected* to be, given the market demand and a specific level of effort in each of the marketing-decision variables.

In Figure 5-2, the curve represents market demand—the amounts that would be demanded at different levels of marketing effort. It is the collective purchase-response function of all prospective buyers. The line *M* represents potential—the volume which could be developed within the defined time period and market given maximum use of all marketing inputs. The market forecast for any level of marketing effort is determined by reference to this curve. Thus at E_1, sales of S_1 are forecast, for E_2, S_2, and so on.

In terms of the fundamental marketing equation,

$$S = f(O, E)$$

where
$S = $ sales
$O = $ opportunity or potential
$E = $ effort

potential is concerned with the value of O; forecasts with the future values of S. While there are many uses of sales forecasts (for example, expected cash flows, production schedules, and decisions following from them), the application of efforts ideally should be based on the nature of opportunities (potentials) and the probabilities of converting these opportunities into sales, taken separately. The use of sales forecasts to allocate effort not only inverts causation (by implying that sales cause efforts) but introduces circular reasoning and tends to

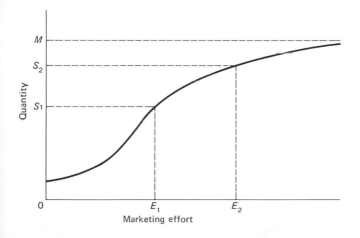

Figure 5-2
MARKET DEMAND AS A FUNCTION OF EFFORT

focus attention on past input-result association. It may even lead to stagnation on the status quo and to self-fulfilling prophesies such as:

> *At time t_1:* We never make sales to industry Q nor do we expect to make any. Therefore, forecast is zero. Hence, we will not call on industry Q.
>
> *At time t_2:* You see we did not make any sales to industry Q. Therefore, our decision was correct in not wasting effort on them.

Market potential, market demand, and market forecasts represent the sums of the opportunities and effort-result relationships of *all sellers seeking to tap a particular market opportunity.*

The set of sellers seeking to tap a particular market opportunity is not the same as a *product-defined* industry. The set of sellers seeking to tap a market opportunity may consist of sellers in different "industries" (when industries are product-defined rather than market-defined) whose products represent alternative ways of fulfilling a market need. At the same time, many members of a product-defined industry should not be seeking to tap certain markets which are of interest to other sellers in that product-defined industry. Strictly speaking, a product does not have potential or opportunity; an application or usage does.

For the firm, it is frequently more significant to examine *company opportunity, company demand,* and *company sales forecast.* These terms have the same meaning when applied to a company as to a group of companies. The relationships in Figure 5-2 apply in the same way. In some cases, notably those in which the products of the various sellers all appeal to the same market, company potential is simply the company's share of market potential, and its sales forecast is its estimated market share for the future period, given a certain level and type of effort—that is, a marketing plan. It is not necessary or even likely, however, that the shape of the company's demand function will be the same as that for the industry because of differences in decision variables used and in the effectiveness with which they are employed.

The concept of market share has limited application for many companies because of the niches which they occupy. Occupying separate niches in the market, they do not face the same set of opportunities as others. Because of product variants and capabilities, it is not unusual that parts of the company potential of one firm lie outside the total potential for which other firms in the same industry are supposedly competing. For example, the attributes of Company A's product may provide A with (a) opportunities which others cannot enjoy, and (b) opportunities in common with rivals in its industry (competitive area). These same attributes may make Company A's product unsuitable for some uses which are within its rivals' potential markets. This applies to all attributes which define a niche, not merely to product attributes. Thus, company potentials may interrelate as shown in Figure 5-3. In circumstances such as these, the concept of market share has little meaning and the distinction between company and market opportunities and demands disappears. To the manager, the concerns are the opportunity for his company and the demand curve which depicts the input-sales relations involved in efforts to tap that potential. To the extent that other members of his industry are concerned with segments of potential outside of his capability or interest, that potential is part of the outside environment, and is irrelevant to the potential of the particular company.

For example, a manufacturer of plastic wrapping materials finds that, in fact, he has several markets. For some applications he shares the market with other plastic wrap manufacturers and with manufacturers of cellophane; for others he shares the market with a partially different group of plastic-wrap manufacturers and several manufacturers of waxed paper products; for still others the competition comes from a few plastic wrap manufacturers and from suppliers of glass containers. In addition, there are many plastic wrap applications for which this particular plastic wrap manufacturer's products are ill-suited. While this manufacturer might meaningfully think of the share of each application market which he is able to obtain, the idea of a total share of a (product-defined) "plastic wrap market" would seem to have little real meaning.

The determination of opportunity (potential) requires the identification of the factors which underlie demand. This requires determination of the uses and potential uses of a product or service. To do so requires more than hope or speculation. For a new product or prospective new applications, for example, assurances from design or sales personnel or other advocates that a product is physically capable of

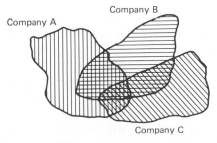

Figure 5-3
POTENTIAL MARKET FOR PRODUCTS OF THREE FIRMS

serving a need are rarely sufficient. The analyst must identify the customer groups for whom the proposed product does or could offer a perceptible benefit over what is currently being used to resolve the same user problem. Extensive field work is often required to determine those applications which, in fact, represent bona fide opportunity for a firm as contrasted with those which merely "could use" its products. The performance of such field work may be an important duty of many industrial salesmen. In small firms it may be a responsibility of key executives or technical personnel. Increasingly, staff or outside analysts may be utilized for this task.

Next, the industries, companies, or individuals to whom these applications have relevance must be identified. Again, field work may be required, although reference sources will often provide important information about the numbers, sizes, and locations of firms engaged in certain types of operations, families of certain types, and so on. For some industries, research firms have extensive computerized, currently maintained, data files from which they can draw relevant data not economically available from more general sources.[3]

If the analyst can relate use and user and can obtain or develop lists of users together with a basis for estimating their prospective usage of the products of interest, market potentials may be determined by the addition of the appropriate building-block units—for example, firms of certain types or families of certain types.

In some situations, the analyst may identify as a market an industry which is well defined, perhaps identical to a four-digit class in the Standard Industrial Classification. Census and similar sources can then be used to determine the number of firms, volume of output, and number of employees in the using industry not only for the United States as a whole but for individual states and many smaller divisions. Employee data for many such industries are available down to the county level. Thus, if the analyst can relate the opportunity for his products to the size of the using firm, he will have a coefficient which will provide the basis for usage per 1000 employees or some similar relationship.

Relating usage to output or to employee size rests on knowledge of the using industry. The analyst has many ways of estimating the significant relationships. Some common ones are: generally known technical relationships (for example, one motor per refrigerator); typical formulations obtained from chemical or engineering sources or knowledgeable technicians (for example, 2 percent by weight of wetting agents in certain compounds); the Department of Commerce's interindustry relations (input-output) studies which show

[3] For example, Dun and Bradstreet; Chilton Research, Mc-Graw Hill, Inc.

in total amount the purchases of each industry from every other industry; and census of manufacturers data showing value of shipments, amounts of certain materials used, and number of workers. Oftentimes, the linkages will not be direct. The skillful analyst will seek out ways to estimate the desired relationships, often through a series of calculations, until he derives the one which relates the information which he can obtain to the market he wishes to measure. Sometimes a few interviews with known accounts will expose relationships.

A bakery supplier, for example, found a stable relationship between the consumption of major ingredients and the number of delivery trucks of retail bankers. Thus, by observing the number of trucks of each prospective account he was able to estimate quite closely their consumption of major ingredients.

The need for a clear understanding of the use situation for a product cannot be overemphasized. Unless particular use situations are well understood, potential may be ascribed to too broad a group— for example, to an entire four-digit industry when, in fact, only certain types of users within that industry represent bona fide opportunity.

Certain surface-active agents are widely used in the manufacture of paints. A "surfactant" manufacturer might, thus, be tempted to relate usage of his product to the generic category "Paint Manufacturing" (Standard Industrial Classification No. 2851). He thus might calculate a need coefficient, such as x pounds of surfactant per ton of paint produced, or z pounds of surfactant per employee per year in paint manufacturing plants. Using a census or file of paint manufacturing plants, he might thus estimate the potential of each plant, and, through aggregation, of each control unit area.

A major source of error in such a procedure would arise from the fact that though large quantities of these additives are useful for some kinds of paints (for example, alkyd-resin paints), they are not currently used in other kinds (for example, lead-in-oil paints) and their use may be completely inappropriate for others. Estimates of potential based on the broad category "Paint Manufacturing" (SIC 2851) thus introduces an assumption that within each (territorial) control unit, the manufacturers produce a product mix substantially similar to the U.S. average for all paint plants. In this instance, such an assumption was so clearly untenable that it was necessary to devise and apply separate coefficients for each type of paint manufacture, including a zero coefficient for plants which did not make relevant kinds of paint products. Failure to recognize these differences in opportunity would have lead to substantial overstatement of opportunity in some areas and understatement in others.

Care must be taken not to confuse past industry sales with opportunity. Usage and purchase data are backward looking *per se.* In laying out territories the emphasis must be on opportunities for *future* product usage. Thus, consideration must be given to possible new usages, loss of some current applications, and similar shifts in opportunities.

Where the analyst cannot identify use or relate use and user, a direct measurement of potential is not possible. The analyst may thus be thrown back on the need to *assume* a relationship between potentials and some (preferably causally) related factor which he can measure. Not uncommonly, forecasting techniques such as multiple regression analysis are employed using past industry sales of the product as the dependent variable and testing possible independent variables as possibly causal. Forecasts are then made of the independent variables and the dependent variable calculated. The reader will recognize that the result is not an independent estimate of potential but an industry sales forecast based on historical association between sales and certain factors believed to be causal. Companies which use this method then derive their "potential" as the maximum of a company demand curve (company effort-sales relation). Some firms derive a company sales forecast from external independent variables in the same way. This method has appeal in many consumer goods industries in which (a) the units of demand are not individually important, and (b) changes in global totals are sluggish. The method also may be used appropriately for industrial products having single uses or if separate forecasts are made for each use. In circumstances such as these, industry sales forecasts and so-called company potentials derived from them may be sufficiently accurate to serve for effort allocation. The method does not, however, attempt to measure or provide for untapped opportunities.

It is quite clear, however, that the development of products increasingly suited to particular use situations, which have been so prominent in industrial markets in recent years, is growing in consumer markets as well. Therefore, demand for more precise methods of identifying and measuring units of potential for consumer products seems inevitable.

POTENTIALS FOR TERRITORIAL BUILDING BLOCKS

The development of sales-force territories requires not only that response functions be understood and that total national or world potential be known, but also that the potential be expressed in the units from which the customer groupings known as territories are to be constructed.

The development of potentials through building-block methods generally permits direct assignment of potentials to units of demand which are either already known or can be located in terms of their industry class, size, or geographic location with little additional effort. Industrial, trade, and population censuses and industrial directories may provide relatively simple bases for determining where, in both geographic and industry terms, the units of demand lie.

Where so-called potential is derived from a sales forecast (for example, through regression), on the other hand, some separate means of locating the opportunity industrially and spatially is still required. At this point, the analyst may return to the causal factors employed to make the sales forecast and apply the particular regression equations to the independent variables in the various industrial or geographic units. For example, if population were the sole determinant of demand for product R, an index of population—the share of total United States population in any geographic area—could be used to assign potential to each area. Most so-called market indexes are based on this premise although several independent causal factors may be combined.

GROUPING PLANNED EFFORTS INTO ASSIGNMENT UNITS

Before the manager is in a position to concern himself with the determination of specific sales territories, decisions will have been made as to the overall markets to be sought, both in terms of geographic area and customer type. The bases of customer grouping (dimensions for territorial definition) will also have been selected. In addition, the average workload to be assigned to each salesman will have been ascertained by some appropriate means.

Design of the geographic element of a territory plan involves selection of a base unit or control unit and a system to lay out the territories themselves.

Determination of Base Unit or Control Unit

The first step in the establishment of the geographic scope of individual territories is the determination of the base unit or control unit which is to be employed to define and delimit geographic areas. The base unit will almost necessarily be expressed in terms of some politically defined unit or combination of units. The largest units in common use are countries, regions (groups of countries or groups of states within a country), and states or provinces. The use of states as the base unit is appropriate in a few industries in which national or state boundaries, in fact, delimit markets (for example, alcoholic beverages, public school textbooks). In addition, the use of states may prove adequate for a firm with a small sales force covering an extensive area without intensive cultivation. New firms exploring as yet ill-defined opportunities may, for example, find such a crude delimitation of areas adequate for their purpose of skimming the market for ideas and initial sales.

More intensive cultivation of a market, however, requires areas that are attuned to market rather than political realities. Boundaries of states of the United States are particularly ill-suited for such purposes because many of the centers of economic activities lie on or near state boundaries and their activities and influence spill over into adjoining states. Hence, areas which have economic, and particularly market, significance are preferred. Because of the need to define such areas in political terms in order that they be understood by those who will work with them, and because nearly all reference data about marketing environmentals are expressed in terms of political reference units, it is desirable to have a base unit which is geographically small, readily identified, and capable of being grouped with other units to form larger economic aggregates. For most of the United States, the unit which best serves this need is the county.[4]

COUNTIES

Counties have the merit of being sufficiently large units. Statistical data are available for them. At the same time, counties are sufficiently small so that groups of them can be aggregated in appropriate fashion to form territories.

The boundaries of counties generally remain fixed over long periods of time. With a few exceptions, the set of counties exhausts the entire area of a state. Thus there is no problem of a remainder as would result if cities were to be the territorial unit. In that case, separate provision for the various areas outside of defined cities would be required.[5]

STANDARD METROPOLITAN STATISTICAL AREAS

Groupings of counties of particular significance for the layout of territories are the Standard Metropolitan Statistical Areas. A Standard Metropolitan Statistical Area is a county or group of contiguous counties (towns or cities in New England) which contains at least one central city of 50,000 inhabitants or more, or "twin cities" with a combined population of at least 50,000, plus contiguous counties which are essentially metropolitan in character and are socially and economi-

[4] In states not having county government, the preference is for the largest civil division below the state level. For Alaska, this unit is the judicial district; for Connecticut it is the town.

[5] Large independent cities such as St. Louis, San Francisco, and Richmond are treated as if they were counties. While the small "independent cities" of Virginia can be so treated, it is generally preferable to treat them as parts of a contiguous county.

cally integrated with the central city. There were 230 such SMSAs in 1970 of which 70 had populations in excess of 500,000 persons. SMSAs are particularly useful in territorial layout not only because they are made up of county building blocks (which the analyst may separate where appropriate) but also because nearly all federal, most state, and many private organizations gathering industrial, commercial, and demographic data use these geographic units in reporting.

TRADING AREAS

For products sold to or through wholesalers and retailers the concept of a trading area is useful. The trading area derives from the movement of people towards goods and the outreach of wholesale and retail middlemen towards people. It is defined as the area which draws its major portion of a particular class of goods from a *trading center.*

A wholesale trading area is the area within which the principal source of supply for retailers is a particular trading center. The scope of a wholesale trading area may be as large as, but no larger than, the effective outreach of the wholesalers in the center.[6] It may be useful to the marketing manager because it determines the retail area which is likely to be served by wholesalers in the trading center. Wholesale trading areas tend to be more extensive than SMSAs because they include tributary nonmetropolitan counties served from the trading center. They tend to be quite stable for many categories of goods, although improvements in the highway pattern now taking place suggest that some secondary centers and areas are likely to decline as the ability of the larger centers to serve wider areas effectively tends to grow.

Retail trading areas vary in size from a few blocks for convenience goods and services (drugs, self-service laundry) to SMSAs and even larger areas for some specialties (bridal gowns, opera tickets, original paintings).

Conceptually, trading areas have the benefit of recognizing the "natural" areas as developed through the operation of market attractions. Their use is facilitated by the availability of a number of trading area maps for some broad goods categories. Manufacturers whose products fall within these categories may find that the areas thus delineated provide meaningful building blocks from which to develop territories. They are also useful as a starting point in selecting places in which retail and wholesale outlets should be sought. One limitation

[6] The trading area may be more confined than the outreach of some wholesalers in the center who are able because of their particular market strengths (for example, controlled brands, effective sales organizations) to enjoy effective outreach into areas which are dominated by other centers.

to their use is the effort involved in delimiting trading areas for a particular product. Existing trading area maps such as *Rand McNally Commercial Atlas and Marketing Guide, Market Areas of the U.S.* (Philadelphia: Curtis Publishing Co., 1961) and U.S. Department of Commerce, *Wholesale Grocery Trading Areas,* often prove helpful although the user must first satisfy himself that the areas delineated by the maps are valid for his situation.

Retail trading areas especially are subject to obsolescence hazards where new transportation facilities (for example, limited access highways) and new regional shopping centers related to them alter the trade flows for various categories of goods.

INTRACOUNTY UNITS

Where large numbers of calls are to be made within a county, smaller geographic units are necessary to delimit territories. Municipalities and other minor civil divisions (townships) may be useful, particularly when it is necessary to create two or more territories from a single rural or partly rural county. In metropolitan areas, the census tract is the most suitable subarea because it provides reasonably small units within even the largest cities and because demographic, housing, and sometimes economic data are available in this unit. As data become available for them, zip code areas may provide useful intracounty or intra-SMSA units.

Laying out Territories

Given the amounts and kinds of efforts to be devoted to the development of various types of accounts (Chapter 4), the location of potential, and the bases to be used for defining territorial groupings, the manager is now able to lay out specific territories. Although, in principle, it would be possible to start at any corner of a map of the entire area to be served and successively carve out territorial segments of the desired size, such a procedure is unlikely to be satisfactory because it fails to take into account adequately the great differences in the size of trading areas and metropolitan units. Moreover, rarely, if ever, does a company start with a designed national or international market coverage plan; rather, it develops markets, often proceeding from strong points into less strong areas. Even if it is desired to approach the entire national market in a single stroke, it is generally preferable to work from major to minor areas in order to preserve the integrity of key metropolitan areas and to facilitate establishing divisional, regional, or other groupings of territories with reference to meaningful locations for such headquarters. Proceeding along these lines, a five-step plan for laying out territories may be envisaged (Figure 5-4).

IDENTIFY KEY TERRITORIAL UNITS

Based on important concentrations of industrial customers or major metropolitan areas the analyst will identify the major centers of market potential. Each of these major centers will contain sufficient workload to require one or more territorial assignments.

TENTATIVE DELIMITATION AND DIVISION OF KEY UNITS

Based on the desired workloads and previously determined estimates of the work required, delimit the outreach of each key territory. The largest key areas may involve two or more such territories.

RANK OTHER MARKETS

All other centers (or markets) which are believed to be sufficiently large to warrant recognition as territorial centers are ranked in order of their estimated return per unit input (in terms of pV per man-month of effort).

DELIMIT SUCCESSIVE MARKETS

Proceeding in rank order, tentatively delimit each market, again based on estimates of work required. This procedure will not provide

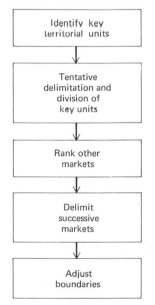

Figure 5-4

**STEPS IN
LAYING OUT
TERRITORIES**

for coverage of the entire national market because (a) some area will lie outside the outreaches thus defined and (b) some areas, despite estimated pV for the area as a whole, will have been "cut short" by the prior incorporation of a portion of the area into another tentative territory.

ADJUSTMENT OF TERRITORIAL BOUNDARIES

Although the concept of equal workloads and equal marginal returns from effort are desirable in principle, the need to recognize the topography of the market requires some modifications. In the first place it is necessary to maintain the integrity of the base units as boundaries. The division of an SMSA or even a trading area may be undesirable in terms of customer service and in terms of evaluating performance and fixing responsibility. A customer in Chicago, for example, might reasonably expect to receive delivery, follow-up, and maintenance services from the seller's Chicago distribution and service facility. An arrangement in which certain blocks in Chicago are assigned to the South Bend, Indiana sales territory and thus serviced out of Indianapolis might provide more equal workloads but is hardly likely to appear reasonable to customers. The maintenance of base unit integrity requires some modification of the ideal of equating workloads in terms of cost of pV efforts.

In addition, if the entire market is to be served, provision must be made to reach those remaining market segments which meet appropriate criteria—that is, to fill out the blank spaces on our territorial map to the extent that they warrant reaching without violating the compactness necessary for good route coverage.

Of course, some prospective accounts may be too costly to attempt to reach, considering their location and possible purchases. Rising solicitation costs tend to make more prospects submarginal, unless the potential business obtainable from them rises at least proportionately.

Improvements in express travel may also make out-of-the-way prospects unattractive.

A rug manufacturer, following profitability studies of its salesmen, concluded that it would be preferable to have its salesmen fly, rather than drive, to certain major cities. This meant the elimination of salesman calls on many accounts in smaller towns lying along previously used motor routes. The possibility of serving these markets with separate salesmen was rejected as being too costly for the volume which could be obtained. Thus the shift to air transportation, in effect, removed certain nonmetropolitan areas from the sales territory being canvassed by the company.

The interstate highway system is likely to have similar effects. The time savings in using the interstate routes may make communities distant from the system uneconomic in terms of the values to be obtained from calls there. For example, in driving between Cincinnati and Pittsburgh, the route through central Ohio (US 40) and the route through southern Ohio (US 50) were roughly similar. The construction of I70 to replace US 40 now makes the drive from Cincinnati to Pittsburgh substantially shorter. Thus communities along US 50 are likely to receive less attention from salesmen and may not be worth the additions to travel time which use of that route requires.

Tentatively established territorial boundaries must be modified to recognize these factors. In an established sales organization, tax and personnel factors also impose constraints on territorial alignment.

DEVELOPING EQUAL WORK-LOAD TERRITORIES WHERE TOTAL NUMBER OF TERRITORIES IS FIXED

In cases in which the marginal returns from sales or service work are likely to be uniform over the market, and geographic coverage of an entire area is required, the determination of territorial boundaries becomes one of equalizing activity (workload) over a prespecified n number of one-man territories. In this context, the problem is to align the territorial boundaries so as to provide equal activity with the greatest possible total compactness in order to reduce travel. S. Hess suggests that this can be approached by minimizing the moment of inertia of the points at which sales activity is to be performed. All activity within the smallest geographic unit which will be recognized for territorial purposes (the smallest building block unit) is for calculation purposes presumed to be located at the center of that unit.

A procedure of Hess makes use of a computer routine originally developed to establish compact legislative districts of equal population. As input data, the procedure requires the identification of all subunits together with the "activity" (work-load) associated with that subunit and the longitude and latitude of its center.[7] In addition, an initial set of trial territorial centers is selected as a starting point. The computer then (1) computes a matrix of squared distances between geographic *unit* centers and trial *territorial* centers, (2) solves a linear program assigning each geographic unit for maximum compactness

---

[7] The Hess program, having been developed to balance the *fact* of population rather than access to it, properly uses the geographic center of each geographic unit as the point to represent that unit. Since the salesman is concerned with *access* to the unit, it may be more appropriate to use the latitude and longitude of the normal access point of such unit (for example, highway interchange, airport) as the "location" of the unit.

and equal activity, and (3) computes a new territorial center and its moment of inertia. This new center is then used as a trial center and the process repeated until no improvement is shown. Maps are then prepared and adjustments are made for factors which were not explicit in the computer program.[8]

MATCHING THE SALESMAN TO THE TERRITORY

To this point it has been assumed that (a) all salesmen are equal in ability and (b) their individual performance is independent of the particular territory to which they are assigned. In this section the matching of individual salesmen, each possessing particular personal capabilities and limitations with respect to specific territories, is examined.

Salesmen of Differing Abilities; Performance Territory-Independent

It has been assumed thus far that any unit of effort would have the same probability of attaining the result—that is, that p is unaffected by the choice of man used.

If, however, some salesmen are better than others, where should they be assigned? To the richest territories or to the weaker territories which "need their abilities the most?" In saying that a salesman is superior, we imply that the use of this unit of resource has greater potential benefit to the company than other resource units. Our earlier concept of pV thus must be modified to reflect the fact that the probability of securing the result V is itself man-dependent.

The goal in assignment is to maximize the sums of all pVs over all salesmen. In the simplest case, this suggests that the salesmen who provide superior values of p will have the greatest favorable effect if they are matched with the largest values of V. This is what the sales manager accomplishes intuitively when he assigns his best men to the most important accounts.

If the better salesmen provide a superior level of p, without regard to where they are employed, it follows that matching top salesmen to top values of V is indicated.

Salesmen of Differing Abilities; Performance Territory-Dependent

The foregoing treatment does not recognize the particular characteristics of individual salesmen which serve to make particular salesmen more effective *in particular assignments*.

In the more common operating situation, the performance of

---

[8] For procedure to avoid split units and insure contiguity and other details see Sidney W. Hess, "Realignment of Sales and Service Districts" (Unpublished paper, Wharton School Management Science Center, July 1, 1968).

a salesman will be affected to some degree by the group of accounts (territory) to which he is assigned. The intercommunicative nature of the personal sales job (Chapter 2) itself suggests that all territories will not be the same in the kinds of problems with which the salesman will deal, the kinds of accounts on which he will call, the kinds of prior relationships which exist and are in the process of modification, and so on. Rather than finding himself in a situation in which Salesman *B* is always the second best salesman, no matter where assigned, the detailer is likely to find that the relative performance of the men will reflect the individual's relationship to the territory. A salesman may do well in one type of assignment but perform less satisfactorily in another for any of a variety of reasons (personal, education, skills, previous assignments, and so on).

To develop an optimal assignment plan the manager must first estimate the profits which would be derived in each territory if a particular man were assigned that territory. Table 5-2 sets forth such a series of estimates for a five-man, five-territory sales operation. In Table 5-2 there is no salesman who would be "best" in all territories, nor is there any territory which is "best" regardless of the salesman assigned. A convenient way to approximate the optimal solution manually is to develop a *loss table,* indicating the amount of profit foregone if the *most* appropriate salesman for that territory is not assigned to each particular territory. The loss table derived from Table 5-2 is shown as Table 5-3.

The goal is to select the pattern of assignments which will minimize the sum of the losses. This can be accomplished by first identifying all zeroes which are unique to both its row and column. (In this case, Evers Territory 4). Next, where there is more than one zero in a

Table 5-2

EXPECTED PROFITS PER TERRITORY
(thousands of dollars)

Salesman	Territory				
	1	2	3	4	5
Anderson	4	5	5	3	2
Brown	6	6	3	5	3
Caldwell	7	8	4	4	3
Davis	3	4	6	6	4
Evers	4	6	3	7	3

Table 5-3

LOSS TABLE DERIVED FROM TABLE 5-2
(PROFIT FOREGONE BY INDICATED ASSIGNMENTS)
(thousands of dollars)

Salesman	Territory				
	1	2	3	4	5
Anderson	3	3	1	4	2
Brown	1	2	3	2	1
Caldwell	0	0	2	3	1
Davis	4	4	0	1	0
Evers	3	2	3	0	1

row, select the zero which avoids the largest loss (in this case, assign Caldwell to Territory 2). Follow this principle until all are assigned. (In this case, Brown is assigned Territory 1; with Caldwell not available, the assignment of Brown results in a loss of only 1; any other man would involve 3; Anderson is assigned to Territory 3 and Davis to 5). In Table 5-3, the minimum total loss is 2. The estimated profit through this assignment is $30,000 (Table 5-2). As a check, the reader should note that the total profit from each territory were the best men available for it without regard to needs elsewhere would be $32,000.

Suppose, in the foregoing example, that Anderson were not available and that no replacement could be secured.

What territory should be dropped? Should the men be reassigned? If so, how?

The foregoing method is intuitively reasonable and has the additional advantage of being sufficiently simple that it can be done easily with pencil and paper. It does not, however, guarantee an optimal solution because of the nonrigorous manner in which the multiple zeroes are dealt with. Algorithms are available which will provide an optimal assignment pattern.[9] In any case, however, the precision of the results is limited by the accuracy of the estimated profit table (for example, Table 5-2) from which all else is derived. The utility of the results is further limited by personnel relations constraints on assignments.

Figure 5-5 summarizes the man-territory matching process.

REVISION OF SALES TERRITORIES

Conditions in the marketplace do not remain static. Both the work to be done in a segment of the market and the sales organization's capabilities for doing it undergo continual change, be it slowly or rapidly. Sales management both must recognize and respond to these changes.

Identification of Needs for Changes in Territories

Market opportunities change. Customers and prospects move. Some users grow; others wither. New applications are developed; others are displaced by alternative ways of meeting user problems.

The firm's situation may change. Developments in the line of products may indicate that different groupings of prospects and customers would be appropriate for an individual salesman to call upon. Attempts to penetrate new types of uses may suggest new responsibilities for the salesman, while old responsiblities must still be dis-

[9] For example, see William R. King, *Quantitative Analysis for Marketing Management* (New York: McGraw-Hill, Inc., 1967), pp. 454–461.

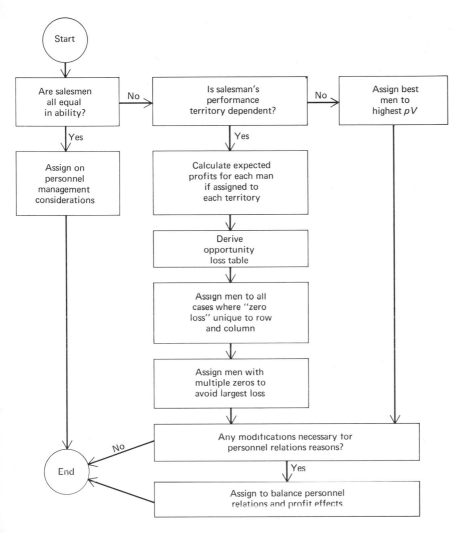

Figure 5-5
MATCHING SALESMEN TO TERRITORIES

charged. Thus new divisions of the total work load must be devised
if some tasks are not to be slighted.

Even if the firm's position has not changed, the role of the salesman in the user's buying process may shift dramatically. When a
particular product is new, much communication may be needed if the
buyer is seriously to consider changing his ways and adopting the
new product; later, little may be required. When the using industries
are in a period of rapid technological growth and change, much technical help from supplier salesmen and technical personnel may be need-

ed; as these same industries mature, their problems and needs change and with these changes the most useful types of interactions with supplier salesmen are altered.

The salesman's own performance does not remain static. Moreover, some men will be more successful than others in maintaining their competence to meet the changing needs of those upon whom they call.

At the very least, these sorts of changes may call for realignment of territories and/or reassignment of men. Often they involve reassessment of what the workload should be. Sometimes they require changes in the bases upon which territories are defined.

As noted in Chapter 3, management should continually monitor the sales job for the purpose of detecting changes which should be made in the job itself. In addition, it must monitor the market to determine when changes in opportunity call for reallocation of effort among geographic areas or user groups. As a minimum, the manager needs periodic analysis of the factors which underlie market opportunity and at least periodic, if not continual, analyses of sales by application, customer types, and so on. Unfortunately, many firms, even those with both the basic data in their records and the data processing capability to analyze them, lack systematic efforts to monitor the types of changes which would reveal needs for changes in territories.

Problems of territorial realignment are likely to be particularly severe if, through managerial default or inattention over a period of years, territories get drastically out of line and, in addition, the salesmen in the richer territories come to believe that they enjoy proprietary rights to their territories. If such a situation is permitted to develop, the company may some day find itself unable to modernize its territorial alignment without wholesale disruption of its sales force and the loss of good men.

Problems of Territorial Realignment and Reassignment

Territorial changes introduce problems of customer relations, human relations, and equity, as well as some administrative ones.

The interactive process which is personal selling is essentially a personal process. The parties are living individuals, not numbered robots. A change in the salesman assigned to a particular account entails a modification of the total interactive process between the buying and selling systems. A new set of relationships must be developed. In some types of selling situations, the establishment of these new relationships, including confidence in the salesman's diagnostic capabilities, may require a prolonged period and substantial effort. Risks of loss of the account may be far from negligible. This is not so much a result of the old salesman having a personal following as of the need to build confidence and relationships anew with the new man.

Salesmen and their families are not bundles of goods. In a pluralistic society, men have many affiliations in addition to those with their employer. Salesmen have wives; children in school; homes they own; religious, social, political, and community groups of which they are parts and towards which they may have responsibilities that they deem important. Consequently, salesmen and their families cannot be moved across the map like so many chess pieces. The disruptive influences of moving would constrain "instant adaptation" even if other factors did not.

In addition, any territorial reassignment or realignment raises problems of equity. Perhaps the most obvious case is that of a fast growing territory in which the salesman's work has contributed in an important way to that growth. If the territory has become too large to be properly serviced by one man, is it equitable to take potential and possibly even earnings (if volume is an important factor in compensation) from the man who may be largely responsible for the happy event?

> What consequences might inequities produce? Is it the actual inequities or the salesman's perceptions of them which matter? How would the problem be different if the growth in territorial potential were entirely the result of environmental developments rather than the salesman's work? Are inequities involved if opportunities change and the territories are not changed?

To minimize the impact of equity problems, it is generally prudent to assure the salesmen that individuals will be treated fairly, and that although changes are sometimes necessary, they will be discussed with the men. Often saved-pay provisions are useful; that is, arrangements in which a man whose territory is reduced or changed is guaranteed that his income will not be reduced for a period of years below that of his recent performance. Thus the salesman is offered a "can't lose" proposition in which he might increase his earnings but is protected from a decline.[10]

Territorial realignments are likely to introduce some administrative problems. If continuity and comparability are to be maintained, historical sales records and territorial analyses of potential, for example, will need to be adjusted to reflect transfers of customers or other segments of potential. One large pharmaceutical company tended to postpone needed territorial modifications because of the paperwork which would be involved.

Problems of territorial realignment are likely to be more tract-

---

[10] This is equivalent to the liberal job security understandings sometimes used in connection with the introduction of labor saving equipment in manufacturing and distribution operations.

able if (a) the original territories were soundly based[11] and (b) re-alignment has not been deferred for so long that the adjustment required would be drastic.

SUMMARY

The development of sales territories is basically a matter of grouping customers and prospects to provide appropriate work units for assignment to individual salesmen. The bases appropriate for defining territories depend on the kinds of relationships which salesmen are expected to develop with different types of customers.

Many factors may be relevant to defining the customer group which should form a "territory." Among them are industry served, type of application, trade position, and location. Commonly, two or more dimensions will be involved in delimiting territories.

The most appropriate bases for specialization of the sales force will reflect the changing relationships between suppliers and customers and, in particular, the life cycle of products: product specialization may dominate in the exploratory phase; application specialization tends to become critical once markets have become identified; cost considerations leading to geographical specialization become more dominant as communicative needs recede.

The development of territories requires sound estimates of potential *and of response functions* as well as knowledge of appropriate work loads. The layout of the territories themselves requires the selection of appropriate control units and a systematic procedure for dividing the total sales area into work units which both meet market needs and provide reasonable work loads.

Once territories are established, the set of territories must be matched with the set of available men. The assignment plan must take into account the strengths and weaknesses of individual men in various territories.

The work to be done in developing and maintaining relation-

---

[11] The problem created by poor original layout is illustrated by a regional wholesale firm which had not assigned men to specific geographic territories. Each salesman cultivated his own accounts. New accounts were secured when a salesman served a new customer at a trade show or the company's showroom or if the salesman was successful in a "cold call" on a prospect. Each salesman developed rapport with his customers who were spread out over several states. Any realignment on geographic lines would require that each salesman give up a number of his best accounts. Yet failure to redesign left the company with unacceptably high travel costs as a result of considerable geographic overlap.

A Pennsylvania dry goods wholesaler had a similar problem with each of its men having customers in each of the areas served by the firm; sales per man-day were well below reasonable expectancy.

ships with a segment of the market undergoes continual change. So does the sales organization's capabilities for doing it. Sales management must perceive these changes and modify territories accordingly.

SELECTED READINGS

Phelps, D. M., and J. H. Westing, *Marketing Management.* 3rd. ed. Homewood, Ill.: Richard D. Irwin, Inc., 1969. Chapter 17. Description of commonly used procedures for determining potentials and making forecasts.

Piersol, Robert J., "Accuracy of Estimating Markets for Industrial Products by Size of Consuming Industries," *Journal of Marketing Research,* Vol. V (May 1968), pp. 147–154. Tests of the use of the index method in which the national market for an industrial product is distributed by the size of consuming SIC industry groups.

Spencer, Milton H., and Louis Siegelman, *Managerial Economics: Decision Making and Forward Planning.* Rev. ed. Homewood, Ill.: Richard D. Irwin, Inc., 1964. Chapters 3, 5, 6, 7. A careful presentation of demand analysis and forecasting.

Spencer, Milton H., Colin G. Clark, and Peter H. Hoguet, *Business and Economic Forecasting: An Econometric Approach.* Homewood, Ill.: Richard D. Irwin, Inc., 1961. Explanations of various econometric forecasting methods.

Talley, Walter J., Jr., "How to Design Sales Territories," *Journal of Marketing,* XXV (January 1961), pp. 7–13. A case illustration of territorial design.

Part II

Providing the Sales Force

6 Obtaining Sales Personnel

The provision of a sales force requires that salesmen be obtained and that they be trained and provided with the tools necessary for the performance of their work. These are substantial tasks. A New York Sales Executives Club study estimated that fifteen major manufacturing industries alone would spend 979 million dollars in 1969 to locate and train 152,000 salesmen, 62,000 of whom would be novices and 90,000 of whom would have had some experience. The average cost of securing and training a new industrial salesman in 1968 was $7,516; for consumer goods manufacturers' salesmen, $5,970, all exclusive of the salaries paid the men during the training period. If these payments are included, total costs are much higher. An oil company manager estimates that his company will have invested about $25,000 in a new man before the man will earn his keep.

The average turnover rate for the fifteen industries studied by the Sales Executives Club was 8.4 percent per year. Approximately 399 million dollars was spent to obtain and train the 62,171 replacements needed.[1] Many firms experience substantially higher turnover rates. In addition, attrition during the first year, when little or none of the procurement and training investment has been recovered, may be substantially higher than for the sales force as a whole. First-year drop out rates of 30 to 40 percent are not unusual.

Flaws in the selection process which require early replacement are costly in terms of financial outlay as well as in terms of less effective performance in the field and a lower level of service to customers.

In addition, recruiting and selection flaws have serious personal, economic, and social consequences for the individuals involved. Some men will be placed in jobs for which they are not suited, only to find it necessary to seek a different position later. Others may lose an opportunity for which they were, in fact, fully qualified. Both the business and the social costs involved impose on the sales manager a responsibility for employing effective recruitment, selection, and training procedures.

The selection and training processes are closely related because the manager, confronted with the need to provide trained manpower for the field, has the choice of obtaining men with considerable prior training who will require limited training or of seeking out relatively inexperienced men and undertaking more of the training after employment. Where even partially trained manpower is in short supply, or completely unavailable as in some underdeveloped economies, it is necessary to accomplish most of the training in-house and to select untrained, possibly illiterate, recruits who have good prospects of being trainable. Conversely, a small firm with needs for only one or two men per year may find a training program excessively costly; it may thus prefer to hire men with as much prior training as would have utility in the new job. For most sales managers, the need lies somewhere between the two. He seeks trainable, quality recruits but is able to build on some prior training, such as that provided by educational institutions or previous experience.

MANAGEMENT PROBLEMS IN OBTAINING SALES PERSONNEL

Several problems are involved in providing a suitable supply of personnel to meet the needs of the sales organization:

1. determining the man-specification and modifying it as the job changes,
2. determining the number of applicants needed,
3. securing an appropriate body of recruits,
4. evaluating the applicants' possession of the desired qualifications,

[1] *Sales Management,* October 1, 1968, pp. 29–31.

5. inducing the preferred candidates to select the job,
6. adjusting the procurement process to changes in the environment,
7. evaluating the procurement process.

DETERMINATION AND ADJUSTMENT OF THE MAN-SPECIFICATION

Most writers on salesmanship and sales management suggest that there are certain basic qualifications or attributes which mark the successful salesman and which therefore should be sought in the candidate. It is not unusual to see lengthy lists of such attributes. Most are more reminiscent of the qualifications of a Boy Scout than the results of careful investigation of the relationships between attributes and performance on the job.

A few have advanced the hypothesis that the presence or absence of a few qualities is sufficient to provide a good forecast of success in a sales job of any kind. David Mayer, for example, has suggested, as a result of his work over an extended period in developing tests for various occupations, that two basic qualities underlie success in selling and that, given these, other attributes are of limited relevance. The two essentials are *empathy* and *ego drive*. The emphasis on empathy is consistent with the view expressed earlier that the salesman is part of an interactive communicative process in which he is not the sole, nor often even the principal, actor. In these circumstances, the ability of the salesman with good empathy to sense the customer's problems and feelings and to interact with him contributes to his success. Mayer argues that ego drive is also necessary so that the salesman is motivated to make the sale for the subjective and monetary satisfactions derived therefrom and so that empathy does not spill over and become sympathy. He reports that measures of empathy and ego drive provide a high level of predictability of sales success in a number of different types of sales situations involving sales of goods and services to consumers.[2] Yet, no applications to industrial sales or sales to the trade are enumerated.

General lists of desirable characteristics or traits may be useful in identifying the minimum qualifications of salesmen for any type of sales job and may thus delimit in some general way the group from which salesmen should be selected. They are rarely, if ever, adequate to provide the man-specification which the recruiter needs. As noted in Chapter 2 there is a wide variety of jobs which fall under the broad rubric of "salesman." Moreover, as noted in Chapter 3, the duties of most salesmen are multifaceted and adaptive to the situations in

[2] David Mayer and Herbert M. Greenberg, "What Makes a Good Salesman," *Harvard Business Review*, July–August 1964, pp. 119–125.

which they find themselves. The selector thus must develop a man-specification for each job in the light of its requirements.

There are two fundamentally different approaches to determining the qualifications for a particular sales job. The first, and most commonly employed, seeks to deduce from the job description those characteristics which are deemed to be requisite for good performance. The second attempts to induce the qualifications of successful salesmen by comparison of the attributes of men who proved successful and those who proved less successful on the job. In this way, it seeks predictability of future success based on attributes measurable at the time of employment. Each of these approaches, while useful, involves difficulties.

Determination of Qualifications from Job Description

If the job analysis has been carefully performed and kept up to date, the resulting job description will indicate the activities the salesman will undertake and the responsibilities he will be expected to assume. It should reveal such job factors as the kinds of persons upon whom the salesman will call, the kinds of relationships he is to have with them, the role of prospecting, the different kinds of services to be rendered to accounts, the amount of travel, the closeness of supervision, and the amount of independent action called for. These, it is argued, provide the basis for determining the aptitudes, knowledge and skills, and motivation needed to perform the job well.

However, the transformation of a job description into a set of qualifications for its performance poses a number of difficulties many of which are not easily resolved. It will be recalled from earlier discussion that the salesman's job involves many activities and that the importance of these activities even for a given sales job is likely to vary from call to call and from day to day. Which of the several duties—some job descriptions list forty or more—are most relevant to determination of the characteristics required for the job?

Job descriptions are necessarily duty oriented. Even a job description which is extremely accurate as to the *activities* that constitute the job does not indicate the *attributes* in the salesman which influence performance. At most, activities provide a basis from which deductive inferences may be advanced as to the attributes having relevance. The number of human characteristics which *could* have a bearing on job performance is very large. Which of these really make a difference in the performance of a particular job?

Robinson and Stidsen suggest that several different kinds of requirements could be deduced from an appropriately developed job description which would reflect full awareness of the role the salesman is to perform:

1. The *physical requirements* of a given task. This is the "things to do" approach from which derive the notions of required appearance, mechanical dexterity, and verbal acumen of the salesman.

2. The *adaptive requirements* of a given task. The concern here is with the range and typology of situations which the salesman is likely to encounter. Attempts thus have been made to match job requirements and individual psychological traits.

3. The *performance requirements* of a given task. Job requirements are defined in terms of the function or role the salesman is required to fill. The concern here is with the purposes of the salesman's activities rather than with the specification of the activities themselves.

4. The *integrative or systemic requirements* of a given task. The job requirements are expressed in terms of the relationship between the selling organization and some category of buyers. Diagnostic and communicative capabilities are relevant.

5. *The strategic requirements* or value dimensions of a given task. That is, the extent to which the salesman must be capable of determining the strategically most effective use of his time and competence and of accepting responsibility for these decisions.[3]

Even if a listing of desirable attributes could be deduced from the job description, two difficulties remain: the amount of each attribute which is required or desirable and the combination of attributes within the individual candidate which is most predictive of success. Job descriptions are rarely of much help in resolving these questions. It is not enough to know that the salesman must possess perseverance, motivation, knowledge, and skills. The selection problem is likely to be posed in terms of the extent to which different levels of perseverance, different kinds and levels of motivation, and different kinds of knowledge or skills result in different performance on the job.

Consider, for example, the matter of motivation. In some situations, the motivation of interest is no more than that which impels the man to carry out his minimal assignments and perhaps to drive towards maximizing his immediate sales. In other situations the man-specification might appropriately take into account the candidate's willingness to acquire new knowledge and behavior patterns. Or it

[3] Adapted from Patrick J. Robinson and Bent Stidsen, *Personal Selling in a Modern Perspective* (Boston: Allyn & Bacon, Inc., 1967), pp. 225–226.

might call for individuals who are likely to become motivated to commit to the firm and to organize and drive themselves towards firm goals. Pursuing such a specification, a firm might seek men who are so motivated that once they are given goals they will move towards them for the satisfactions to be derived from attaining them.[4]

Finally, it must not be overlooked that it is the whole man with whom the personnel in both the buying and selling organizations must work, not the individual parts of the man as depicted by his individual attributes.

One may conclude that job descriptions based upon sound job analyses may provide some basis for indicating the aptitudes, knowledge and skills, and motivation which might be desirable in salesmen. However, by themselves, they are far from providing the man-specification which the sales manager needs for this portion of the selection process. In particular, job descriptions can provide an indication of the kinds of competence in intercommunicative work that are likely to be important to a particular sales job but they do not yield the man-specification of the individual in whom that competence is to be found.

Determination of Qualifications by Analysis of Men Previously Hired

In order to identify the characteristics of salesmen which are associated with success on the job, a large number of attributes of salesmen who have actually been hired by the company are examined and related, through correlation procedures, to their subsequent success. In its simplest form the attributes of the better salesmen are compared with those of the weaker ones. A wide range of factors may be considered, including factual data on the candidates' life, family status, education, experience, economic attainment, attitudes, physical characteristics and aptitudes, and psychological and sociological characteristics. The goal is to isolate those factors which would have had a high probability of forecasting success or failure of the candidate. In rating the applicant, a number of points are assigned for each factor, based on the presumed relationship between that factor and success.

Studies in this area generally reveal some association between one or more attributes observable or measurable at time of hiring and success.

Merenda and Clark found in the study of 522 life insurance agents that certain personal history variables (number of children, educational level, offices held, life insurance owned, and amount of minimum monthly living expense) were significantly correlated with success. Other personal history variables investigated (age, marital status, military

[4] See Chapter 1, pp. 24–26.

service, educational expenses earned, organizations belonged to, years previous work experience, time at present residence, amount of un-earned monthly income, amount of outstanding debts, attendance at courses, employment of wife, previous sales experience, number of friends, number of friends in professional or managerial class, and typical recreation) lacked predictive value, except in providing outer bounds for acceptable ages. The same study found that certain tem-perament characteristics (for example, aggressiveness, sociability) were good predictors of success. The best predictive efficacy was ob-tained by utilizing the personal history and temperament characteristic variables in concert.[5]

Another large company, upon studying the records of recruits who had been with the company for three years, found that none of those without college experience had been promoted and that those who had completed college had a promotion rate three times that of those who attended but did not complete.[6]

The development of predictors of success requires that the job behaviors which are deemed to represent success and those which represent nonsuccess must first be identified. This is not always easy. Sometimes the attainment of a specific goal or the occurrence of a specific behavior is sufficient to separate the "successful" from the "unsuccessful." Often, even with reasonably good methods of evaluating performance, it may be necessary to accumulate perform-ance information for many months or years before the investigator can characterize a particular salesman's success. As salesmen increasing-ly become cultivators of communicative relationships rather than individuals who secure a sale, the problem of determining perform-ance within short time periods becomes increasingly difficult.[7]

After the job behaviors which represent success and nonsuc-cess have been identified, a search is made for predictors which have a high expectancy of association with particular behaviors. As there may be more than one route to success, it is generally preferable to seek to predict behaviors which represent success, rather than suc-cess itself. The predictors themselves may be personal history factors or attributes measured through observation or tests.

In order to judge how useful any given predictor may be for personnel selection or placement, we need to know at least two

[5] Peter F. Merenda and Walter V. Clark, "The Predictive Efficiency of Temper-ament Characteristics and Personal History Variables in Determining Success of Life Insurance Agents," *Journal of Applied Psychology,* Vol. XLIII, No. 6 (December 1959), pp. 360–66.

[6] Derived from data in Andrall E. Pearson, "Sales Power through Planned Careers," *Harvard Business Review,* January–February 1966.

[7] Problems of evaluation are examined in Chapter 13.

things: (1) the relative odds that persons with various predictor values will exhibit particular job behaviors or job outcomes; and (2) the degree of confidence that can be placed in these odds.[8]

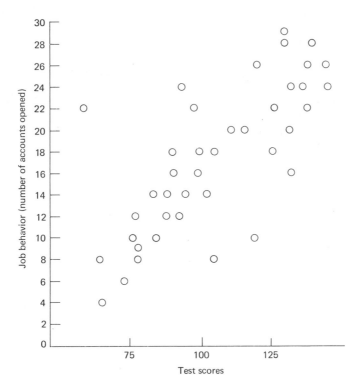

Figure 6-1
SCATTERPLOT OF TEST SCORES AND JOB
BEHAVIOR

USE OF SCATTER DIAGRAMS TO IDENTIFY POSSIBLE PREDICTOR VARIABLES

As the number of attribute and/or personal history variables which *might* be predictive of behavior is very large, it is generally prudent to examine possible relationships by means of a scatter plot before undertaking more detailed analyses. In this way those factors which *appear to be* related to certain job behaviors can be isolated.

Figure 6-1 shows the relationship between number of accounts secured and a test of sales aptitude. The results appear to show a

[8] Marvin D. Dunnette, *Personnel Selection and Placement* (Belmont, Cal.: Wadsworth, 1966) p. 125.

relationship. We say "appear to show" rather than "establishes" because the scatter plot assumes that all other factors which might
affect job behavior have been held constant (that is, that other factors
which might affect behavior are equal).

Now consider Figure 6-2 which shows, for the same salesmen,
the relationship between educational level and job behavior. These
results appear to show that educational level is highly related to job
performance.

*Based on the data in the two charts, which "predicts" job per-
formance? What might the test be measuring?*

Interrelationships among various possible predictor variables
can sometimes be identified by a multidimensional scatter plot such as
shown in Figure 6-3.

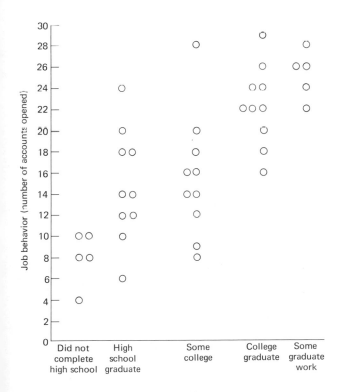

Figure 6-2
   **SCATTERPLOT OF EDUCATIONAL LEVEL AND JOB
   BEHAVIOR**

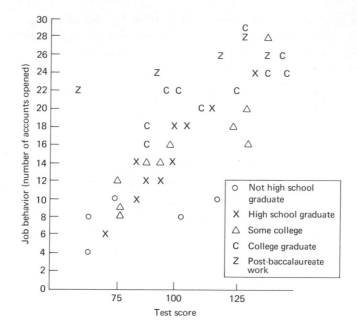

Figure 6-3
MULTIDIMENSIONAL SCATTERPLOT SHOWING RELATIONS AMONG TEST SCORES, EDUCATIONAL LEVEL, AND JOB BEHAVIOR

If a salesman opening fourteen or more accounts is considered successful and one opening twenty-two or more accounts is considered highly successful, could you suggest a sequential decision procedure which would provide high expectancy of identifying likely successes and failures? Would this procedure be more effective than a weighted point system in which points were given for both test scores and educational level?

EXPECTANCY TABLES

One way to determine the odds that a certain behavior will occur, given the value of a predictor variable, is by developing an expectancy table based on the experience of all persons obtaining a particular score on the predictor variable. Examples of this procedure are shown in Figures 6-4 and 6-5.[9]

Figure 6-4 shows the relationship between a composite score based on tests and biographical responses and success of Standard

[9] The examples are from published research. Similar investigations for sales positions are generally not published.

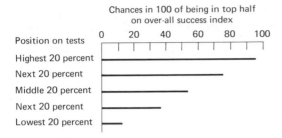

Figure 6-4

EXPECTANCY CHART SHOWING CHANCES OF BEING IN THE TOP HALF ON THE STANDARD OIL COMPANY (N.J.) OVER-ALL EXECUTIVE SUCCESS INDEX ON THE BASIS OF COMPOSITE TEST-BIO-GRAPHICAL SCORES

SOURCE: H. Laurent, *Early Identification of Management Potential.* Social Science Research Report. (New York: Standard Oil Company (N.J.), 1961). Basis: 443 executives.

Oil Company (N.J.) executives as measured by promotion rate and job effectiveness ratings.

For some jobs, information on the application blank may prove to be highly predictive. The Minnesota Mining and Manufacturing Company studied the biographical histories of female office workers to ascertain which factors distinguished long-term from short-term employees. Points were then assigned to these factors and the points summed up to provide scores. The relationship between these scores and tenure is shown in Figure 6-5.

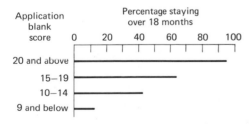

Figure 6-5

EXPECTANCY CHART SHOWING RELATIONS BE-TWEEN BIOGRAPHICAL SCORE AND LONG SER-VICE FOR FEMALE OFFICE EMPLOYEES

SOURCE: "Development of a Weighted Application Blank to Aid in the Selection of Office Employees," Research Report No. 7, *Personnel Research*, Minnesota Mining and Manufacturing Co., 1956. Basis: 83 workers.

As a sales management example, suppose that fifty applicants for a summer sales job are given a test for dominance. All are hired. Nine fail the training course; another twenty-one quit before the end of the summer. Twenty complete the job. Figure 6-6 is a scatter diagram which shows the relationship of the test scores to job outcomes.

Based on Figure 6-6, what are the odds that (1) applicants scoring 3 or below will pass the training course? Complete the summer? (2) Applicants scoring 9 or 10 will pass the training course? Complete the summer?

If you wished to limit hiring to men with at least a 50 percent chance of continuing until the end of the summer and the test was your only predictor, what acceptance/rejection policy would you employ? How might you explain the nonlinearity of the results?

REFINEMENT OF PREDICTORS

Once relevant predictors have been identified they can be employed in sequence or in combination to improve predictive capability. Multivariate statistical techniques such as regression and discriminant analysis can be used to isolate and assess the importance of the factors associated with differences in performance. Because in many sales situations there may be alternative routes to success, and because many predictor-behavior relationships may be nonlinear, such

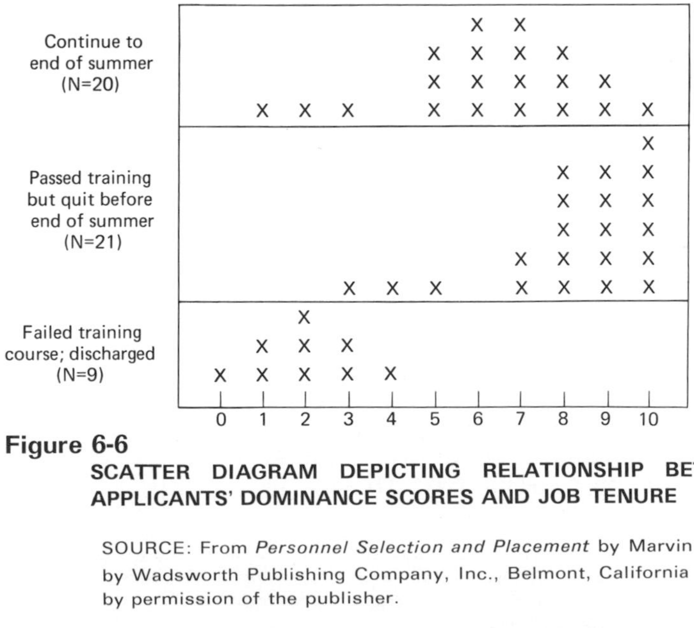

Figure 6-6

SCATTER DIAGRAM DEPICTING RELATIONSHIP BETWEEN SALES APPLICANTS' DOMINANCE SCORES AND JOB TENURE

SOURCE: From *Personnel Selection and Placement* by Marvin Dunette. © 1966 by Wadsworth Publishing Company, Inc., Belmont, California 94002. Reprinted by permission of the publisher.

techniques may or may not provide better predictions than simple expectancy charts or scatter plots.

NEED FOR ADEQUATE DATA INPUTS

Significant operational limitations in the development of predictor variables in many organizations result from the selection process itself. Because only some of those for whom predictor data may be available are actually hired, the analyst has no behavior information on those who, for one reason or another, were not selected or who chose not to accept the company's employment offer. If a firm has never hired persons of a certain race or religion or of a certain age, height, background, intelligence level, or test score for its sales force, it has no behavioral data on which to draw. If only a few special individuals from such groups have been hired, the inclusion of such individuals may be far from representative of the applicant population possessing that attribute.

The development of an adequate set of predictor variables requires that all (or a random sample) of the applicants about whom predictions of success or failure are to be made must be hired so that data on their behavior can be generated.

VALIDATION

In the foregoing discussion predictor variables have been developed by analysis of the results of past performance. How much confidence can we have that the predictions will apply to future applicants? The answer will depend on three questions:

1. Since the predictive relationship was drawn from a sample of the universe of possible applicants, how reliable are the conclusions drawn from that sample?
2. Do past applicants, on which the analysis has been based, validly represent the body of future applicants?
3. Will the relationships themselves remain stable, or will the changing nature of the job itself render the results invalid for future selections?

The first problem can be resolved by assuring first that the study from which the predictors were derived was based on a sufficient number of cases to provide statistically significant results. More importantly, such studies should be cross-validated. That is, the study should be replicated with a similar group to ascertain if the results hold. This can be accomplished by selecting a study sample somewhat larger than that needed to assure statistical stability and then dividing

the enlarged sample on a random basis into a study part and a validation part.[10]

The second and third problems arise because the applicant
group may not be stable and because the job itself changes. An ongoing program to relate predictor variables to job behaviors is desirable if validity is to be maintained.

It should be clear at this point that determination of desired
attributes by the study of persons previously hired requires careful
design of the research, starting preferably with a hiring policy which
has not loaded the test group with persons possessing attributes
whose relevance is based on no more than custom, belief, or unstructured experience. A system is needed for evaluation of the performance of better and poorer (successful and less successful or unsuccessful) salesmen over a sufficient period so that long-term success
(as contrasted, for example, with success in completing the sales
training program or success in the first few months on the job) can be
measured. The outcome of the process will reveal what attributes
would have been good predictors of success among those hired at the
original hiring date. These attributes can then be sought in new prospective employees, *provided* both the applicant group and the sales
job have remained unchanged. These last conditions are never literally
true and often not even approximately true in a dynamic society.

Consider the following situation:

> A company hired a large number of students graduating from
> leading graduate business schools in 1966. Most of the students had
> completed undergraduate work in liberal arts or engineering between
> 1962 and 1964. After a five-year period of observation, the company
> in 1971 identified the "best" and "poorest" among those hired in 1966.
> Correlation analysis indicated those factors which would have been
> good predictors of success of the "class of 1966." When it turns to
> employ the results, however, the company is faced with two additional
> problems. The graduate schools' 1972 classes, from which selections
> are to be made, will be substantially different from the class of 1966 in
> terms of the candidates' backgrounds and educational experience. These
> differences result from changes in the education and experience of
> individuals applying to graduate business schools, and in the schools'
> admissions practices and curricula. As a result, the class of 1972 will
> be much different from the class of 1966; yet the company cannot select
> from the class of '66. The causal factors which distinguished successes
> from failures of the class of 1966 may, or may not, be applicable to can-
> didates from the class of 1972.

[10] The two parts need not be of the same size. Commonly, the test group is
larger in order to assure greater statistical stability; the validation part can be
smaller as it is required only to confirm patterns developed in the analysis of
the test group.

Even more serious, the sales job for which the men are to be hired has changed over the years. Since 1966 both the company and its principal products have become better known. Thus the need for acquainting prospects with the firm's capabilities and those of its products is less critical. At the same time, the entry of strong new competitors has increased the importance of service and, in particular, of precisely tailored application advice. In short, the company has developed a program to tell it which members of the class of 1966 to hire to do the kinds of work to be undertaken during the period 1966–1971. What it needs are guidelines for hiring from the class of 1972 for the kinds of work which will need to be undertaken in the mid-1970s and beyond.

The limitations and difficulties in identifying those attributes which distinguish successful and unsuccessful salesmen requires that research in order to identify such characteristics must be done with considerable care and with full appreciation of the limitations involved. Nevertheless, such comparisons can provide standards which meet the pragmatic test of workability.[11]

The determination of the qualifications desired in salesmen no more provides a going sales force than does the decision to employ a certain type of wholesaler or retailer create a dealer organization. Having determined what it believes to be the qualifications needed for the best performance of the job, the firm must then determine the number of men which it will require over various time periods. It must locate sources of possible candidates, determine which of these "possibles" should be encouraged to become applicants, and induce them to apply. These activities constitute the recruiting process. Unless they are performed well, the applicant pool from which those candidates offering the best prospects of success will be selected will not contain a sufficient number of good applicants to assure the firm that it will be able to actually hire enough qualified men to meet its needs.

DETERMINATION OF THE NUMBER OF APPLICANTS NEEDED

In the past it has sometimes been possible, for certain types of sales work, to hire personnel as the need for them becomes apparent. Such practices are becoming increasingly less workable in conditions of tight labor markets for able people and as sales work increasingly takes on the role of a highly individualized intercommunicative process. As a consequence, except for the most perfunctory types of selling tasks (for example, sales jobs of types 5 and 6 in Chapter 2)

---

[11] For useful techniques in identifying and validating predictors see Dunnette, especially Chapters 6–8.

provision must be made for the development of sales forces as a deliberate personnel-planning activity. A personnel plan for the sales force must reflect answers to such questions as:

How many salesmen are needed for present tasks?

How many will be required next year?

Will changes in the sales situation, such as increased competition, require an intensification of the personal selling effort?

Will the geographic area currently serviced by the company be extended in the foreseeable future?

What impact will new product introduction have on the size of the sales force?

Will changes in the nature of the organization's business entail a different type of sales situation or a reaching into different markets?

What should the age and experience profile of our sales force be five years hence?

How long does it take for a man to become fully qualified for the most demanding present and future sales assignments?

What attrition rates may be expected from such causes as transfer or career advancement within the company, resignation, retirement, death, discharge, or obsolescence as the job changes beyond the capability of individuals to adjust?

A good personnel plan will indicate the needs for personnel modifications, year by year, for several years ahead, and for personnel inputs, year by year, in order that fully qualified manpower will be available when it is needed.

If the company can forecast the scale of its sales operations for an extended period and the survival rates of its men, it can determine the number needed to be drawn into the sales force each year.

Operations researchers working for the Northwestern Mutual Life Insurance Company took these data and analyzed turnover as a Markov process. Then they developed an elaborate model for simulating the effect of various alternative recruitment patterns on the composition of the future sales force and sales. For a given sales target, they were able to recommend the minimum number and types of agents to obtain each year.[12]

In order to obtain a given number of new employees, the firm will need to recruit a much larger number of applicants. The relation-

---

[12] Joe Midler, "A Simulation Model of Sales Force Development with Application to Manpower Replacement, Sales Forecasting, and Corporate Growth" (unpublished, 1957). Cited in Philip Kotler, *Marketing Management: Analysis, Planning, and Control* (Englewood Cliffs, N.J.: Prentice-Hall, Inc., 1967), p. 510.

ship between the number of applicants and the number of men eventually hired will depend on (a) the approval or selection rate—the proportion of applicants who are approved for employment, and (b) the acceptance rate—the proportion of these who accept and join the firm. The approval rate will reflect the selection process—the means by which the firm determines how the candidates' qualifications measure up to the desired standards. The acceptance rate will reflect conditions in the labor market and in particular the alternative opportunities which each candidate possesses, including the alternative of not taking commercial employment at all.[13]

Approval rates can be determined from recorded experience. Acceptance rates can also be derived from experience but are subject to significant fluctuation with market conditions; thus a predictive model requires more than the mere application of the most recent acceptance experience. Where the firm derives recruits from diverse sources, different approval and acceptance rates may be expected to apply to recruits from each source.

By applying estimated approval and acceptance rates to the number of men to be drawn into the sales force during any time period, the number of applicants desired can be determined:

$$D = \frac{R}{SA}$$

where

D = desired number of applicants
R = required number of hires
S = selection ratio (percent)
A = acceptance ratio (percent)

How many applicants are needed if a company needs 48 new men per year and expects to select 40 percent of those applying and to experience an acceptance rate of 60 percent?

It is desirable to have a sizable number of potentially qualified applicants in order to have a large body from which to choose. This not only increases the likelihood that able candidates will be among those recruited, but reduces the need to accept a low minimum standard of acceptance. The optimal number will be based on a trade-off between recruiting costs and the probability of securing applicants with given levels of qualification. The latter is likely to increase as $\sqrt{N}$ increases, where N is the number of applicants.

[13] The alternative of not taking commercial employment is especially relevant for certain types of sales jobs (for example, type 6, Chapter 2) which seek to draw on the marginal labor force (housewives, persons on public assistance, retired persons).

One of the more difficult parts of personnel planning is envisaging the kinds of work in which the sales force will be engaged—that is, the nature of future buyer-seller communicative relationships for which sales personnel will be employed. Such a forecast is essential to making adequate provision for manpower obsolescence as the job changes. Without it, the company risks finding itself with a full complement of men prepared to do a job that has become passé.

Forecasts of the nature of changes in communicative relationships with customers and prospects are much more difficult to make than projections of total personnel requirements. Nevertheless, examination of the stages in the life cycle of various products and product lines, estimates of progress of developmental products, and judgments about the nature of likely acquisitions and strategic changes can provide some guidance as to the kind of buyer-seller relationships which will be required in future years. One way to hedge against the consequences of present uncertainties about the nature of future tasks is to seek out personnel with superior capabilities for adaptation to new situations.

SECURING AN APPROPRIATE POOL OF RECRUITS

Any selection process requires a candidate pool of adequate size and composition. The recruiter must determine the sources from which applicants are to be drawn and must communicate with these groups in such a way that sufficient numbers will wish to apply.

Candidate Sources

Any source may produce a good candidate. The appropriateness of a particular source will depend upon the job being offered and the opportunities which possible candidates see in it. The sales organization can determine, on the basis of its own historical records, those sources which have yielded the most fruitful number of prospects who qualified as salesmen and who proved to be successful on the job. Its choices may be constrained by the scope of feasible training activity. Thus the small organization may find candidates with maximum prior training and experience preferable to the operation of an extensive training activity.

> A bearing manufacturer which requires only one or two men at a time prefers candidates with technical degrees and some selling experience. Local managers are expected to seek out such men on the basis of criteria established centrally. Training can thus start at a more advanced level.

The choice of sources will also be constrained by market conditions.

A power equipment manufacturer prefers technical graduates from leading electrical engineering schools. However, the interests of students in these schools has shifted in recent years from power generation and transmission to electronics and communications. The company has had to turn to other sources.

A paper goods manufacturer and an oil company both find that they are unable to attract graduates of certain prestige schools into their sales forces. They now seek men from less well-known schools.

In appropriate circumstances, any of a wide variety of sources may be drawn upon for candidates.

EMPLOYEES IN OTHER DEPARTMENTS

Employees in other departments of the company may have interest and aptitudes for sales work. Such recruits are already familiar with the company as a result of their present duties or through participation in training programs. In addition, the evaluation of their qualifications is facilitated by their history with the company and their personal relations with their supervisors and executives.

Many excellent salesmen of highly technical products have been recruited from the ranks of the engineers who developed them. In addition, experience in engineering, production, quality control, and so on can be expected to give a man a familiarity with the trials and tribulations of these jobs that will help him to empathize with persons in similar positions in the customer's organization. Since persons in these positions are very often the prime decision makers with respect to the salesman's offering, such empathy can be highly beneficial.

EDUCATIONAL INSTITUTIONS

Educational institutions are especially relevant where technical training at an academic level is required but are also important as a source of men who have demonstrated some capacity for acquiring learning and for adjusting to their environment. In a tight labor market, obtaining recruits from educational institutions reduces the hazard of obtaining an undue proportion of recruits who have not been fully successful in their prior jobs. With the growing recognition of the need to utilize fully the abilities of the entire population, including those who do not go on to college, one may expect increased activities in the way of recruiting at the high school level. While most recruiting at educational institutions yields only inexperienced recruits, the presence of veterans of military service on campuses and the rise of alumni placement offices on some campuses suggests that more mature candidates can sometimes be obtained from these sources.

PERSONS EMPLOYED BY NONCOMPETING FIRMS

Persons employed by noncompeting firms calling on the same types of customers may offer a promising source if they can be reached by advertising or as a by-product of contacts with suppliers and customers. Such men may be interested in bettering their positions if they feel that their present employer is not fully recognizing their present worth.

SALESMEN OF COMPETITIVE FIRMS

Salesmen of competitive firms have knowledge of the industry and thus may need less training. However, their willingness to shift from one company to another may indicate a low loyalty level which is likely to lead to further shifts. Generally, it is undesirable to initiate recruitment of personnel from a competitive firm. On the other hand, an applicant who leaves a competitor for personal reasons (for example, personality clash with new management, unwillingness of family to relocate as required by present employer) should not automatically be barred from consideration. Despite the hazards of hiring from competitors, some small firms still follow this practice because they feel that they are unable to conduct suitable training programs; hence they rely on larger competitors to provide a major portion of the training for them. However, because the firm being raided is in a position to possess superior knowledge about its men, it is commonly able to retain its best men by matching offers or other inducements. Hiring from competitors also raises ethical questions, especially if the man is expected to bring privileged information or even accounts.

PERSONS IN OTHER LINES OF WORK

Persons in other lines of work or not in the labor force at all may be interested in bettering their position through a new job. Men and women complete military service; housewives whose children have reached a certain age become available for employment; persons retiring or separated from a company because of merger or dissolution are available for other opportunities. These and other persons not presently employed are generally reached through advertising in newspapers, or the trade press, or through employment agencies or the placement activities of organizations with which they have been affiliated. These sources provide an important supply of recruits for some types of selling jobs; for others they are unlikely to uncover the needed experience and skills.

Pool Generation

Substantial efforts may be required to interest qualified persons in applying. In an environment in which people choose jobs on a variety of noneconomic as well as economic criteria, general corporate advertising and public relations programs which affect the possible job seeker's image of the company may be as important as communications relating to the specific job.

The sellers' market in able personnel in the past decade has made it difficult to interest many otherwise qualified applicants in the idea of a sales career. College students, in particular, have a low level of predisposition towards selling work. While the causes of this low predisposition are numerous and complex, the recruiter must recognize its existence and seek to overcome it if he is to tap the college graduate market for his men.[14]

The selection pool is narrowed not only by prospective candidates' avoiding sales jobs, but also by their decisions, for whatever reasons, not to consider employment with a particular organization. A recruitment program must, therefore, consider the various factors which influence prospective candidates' image of the company as an organization with which they would like to be associated. Such images may be the consequence of company practices in employment, in community affairs, or in its dealings with suppliers or customers, or may reflect ideas of the social worth or status of an industry or type of work. That impressions of a particular profession, industry, or firm are based on incorrect or false perceptions is largely beside the point. Such images limit the candidate group, often in an important way. As outsiders are generally ill-informed about what an organization is really like, the recruiter may find it necessary to determine the impressions about his firm which are extant in the relevant community and to initiate or encourage the dessemination of information to overcome uninformed or erroneous ones.

EVALUATION OF THE APPLICANTS' POSESSION OF THE DESIRED QUALIFICATIONS

The qualifications needed to perform sales work consist of aptitudes, knowledge and skills, and motivation. The determination of the particular aptitudes, knowledge and skills, and motivation appropriate to a particular sales job—itself a difficult task—has been explained. At this point it is assumed that the qualifications desired have been determined. We turn to the problems of determining the extent to which various applicants possess them.

[14] Among possible contributing causes are (1) students' experience with selling is almost always with the lowest level and least socially rewarding types of selling jobs; (2) the lack of understanding of the sales process and even the marketing process on the part of students and many academic personnel; and (3) a bias in segments of the academic community in favor of elitism (prescription of what is best for others by a self-constituted elite) as opposed to consumer sovereignty.

Some (of the desired) characteristics are *observable* through interviews, others are *inferable* from (the applicant's) past experience, while (the presence of) still others may only be *determinable* through testing procedure.[15]

For these reasons a combination of methods is generally used to ascertain the presence or absence of desired attributes. These methods may include forms for the collection of factual and historical information about the applicant, one or more interviews, inquiry of persons familiar with the applicant or his work and a variety of tests or examinations. In evaluating these tools it should be emphasized at the outset that the sales manager is not interested in the tool itself. Tools (for example, psychological tests) are not "good" or "bad." Interest should be centered on what information the tool can provide to assist in evaluating the candidate's aptitude, knowledge, skills, or motivations. For this reason, the following discussion is organized in accordance with the subject matter of the information sought rather than with the tool used to obtain it.

Determining Aptitudes

Aptitudes for selling may be associated with (a) physical attributes such as height, appearance, general health and voice; (b) psychological attributes such as perception, tact, empathy, personality, self-esteem, and attitude; and (c) prior training.

Interviews are useful in appraising a few of the physical attributes such as appearance and voice and may convey some impressions of such psychological attributes as the candidate's perception and personality. In addition, interviews may be used to secure amplification of information on the personal history record or application blank.

Because the data obtained through interviews is largely subjective in character, it is desirable to make it clear to the interviewer that he is attempting to measure the attributes of the candidate, not to relate the candidate's attributes to sales success, a separate matter which has been examined above. The goal of the interview should be to appraise, as objectively as possible, those attributes of the candidate which can best be appraised through observation and oral communication. Unless these goals are well understood by the interviewer, there is a real danger that the interviewer will seek to forecast the success of the whole man—possibly even by measuring him against his own image or that which the interviewer considers to be the image of the successful salesman—rather than by appraising the

[15] D. M. Phelps and J. H. Westing, *Marketing Management* (3d. ed.) (Homewood, Ill.: Richard D. Irwin, Inc., 1968), p. 639.

presence of the specific attributes in the candidate which the interview is intended to appraise.

To the extent that the overall image presented by the salesman contributes to his success, it is the image perceived by the prospects and customers with whom he will communicate rather than the image perceived by the sales manager or employment interviewer that is the relevant one. *Because the customer's perception of the salesman on a sales call depends on the respondent's perception of his own role and the role of the salesman, it is unlikely that a customer's perception will be the same as, or even remotely similar to, the image which an interviewer might have of a successful salesman.* Hence the interviewer should guard against tendencies to evaluate the total image projected by the candidate and confine himself to appraisal of those specific attributes which have been determined to be relevant to sales success and which are best observed through interviews.

Interviews should always be planned and structured. In this way the interviewer has before him an organized plan to obtain the information and impressions which he seeks. Moreover, interviews at different times and by different interviewers will have a common thread so that the results can be compared. The structure should not be so rigid, however, as to foreclose the applicant's opportunity to raise matters which he deems important.

The interviewer's observations and judgments concerning the attributes of the candidate should be recorded on appropriate rating forms *immediately* following the interview. Because of the high decay rate of the kinds of observations obtained through interviews, information which is not recorded until an hour or more later or following intervening interviews or other activities is likely to be excessively general, impressionistic and of limited accuracy. Tape recording of the interview may assist the interviewer in recall for review but does not eliminate the desirability of prompt recording of observations and judgments.

Because of the subjective character of most information obtained through interviews, it is generally desirable to have each candidate interviewed and rated independently by two or more interviewers.

Personal history forms, which may be combined with application blanks, provide information from which the evaluator may infer some indication of attributes. A record of physical illness may suggest health limitations to a sales career. The nature of prior jobs and the reasons for separation therefrom may cast light on the ability of the candidate to succeed in certain types of work. In general, however, the personal history record, while useful in evaluating candidates' knowledge, skills, and motivations, as discussed below, has only limited use in the direct appraisal of aptitudes. Indirectly, however, the personal history record may act as the source of data which have been established through appropriate analyses to have a *valid* relationship to expected sales achievement.

References provide a source of information about the applicant based upon the observations of others about his qualifications. Their utility depends on (a) how well the reference knows those things about the applicant which the evaluator wishes to know, and (b) the extent to which he is willing and permitted to furnish the inquirer with his best judgment.

Prior employment references are often in a position to appraise the aptitude of the applicant, especially if the reference has employed the applicant in similar work. Personal, as well as employment, references may be queried about the psychological attributes and prior training of the applicant. To be of significant value the inquiry should be directed from the prospective employer to the reference with specific questions designed to elicit information about specific attributes. Allowance must be made for the fact that the names given as references by the applicant may not represent the universe of persons who know or work with him but are quite likely to be biased in the direction of those whom he would expect to speak well of him. Statements received must be evaluated with this factor in mind. Moreover, the failure to give as reference an individual known to have had close contact with the applicant raises questions of the reason for the omission.

Tests of many types are used to measure the psychological attributes of candidates. Some tests are designed to measure single attributes such as intelligence, self-confidence, dominance, extroversion or empathy. Others seek to measure the total psychological make-up of a person, generally by relating the profiles of several personality traits to those of successful and unsuccessful salesmen. Still others seek to relate the profile of the candidates' interests, as self-described, with those of successful salesmen.[16]

The utility of tests in the selection process rests largely on (a) whether the relationship between particular attributes and sales success has been validly established, and (b) whether the test validly and reliably measures the presence of the attribute.

Much of the controversy over the use of tests in the selection of salesmen springs from a failure to distinguish clearly between these two aspects of test utility. Some users attempt to combine the two and thus seek to associate test scores directly with sales performance.

[16] For details of various available tests and professional reviews of each, see Oscar K. Buros (ed.) *Mental Measurements Yearbook* (6th ed.) (Highland Park, N.J.: Gryphon Press, 1965). Recent findings and critiques are summarized in *Annual Review of Psychology* (Palo Alto, Cal.: Annual Reviews, Inc.)

The result is often disappointment. This should not, however, dissuade the sales manager from using tests to measure attributes if (a) significant association between attribute and success has been established, (b) the *desired amount* of the attribute has been determined, and (c) a test exists or can be developed which can reliably and validly measure the attribute.

For example, *if* it has been determined that an IQ below 90 or above 130 is incompatible with a reasonable probability of success in a particular sales job, a standard IQ test can be used to measure which candidates fall within the acceptable range of 90–130.

Many of the tests used for forecasting sales success have not been adequately validated for the particular application. Such validation would require that hiring be made without any consideration of the test scores and that records be maintained so that subsequent performance could be correlated with the test scores. This could be accomplished by hiring all those who took the test or by selecting a sample which was either random over the test scores or, at least, gave no consideration to the tests in selection. In many instances, no particular validation procedure is employed, the user relying instead on the fact that the test had been validated for some other group (for example, students) in a different situation. In other cases the user relies upon association which has been developed between test scores and sales success of those *hired,* completely ignoring that portion of the test group which was not hired and for whom success/failure data is therefore not available. Even further removed is the attempt to relate applicants' test scores or profiles to those of persons previously successful in that line of work. For example, it may be determined by testing that the candidate has interests similar to those of successful salesmen. Hence, he should be hired in preference to another candidate whose interests opposed those of the profile of successful salesmen. The reader will recognize such a procedure as but another extension of the practice of hiring in perpetuation of past operations and without regard for the factors which are causal to success or even surrogates for such factors. This leads to conformity and tends to discourage those who differ in some way from those hired previously. Until a better understanding of the attributes relevant to success in particular sales jobs is obtained, one can hardly expect the development of tests to measure validly their presence.

Existing tests are open to the hazards of "faking"—that is, the pattern of answers may reflect in part the applicants' interpretation of the test questions, and the taker may attempt to infer what he believes to be the "right" answers so that answers represent what the applicant wishes the grader to perceive rather than his true feelings.

The salesman selector is thus faced with a dilemma. He believes, probably with good cause, that relationships do exist between the psychological attributes of salesmen and their success. Yet, in the present state of the art, we know very little about *how much* of *which attributes* is relevant to which job. Under the circumstances, he is tempted to accept any aid that is forthcoming, including the use of tests which appear to show historical association with success, despite the lack of proved causation. One hesitates, therefore, to fault the use of individual tests or test batteries where acceptable correlation between test results and performance is shown to have existed. Such usage, however, should be with the full realization that it represents an improvisation until causal relevance can be determined and tests to measure relevant attributes can be developed and validated.

Tests are generally more useful as a screening device to reject the unqualified than as a means of choosing among qualified applicants. The reliability of test results can be increased by employing more than a single test of each attribute (for example, more than one personality test). Validity can usually be increased through the use of a battery of tests. The Klein Institute of Aptitude Testing, New York, is one organization that offers such batteries in addition to its own "sales aptitude" test. Tests should be administered and the results interpreted by professionally qualified personnel. Unfortunately, such specialized personnel is rarely found in sales management offices or personnel departments or among those with minimum professional training (for example, undergraduate majors in psychology) who are likely to be available to the sales manager. No doubt a part of the disillusionment with testing is a consequence of subprofessional execution.

Physical examinations prior to hiring are a desirable precaution against placing persons with physical impairments in positions in which they are not likely to remain well suited over long periods. Such examinations provide a service for the applicant as well.

In summary, it may be noted that several aptitudes are requisite for good performance in sales jobs. Interviews, personal history records, and various physical and psychological tests serve to provide evidence about some of them. For others, valid measures do not yet exist. To fill these voids, sales managers may use tests or factor rating schemes which have demonstrated historical association with sales success even though causal relationships have not been established.

Determination of Knowledge and Skills Possessed

In selecting personnel for sales positions, the knowledge and skills possessed by the applicant, the candidate's skill in applying his knowledge to customer problems, and the applicant's ability to acquire new knowledge and skills are all relevant. To determine the presence of these factors, reliance is placed on inferences from personal history, the testimony of references, and formal tests.

The interview is of limited value in assessing knowledge or the skills to apply this knowledge. However, it may be useful in eliciting information about the applicant's experience which would assist the interviewer in evaluating the relevance of knowledge acquired through work experience to the proposed job.

The personal history record sets forth the educational, training, and experience process to which the applicant has been exposed. It provides some basis for inference as to the level of knowledge and skill attained. However, the extent to which relevant knowledge has been acquired is known only in a very general way. The level of education attained may also indicate the ability of the candidate to acquire additional knowledge. A limited level of formal education does not, on the other hand, suggest by itself limited capability in this respect.

There are very real limits to the amount of knowledge and skill which may be inferred from the candidate's experience. The mere fact of so many years of experience provides little to answer such questions as: How successful was the man on the job? Did he grow with the job or did it grow while he stood still? Was the degree of success observed because of, or in spite of, his knowledge and skill? What relationships exist between the knowledge and skills in the present or former job and those which the man-specification suggests are important for the proposed job? Will the past experience aid or hinder training in the new position?

References supplement personal history information. In particular, references may indicate the circumstances of an individual's separation from prior employment and the prior employer's attitude towards rehiring.

Present knowledge and some types of skills can be determined at least partially by *tests*. Unfortunately, even tests of knowledge, such as those of product properties and product applications, are limited to examining a sample of what the candidate knows. More seriously, conventional tests, even if they measure knowledge well, do not reveal the extent to which the applicant has the skill to apply his knowledge to customer problems or measure the skills involved in the intercommunicative process.

Determination of Candidates' Motivation

Motivation may be associated with many of the psychological attributes of the candidate and with the socioeconomic situation in which he finds himself.

As candidates' motivations cannot be ascertained by observation in the usual sense, *interviews* are of limited value in assessing them. A skilled interviewer can, in some cases, uncover the nature and strength of underlying drives and their causes, but such abilities are rare among interviewers of job applicants. For the most part, the level and nature of motivation must be inferred from his *personal history* and socioeconomic situation. A historical record of advancement—not necessarily confined to job advancement—suggest at least some level of drive. Some socioeconomic variables found in personal history data may be found by analysis to be associated with high, or low, motivation. A case in point is the sometimes-cited argument that men with dependents are motivated by the need to meet their responsibilities. While such arguments may appear to be logical, the alleged association should be tested before reliance is placed on items of personal history information as measures of motivation. References, especially if they can be contacted orally, can sometimes provide clues to an applicant's motivation.

In addition to their usefulness in measuring aptitudes, *psychological tests* may be used to measure psychological attributes such as ego-drive which are believed to imply motivation. Mayer and Greenberg allege their tests to be effective in this respect.[17]

Problems of Staffing in Organizations of Modest Size

Managers of sales forces of moderate and smaller size commonly find the hiring of new salesmen to be an intermittent rather than a regular process. With only a few men being hired each year, they have only a small body of experience upon which to draw for indicators of success or failure. Objective standards are thus hard to establish.

Instead of a regular system of recruiting, applicants may be sought only as the need demands. Urgency may require the use of those sources which can produce at least a few applicants quickly; the field from which choices can be made is thus limited both quantitatively and qualitatively. Too frequently, hiring occurs in a crisis situation—a vacancy has occurred and a new man is needed immediately lest a territory go uncovered. In these circumstances, it may be impossible to obtain full benefit even from properly chosen selection tools.

Hiring for such sales forces is likely to be done by the sales manager who, despite his other qualifications, is not a specialist in personnel recruitment and qualifications evaluation. For the sales manager, filling force vacancies may be viewed as an extra and not particularly rewarding task. Because objective standards may not exist, evaluation of personal history factors is likely to be highly subjective. Instead of by specialist interviewers, the candidates will be

[17] Mayer and Greenberg, "What Makes a Good Salesman."

interviewed by the sales manager or by one or more executives of the firm. Commonly, such interviews are unplanned and the interview goals only vaguely stated; as a result they yield little more than impressions of the applicant.[18]

Small size does not, however, require the abandonment of the search for relevance and objectivity in selection. The sales job *can* be carefully defined. Objectivity can be sought in the man specification. Personnel needs can be anticipated at least partially. Performance records can be maintained and analysed. Interviews can be preplanned and designed for securing specific data. Evidence of applicant capabilities can be examined. For some measures outside help (for example, for psychological testing) can be employed. In short, even the manager of a small sales force can do better than a list of preconceived and untested qualifications, an unverified test, and a subjective, unplanned interview to determine if the man "seems" like salesman material.

INDUCEMENT OF SELECTED CANDIDATES TO JOIN THE FIRM

Today, the candidate commonly selects the job.

The problems of securing applicants in a seller's market for personnel and one in which some of the source groups have a low predisposition towards selling have already been noted. After applicants have been obtained and the firm chooses those whom it would like to hire, it must still convince them to come with the company. This is a sales job of no mean proportions in a market in which able candidates have many attractive alternatives available to them.

While compensation, fringe benefits and possible advancement cannot be ignored, it is becoming increasingly evident that opportunities for self-fulfillment and for contributing to socially worthwhile goals are important considerations for many jobseekers. Hence, job satisfactions are likely to receive increased attention in efforts to sell the job to the desired applicant. As in other selling situations, presentations should not over-represent the attractiveness of the offer. The entire recruiting and selecting process must be conducted with the view to developing the desire of the candidate to become a salesman with the firm as much as to determining which applicants would make

[18] Many of the recruiting and selection problems of small sales forces also occur in larger organizations where these duties are relegated to local field managers rather than being centralized at the home office. In a study of salesmen, Pearson found that men hired at headquarters tended to have better records than those hired in the field. A larger proportion of MBAs were hired. Turnover was 50 percent lower. He attributed these differences to the tendency of field managers to settle for anyone capable of filling the vacancy— that is, selecting from a minimal field—and their tendency to hire in their own images. (Pearson, "Sales Power Through Planned Careers," p. 106.)

the best salesmen. In the final decision process, the candidate selects; moreover, the climate should be such that he feels that he has done the selecting.

ADJUSTING THE PROCUREMENT PROCESS TO CHANGE

In a changing world, sales jobs rarely remain static over long periods. Some changes will be dramatic (for example, changes in products, markets to be reached, or underlying relationships with dealers or users). Others will be more evolutionary, as the nature of buyer-seller relationships changes. In still other situations, personnel planning for the long term may suggest a preference for persons with demonstrated adaptive capabilities rather than specific technical training. Such a situation well might pertain, for example, in a firm expecting to undergo major changes in its markets or in its relationships with its customers.

Outside factors may play a considerable role in the qualifications which should be sought or can be obtained. At times, for example, a tight situation in engineering graduates may make it advisable to select less technically trained people rather than suffering a lack of manpower or being required to select from the less qualified recruits possessing the specific technical degree desired. At other times, political, public relations, or public service considerations may suggest modifications of practices to deal with matters of important public concern (for example, minority group hiring).

EVALUATION OF THE PROCUREMENT PROCESS

The efficacy of the process of obtaining desirable sales force personnel rests on how well the recruiting and selecting work has produced the best possible selectee group. Since the firm cannot know wth certainty how the persons not recruited or not selected might have performed, there is no absolute measure of the quality of the selection process, no means of determining an optimum in the literal sense. It is possible, however, to obtain measures of relative performance by examining some of the consequences of the selection process, such as the percentage of those who succeed and fail during the training program and subsequently on the job, and the turnover of personnel, and (indirectly) through measures of the performance of the sales force as a whole. An easily monitored measure is the percentage of those hired who are still with the firm and considered to be successful after one year and at the end of two, three, or more years.

In addition to overall evaluation of the selection process, it is desirable to evaluate the effectiveness of the factors being used as predictors of success. By maintaining records of performance of those selected, the analyst can seek measures of association between that performance and various candidate attributes that were observable, inferable, or measurable at the time of hiring. In this way the factors which correlate with success can be isolated and those which appear to have little relationship can be passed over in the selection process. However, it is well to continue to record data on factors not currently used. In a changing world, the relevant factors may easily change, and data for subsequent analysis is thus preserved. Comprehensive records when matched with performance provide needed feedback to those who must determine the attributes to be sought in candidates. Because both the sales job and the attributes of the population from which the applicants are drawn are always changing, such a feedback and accompanying analysis would be necessary even if a firm had ascertained at some point that certain factors were, at that time, the best predictors of sales success.

SUMMARY

The procurement of a sales force bears a close resemblance to the establishment of a dealer organization. The types of candidates to be sought must be determined. Then particular individuals must be identified as candidates. The candidates must be qualified through appropriate evaluation procedures. Those considered by the firm to be qualified must be induced to accept positions in the firm's marketing organization. And, finally, satisfactory working arrangements must be developed so that, in fact, the individuals become members of the team committed to its success.

Procedures to accomplish each of these activities must be developed to operate dynamically. Change is continual in both the world of the sales job and the population from which candidates are derived. The man-specification which underlies the entire process changes not only with the job itself but with increases in the firm's understanding of the factors which contribute to success in developing and maintaining profitable communication with its customers and prospects. Sources of recruits and means for obtaining their interest change with the situation in the markets for people and in the predisposition of different groups toward sales work. Despite progress in the development of tests and rating systems, measures for determining the attributes of humans are far from precise. Although tests and other rating systems can provide useful information about aptitudes, motivations, knowledge and skills, continued testing of these tools and evaluation of their utility in the selection procedure is required.

SELECTED READINGS

Barrett, Richard S., "Guide to Using Psychological Tests," *Harvard Business Review,* September–October, 1963, pp. 138–146. This article plus the two Gellerman articles listed below summarize the dispute over testing.

Dunnette, Marvin D., *Personnel Selection and Placement.* Belmont, Cal.: Wadsworth Publishing Company, Inc., 1966. A well-written explanation of selection tools drawing on easily explained statistical techniques.

Gellerman, Saul W., "A Hard Look at Testing," *Personnel,* Vol. XXXVIII, No. 3 (May–June 1961), pp. 8–15. See Barrett.

Gellerman, Saul W., "Personnel Testing: What the Critics Overlook," *Personnel,* Vol. XL, No. 3 (May–June 1963), pp. 18–26. See Barrett.

Mayer, David, and Herbert M. Greenberg, "What Makes a Good Salesman," *Harvard Business Review,* July–August, 1964, pp. 119–125. Use of psychological tests which their sponsors believe particularly effective.

Phelps, D. M., and J. H. Westing, *Marketing Management* (3rd. ed.). Homewood, Ill.: Richard D. Irwin, Inc., 1969). Chapter 23, "Recruitment and Selection of Salesmen." Commonly used selection aids and their application in sales management.

Robinson, Patrick J., and Bent Stidsen, *Personal Selling in a Modern Perspective.* Boston: Allyn & Bacon, Inc., 1967. Chapter XIII. Concepts for selection and training when the salesman is viewed as a system of action.

7 Initial Training

Training is essentially a competence-development process.

The outcome of the selection process (Chapter 6) is the provision of a supply of recruits possessing the potential to become effective salesmen. The role of training is to transform these human resources into a staff of qualified personnel.

Personal selling activity that is largely anchored in personalities retains at most only a limited role in modern markets. Hence the attributes which the recruits bring to the job are no more than the human raw material upon which professional development can be based. For nearly all types of selling, a substantial competence-development process is required if the salesman in the field is to be of value to those upon whom he calls and, ultimately, to his employer.

Rapid product diversification, expanding market uses and potentials, dynamic channels of distribution, and more exacting purchasing requirements all demand . . . a salesman keenly sensitive to his customer's needs, and equipped with . . . knowledge that will permit him to provide counsel to his customer to the mutual advantage and profit of both parties. Well calculated sales training and development programs . . . are an economic necessity for all who wish to compete.[1]

Although training costs have risen rapidly in the past two decades, the consequences of inadequate or inferior training have become even more pronounced. Costs of keeping men on the road and providing sales-force support have multiplied. Moreover, many of these costs, such as travel costs, communications, and the provision of sample kits or demonstration equipment, are likely to be as high for the ineffective performer as for the effective one. Indeed, some costs, notably supervision and the costs of correcting errors and overcoming the unfavorable consequences of salesmen's activities, are likely to be greater for the poorer salesmen than for the better ones. Hence, it is not surprising that training has come to play a major role in the management of sales forces and a major responsibility of sales managers at many levels.

More sophisticated products, more complex customer problems, wider customer alternatives, and rapid changes in product offerings and market needs all call for a higher level of training if customers are to be adequately served. In addition, the changed role of the salesman has significantly raised the standard of performance which is acceptable to customers when salesmen are employed. The less demanding and less interactive parts of the communicative process have been transferred to unidirectional media (for example, television, direct mail); to labels, tags, and other aids to self-selection; or to data processing and transmitting systems. Personal selling, as noted in earlier chapters, thus is left with those activities which it can do best—that is, intercommunicative processes involving multidirectional communication and mutual understanding. But these activities require a much higher level of sales personnel competence than many of the activities which have been displaced. In response, training programs have become more widespread, have increased in scope and duration, and have become more costly. Some of the sharpest growth has been in the retraining of experienced personnel as knowledge expands and the serving of markets requires higher levels of proficiency.

The median initial training period for 164 organizations having training programs of fixed duration was found in a 1967 National Industrial Conference Board study to be six months or longer.[2] The costs of compensating trainees for such periods and maintaining their

---

[1] *Cost and Profit Outlook,* April, 1953, p. 1.

[2] This includes on-the-job training time. *Training Company Salesmen* (Experiences in Marketing Management, No. 15) (New York: National Industrial Conference Board, 1967), p. 7.

motivations are substantial even without consideration of the costs of the training activities themselves. Thus cost considerations also demand that the job be done well.

MANAGERIAL PROBLEMS OF INITIAL TRAINING

The nature of a sales-force training system is shown in Figure 7-1.

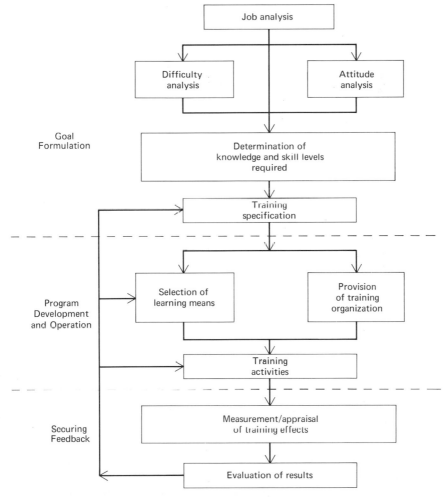

Figure 7-1
SALES-FORCE TRAINING SYSTEM

The sales manager must deal with four types of problems in establishing and maintaining a viable training system. These are:

1. formulating goals and the development of training specifications;
2. selecting appropriate training means to meet the specifications;
3. formulating and creating an organization for sales-force training;
4. securing feedback on the performance of training activities.

The tools to deal with each of these problems will be examined in the succeeding sections of this chapter.

FORMULATION OF RELEVANT TRAINING GOALS

Development of the salesman's competence is largely a matter of developing his communicative, diagnostic, and prescriptive skills and providing him with the knowledge to employ those skills effectively.

Communicative skills are largely matters of perception and evaluation. The competent salesman is able to perceive and evaluate both the buyer's and his own role in the interactive process; how these roles differ in the case of interactions with different individuals; and how they change over time even with the same individual. Even so-called persuasive skills contain important elements of the salesman's ability to perceive the feelings and thought processes of the other parties and how these individuals use the salesman to fulfill their needs.

Diagnostic skills are the stock-in-trade of the problem solver. Training must develop the salesman's ability to understand the buyer's needs from such cues as are made available and to develop new cues as opportunities present themselves during the interaction. The salesman also needs to understand the behavior of individuals within the salesman's own firm with whom he interacts in various ways. This group includes the personnel to whom he provides information, those who provide intelligence and service support for him, and those who service his accounts.[3]

Prescriptive competence rests on the base provided by diagnostic and communicative skills plus an appropriate level of knowledge of the problem-solving capabilities of available products. This includes: knowledge of the company, its products, and its policies; knowledge of competitors, their offerings and policies; knowledge of markets and applications; and knowledge of the relevant experiences

[3] The role of supervisory, controllership, and technical personnel and house staff in supporting the individual salesman's work in the field is discussed in Chapter 10.

of others, both within and outside his firm. This knowledge must be provided in such a way that it is fully understood and retained by the trainee and made a part of his own "knowledge bank" for use in the conduct of his duties, including the solution of customer problems.

While all training programs should be concerned with the development of communicative, diagnostic, and prescriptive skills, the specific knowledge which should be acquired, the types and levels of skills which need to be developed, and the kinds of habits which need to be created are specific to the particular sales situation—that is, to product i, for user category j, in buying situation k.

If training is to develop skills, it is necessary to determine the specific skills which are needed, the skill levels which need to be attained and the present skill levels of the trainees. In the case of work habits, desirable habits must first be determined and compared with the present habits of the trainees, or those likely to develop in the absence of training. The training program can then be designed to generate the desired skills and habits.

Similarly, if training is to provide the salesman with a usable knowledge bank, it is first necessary to know both what this bank *should* contain and what the salesman *already knows.* The training program can then be designed to fill gaps in the salesman's knowledge.

The development of a sound training program thus starts not with the examination of training techniques but with research on the sales job, on methods of effective salesman performance, and on the impediments to performance which must be forestalled by the training process. As the presence of different impediments will vary among the trainees, portions of the training experience may need to be tailored to individual men or small groups.

A program of research for training program development will involve job analyses (what the job should be) and duty analyses (what the job presently is). In addition, the research program should embrace difficulty analyses in order to identify the problems which salesmen encounter in the field and with which the training must prepare them to cope. It may also be useful to analyze the attitudes of trainees in order to ascertain their present perspectives and the attitudes of salesmen in the field as a means of identifying areas in which previous training goals have either been inadequate or insufficiently attained. Although attitude problems may arise from many factors quite unrelated to training (for example, compensation; personal relationships with supervisors), many attitude problems reflect limitations of the salesman's knowledge or skills and are thus amenable to improvement through training. Examples of the latter are unhappiness over product or service as a result of imperfect understanding of them; belief that certain customer personnel cannot be reached as a result of failure to keep the salesman's technological knowledge on a par with that of the customer personnel or his problem-solving skills in line with those which the customer expects; lack of confidence in the company because of poor understanding of its operation; and displeasure with compensation resulting from a misunderstanding of the compensation plan or from low earnings resulting from poor work habits.

Job Analyses

Job analyses for the determination of training goals need to be concerned with what the sales job *should be,* rather than what it *has been.* Of particular import is the need to determine: (1) the information needs of buyers and those who are or might become buyers or buying influences; (2) those characteristics of the persons upon whom the salesman will call which affect the knowledge and skills that the salesman should possess; and (3) the kinds of relationships which the salesman will be expected to develop.

As both industrial (including institutional) and consumer markets become more sophisticated, the task of maintaining viable communicative relationships with buyers becomes more complex. Buyers expect salesmen to be more informative, knowledgeable, and accurate. Particularly in industrial and institutional buying, different purchasing influences can be expected to have different perspectives of the need to be fulfilled and of what a desirable product should offer them. Thus they look at the same product through different eyes.

The production manager of the buying organization may view a new component under consideration in terms of its effects on assembly cost and reliability of supply. Quality control may be concerned with the uncertainties introduced by the proposed change itself. Purchasing personnel are concerned with relative costs and the risks associated with shifting to a supplier whose performance is unknown. The sales manager is concerned with the effect of modification on the attractiveness and suitability of the changed end product for his customers and thus the effect of the specification change on sales. Customer service is concerned with expected breakdown rates, possible misuse by customer personnel, the costs of adding new items to the repair parts inventories, and of additional training of maintenance, repair and service personnel. Thus each possible buying influence employs his own criteria in evaluating the worth of the salesman's offer. Moreover, the different purchasing influences bring to the interview situation different personalities, information states, and predispositions with which the salesman must be prepared to deal.

This multiplicity of purchasing influence is not limited to industrial goods. It also applies to the different criteria and perspectives of the people who buy for wholesale and retail organizations and to those various members of a household who participate in or influence the purchases of ultimate consumers. The salesman's communications responsibilities involve all of them. Hence, his competence must embrace the ability to deal with these diverse perspectives and predispositions. Job analyses must identify all of them if training is to nurture that competence.

Effective communication is a two-way street. Each side must not only send and receive messages, it must achieve an understanding of the meaning that the other intended to convey by his message. To achieve this understanding, the recipient must attach the same meaning to the words or other elements of the message that the sender of the message attaches to them.[4] The more familiarity the sender and the recipient have of each other's background and environment, the more likely it is that they will achieve a high degree of understanding.

There is little a sales organization can do to give its customers a better understanding of its background and environment other than what it normally does by way of sending out sales messages. But it can do something about the understanding that its sales force has of the background and environment of its customers. Such understanding at increasingly sophisticated levels is essential if the sales force is to achieve good communication with its customers and thus establish and maintain high quality communicative relationships.

Job analyses must determine which kinds of knowledge of customer background, environment, and problems will be most useful to the salesman. Mere knowledge of who the buyers are and where they are located will rarely suffice. The salesmen need to know buyers' rationale, their information sources, and how they process information which they receive. They must possess the perceptive skills to determine when these things change.

In summary, job analyses for training-program design require much more than a mere description of the duties which have been or are to be performed and high-sounding, but often vacuous, statements of sales-force purpose. In a training context, the job analyses must reveal the kinds of competence which are required for job performance, the different elements of which that competence is composed, and the levels of each kind of competence which should be sought.[5]

---

[4] Wilbur Schramm, "How Communication Works," in *The Process and Effects of Mass Communication* (Urbana, Ill.: The University of Illinois Press, 1954), pp. 3–10.

[5] Specific techniques for the conduct of job analyses are examined in Chapter 3.

Difficulty Analysis

One authority believes that the meat of training programs should deal directly with the problems and difficulties which the salesmen will encounter in the field.

> . . . Whereas the activities of the salesmen determine the content of the training program, it is the difficulties that prescribe where emphasis shall be established; in short, how the skeleton shall be covered.[6]

Difficulty analysis attempts to identify the areas in which salesmen in the field experience difficulty. Data on difficulties may be obtained through interviews with present salesmen. In the selection of salesmen to be interviewed, particular emphasis should be given to men with limited experience—for example, those in the field for less than three years—as the difficulties which the new trainees will encounter are more likely to be similar to the difficulties of these men than those of the more experienced older hands. Phelps and Westing hold that about 30 interviews are all that are required to bring out just about all the difficulties that have real significance.[7]

Interviews with customers may provide insights as to what buyers perceive as the main problems of working with company salesmen. This source is likely to be most useful in industrial buying situations in which buyers may be quite cognizant of the shortcomings of those who call on them.

Although difficulty analysis has, in the past, been employed chiefly to identify salesmen's difficulties in their relationships with those upon whom they call, difficulty analysis may well be appropriate in examining other facets of the salesman's job, including his information gathering and reporting activities and his relationships with his supervisors.

Information on difficulties which salesmen encounter in the field may also be obtained from supervisors. In reporting difficulties which arise in the salesman's work with customers, reports from supervisors are, of course, secondhand and subject to perceptual bias; consequently, they should not be accorded as much weight as information reported directly by the salesmen. Nevertheless, supervisors may be a useful and economical supplementary source of insights into problems which salesmen encounter. In dealing with the information-gathering portion of the salesman's job, supervisors may be in a position to testify directly on the difficulties which salesmen under their supervision appear to be encountering.

[6] Saul Poliak, *Rebuilding the Sales Staff* (New York: McGraw-Hill, Inc., 1947), pp. 253–54.
[7] D. M. Phelps and J. H. Westing, *Marketing Management* (3rd. ed.) (Homewood, III.: Richard D. Irwin, Inc., 1968), p. 675.

In short, the examination of the difficulties which salesmen encounter in their daily work is essential to formulating goals for any training program which is to be problem oriented.

New difficulties are likely to emerge as customers' problems, competitive activities, environmental conditions and the status of the firm's own products and strategies undergo changes. Difficulty analyses should be undertaken periodically, preferably at least once a year.

Attitude Analysis

Attitudes held by recruits toward the firm, toward themselves, and toward the job as they perceive it may affect the learning process as well as the trainee's subsequent performance on the job. Attitudes about the company, the job, company policies and products, individual personnel, and customers are quite likely to affect behavior on the job. They also may be the result of on-the-job behavior and experience. To the extent that attitudes affect or are affected by behavior, they need to be determined so that training activities can be undertaken to modify them if necessary.

ANALYSIS OF THE ATTITUDES OF THE PRESENT SALES FORCE

Present salesmen's attitudes toward the company and its offerings, toward other personnel within the firm, toward customers and prospects, and toward their jobs and their various duties may uncover attitudes or perspectives within the present sales force which adversely affect some facet of performance. In some instances, corrective action may be taken to deal with the underlying causes; in others, the modification of such attitudes or perspectives may become a goal of retraining activity or operating supervision.[8] The training program for new salesmen well may seek to create esprit de corps and understanding and thereby forestall the development of attitudes which might impair maximum performance.

Research into the attitudes of present salesmen is less concerned with ascertaining modal or average perspectives than in identifying possible causes of friction and attitudes which are likely to impair effective job performance. For this purpose, detailed interviews with salesmen along the lines suggested for difficulty analyses may be useful. At this stage, measures of the extent of an attitudinal problem are of less concern to the researcher than identification of the areas in which attitudinal problems exist. If problems appear to be significant, standard survey methods, including projective techniques, may be employed to determine their extent, if such information is needed.

[8] These topics are treated in Chapters 8 and 12 respectively.

ANALYSIS OF ATTITUDES OF RECRUITS

If training entails the processing of recruits into trained sales-men, the attitudes held by the recruits at the time of employment constitute an important dimension of the "raw material." For purposes of program design, the analyst seeks to determine the attitudes and beliefs held by the recruit group to be trained. The training program will then seek to modify these attitudes where this appears appropriate.

Scaling techniques, such as the currently popular semantic differential, can be employed to determine the attitudes of recruits.[9] Whereas the study of attitudes of present salesmen is undertaken largely to identify problems, the study of the attitudes of recruits is to determine the attitude status of the group as a base-line for training program design.

Determination of Knowledge and Skill Levels Required

The results of job, difficulty, and attitude analyses suggest the kinds of competence which are required for salesmen. They should suggest the communicative, diagnostic and prescriptive skills needed for competent performance. In addition, they should indicate the kinds of information about products and their manufacture, about the company and its background and policies, and about users and their problems that are useful in the salesman-buyer interaction in contrast with those kinds of information which, despite their interest to company executive or technical personnel, have little real relevance to the salesman's competence.

In addition, the analyses may indicate the impact of competence

[9] For a brief summary of useful scaling techniques, see Engel, Kollat, Black-well, *Consumer Behavior,* pp. 170–173. For a good overall text, see Allen L. Edwards, *Techniques of Attitude Scale Construction* (New York: Appleton-Century-Crofts, 1957). For detailed descriptions of the individual techniques see (a) Equal appearing interval technique: L. L. Thurstone, etc. *The Measurement of Social Attitudes* (Chicago: University of Chicago Press, 1929); pp. 129–134. (b) Method of Summated Ratings: Rensis A. Likert, "A Technique for the Measurement of Attitudes," *Archives of Psychology,* No. 140 (1932), pp. 1–55. (c) Semantic Differential: C. E. Osgood, G. J. Suci, and P. H. Tannen-baum, *The Measurement of Meaning* (Urbana, Ill.: University of Illinois Press, 1957). (d) Q-sort: William Stephenson, *The Study of Behavior: Q-Technique and Its Methodology* (Chicago: University of Chicago Press, 1953). (e) Scalogram: Louis Guttman, "The Basis for Scalogram Analysis," in Samuel A. Stouffer (ed.), *Measurement and Prediction* (Princeton, N.J.: Princeton University Press, 1950). (f) Coombs unfolding technique: C. H. Coombs, "Psychological Scaling without a Unit of Measurement," *Psychological Review,* Vol. 57 (1950), pp. 145–158. (g) Non-metric scaling: Paul E. Green and Frank J. Carmone, *Multidimensional Scaling and Related Techniques in Marketing Analysis* (Boston: Allyn & Bacon, Inc., 1970).

limitations on the performance of a sales force—that is, the extent to which lack of knowledge or skills or unsuitable attitudes or work habits contribute to performance problems.

The analyses will not, of course, fully reveal all of the specific knowledge which is required, nor the precise levels of skill attainment which are desirable. Rather, they indicate the kinds of pitfalls which the salesman must be trained to avoid and the kinds of information and skills which promise to have meaningful payoffs. In any event, the knowledge and skill requirements must be set forth in specific, not merely general, terms. What levels of diagnostic, prescriptive, and intercommunicative skills must be attained before the salesman is properly qualified for a territory of his own? Precisely what kinds of information about which products and processes are relevant for the salesman and actually needed for his work? Which parts of the needed technical knowledge must be internalized and which parts can be made available to him in the form of reference source materials (for example, manuals)? What knowledge of using industries' technology and problems is needed if a salesman is to be of value to those upon whom he calls? Although considerable judgment will often be involved in decisions on these questions, the findings of analyses of the types suggested provide a substantial aid and an important step in the direction of objectivity.

A common, although not always recognized, problem of many training programs is that they are excessively inward-looking in examination of the knowledge needs of the salesmen to be trained. Emphasis is on product *features* rather than user *benefits.* As a consequence, programs to provide technical competence tend to concentrate on the seller's offerings and to slight the need to provide technical competence in understanding the problems of the using industries. Similarly, programs to develop selling skills tend to be heavily prescriptive—how to do it—rather than diagnostic—how to better understand the interactive process.

The Training Specification

Comparison of what the salesman needs to know and the abilities which he needs to possess with the knowledge and skills possessed by recruits will indicate the job which lies ahead for training. The training specification is, thus, a performance specification; it tells what training must accomplish. Although the preparation of formal training specifications is not common, the idea of determining, as precisely as possible, the nature of the gap between what the new employee brings to the job and the competence requirements of that job is fundamental to sound program development.

Although the specifics of the training program must be tailored to the requirements of the specific firm, some coverage of a number of areas may be appropriate.

SKILL DEVELOPMENT

DEVELOPMENT OF INTERCOMMUNICATIVE SKILLS Acquisition by salesmen of a method of looking at behavior and understanding the communication process; ability to understand their own behavior and attitudes and what other parties are trying to communicate, both explicitly through words and actions and implicitly; development of ways of thinking about human behavior so the salesmen can make better observations about themselves and their relationships with others; development of a frame of reference so that each salesman can derive understanding and skills from his own experiences.

SKILL DEVELOPMENT IN THE CONDUCT OF SELLING TASKS Development of skills in perception and diagnosis of customer problems and of habits in thinking about such problems; development of skills in prospect identification and qualification, planning presentations, probing for cues; understanding and dealing with latent and expressed objections, closing sales, achieving customer satisfaction.

SKILL DEVELOPMENT IN THE PERCEPTION OF USEFUL MARKETING INFORMATION, ITS CONVERSION TO INTELLIGENCE, AND ITS TRANSMISSION TO OTHERS WITHIN HIS ORGANIZATION.

KNOWLEDGE OF COMPANY OFFERS

KNOWLEDGE OF COMPANY PRODUCTS Extent of line; performance properties; uses; specifications; methods of manufacture and modification; quality control systems; limitations in usage; causes of failure.

KNOWLEDGE OF THE ECONOMIC BASES UPON WHICH THE COMPANY'S PRODUCTS ARE SOLD Benefits to buyers and users; applications to user problems; relative merits of company products and substitutes therefor.

KNOWLEDGE OF ENVIRONMENT

KNOWLEDGE OF COMPETITION Competitors' products, pricing, and selling policies; relative merits of product and service offerings.

KNOWLEDGE OF CUSTOMER PROBLEMS Recognized and latent problems of various using industries and customer groups; current and prospective changes in using industries which have impact on their problems.

KNOWLEDGE OF CUSTOMER RATIONALE Working and thought patterns of various specifiers; motivations, problems, and concerns of different groups of buyers; other buying influences.

KNOWLEDGE OF MARKETS   Nature of various markets for company products; changes occurring in various markets.

KNOWLEDGE OF MEANS OF AUGMENTING MARKET KNOWLEDGE Means of perceiving information of marketing significance and transforming it into intelligence useful for the salesman and for others in the organization.

KNOWLEDGE OF COMPANY AND POLICIES

KNOWLEDGE OF SALES POLICIES AND REASONS THEREFOR Policies on confinement of lines and restricted or exclusive distribution; terms of sale; return, allowance, and cancellation policies; policies on protection of customer stocks (for example, reimbursement if market or suggested retail prices are reduced); bases of customer classification in applying sales and pricing policies.

KNOWLEDGE OF COMPANY HISTORY AND ACCOMPLISHMENTS Key elements in firm development; importance in social and economic structure; role in the community; major marketing and nonmarketing policies in dealing with customers and the general public.

KNOWLEDGE OF OPERATIONS

KNOWLEDGE OF SUPPORT ACTIVITIES PROVIDED THE SALESMAN Nature and scope of other elements in the marketing mix which support or augment the salesman's work such as advertising, warranty and service practices, staff support groups, and the internal supervisory and communication systems.

KNOWLEDGE OF SELLING METHODS AND TECHNIQUES Most effective methods of identifying "suspects" and qualifying them as prospects; relative effectiveness of different approaches; most effective means of presentation, handling objections, and closing. If possible, training materials in these areas should be based on objective studies of results using alternative methods; at the very least they should be based on some experience within the particular sales organization.

KNOWLEDGE OF PROCEDURES   Proper handling of nonselling duties such as handling inquiries, quotations, and correspondence; maintenance of records; preparation of reports.

WORK PATTERN DEVELOPMENT

DEVELOPMENT OF EFFECTIVE WORK PATTERNS   Development of skills and work habits in such areas as effective use of time, routing, sales planning, call frequencies and coverage, report preparation; discharge of service and accounting duties; if within the salesman's responsibility, skill in such additional duties as sales forecasting and credit evaluation.

Product knowledge dominates many training programs. In part, this reflects the need for the salesman to be well-versed in his products and their strengths and weaknesses if he is to have any real value in aiding those upon whom he calls to make selection decisions. However, some portion of the heavy emphasis presently found on product attributes in some programs is, no doubt, merely a reflection of a firm's own product orientation with its relatively little concern with study of users and prospective users and their problems. In this environment it is not surprising that so many sales training programs devote relatively little time to orienting the trainee to the problems and perspectives of potential buyers and users. As firms increasingly accept a service-to-the-market perspective, however, training programs can be expected to move in the direction of much greater attention to transmitting knowledge about customers and their buying problems and to assisting the trainee to develop and internalize means of perceiving and digesting information about users and their problems.

SELECTION OF APPROPRIATE TRAINING MEANS

The selection of the most effective training means and the specific training practices to be employed rest on an understanding of the learning process and of the conditions under which learning will be motivated to take place.

The Learning Process

Learning is a process of discovery of information and ideas and their *transfer* into behavior. The learner is an active part of this process, not merely a passive sponge to receive the wisdom that is poured into him by an author or instructor. Training programs must be designed in terms of the process by which the learner learns— including those things which motivate him to learn—rather than in terms of the teaching methods with which the trainer is more comfortable or which the literature reports as more popular at the moment.

This does not mean that the learner should be left to his own devices to learn what he wishes and in the manner which suits his pleasure. Such unstructured "sink or swim" tactics are unlikely to produce a high level of learning. The student does not know what is to be learned, nor why. Thus he could as easily acquire misinformation as valid information and develop poor habits as easily as sound ones.

Training is a participative process. The trainer has a major role to play in it. Training programs are essentially systems through which trainees' motives are activated and the learner is guided in self-development.

As an interactive process, the learning process is significantly influenced by what the trainee and trainer each bring to the situation, by the objectives of the learning process and how they are perceived and communicated, and by the methods employed to bring about learning.

Because the trainee, rather than the trainer or the method, must be the central focus of any training activity, it is good to emphasize what he brings to the training situation in the way of experiences, predispositions, attitudes, and perspectives. Robinson and Stidsen suggest five elements which are significant in understanding the trainee's position.

1. A certain level of awareness and perception of the training process and his own place in it, as well as a set of expectations concerning the benefits he is likely to receive from the process. *The resources which an individual is willing to allocate to the learning process will in large measure determine the outcome of the process.* In the case of non-volunteers one of the first tasks of the training process may well be the development of such awareness.

2. An attitude toward the specific trainer or trainers in general and an internalized concept of learning in relation to himself. *The individual's attitudes toward the learning process and teachers may have either a positive or a negative influence on the learning process itself.* In general, learning is a disturbing experience to the individual primarily because it involves him in a change of his existing modes of thought and behavior. In the case of a negative attitude to trainer and learning, the trainer may have to "sell" both himself and the process to the individual learner.

3. A concept of a desired outcome of the learning experience and a set of expectations about the value of the exercise for the trainee.

   In general, it may be postulated *that individuals will accept a higher degree of responsiblity for their own learning if the experience is related to their goal structure.* In a limited number of cases learning may take on a functional autonomy in itself and the individual will be learning for the sake of learning. In most cases, however, the learning experience is probably perceived as a means to an end. In such cases it is important that the individual's perceived purpose is recognized. . . .

4. A certain ability and willingness to internalize the results of the training process. . . . Indeed, *the essence of a learning process is the transfer of new knowledge and behavior repertoires from an overt to an internalized state.* The achievement of this transfer may be a difficult and painful process which in any case involves the participation of the trainee. . . .

5. A certain predisposition for or against committing himself to the outcome of the process. . . . *Learning has not occurred until the trainee has identified with or committed himself to the results of the experience.* The process of commitment (requires) . . . internalization of the acquired knowledge as a "useful" and "reliable" guide for future behavior. The test of commitment is the individual's ability to generalize the experience to new situations.[10]

In this context, the essence of the training process is the self-development of the competence of the trainee, under motivation and guidance of trainers. The development of this competence entails an increase of the trainee's knowledge not only of products and services but also of himself, of intercommunicative processes, and of the barriers to them.

Since learning is a self-development process, learning programs must fully recognize individual differences. Each learner can be expected to have perceptions, attitudes, capabilities, and skills which differ in some way from every other learner. His learning experience thus will be laid in a somewhat different context and will start at a different point.

[10] Patrick J. Robinson and Bent Stidsen, *Personal Selling in a Modern Perspective* (Boston: Allyn & Bacon, Inc., 1967), pp. 233–34.

Several properties of the learning process which are useful in the design and execution of training programs will be noted briefly.

Learning is a purposeful process. It must make sense to the learner or his motivation will be lost. Learning is enhanced if the learner knows what he is to learn and why. Thus, to maintain motivation, purposes must be kept in focus and progress towards learning goals made evident.

Learning involves self-activity by the learner. To maximize this activity it is often useful to involve the maximum number of senses appropriate to the learning situation. Mere numbers of senses will not, of course, compensate for inadequacy of purpose or irrelevancy of materials, but they may facilitate the learning process where other factors are properly aligned.

Learning is growth-like. Hence the pace of learning will depend on where the learner is, how closely the new information is related to the old, and the capacity of the learner to acquire more knowledge or develop greater skill of a particular type.

Learning is affected by the physical, social and emotional environment. Unfavorable environmental factors (for example, a poorly ventilated room, hostile classmates, a teacher with whom the student has not established rapport) tend to impede learning or even prevent it.

Learning must be satisfying. The satisfactions may come from the learning itself—for example, the pleasures of knowing and grasping certain concepts or of having accomplished a difficult task. Often external satisfiers may be called for (praise, reward, recognition of accomplishment) because the satisfactions from the learning process may be only indirect and long term (for example, the results of a program to increase salesmen's understanding of products or customers and for which the money payoff is remote in terms of time).

Learning involves changes in behaviors, not merely data storage. Mere memorization, for example, is not learning if the learner fails to transform what has been "recorded" into generalizations relevant for his behavior. Teaching methods which stimulate functional understanding are thus preferable to those which merely transfer undigested data from the teacher's notebook to the student's notebook via the teacher's mouth, the student's ears, and the student's pencil. Teaching techniques which emphasize use situations and those in which the learner discovers generalizations and their applicability are, thus, often effective as learning devices.

Motivation

Since learning is an active process, it cannot take place in any significant way without motivation; the learner must want to learn.

Motivation is internal to the person motivated. One cannot motivate someone else although supervisors and other trainers may provide incentives which, *if considered relevant and significant by the trainee,* may cause the trainee's motives to be activated.[11]

INTRINSIC MOTIVATORS

The most useful devices to arouse motivations lie in the knowledge itself and the values which the learner perceives it will have for him. The skillful instructor will find ways to arouse these motivations in his students.

An important source of motivation for sales trainees is knowledge that the material to be learned or the skill to be acquired has a discernable payoff in terms of the salesman's goals. It is not enough for the instructor to allege that materials to be mastered have value; their value must be perceived by the trainee if it is to activate motivation.

The instructor may suggest short-term learning goals, for example, by showing the utility of certain concepts to the salesman's work or what the student should gain from a certain exercise or chapter. He might, for instance, present an example in which the habitual application of a safety rule learned through drilling prevented a disaster, or in which conformity to a seemingly ridiculous and unnecessary procedure required by the company actually saved several salesmen from considerable embarrassment and loss of important accounts.

Some firms believe that relevance of training materials to the recruit is increased by exposure to problems in the field. These firms defer much training until the man has had a few months in the field as a junior.

Trainees' motivation can be strengthened by feeding measures of progress back to the trainee during the learning experience. Prompt knowledge of his learning progress—for example, from a test or from observations of his behavior—acts to motivate the trainee, especially if the results show a large measure of success.[12] Since knowledge of success reinforces learning and motivates more effectively than knowledge of failure, it is desirable to sequence training experience so that the trainee will enjoy, and learn of, successes early in the experience.

[11] See Chapter 12 on the role of supervisors in providing incentives for salesman motivation.

[12] Feedback tends to be more favorably received by trainees who have high levels of aspiration, strong self-esteem needs, and strong desires for accurate evaluation. (Bernard M. Bass and James A. Vaughn, *The Psychology of Learning for Managers* (American Foundation for Management Research, 1965), pp. 28–29.

EXTRINSIC MOTIVATORS

Where adequate intrinsic motivators are not available, devices not related to the knowledge itself or its value to the learner may be useful. The prospect of receiving praise or recognition from the instructor or from peers or of being recognized as out-performing peers appeals to self-esteem motives and may encourage the student to work actively at the learning process.

Criticism and other forms of punishment for failure to learn and exhibit desirable behaviors may also serve as extrinisic motivators. However, the available evidence suggests that the results of punishment (including criticism) are less predictable, less permanent, and less effective than rewards for success in learning.[13]

In general, extrinsic motivators are less likely than intrinsic motivators to be effective over the long term as they focus on the extrinsic stimulator (the reward) rather than the substance and goals of the training.

Because different means are appropriate for acquiring knowledge, developing skills, and acquiring habits, appropriate learning means for each of them will be examined separately.

Learning Means: Acquiring Knowledge

Choices from among the wide variety of instructional methods available must give substantial weight to selecting the methods which will best assist and encourage the trainee to gain the desired knowledge. Consideration must also be given to costs, especially the value of trainer and trainee time consumed in training activity. For these reasons a variety of methods are likely to be employed as a coordinated program.

STRUCTURED PRESENTATIONS

The acquisition of knowledge is largely a matter of grasping concepts and principles which have been derived from the experience of others. If motivation can be sustained, this can be accomplished most rapidly and economically through transmission of the experience in some structured form such as readings, lectures, motion pictures, programmed instruction materials, or some combination thereof. If the materials are well prepared, the trainee can be exposed in a limited time to many more ideas and a richer scope of experience than he could obtain by personal observation or by listening to unstructured anecdotes reported by others. However, because they are largely unidirectional—that is, they communicate only *to* the trainee—these

---

[13] Bass and Vaughn, pp. 49–51.

instructional tools are likely to be effective only if they are employed in ways which induce substantial activity on the part of the learner. Unless sufficient learner activity can be obtained, readings and lectures may produce no learning experience even though the pages have been turned and the chairs have been occupied.

"Programmed instruction" seeks to overcome this problem by requiring the trainee to respond at frequent intervals, by providing feedback to the trainee based on his responses, and by using these responses to direct his following steps.

Programmed instruction entails individual learning, without either a teacher or the pressure of group norms. Material is usually presented in logical sequence in small increments. The student proceeds through the material at his own pace, examining new material, making choices which reveal his grasp of the material, and receiving immediate feedback on his performance which provides reinforcement when he is correct or redirection when he errs. This participation and prompt feedback aid in making study of the material a participatory process, although they do not, in themselves, guarantee that the knowledge will be acquired and the concepts mastered and internalized. These require that sufficient motivation be maintained—for example, through one or more of the means which have been suggested above—to sustain and encourage learning activity.

Structured presentations are likely to be most useful in furnishing information on company products, company history and accomplishment, economic bases of company products (for example, performance benefits vis-à-vis alternatives available to users), and company policies and procedures. They may also be useful in communicating some types of market knowledge and some concepts of selling methods and techniques if the trainee can relate effectively to the materials presented and sees the significance of their mastery to his own goal attainment.

CASES AND CONFERENCES

Experience can also be presented in a less structured way in the form of cases or through conferences in which salesmen exchange ideas and individual experiences. One advantage of cases and conferences is the greater involvement of the trainees. Moreover, discussion facilitates the discovery process and encourages transfer. In addition, ideas presented at conferences in which the participants exchange experiences are likely to enjoy high credibility and be considered as highly relevant to the trainee's own situation. However, the total scope of ideas and knowledge which can be presented in this way is likely to be seriously inadequate to the needs of initial training. Conferences are extremely useful for retraining (Chapter 8) and may be useful to maintain a perception of relevance and add elements of participation in an initial training program.

Case problems afford the trainee the opportunity to learn from a simulated situation and force him to play an active role. His part in case learning is largely unstructured. Whether or not he will acquire useful knowledge from case work will depend upon the information contained in the case itself and the skill of the instructor or moderator in focusing case discussions on significant principles.[14]

Case problems may be useful in communicating information and concepts about the market, the problems and behavior of customers, and the use of various selling techniques. In addition to their limited use as a vehicle for acquiring knowledge, cases are often useful in assisting the trainee to develop skills.

UNSTRUCTURED EXPERIENCE

Completely unstructured experience gained by the trainee can be a forceful teacher. Learning through experience on the job has convincing relevance. Unfortunately, it is slow and prohibitively costly in terms of the underutilization of human resources over a long learning period as well as in terms of its effect on customers in the interim. Hence, it is unsuitable for initial knowledge acquisition.

New salesmen can also learn through observation of others, although this requires a perception of what is significant and what is correct which the trainee, unaided, cannot normally be expected to possess. Lectures of the "let me tell you how I did it" type are a form of unstructured experience sometimes found in training programs; they combine the disadvantages of the lecture method with those of "sink or swim" on-the-job training without providing the advantages of either.

An effective program to assist and motivate trainees to acquire various kinds of knowledge which they will need for the performance of their jobs is likely to require a number of training methods. Lecture sessions or readings for the transmittal of digested, organized knowledge may be interspersed with various other techniques to provide participation, to maintain motivation, and to insure that the relevance of the materials which the trainee is expected to master is perceived.

Learning Means: Developing Skills

For the most part, the learning methods which are most suitable for the acquisition of knowledge are quite inappropriate for the acqui-

---

[14] For discussion of the uses of the case method and claims for its efficacy see Milton P. Brown, Wilbur B. England, and John B. Mathews, Jr., *Problems in Marketing* (New York: McGraw-Hill, Inc., 1961), Introduction, Chapter 1.

sition of skills. Lectures, films, and classroom demonstrations can be used to provide information about useful techniques, but skill development itself requires actually doing, not learning about, an activity. Types of classroom activity which can contribute to skill development are role playing, case work, and business games.

ROLE PLAYING

In role playing the trainee is placed in a realistic situation and asked to simulate selling to a prospect—either the instructor or another trainee. Both the instructor and the other trainees may criticize the performance. The trainee learns that doing is quite different from possessing knowledge of what should be done. In addition, he may be able to utilize comments by the instructor and his peers to better his subsequent performance. The observer-trainees will hopefully learn from their observations. Advocates of role playing also point out that it is better to have the trainee's errors made in the classroom than on real customers or prospects in the marketplace.

A large chemical company uses role playing to develop sales trainee skills. Each observer prepares an evaluation form which goes only to the trainee. Sessions are taped, sometimes with videotapes. Sometimes the tapes are played back with intermittent stops for class discussion and interpretation. The complete tape is furnished to the trainee for two weeks for his own study and review.

The company has found several guidelines useful in securing maximum benefit from role playing sessions:

1. Pick a good man to lead off.
2. The saleman-trainee must *never* be embarassed. If necessary, the individual acting as "buyer" must help prevent "salesman embarrassment" through his own behavior and, if the situation requires it, even by "aside" suggestions.
3. All observers should be required to submit an *unsigned* evaluation form which *must* include constructive comments as well as ratings or answers to short answer evaluation questions. See Exhibit 7-1, for an example evaluation form.
4. The trainer should open the class discussion by asking about the good points in the presentation. The trainer himself should never take a position.

Role playing undoubtedly has a useful role in the initial stages of skill development. Yet its limitations must not be overlooked. A classroom, no matter how well equipped, is not an office or store. Classmates and instructors are not customers; their behavior cannot safely be assumed to be that of customers. Benefits to the observing members of the class are based on the dubious premise that each observer understands what is done incorrectly and why it is incorrect *and* can from such observation modify his own methods of operation.

Exhibit 7-1

EVALUATION FORM—SALES PRESENTATION

Salesman _____ **Date** _____

Elements of the Sale   **YES   NO**

1. Approach

a.   Did salesman handle salutatory aspects effectively?
b.   Did he utilize proper strategy in first minute?
c.   Did he present a benefit statement during the strategy phase?

2. Presentation or Demonstration

a.   Was presentation perfectly *clear* to prospect?
b.   Did salesman properly emphasize features *and* benefits?
c.   Did he adequately utilize sales aids (product samples, visual aids, product literature, and so on) where applicable?
d.   Did he invite and obtain participation by the prospect?
e.   Did he listen effectively?

3. Objections

a.   Did salesman adequately analyze objections (equivocal vs. honest)?
h   Did he handle the price objection effectively?
c.   Did he utilize the "Yes—But" technique (indirect denial) when appropriate?

4. Close and Departure

a.   Did salesman show mastery of several closing methods?
b.   Did he ASK FOR THE ORDER?
c.   Was his departure smooth and poised?

5. The Complete Sales Interview

a.   Did the salesman appear to understand the basic problems—that is, did he show knowledge of prospect's needs and personal characteristics?
b.   Did the salesman maintain control of the interview without the use of "high-pressure" selling?
c.   Did he exhibit proper speed of delivery, voice, diction, and gestures?
d.   Did he appear to be genuinely interested, sincere, and properly enthusiastic?

Constructive Comments:

A more fundamental objection to role playing as it commonly operates is the tendency to focus on prescription rather than diagnosis. *Communicative skill is largely a diagnostic process*—understanding what is happening to the ideas, preconceptions, beliefs, and so on of the various individuals involved. Unless the trainer can foster this spirit of inquiry, role playing very easily becomes prescriptive. Each observer (possibly even the trainer) seeks to judge what is right or wrong in the presentation and how they would act differently. Role playing in this manner is thus little more than a form of practice in the application of selling rules or guide lines. Worse yet, it can easily encourage the development of manipulative skills rather than cultivate the diagnostic capabilities of the trainees.

The above difficulties are not necessarily inherent in the role-playing technique. Role playing can be oriented toward *diagnosis of what is occurring* and away *from judging what is right or wrong* in the actions of the salesman. A skillful instructor can lead the discussion toward diagnosis and interpretation. In this way the players can be aided to learn more about themselves, and the observers can develop habits of perception and skill in understanding what occurs in the communication process. One advocate of role playing recites this experience in a firm employing a large sales force in a highly competitive industry:

> In the beginning the salesmen—particularly the older, more experienced ones—were skeptical of the value of role-playing. Agreement was finally reached, however, to experiment with the plan on an informal basis in one department. At first the salesman acting the part of the "buyer" played the role as he himself felt. The acting was somewhat stilted. The players were rather embarrassed, and a number of jokes and humorous comments were made. The ensuing discussions were restrained and brief.
>
> But soon the atmosphere changed. The initial embarrassment was gone. The participating salesmen began to get deeply involved in what they were doing. So did the observing salesmen. The formal discussions waxed hot and heavy, continuing in informal groups for days afterward. One salesman suggested acting out the part of a real buyer whom he had recently come in contact with. This was done, and it worked out very well.
>
> At times the discussions wandered. At times they got out of hand. But for the most part they were remarkably beneficial. The salesmen gradually became more consciously aware of the assumptions, perceptions, and feelings that they were bringing to a particular situation, and of how these feelings and attitudes were inextricably interwoven into their relationship with a buyer. They also became more perceptive of the feelings and emotions of a buyer. And they began to recognize the nature—and consequences—of the term "involvement."
>
> In the particular situation of the company making this experiment the problem of price negotiation has continually loomed large. Quite naturally, therefore, the bargaining process arose in almost every role-playing situation. Initially, the natural tendency of the discussion was to focus on the "best" method of bargaining with a buyer—a natural error in this day of "how-to-sell" books. Consequently, a strong effort

was made to guide the discussions away from a "right-wrong" basis to a "what happened" basis, which was found to be far more profitable.[15]

Although more applicable in management than in sales training, the trainer may employ the technique of role reversal if a strong conflict occurs between two persons. The individuals are asked to change sides and continue the scene. Hopefully, each player will acquire some insight into the other's feelings and wants.[16]

CASE PROBLEMS

Case problems provide another vehicle to simulate the market situation in a classroom. They are useful in assisting the trainee to develop diagnostic, analytical, and decision-making skills by simulating a problem situation. As in the case of role playing, trainee behavior may be conditioned by the fact that the game is not being played with "real bullets." Fruitful use of case problems requires an instructor who can moderate the discussion to avoid a situation in which "the blind lead the blind" and at the same time remains sufficiently detached from the meeting so that the trainees can participate fully and interact as if the instructor were not present.

Case problems are especially useful in the development of skills in perceiving customer problems and in defining alternative approaches to the problems of human interactions. They are less useful in developing solution skills.

BUSINESS GAMES

One objection to case problems is that the participants do not learn the outcome of their actions. Did the chosen course of action prove to be a wise one? If so, why? If not, why not? Feedback of this kind would extend the learning experience from experience with the group decision process (the case discussion) to experience with the outcome. Operational gaming seeks to overcome this deficiency in case problem instruction by providing outcome feedbacks for all actions taken. While this provides an added element of learning, it should be noted that the feedback provided is primarily a reflection of the manner in which the computer has been programmed. Players may focus on winning the game, rather than learning principles and their transfer into their behavior patterns.

[15] John M. Frey, "Missing Ingredient in Sales Training," in Kenneth R. Davis and Frederick E. Webster, Jr. (eds.), *Readings in Sales Force Management* (New York: The Ronald Press Company, 1968), pp. 382–383.

[16] For an examination of the role-reversal technique see B. J. Speroff, "The Group's Role in Role Playing", *Journal of Industrial Training,* VII, No. 1 (1953) pp. 3–5.

FIELD TRAINING

All off-the-job training techniques are subject to problems with transfer and reinforcement. Transfers of learning to the job setting are rarely 100 percent. Reinforcement from successful application in the job situation is weak or nonexistant. New learning will occur as problems are encountered. Some portion of every trainee's learning experience will come from field, or on-the-job, training whether planned or not.

In the most primitive form of on-the-job "training," the salesman is assigned a territory and sent out to learn in the "school of hard knocks." Although this is indeed a learning experience, it should not properly be called training because there is no trainer providing guidance and little or no control over what the recruit learns. To be sure, some who try will uncover methods and develop work habits to become effective salesmen. Many will fall by the wayside with the accompanying waste to the company (in territories and customers inadequately served), to the men involved (in career time wasted), and to society (in improper use of valuable human resources). Even those who succeed may develop their skills and habits by a more circuitous route and over a longer period than if they had been provided with proper training.

A practice not yet extinct is that of sending trainees into the field with more experienced men in order to learn intercommunicative skills through osmosis by observation of successful men.[17] This practice appears to rest on a number of dubious premises: (1) the salesman being observed possesses exemplary skills and employs them without exception in his daily work; (2) the trainee in observing the senior man at work will perceive the critical elements in each of his activities so that he knows what makes the senior successful in each part of his job—that is, the trainee can perceive the various parts of the senior's work sufficiently well to identify those factors which led to success from those which did not; and (3) skills can be developed through observation of a skillful person at work.

> The most careful observation of the skill of the leading batters of the National and American Leagues over several years has not improved the author's skill with the bat.

[17] Trainees may be sent into the field with experienced men for other reasons. The S.S. White Company has each trainee spend two days in the field with one of the company's hardest working salesmen. This is undertaken at the outset of the training program. Both the salesman and the trainee are asked to report on the experience. Some trainees find that the job thus revealed is not to their liking. This avoids having the man devote career time and effort to a position from which he will soon withdraw; it saves the company a minimum of $5000 in training and carrying expenses.

Training to develop skills must involve acting by the trainee in such a way that the action can be modified and improved upon until the requisite level of skill is attained. This can be accomplished through coaching on the job. The coach can be a member of the training staff, a line supervisor, or a senior salesman charged with training responsibilities. The coach travels with the trainee and observes both his planning activities and his performance during interviews. After each call, and at other times when appropriate, the observer reviews the trainee's procedures step by step indicating strong and weak points and alternative ways of dealing with various situations. The trainer will also point out and commend good performance so that such learning is reinforced.

The demonstrator-observer system is a somewhat more formal variant of this procedure. It is particularly suitable in selling situations where many calls are quite similar in form or purpose, such as calls made on retail stores or on consumers. The trainer alternately acts as demonstrator and observer on successive calls, with the trainee's role alternating between observer and actor. The trainer demonstrates proper procedure on the first call. After the call he reviews his activity with the trainee. The trainee takes the second call, attempting to employ similar techniques. Often he will find that the situation is not, in fact, identical so that he will need to use his own initiative to complete the interview. Whether this is necessary or not, the trainer in a post-interview discussion will point out strong and weak points in the trainee's efforts. On the third call, the trainer again assumes the role of demonstrator, and so on. One advantage of this method in the hands of an able trainer is that the trainee's experiences in the calls in which he is the actor serve to establish the relevance of what the trainer is doing in the following calls. This method thus tends to support trainee motivation more effectively than field arrangements in which the trainee is either permanent observer or permanent principal actor. A hazard of this method is that the trainer will emphasize the "how to" of the interview rather than developing the trainee's abilities to perceive and gain understanding from his own experience. Careful training of the trainers is thus a necessary prerequisite.

Coaching on the job is expensive. To be effective it virtually demands a one-to-one student-teacher ratio and a sufficient time period for the trainee to develop at least a minimum level of perceptual skill and skills in the performance of his various duties.

Job rotation, in which the trainee is moved from assignment to assignment, is also employed as a training device to broaden the trainee's experience. Its effectiveness, like that of other on-the-job training, depends on whether training, rather than mere exposure, actually takes place.

Learning Means: Developing Work Habits

Desirable habits, like skills, are acquired by doing, not merely by knowing, what is correct. Most of us know things which we should do (arrive at meetings on time; treat others courteously; embrace the Golden Rule). Such knowledge alone does little to create the habits of thought and action necessary to translate these admirable traits into practice.

Where the salesman is conceived as a territory manager, the habits which need to be developed will embrace a wide range of activities such as systems for rating accounts, routing and scheduling, overall planning of the use of his time, preparations for individual calls, record keeping, reporting, and the development of budget making, pricing, and collecting habits which contribute to favorable performance.

Many of the techniques useful for skill development can also be employed to mold work habits of trainees. In addition, the administrative procedures of the organization should serve to point out poor work habits (for example, improper hours, poor reporting, lack of reliability in meeting arrangements with customers) so that the supervisory process can be employed to correct them.

The variety of knowledge and diversity of skills which must be acquired by the salesman can be secured only through an assortment of learning methods. The principal methods useful for different portions of the trainee's learning experience are listed in Exhibit 7–2.

Learning through unaided experience and learning by observing succesful salesmen in action are not included in the figure. Why not?

ORGANIZATION FOR SALES FORCE TRAINING

Training is basically a line responsibility. However, the importance of the training job and the demands which its performance place on the executives involved usually require that a training unit of one or more individuals be employed to act in a staff capacity for training activities. In the absence of such a provision, training responsibilities are likely to be diffused among the various line managers with the risk that they will be treated as secondary activities by the various regional, district, and local managers. Training is too significant in modern markets to be relegated to that status.

Even in a small organization much planning, investigation, and evaluation work is necessary if proper programs are to be developed and carried out. This work is unlikely to be done well if relegated to the status of an ancillary responsibility of diverse, busy line managers. Hence it is desirable to have overall responsibility for the de-

Exhibit 7-2

SALESMAN TRAINING METHODS

Learning Area	Structured presentation*	Role Playing	Cases	Games	Conferences	Structured Experience †	Coaching on-job	Demonstrator-Observer
Knowledge								
Products	✓							
Economic bases	✓✓		✓		✓			
Customer problems	✓✓	✓✓	✓✓		✓✓✓			
Customer rationale	✓✓	✓	✓✓		✓			
Markets	✓		✓					
Augmentation of market knowledge	✓✓	✓	✓✓		✓			
Sales policies	✓✓		✓✓					
History	✓							
Support activities	✓✓	✓	✓		✓			
Procedures	✓							
Skills								
Intercommunicative		✓✓✓	✓✓			✓	✓✓✓	✓✓
Selling methods		✓✓✓	✓✓✓	✓		✓	✓✓✓	✓✓✓
Intelligence				✓✓			✓	✓
Work habits							✓	

*Includes lectures, audio and/or visual presentations, readings, manuals, workbooks, and programmed instruction

† Includes job rotation and other specific training assignments under direction of, but not necessarily in the presence of, a trainer.

velopment and operation of training centered in a single individual, even if a separate staff to actually conduct training is not provided.

In firms where the training of salesmen is substantially similar to the training of other personnel or where newly hired personnel go through an indoctrination and acclimitization experience before being assigned to a particular functional activity, initial training may be under the cognizance of the personnel department. Even in such firms, however, the growing role of the marketplace in fashioning what the salesman will need to know and the skills which he will require suggests that the major portion of the training activity be placed under the jurisdiction of a senior marketing executive.

Relationship of Training Staff to Line Sales Organization

The provision of a training responsibility distinct from the line sales organization does not imply that training as an activity should be separate from that organization. In fact, the director of sales training, whatever his title or organizational position, must derive the training specifications from the needs of the line organization in the field.

Research to determine training goals, the selection of training methods, the planning of training activities, and the evaluation of training work are essentially staff activities which should be under the cognizance of the training director. The actual execution of training programs is likely to be divided between the training director and his staff and the line organization in the field.

Certain parts of the training experience, including on-the-job field training and learning experiences from job rotation are necessarily performed in the field. Other parts of the program may appropriately be conducted either by the training staff or by line personnel. The most effective division is likely to rest on the relative importance of understanding of the market and its problems on the one hand and training expertise on the other. Field sales personnel may have a grasp of market realities and the needs and problems of particular customer groups which makes them uniquely suited to dealing with these matters. On the other hand, since training activity is rarely the principal interest or activity of field managers, they are likely to be less proficient in the training process itself than members of the training staff. These circumstances suggest that training activities which do not require the particular expertise on specific market problems which can be found only in the field organization should be conducted by training personnel. Large sales organizations frequently have a separate marketing training or sales training unit which develops and executes programs to train both salesmen and field sales managers and to maintain their level of competence.

Centralized versus Decentralized Training

The locale at which training takes place rests on the types of material to be presented and the costs of bringing salesmen from a wide area to a central place. Where the number of trainees warrants the cost, a well-staffed training school at company headquarters offers the advantage of specialization, detachment of trainees from non-training activities, and the ability to use other headquarters personnel, and perhaps plant facilities, as part of the training activity. Where exposure to plant operations is necessary, at least a part of the training experience must clearly be at a location where such operations can be observed.

For the same reason, most skill development portions of the training program are best conducted in situations as close to those which the salesman will encounter in the field as is possible. Many skill development activities are best performed on the job or in local offices on a scheduled basis running concurrently with work on the job.

Cost considerations often limit the extent to which it is feasible to bring trainees to a central point. In addition to travel costs and the costs of maintenance at the training facility, the opportunity cost of time absent from the field may be substantially higher where travel is involved. However, air travel has reduced these costs somewhat, thus making centralized training somewhat more feasible for many companies.

Many of the benefits of centralized training can be secured without bringing the salesman to the central location. Teams of training personnel can move to various locations around the country. Training films and training aids can be prepared centrally and distributed for use in local areas by a decentralized training staff.

Selecting and Training Trainers

Teaching others is a different kind of activity than branch management or successful cultivation of a market. Success as a branch manager, for example, may be quite unrelated to an individual's competence as a trainer, or even as a salesman. Many successful salesmen may have only limited understanding of why they are successful and no experience in the often tedious process of inducing and assisting others to learn and to develop skills. The salesman may possess great ability to diagnose customer problems, but little ability to diagnose learning difficulties of junior salesmen or trainees. Some hold, in fact, that teaching skills are more difficult to develop than is technical knowledge and that, therefore, it is easier to teach a skilled teacher the technical subject matter than to make a teacher of a knowledgeable salesman.[18] On the other hand, training specialists well may be so remote from the "firing line" that they simply do not understand the problems that the salesmen will face in the marketplace and for which the recruits are being trained.

Regardless of the background of the individuals selected to serve as trainers, some training of the trainers is indicated. If professional trainers are used, some field experience will be necessary if they are to maintain relevance to the real world in their teaching and thus retain the confidence and respect of the trainees.

The more ubiquitous problem is providing training competence for line personnel who are to have training responsibilities. As a minimum, such persons must be given sufficient time to prepare for and perform their training functions and sufficient training in the learning-teaching process that they can effectively utilize their own knowledge and experience and the various training materials provided them.[19]

Training First-Line Sales Managerial Personnel

The duties of first-line field sales managers differ markedly from those of salesmen. The knowledge, techniques and skills which are required for the effective performance of these duties differ in kind as well as degree from that required for sales work. Yet most first-line sales supervisors receive little formal training to equip them for their new tasks. In some cases all they receive is that which results from their own unstructured experience and, perhaps, some unstructured interaction with peers.

The procedures suggested earlier in the chapter for formulating training goals for salesmen and the principles for selecting appropriate learning means can be employed to develop training programs appropriate for the responsibilities of sales management personnel at various levels.[20]

[18] For an example, see "Building the Sales Training Program," in *Practical Techniques in Sales Selection and Training* (New York: American Management Association, 1945), pp. 33–41.

[19] For guidelines for the training of supervisors and other trainers in training techniques, see William McGehee and Paul W. Thayer, *Training in Business and Industry* (New York: John Wiley and Sons, Inc., 1961), Chapter 8.

[20] For a description of current practice in training field sales managers see Robert F. Vizza, *Training and Development of Field Sales Managers* (New York: Sales Executives Club of New York, 1965). Briefly summarized in Velma A. Adams, "Field Sales Managers Cry: 'Give Us More Training'," *Sales Management,* Vol. 94, No. 8 (April 16, 1965), pp. 25–27.

EVALUATION OF TRAINING PROGRAMS

Evaluation of training programs is necessary both (a) to determine if the effect of a program warrants the cost and (b) as feedback useful for improving the programs.

The ultimate measure of the value of a training program is the effect which it has on the level of competence of the trainees. However, competence itself is difficult to measure. In addition, attained competence is often at least as much the result of what the trainee brings to the job as of the training process. Moreover, many training programs, especially new ones, will not have been in operation for sufficient periods or with sufficient numbers of men to obtain accurate measures of their effects. Consequently, sales managers need both measures of training program effect and means of appraising existing and prospective programs when such cause-effect measurements are not available.

Measurement of the Effects of Training Programs

The effects of training programs may be measured at three levels: (1) whether the trainee learned what he was supposed to learn; (2) whether the learning affected his subsequent behavior on the job; and (3) the extent to which changes in job behavior affected the attainment of job goals, for example, greater sales.

MEASURES OF LEARNING

The extent to which knowledge and skills have been acquired and attitudes changed can be measured by testing the trainees both before and after the training experience.

A variety of types of tests can be employed. Written tests are most suitable to measure knowledge and attitudes; role playing may be appropriate to ascertain changes in the way the trainee handles himself. To eliminate the effects of the testing procedure itself, separate, but equivalent, "before" and "after" tests are desirable.

Testing involves a number of problems. The test materials must be a reliable sample of the subject matter being tested; the test must validly measure what it purports to measure; and distortions introduced by the presence of observers or perceptive biases of the observer in grading the student must be avoided.

Similar tests at a later date can be used to measure retained benefits. High levels of retention suggest that the material was learned well and may have been reinforced through usage by the trainee and through system reinforcement—that is, rewards for usage. Low retention, especially following high scores on tests given at the immediate conclusion of the training, suggests that the material was not successfully internalized and/or that it lacked relevance or consistency with system behavioral norms. ("Never mind what the instructor said, this is the way we do it in this division!") As a result, the learning decayed rapidly.

An example of role playing tests to determine if managers' discussion skills were improved is described in a Xerox Learning Systems validation report:

> "Role play situations are used not only as part of the training, but also as tests to evaluate the trainee's application of the skills taught by the course. These tests required each participant to act the role of the manager in a specially constructed true-to-life sales and marketing problem situation with another trainee or an administrator playing the role of the "subordinate" according to detailed directions.
>
> "The test sessions were taped and later scored utilizing a scoring key which was developed to reflect the principles taught in the course. . . .
>
> "Five test episodes were used. These were administered in such a way that no one participated in the same episode more than once. Each episode was used approximately the same number of times as a pretest, posttest and retention test. The tests proved to be reasonably comparable—no significant differences were found between scores on different tests taken at the same time (that is, as a pretest, and so on)."[21]

In this example, involving executives from four companies, the median score before training was 27; after training, 84. A retention test five months later of trainees from one of the companies yielded a median score of 84.

Testing can measure the extent to which the trainees have acquired certain knowledge or mastered certain techniques. It does not, however, reveal whether the best training methods have been employed in providing the training experience. The latter requires experimental or observational study of alternative training means.

Moreover, although testing can reveal whether the student has mastered the subjects chosen for him, it does not measure whether or not these choices were the correct ones—that is, whether the program design was relevant to the competence needed.

MEASURES OF CHANGES IN BEHAVIOR

Measures of what has been *learned* do not reveal whether the learning has affected the trainees' *subsequent behavior* on the job:

The trainee may have acquired specific knowledge through rote memory, but has not generalized that knowledge.

[21] *Problem-Solving Discussion Skills for Sales/Marketing Managers: Validation Report* (New York: Xerox Learning Systems, Xerox Corporation, n.d.). To avoid halo effect, the evaluators are not told which tapes are pretest, which posttest, and so on.

The trainee may have learned a skill applicable to a very specific situation but has not learned to apply the same skill to similar but not identical ones.

The trainee may have learned well, but is unwilling or unable to transfer the learning to his daily work on the job (for example, failure to apply new product knowledge to customer's problem).

The "system" may be such as to constrain or bar the exercise of newly acquired skills (for example, line management or peer group pressures induce retention of old ways).

Measures of the extent to which learning has not only occurred but has been transferred into on-the-job behavior are more meaningful in evaluating a training program than mere measures of what has been learned. Unfortunately, such measures are also more difficult to achieve.

Basically, measures of changes in behavior require the observation and evaluation of the salesman at work, both before and after the training experience. The observations differ from those in a role-playing test in that the situations observed are real, that is, on-the-job, rather than artificially controlled.

A major problem in observing behavior is making sure that the presence of the observer does not affect behavior, either in selecting the sales calls or other activity to be observed or in the conduct of the work itself. The confidence of both salesmen and line management is necessary if contamination from observer presence is to be avoided.[22] For some types of sales situations, such as selling in stores, the observer difficulty can be avoided by having the observers pose as shoppers.

As in any study involving the observation of human behavior, perceptual bias on the part of the observer represents an additional hazard. Its effects can be minimized by providing that to the greatest extent possible, observations be of specific acts (e.g., Did the salesman ask "such-and-such") rather than confining reports to impressions.

MEASURES OF OUTCOMES IN TERMS OF COMPANY OR SALES FORCE GOALS

The ultimate merit of a training program is its effect on the results obtained from the salesman's behavior. It is only at this point that the economic value of the training program can be measured for comparison with its cost and the cost-benefit relationships which might be afforded by alternative programs.

[22] Ault suggests that the danger from bias in the selection of sales calls to be observed is likely to be a more serious hazard than the presence of the observer during the interview itself. (Leslie H. Ault, *Justifying Industrial Training.* Working paper. Xerox Learning Systems, 1967, p. 16.)

Training effects can be measured by observational studies in which the performance (for example, sales) of those receiving the training is compared with an untrained group or their own earlier performance. The large number of possible confounding factors— non-random selection of men for training, changes in outside factors affecting sales, and so on—limit the validity of observational studies and suggest that experiments may be more useful.

In an experiment to measure the training effect, experimental and control groups should be selected randomly in order to control the extraneous factors such as developments in the individual terri- tories, age, experience, and tenure of the salesman and his attitude towards training as such. The training effect is measured by com- paring the sales result of the experimental group with that which would have occurred had the group experienced the same rate of change as the control group. Thus

$$TE = \frac{CES - CCS}{100 \pm CCS}$$

where

TE = training effect,
CES = change in experimental (trained) group sales (percent),
CCS = change in control group sales (percent)

In one case, sales of specialty industrial chemicals by men in the training group increased 13.4 percent while those of the control group rose by only 6.4 percent:[23]

$$TE = \frac{13.4 - 6.4}{100 + 6.4} = \frac{7.0}{106.4} = 6.5 \text{ percent*}$$

Given the sales increase, the profit consequence can be derived. The value of the training can then be expressed in terms of return on investment, or in terms of the percent increase in sales or number of salesmen who need to show a given improvement, say 2 percent, to break even on the program. It can also be expressed in terms of a pay- back period.

The use of a profitability measure does not eliminate the need for other measures of training effects. An index of relative sales per- formance measures only the total effects. The analyst has no way of determining whether all of the effect was the result of some part of the program. Perhaps the result was achieved despite the adverse effects of some elements. Perhaps the Hawthorne Effect played a major role— that is, the mere fact that training was provided. Thus measures of

[23] From Xerox Learning Systems, *Professional Selling Skills: Program De- scription and Validation Results* (New York: Xerox Corporation, n.d.).
*.95 level of significance.

total effects on the attainment of sales-force goals, while useful for determining the economic worth of a total program may be less helpful than partial measures in measuring the desirability of particular elements in the program.

An experiment, the results of which are measured in terms of sales or profits, must take place over time. Only one, or at most very few, experiments can run concurrently. In the meantime, the control group remains unexposed to the training. Even if latent demoralization problems can be avoided through careful discretion and explanations, the company foregoes the benefits which these individuals might have secured through training.

If, after a six-month test, a validation study determines that a training program produces a 10 percent increase in sales, the company has foregone that increase insofar as the control group is concerned. Managers are sometimes understandably reluctant to forego the assumed benefits of training for the sake of an experiment.

Appraisal of Training Programs

In the absence of experimental or observational studies to measure the effects of training experiences on the competence of the trainees, evaluation of training must rest on appraisals of the programs themselves.

It is relatively easy to appraise teaching methods: the teacher may himself have a feel for whether an approach has succeeded; feedback can be obtained from student tests of the material and from student appraisals of program materials and presentations. But the more significant questions in appraising a training program lie not in the area of the best way in which to teach but in the appropriateness of the training goals—in determining what constitutes competence for a particular sales job and what contribution training can provide to its attainment. A number of critical questions may be raised in appraising a training program.

> Have the goals of the program been determined by careful comparison of the trainees' ambient knowledge and skill status with knowledge and skill needs, determined as objectively as possible, as contrasted with a "desk-top" program design based upon what executives, supervisors, or technicians believe the salesman should know?
>
> Does the training program place emphasis on customer and market problems appropriate to the degree of market orientation intended for the sales force?
>
> Is the program well balanced in terms of the trainees' needs?
>
> Does the program adequately recognize individual differences in the trainees' backgrounds, experience, aptitudes, and competence? Is it sufficiently adaptive to build on these differences so that each man can progress and will be motivated to do so?

Does the training program provide both the competence necessary for effective job performance in the immediate future and the opportunity and incentive for professional growth?

Is the program oriented to the problems which the salesmen will face in the particular sales work to which they will be assigned?

Does feedback from the market on changing conditions in the field reach the training personnel? Is it reflected in continual program modification?

Are teaching techniques well chosen in the light of existing knowledge on the learning process?

Training programs do not always meet these criteria well. In many firms a product and production orientation still predominate. Major portions of time are devoted to the company and its products. Relatively little time is devoted to an understanding of customers and their problems, yet this is often a major (sometimes *the* major) part of the salesman's job. Technical training is commonly heavily loaded with the technology of the selling industry. Relatively little, often no, attention is devoted to the technology of the using industry and the technological and other problems of various types of users. Many programs do very little to develop the trainee's skills in understanding technological developments in using or prospective using industries or in developing skills in perceiving the rationale and thought processes of buyers.

This behavior is understandable; it is easier to teach the salesman what we are familiar with than what we are unfamiliar with. Moreover, as these are the things that are important to us as sellers, it is easy for those who design programs and prepare training materials to conceive of the salesman's technological needs in terms of "What the salesman needs to know about our product X" rather than "What the salesman needs to know about the problems of using industry Z."

Nevertheless, the heavy emphasis on the selling firm and its offerings and the rather limited treatment of customer firms and their problems so often found in training programs cast doubts on the appropriateness of many such programs to a market-oriented economy. If a company's sales efforts are to be oriented towards its market, training programs must be appraised in terms of their contribution towards serving that orientation.

SUMMARY

The development of a viable training system entails (a) the formulation of training goals and the establishment of training specifications for the particular job, (b) selecting appropriate means to meet these specifications, (c) creating a training organization to administer the training activity, and (d) measuring the results of training and feeding such information back into the planning process.

Developing salesman competence is largely a matter of developing his communicative, diagnostic, and prescriptive skills and providing him with a knowledge bank to assist him in applying those skills.

Before training goals can be established, jobs must be analyzed to ascertain what the salesman should do and the impediments to optimal performance which will exist in the absence of training. Such analyses embrace not only an examination of duties and methods of performance but also difficulties encountered and attitudes which may influence job performance.

Training programs must be designed in terms of the process by which the learner learns, including those things which impel him to learn. Training is a participative process. Training programs are essentially systems to activate the trainee's motives and guide him in his self-development. Diverse means are generally appropriate for the development of different types of skills and for the acquisition of knowledge.

As sound training programs require much planning, investigation, and evaluation work, training is unlikely to be done well if treated as an ancillary responsiblity of a line executive. Hence, even in small organizations, much can be said for at least one individual with responsibility for the development and modification of training activities, even if the actual conduct of training is left to the line organization.

Evaluation of training programs is essential both to determine if a program warrants its cost, and to provide feedback useful for program improvement. Training effects may be measured at three levels: (1) the extent to which the trainees learn the material, (2) whether learning affects subsequent performance on the job, and (3) the extent of influence of the training experience on attainment of job goals, such as sales. Under appropriate conditions all of these can be measured. Tests of various types can measure the extent of learning. Observation can detect changes in behavior on the job. Analysis of sales or other results can measure the overall outcome of a training experience, especially if experimental conditions can be established. Although far from an adequate substitute for training program validation through measurement, program appraisals may be useful when measurements cannot be obtained.

SELECTED READINGS

American Educational Research Association, *Handbook of Research on Teaching*, N. L. Gage, ed. Skokie, Ill.: Rand McNally & Company, 1963.

Bass, Bernard M., and James A. Vaughan, *The Psychology of Learning for Managers*. American Foundation for Management Research, 1965. Relevent learning principles and methods.

Costello, Timothy W., and Sheldon S. Zalkind, *Psychology in Administration: A Research Orientation.* Englewood Cliffs, N.J.: Prentice-Hall, Inc., 1963. Especially Chapters 11 and 12. Findings on the learning process and on effecting change in perceptions and ideas.

Crissy, William J. E., Gary A. Marple, and Earle Conant, "Field Assignments for Individual Managerial Development," *Business Topics,* Winter, 1963, pp. 49–63. Reprinted in Milton Alexander and Edward M. Mazze, *Sales Management.* New York: Pitman Publishing Corporation, 1965, pp. 279–295.

Lapp, C. L., *Training and Supervising Salesmen.* Englewood Cliffs, N.J.: Prentice-Hall, Inc., 1960. An easy-to-read guidebook.

MacDonald, Morgan B., Jr., and Earl L. Bailey, *Training Company Salesmen* (Experiences in Marketing Management, No. 15). New York: National Industrial Conference Board, Inc., 1967.

National Society of Sales Training Executives, *The New Handbook of Sales Training,* Robert F. Vizza, ed. Englewood Cliffs, N.J.: Prentice-Hall, Inc., 1967. Modern handbook embracing all aspects of sales training.

Robinson, Patrick J., and Bent Stidsen, *Personal Selling in a Modern Perspective.* Boston: Allyn & Bacon, Inc., 1967. The nature of competence in selling.

Ruder, E. F., *Getting the Sales from Sales Training.* St. Louis, Mo.: Sales Executives' Publications, 1958. Explanations of training techniques and applications. Includes chapters on memory, reading, and speech improvement.

Stanton, T. F., *How to Instruct Successfully.* New York: McGraw-Hill, Inc., 1960. A practical guidebook, especially useful for the part-time instructor.

Sunbury, David H., and C. Clark Thompson. "Training Company Salesman," *Business Record,* Dec. 1961. Reprinted in Milton Alexander and Edward M. Mazze, *Sales Management.* New York: Pitman Publishing Corp., 1965, pp. 266–278. Company practices in sales training.

Webster, Frederick E., Jr., "Interpersonal Communications and Salesman Effectiveness," *Journal of Marketing,* XXXII (July 1968), pp. 7–13. Salesmen's needs for perceptual skills.

8 Maintaining the Level of Sales-Force Competence*

Like the athlete in his prime,
Competence is a fleeting thing.

The needs and problems of consumers and using industries change rapidly in response to onrushing technological, economic, and social change.

New knowledge is being generated at such a rapid rate in the scientific, engineering, and management fields that without constant effort men trained in these fields find that within a relatively short time their knowledge is old-fashioned and out of date.

Much of the knowledge possessed by the salesman after his formal training becomes obsolete within a few short years. Other

*This chapter was prepared in collaboration with Norman H. Fuss, Jr., of Cresap, McCormick and Paget, Inc., and utilizes a number of concepts and examples developed in Norman H. Fuss, Jr., *Combatting Technical Obsolescence in the Industrial Sales Force* (Unpublished M.B.A. thesis, University of Pennsylvania, 1969).

parts are lost through decay. Skills, like knowledge, also become obsolete as the needs for them change. They, too, decay from lack of use or inadequate maintenance. Thus do highly competent men lose their competence.

THE PROBLEM OF COMPETENCE MAINTENANCE

Perhaps the most evident forms in which declines in competence can be observed are those which result from knowledge obsolescence. It is a potential problem in all fields but it is usually the technologically oriented fields of industrial marketing in which it is first noticed. The problem of knowledge obsolescence among scientists, engineers, and managers is one that is widely recognized in industry.

Many companies, especially those in technologically-oriented industries, have begun to recognize that they have a large investment in their technically trained personnel and have undertaken programs to preserve and even upgrade their technical competence. Scientists and engineers are encouraged to attend conventions, seminars, and refresher courses in their fields at company expense and to be active in their respective professional societies. In addition, on-the-job training programs, in-house seminars and classes, and tuition-aid programs are established to help these people maintain their technical competence.

Managers are sent to courses, seminars, and management conferences conducted by schools of business and by various professional societies. Some are even sent at company expense to advanced management training schools. The purpose of all of these programs is to keep these men up-to-date in their fields; to avoid knowledge obsolescence.

Parallel programs aimed at maintaining the technical competence of the salesmen who will call upon these scientists, engineers and managers are much less common.

For the sales force to perform its function in the most effective manner in today's markets, it is often essential that its members establish and maintain intercommunicative relationships of the highest quality not only with the purchasing agents and buyers in their customer's organizations, but also with the engineers, scientists and managers. To do this, they must understand not only the present technology of their products and those of the users but also the direction of technological change and how these changes are likely to affect the operations and needs of their customers.

The quality of the relationship that can be established with technical and managerial personnel depends to a great extent on the technological level at which salesmen and customers can communicate with each other. In general, the higher the technological plane on which intercommunication can take place, the greater will be the benefits derived by both parties in the relationship. Thus the maintenance of the technical competence of their sales forces at a high level should be of particular concern to sales-force managers, especially those selling to industrial markets.

To prevent knowledge obsolescence, updating is required in a number of areas. Most obvious, and most frequently provided for, is the need to educate the salesman in the properties and capabilities of new products in the line and in the markets which are envisaged for them. A production-oriented company might be expected to go no further.

Less obvious, but perhaps more important in a customer-oriented world, is the need to develop and maintain the salesman's understanding of current and prospective changes affecting customer industries. To effectively sell complex products, the sales force must be able to match these products to the needs of customers. To establish and maintain mutually satisfactory intercommunicative relationships of high quality, the salesman must have something of himself to offer the customer. This demands that he understand the customer's operations and problems. In this context, the salesman's knowledge of the customer industries' technology and advances in the basic sciences and in related areas which are likely to affect technological advancement in the customer industries is required. Moreover, to successfully accomplish the intelligence portion of his responsibility, the salesman must be sufficiently well versed in developments in the using industries to be able to perceive the significance of what he observes in those industries.

When is a salesman's performance impaired by obsolescence? How much decay can occur before the salesman's performance in serving his customers is impaired? Clearly this will depend on the demands of the job.

Presumably the salesman's fund of knowledge begins to decay as soon as it is acquired. The decay rate will depend in part on the rate of introduction of new knowledge in his field. It is generally held that scientists' and engineers' funds of knowledge acquired through formal education have, on average, a half-life of about ten years. That is, roughly 50 percent of what they learn during their formal educational experience will have been supplanted by new knowledge within 10 years.[1] We do not have reliable estimates of half-lives for salesmen in various fields. However, it seems reasonable to assume that they are

[1] See, for example, Roger W. Christian, "Personal Obsolescence," *Factory*, Vol. 122, No. 10 (October, 1964), p. 108. *Steel* magazine estimated in 1964 that an engineer who received his diploma in 1951 was "old" by 1964. ("Memo to Engineers—Better Keep Pace," *Steel*, Vol. 115, No. 10 (October, 1964), p. 25.)

approximately the same as those for scientists and engineers in the same industry. They well may be shorter than ten years in industries in which applications are changing rapidly. Moreover, sales performance may be seriously affected before one-half of a man's knowledge fund has become obsolete.

The need to up-date knowledge and skills is not confined to sales forces selling to technologically advanced industries although it is here that it is most readily noticed. The output of the technologically advanced industries permeates the economy. The customers of these industries use new materials, employ newly available technology, and in turn change both their own needs and outputs. Hence the problems and information needs of buyers of less sophisticated industrial products and of many consumer products—for example, textiles, home furnishings, home maintenance products, entertainment goods, packaged foods—undergo continual change.

Even in such less technologically oriented sales situations, the decay of the salesman's knowledge and understanding and the changing nature of customers' problems and the offerings available to resolve them create obsolescence problems within even a well-trained sales organization.

> A manufacturer of commercial office machines found that the technology of his products changed so rapidly that men in the field three or four years did not know as much about the product line as his new sales trainees.

> Retailers of carpet find that salesmen well trained in the properties of natural fibers and early synthetics become less than satisfactory advisors to consumers who, faced with a bewildering variety of natural and synthetic fibers, seek guidance in the choices for particular use conditions (for example, heavy wear) or subject to particular hazards (for example, TV dinners, alcoholic drinks, pets, muddy feet, high humidity).

Not all developments affecting the sales job are technological in nature. Changes in the environment in which customers operate, such as changes in their relationships with other firms, with labor, or their entry into new markets, or changes in the economic or legal environments in which they operate may significantly affect customers' problems or the buying influences' perceptions of them. The salesman's understanding of these forces and factors must be kept up-to-date if he is to be an effective perceiver and intercommunicator with those upon whom he calls.

In many situations offsetting knowledge decay is not enough. Customers expect, and competitive conditions permit them to demand, increasingly higher levels of competence from the salesmen with whom they will deal.

If the effectiveness of the sales force is to be maintained, men must be provided with new insights about customer industries and customer behavior as they are developed. As more is learned of the interactive process and especially of the salesman's ability to influence it, the salesman's understanding in these areas must be expanded and his work habits modified to reflect this type of new knowledge as well. As feedback from operations and the outcomes of a firm's own experimental and observational studies are analyzed, findings of significance to the sales job must be brought to the attention of salesmen in forms which they can use.

CAUSES OF SALESMAN OBSOLESCENCE

The basic cause of knowledge obsolescence is a failure of trained people to keep up to date on the latest bits of knowledge added to their fields.

In the same way, skill obsolescence results from a failure to develop and modify perceptive, diagnostic, prescriptive, and communicative skills as the needs of the buyer-seller intercommunicative process change.

In many cases obsolescence in the sales force is the result of an evolutionary process spanning many years. In other situations, revolutionary events such as shifts in products or markets or in salesmen's assignments, render the salesman's knowledge and skills partially or totally obsolete overnight.

Evolutionary Obsolescence

Evolutionary obsolescence is caused by the steady accumulation of many small advances in the field in which the sales force is working or by the gradual decay of knowledge or skills possessed by a sales force.

An example of the evolutionary type of knowledge obsolescence is that of the salesman who has been working in a technical field for some years but who has not kept himself abreast of the latest developments coming out of the universities and research laboratories. Eventually his basic fund of knowledge begins to get old-fashioned and he is no longer able to communicate effectively with the younger men in his field when they begin to discuss these newer developments.

Another example of evolutionary obsolescence is that of the salesman who, though at one time well-versed in all of the technical aspects of his company's products and their use, has, over the years, neglected to keep himself as well informed on the newer products that his company had added to its offerings.

There is a marked tendency for the life span of products to become shorter. As the product life span becomes shorter and new products are introduced at an ever-increasing rate, that portion of the obsolescence problem attributable to this type of evolutionary change is also likely to become more significant.

Evolutionary obsolescence may also be caused by evolutionary changes in the markets served by the sales force. The same factors that cause evolutionary change in the technology of the sales force's own company cause similar changes in the technology of its customers.

To maintain effective intercommunicative relationships, the sales force must have a firm grasp and understanding of its customers' technology as well as its own. It is entirely possible for a sales force to be quite well-versed in its own products and internal technology and yet be technically obsolescent in that it has not kept abreast of the evolutionary changes in the markets that it serves.

Evolutionary obsolescence may be brought about by decay in the salesman's fund of knowledge as well as by his failure to acquire new knowledge. Portions of his knowledge may not be utilized for some time. As a result, their relevance to him diminishes, retention declines, and the fund decays. The man can then no longer draw on what he used to know. Decay affects skills and work habits as well as both nontechnical and technical knowledge.

Revolutionary Obsolescence

Revolutionary obsolescence is that caused by important shifts in the field in which the sales force is operating or by additions to this field.

Revolutionary obsolescence can be caused by shifts in, or additions to, the product line being handled. A company may introduce and assign to its sales force a new line of products having few if any similarities to its older product lines. By that act, the knowledge fund of the sales force is made obsolete to the extent that it is insufficient to effectively sell the new product line. Similar situations occur when radical changes in using industries or consumption patterns significantly alter users' needs or problems. These types of revolutionary change are usually the result of a technological breakthrough in either supplying or using industries.

The development and diffusion into the economy of major technological developments that create entire new markets and marketing opportunities while destroying old ones is taking place at an increasingly rapid rate.

The overall elapsed time for technological developments (to reach commercialization) has declined during the last 60 or 70 years from a mean of 37 years in the early twentieth-century period, to 24 years in the post World War I period, to 14 years in the post-World War II period.[2]

Where in the past it was not at all unusual for a salesman to go through his entire working life without being affected by any major changes either in his industry or in that of his customers, the chance of this happening today is small. The average period for development and diffusion of major new technological advances is even now much less than the working span of a man. The same may be said of changes in wholesaling and retailing methods, retailer problems and consumer buying perspectives. Unless companies are willing to abandon large numbers of men in the prime of their working life, they will be forced to develop and institute better and more widespread means of retraining their existing personnel, including their sales force, to adjust to these major revolutionary changes in their environment that will occur with increasing frequency.

Revolutionary knowledge obsolescence may also occur if an existing sales force is assigned to sell its present product line to new markets—that is, to different types of users or for different application. It is faced with an obsolescence problem in that it must expand its basic fund of knowledge to include the environment, problems, and technology of the new market if it is to perform its sales function effectively in that new market.

Factors Contributing to Obsolescence Problems

Personnel and sales management factors may tend to aggravate salesman obsolescence problems.

One significant factor is lack of interest. Many men, after they graduate from school, lose interest in studying. They become interested in other things and simply do not take the trouble to keep themselves abreast of their fields.

Lack of opportunity also deters many men from keeping up-to-date. For many technical graduates, once they leave the academic world and enter the world of business, there is very little time to devote to study. Moreover, it has been generally accepted that one is on the job to use his knowledge, not to acquire more.

This attitude seems to be especially strong in the sales function. Many sales managers even today seem to believe that, since the salesman's job is to communicate with customers, he should spend as much time as possible doing that. They look on time spent in "nonproductive" activities such as refresher training as time wasted.

[2] Frank Lynn, "Our Accelerating Technological Change: Its Impact and Effect," *Management Review,* Vol. 56, No. 3 (March 1967), p. 68.

This is not an entirely unreasonable attitude when one considers the importance of establishing and maintaining meaningful intercommunicative relationships with customers. But a meaningful intercommunicative relationship obviously depends on the *quality* of the communication involved as well as its *quantity.* In any sales force, a balance will have to be struck between the requirement that salesmen spend time with their customers and the requirement they be able to communicate with them effectively.

In part, the relative scarcity of programs aimed at maintaining the technical competence of salesmen may be due to the greater cost and difficulty of assembling field personnel and removing them from daily operations as contrasted with the ease of assembling laboratory personnel and conducting programs with a minimum of interference with daily operations. In addition, however, one may suspect a lack of appreciation for the need to maintain the competence of the salesman's side of the communication system and the fact that serious knowledge-obsolescence problems in sales forces are relatively recent and, even today, not widely recognized.[3]

MANIFESTATIONS OF SALESMAN OBSOLESCENCE

Knowledge obsolescence is probably one of the root causes of many of the problems that confront the managers of sales forces. Many of the problems that are usually attributed to a lack of morale or motivation can often be traced, at least partially, to knowledge obsolescence.

One manifestation of knowledge obsolescence that occurs in industrial selling is that of the salesmen who, over the years, call less and less frequently on the technical personnel of their customers and more and more frequently on the nontechnical personnel. Such behavior may indicate that the salesmen are uncomfortable talking to engineers and scientists, perhaps because they feel a lack of confidence in their ability to communicate effectively with these people.

> Unless the salesman is fully confident of his ability to carry on a technical conversation with a specifying engineer, he will avoid such contact and tend to devote his time to non-technical personnel.[4]

Such behavior has the effect of depriving the company of some of the more valuable intercommunicative relationships that it must have if it is to sell effectively to, and draw sound intelligence from, the industrial marketplace.

[3] Some of the factors which have enabled many companies to avoid serious man obsolescence problems are discussed below.
[4] Frank A. Gonochio, Regional Manager, Kaar Electronics Corporation, in "How Can We Get Our Salesmen to Spend Enough Time with Design Engineers?", *Industrial Marketing,* Vol. 53, No. 1 (January, 1968), pp. 21–22.

Another manifestation of knowledge obsolescence that is closely related to the above is the tendency on the part of many older salesmen to call primarily on the older men in their customers' organizations in preference to the younger men. The younger men are likely to be the ones actually involved in doing the testing and evaluation work that is necessary before the company's products can be approved and used. Their technical training is likely to be much more recently acquired and consequently more up-to-date than that of the older men, and they are likely to be more eager to engage the salesmen in detailed technical discussions. The older men are likely to be their supervisors or group leaders. The technically obsolescent salesman can be expected to find it more comfortable to talk to the older men for several reasons in addition to the obvious one of the similarity in ages. First, the older men in purchasing firms well may be as technically obsolescent as the salesman, having neglected to keep up with their field over the years. Secondly, even if they have kept up with developments in their field, they are less likely to want to engage in technical discussions with salesmen, leaving that duty to their younger subordinates who will be doing the actual evaluation work, contenting themselves with reports on the results of work done. Knowledge obsolescence which leads to behavior of this type is especially critical for firms whose future profits are tied heavily to new products and applications.

The younger scientists and engineers are frequently the true decision makers in a company because, even though it is the older, supervisory personnel who sit on the specification and buying committees, they depend heavily on the work and reports of their younger subordinates for the information on which they base their decisions. Salesmen who confine their calls largely to older supervisory personnel will, for all practical purposes, be communicating with these influentials on a second-hand basis. By neglecting to maintain direct intercommunicative relationships of a high technological level with the younger personnel, the technically obsolescent sales force can easily become ineffective in the critical innovative aspects of customers' operations.

Most sales force managers can point to salesmen (usually older salesmen) whose sales consist primarily of the older, well-established products with high volume, low margins and low requirements for technical assistance. These men are often among the leaders in terms of annual sales volume, but may be well below the mean in terms of profitability on their sales and in terms of sales of new products. When questioned about their low volume of sales in the newer product lines their normal reaction is to point to their large volume in the older products and assert that they don't have time to protect the large bird in the hand and go after the small bird in the bush as well.

Most writers classify a situation of this type as a motivational problem and ask "How do you motivate the older salesman to sell the newer products?" A better question might be "How do you motivate anyone to work in an area in which he feels uncomfortable or perhaps even incompetent, especially if there are other areas in which he does feel comfortable on which he can spend his time?"

A corollary to this is the unwillingness of some salesmen to attempt to sell the old products in new markets or for new applications. Again, one of the root causes of such behavior may be obsolescence of sales-force knowledge. Here it is not unfamiliarity with the product but rather unfamiliarity with the technology of the application. No matter how well he knows his product, the salesman will experience some degree of reluctance to attempt to sell it for use in an application with which he is not familiar. The company suffers from this reluctance in that it is unable to expand sales into profitable new markets as rapidly or as deeply as it might under more favorable circumstances.

FACTORS LIMITING THE MAN-OBSOLESCENCE PROBLEM

A number of factors operate to limit the extent and reduce the consequences of knowledge obsolescence. However, their ability to limit the knowledge obsolescence problem seems destined to decline at the very time that the consequences of such obsolescence for sales management seem certain to grow. The presence of these factors may, however, help to explain why the problems of knowledge obsolescence have not gained the attention which their present and future importance appears to demand.

Limitations of Dimensions of the Sales Job

Any sales job may be conceived as having two dimensions — breadth and depth. One or both of these dimensions may be kept limited for training, control or administrative purposes. One consequence of thus limiting the scope of the salesman's job is to reduce the effects on performance of such competence, and especially knowledge, deficiencies as the salesman might have.

BREADTH OF SALES JOB

The breadth of the sales job may be thought of as that dimension representing the number and size of the product lines and market segments for which a salesman is responsible. Other things equal, a sales force having responsibility for four different product lines has a *broader* job than one having responsibility for only two.

Similarly, a sales force selling to several markets has a broader job than one selling to a single market.

DEPTH OF SALES TASK

The depth dimension under this conceptualization is related to the degree of technical sophistication that the sales force is expected to maintain. Given two sales forces that are equal in all respects except that one is responsible for only that technical information that is normally found in product data sheets while the other is responsible for advising the customer on application methods and techniques as well as on product characteristics, the latter would be considered to have the deeper responsibility.

JOB DIMENSION AND MAN OBSOLESCENCE

The potential magnitude of the knowledge obsolescence problem in any industrial sales force may be thought of as being proportional to the breadth of the sales job times its depth—or, the "area" of the job. A graphical representation of this way of thinking of the competence requirements of a sales force is presented in Figure 8–1.

This conceptualization suggests two possible methods of reducing the magnitude of the knowledge obsolescence problem:

1. reducing the breadth dimension of the salesman's job;
2. reducing the depth dimension of the salesman's job.

By reducing one of the dimensions of the sales job, the "area" of the job, and hence the magnitude of the problem is reduced. Both of the above methods are used.

REDUCTION OF BREADTH THROUGH SPECIALIZATION OF THE SALES FORCE

The divisionalized and departmentalized structure of many large companies, while installed primarily for control purposes, serves

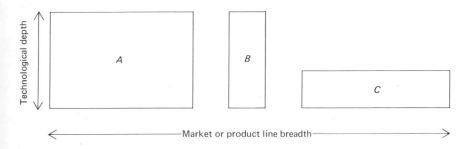

Figure 8-1

THE CONCEPTS OF BREADTH AND DEPTH IN A SALES JOB

to some extent to reduce the magnitude of the problem of obsolescence in the sales force by reducing the breadth of the sales job. This reduction in breadth is accomplished by limiting the fields for which any sales force within the company has responsibility. When the field for which a particular sales force is responsible is limited, the amount of information which it must keep abreast of is also limited. As the sales force becomes more and more specialized to particular product lines and market segments, the problem of combatting knowledge obsolescence becomes progressively smaller.[5]

In practice, specialization of the sales force may be along either market segments or the company's product lines. In larger companies both bases for sales-force segmentation may exist together.

> For example, in the duPont Company the elastomer chemicals department is based primarily on a separation of the market segment represented by users of elastomeric materials and their modifiers from the rest of the world. The department is responsible for marketing anything in the duPont product line that the users of elastomeric materials and their modifiers might need.
>
> On the other hand, the plastics department is based on a separation of the various lines of plastic materials made by duPont from its other product lines. The department is responsible for marketing any plastic material made by duPont to anyone who might want it.

Of course, further subdivision within the primary divisions of a company, along either product or market lines, is widely used and has the effect of further reducing the breadth of the sales job and therefore the magnitude of the knowledge obsolescence problem in the sales force.

As transportation becomes easier and quicker, it seems probable that the trend toward the use of smaller, more highly specialized sales forces will continue.

A refinement of this policy of sales force specialization is used by some firms to avoid one of the major symptoms of knowledge obsolescence in the sales force—that of lack of familiarity with the newer product lines. This is to establish a new sales force for each new product line.

The introduction of a new product line implies a broadening of the sales job. To perform its job well, it is necessary that the sales force broaden its fund of technical knowledge to include the new product line. Moreover, if the sales force is expected to introduce a new product to the marketplace, the magnitude of the problem is greater than if it is only expected to service the new line after it has

---

[5] An extreme example of such specialization is that of a salesman for the Union Carbide Company, whose product line consisted of one grade of polyvinyl-choloride resin and whose market segment consisted of one wire coating plant of the Western Electric Company.

become established, since the depth of technical knowledge required to educate the market to the benefits and usefulness of the new line is greater than that required to sell the line after it is established and the market is familiar with it.

Some companies avoid the technical obsolescence problems associated with a new product introduction through the "task force" approach. A group is assigned to the new product with a charter to do whatever is necessary to bring it through development and into the market. The product introduction is handled by this group and the product's first salesmen are often the engineers and scientists who worked on its development. This procedure has the advantage that during the earliest stages in the product's life, when the sales job is primarily missionary in nature and when the ability to provide the prospective customers with prompt, accurate and complete technical information is of extreme importance, the men in the field are as well qualified to provide this information as it is possible to be.

If the new product achieves market acceptance, new men may be brought in and trained to staff a new sales force for the product, or, alternatively, the new product may be assigned to an existing sales force with the task group conducting training sessions to bring this force to the level of technical competence necessary to perform the less demanding duties associated with servicing an already established product. The former method is used primarily when the new product is a substantial departure from the established lines which the company is selling. The latter method is used primarily when the new product represents only a slight departure from one of the company's established product lines.

A recent study of the chemical industry showed that, in general, the use of special groups to handle or assist in handling the introduction of new products is greater among firms where the technical aspect of the sales job is more important than among sales organizations in which the technical aspect is less important.[6] It is reasonable to assume that this tendency also holds true for other technologically oriented industries.

REDUCTION OF DEPTH THROUGH LIMITED JOB SCOPE

The problem of knowledge obsolescence can also be reduced by defining the sales job in such a manner that the field sales force is required to do little or nothing that requires a substantial degree of technical competence. Firms employing this method characteristically assign primary responsibility for communication with customers' personnel dealing with technical matters to some group of technical

[6] Fuss, *Combatting Technical Obsolescence in the Industrial Sales Force,* p. 146.

specialists such as product managers or the staffs of technical services laboratories.

> In a mail survey of chemical manufacturers, 25 of 59 respondents placed primary responsibility for communicating with customers' technical personnel with a staff of technical specialists, one placed it with R & D personnel and 33 left this responsibility with the field sales force.

Where the primary responsibility for technical communication lies with such a group, the role of the salesman is largely that of "people broker"—to put the customer's people into contact with the proper people in the salesman's organization. In this situation, the technical competence needed is limited to sufficient familiarity with the area to be able to determine the proper individuals to bring together.

This type of organizational structure has an additional advantage from the point of view of combating knowledge obsolescence in that the members of the technical support group that have responsibility for the technical aspects of the sales job are normally located in some central laboratory, research, or engineering facility. As a result, they can easily take part in the programs conducted to prevent technical obsolescence in the company's scientific and engineering staff without having to be brought in from the field.

An organization of this type appears suitable in three kinds of situations. One is in the case of mature products. Here the customer is generally well informed about the products, their handling, and their uses in his operations. The need for technical aid is sporadic and limited. As price and order filling services are likely to be the important factors in sales, there is little that a technical salesman can do to influence decisions which a nontechnical man could not accomplish. The infrequent technical matters can readily be referred to the technical support group.

A second case in which a division of responsibility may be called for is the situation in which the need to fully utilize scarce technical manpower resources overrides the desirability of placing responsibility for communication in a single channel. This situation is likely to exist for highly innovative developments at the time major innovations are introduced and before a sufficient staff of technically able people will have been developed. However, the continued use of separate staffs beyond the innovative phase raises problems of divided responsibility in dealing with customers. Any firm that regards communicative interaction as the central aspect of the salesman's job should have reservations about permanent organizational arrangements which separate technical communications responsibility from other sales communication responsibilities.

A third type of situation is sometimes found in the case of

complex designed-to-order equipment and the contracting of research and development work. In many such cases a wide variety of different types of technical expertise may be needed for assisting the prospective customer in defining his needs and for the selling firm to develop proposals to meet them. No one sales or technical person or group will possess all of the needed expertise. In this situation, the salesman must serve as a people broker. A substantial breadth, though not necessarily depth, of technical know-how is likely to be needed even by the salesman, however, because the task of identifying the individuals in both organizations who should be brought together is likely to involve considerable understanding of the technical questions involved, but not necessarily of the answers to them.

A potential weakness of this type of organizational arrangement is that dual channels of communication may develop with the customer going directly to the technical information source. With two separate channels of communication available, the customer has to choose which channel to use for particular information. In areas where technical questions are infrequent, separating responsibility for technical communication from other communication responsibilities probably causes few problems. But as the technical aspects of the selling job become more important and the division between what is handled by the field sales force and what is handled by the technical staff becomes less well defined, the problems that the customer encounters arise more frequently. The role of the salesman as problem identifier, problem interpreter, and problem solver for the customer and for his own firm, are increasingly compromised, and as a result he may fail to provide a good channel of communication for either the customer or the firm that employs him.

In summary, one method that some companies appear to use to reduce the magnitude of the problem of knowledge obsolescence in their sales forces is to reduce the depth of the sales job by defining out of it most of its technical responsibility.

Changes in Duties Over Time

An unusual method of reducing the problem of technical obsolescence in the sales force is used by one department of a large diversified chemical company. The department sells in a market where the provision of technical information and assistance to the customers is a major part of the total sales job.

This department hires only recent college graduates having technical degrees. After a short training program to familiarize him somewhat with the technology of the department's products and the technology of its customers, each man is assigned to a field office. Here he gradually takes on an increasing amount of responsibility for technical communications to customers. During the early portion of this field assignment the salesman is given responsibility for communications of relatively minor importance and expected to devote most of his effort to becoming more expert in the technical aspects of the job. To this end, he makes frequent trips to the company's laboratories and makes trips to customers' plants with more experienced men, in addition to the study of written material.

As a new man becomes more expert in the technical aspects of the department's sales job, the proportion of his effort devoted to study decreases and the proportion devoted to the provision of technical assistance to customers increases. After two to three years of this on-the-job training the new man reaches the status of an expert on the technical aspects of the sales job, and for the next three to four years he devotes the bulk of his efforts to serving as a technical expert in support of the salesmen having account responsibility. During this period his responsibilities lie almost 100 percent in the technical area.

Somewhere between 7 and 10 years after joining the department, the salesman is brought back to the company's headquarters to spend two or three years as a product manager. During this period his technical responsibilities decrease sharply while his account responsibilities increase sharply.

After serving as a product manager, the man is sent back to the field, this time with substantial account responsibility. He may still devote a significant portion of his effort to the technical aspects of the sales job, but this proportion decreases over time until, when he has been with the department 20 years or more (by this time he is probably a regional manager but still with account responsibility), he is devoting almost all his effort to the nontechnical aspects of the job and depending on the younger man just starting through the process for the needed technical expertise. (See Figure 8-2 for a graphical representation of this process in terms of the individual's total effort.)

While not designed for that purpose, this career progression plan has the effect of avoiding much of the potential problem of technical obsolescence by the simple expedient of changing the individual's job description over time in such a manner that the changes in the importance of the technical aspects of his job closely parallel his competence to deal with them.

In effect, use of this system implies a recognition of the fact that, unless something is done to prevent it, a man's technical competence declines over the years. The system, therefore, chooses to change the man's job to compensate for the changes in his technical competence in preference to attempting to maintain that technical competence.

In some respects this program resembles the organizational arrangement in which the field sales force is backed up by a staff of technical specialists who have the primary responsibility for communicating with customers' technical personnel on technical matters.

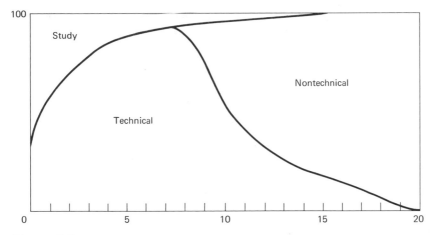

Figure 8-2

ALLOCATION OF DUTIES OVER 20-YEAR CAREER (PERCENT OF TOTAL EFFORT)

SOURCE: Diversified chemical company

However, here the technical specialists are assigned to field offices rather than to some central facility; they are considered to be part of the field sales force and are eventually expected to take on account responsibility. In most other organizations the technical support group is considered separate from the field sales force and its members are not usually expected to become field salesmen.

This system appears to have some substantial advantages in terms of reducing the problem of technical obsolescence in the industrial sales force. However, the circumstances under which it can be used seem to be rather severely limited.

In particular, this system seems to require a well-defined market in which the amount of effort needed is exceptionally constant over the years. If the amount of effort were to vary over a wide range, or if the relationship among the areas (technical and nontechnical) in which effort must be expended were to change substantially, it would probably become necessary to modify the make-up of the sales force and thus destroy the symmetry of experience that is necessary for the regular progression through various changes in job description that is essential if the system is to function smoothly.

In addition, the system presumes that the same individual can perform effectively in both technical and nontechnical (management) work.

Another seeming requirement for the smooth operation of this system is stability of the personnel in the sales force. If a situation should develop in which there was a large change in the proportion of the sales force in any particular experience level segment (for example, as a result of unexpected turnover) serious problems could result because of either a lack of personnel in one experience group which would lead to an insufficient number of men to handle a particular job description, or an over-abundance of men in a particular experience group which would eventually lead to difficulty when the group reaches a level of experience at which there are considerably fewer jobs than there are men ready to fill them.

Systematic changing of duties as men grow older seems to provide a way to reduce the problems of man obsolescence where the size of the sales force and its duty mix are stable and predictable over long periods. Unfortunately, few sales forces meet these conditions.

Turnover of Sales Personnel

A major factor which has kept the knowledge-obsolescence problem within bounds in recent years has been the relatively short tenure of many salesmen, especially in technical fields. In part this is the result of sales jobs being used as a training ground for other positions in the firm's organization; in part it is the result of the rapid growth of many sales forces with the bulk of the additional manpower requirements met with younger, less experienced men. In part, too, the short average tenure of many sales forces, particularly in industrial selling, reflects the difficulty of the work and other factors which produce personnel turnover. The overall effect of these personnel changes is that in many organizations a large proportion of the salesmen have not been in their positions long enough for serious obsolescence problems to develop.[7]

Thus, inexperience of sales-force personnel, despite its many disadvantages on other grounds, does serve to limit the obsolescence problem in the short run.

The factors considered in this section—organizational forms which limit the breadth and/or depth of the salesman's job, career planning which modifies the duties of individuals over the career cycle to compensate for changes in their competence, and the impact

---

[7] Fuss' study of chemical sales forces, for example, found that only one-third of the salesmen employed by 61 chemical organizations has as much as ten years field sales experience. The obsolescence problem seems concentrated in this group, although it is not limited to it. There appears to be a definite correlation between a manager's perception of an obsolescence problem and the experience level of his men. The median percentage of sales-force personnel having more than ten years experience was 50 percent for the 13 sales managers who considered technical obsolescence of their men to be a problem. In contrast, the median was only 33 percent for the 34 managers who perceived technical obsolescence as only a minor problem and only 10 percent for the 12 managers who considered it no problem at all. Fuss, pp. 40–43.

of the short tenure of most salesmen—all serve to reduce the magnitude of the obsolescence problem of a firm and to moderate its seriousness. They do not, however, deal at all with the central problem of preventing or overcoming obsolescence so that a company may enjoy the benefits of an experienced sales force and unified interactive communications with customer organizations without suffering the consequences of obsolescence. To accomplish this, the firm must move actively to maintain and increase the competence of its people.

METHODS TO COMBAT KNOWLEDGE OBSOLESCENCE

Much of what has been said about the formulation of relevant goals for initial training applies as well to programs to maintain the competence of men who have been in the field for some time. Except for the more obvious needs for an updating of technical knowledge, job analyses are needed to determine what kinds of knowledge are most pertinent to the salesman's changing job. Difficulty and attitude analyses are useful to isolate problem areas. Programs must be designed with understanding of the learning process. Motivation must be secured. Learning techniques must be selected which afford the most effective way for the salesmen to acquire the new knowledge and improved skills sought and to promote his motivation to do so.

Motivation problems can easily arise with older, experienced salesmen, especially if the training group ignores or does not fully grasp the salesman's perception of himself and his job. Experienced men will resent and, in fact, resist any type of approach which implies that they are beginners or have been overlooking fundamentals which are necessary in the sales task. Moreover, their experience in the field is likely to have given each student his own sense of what is, and what is not, relevant to his job.

These potential difficulties can become aids to motivation if the training program can be presented in a format and with content which strikes the salesmen as relevant. Courses and teaching materials centering on problem solving are often effective. Peer-group participation and the interchange of ideas is likely to be more meaningful in such a problem-solving context and may be more effective in retraining than in the initial training of recruits who are likely to have a somewhat limited experience with real problems in the field. Short courses may be more effective than longer schooling. The communication of sales fundamentals and the development of skills and habits may need to be kept in the background. Training goals in these latter areas may need to be sought as by-products of trainee problem-solving activity.

A wide variety of instructional methods are employed, usually in combination, to achieve retraining objectives and maintain sales-force competence. These include sales meetings; literature, manuals and other issue materials; refresher courses offered by company or outside personnel; and sending the salesmen to outside courses and seminars. Their effectiveness rests on a careful identification of objectives and the formulation and execution of plans to achieve them.

Sales Meetings

Sales meetings are widely used. Commonly, the major portion of such meetings deals with administrative and supervisory matters, but some firms devote an important part of such meetings to new product and market information. The level of such presentation is often to "introduce and promote;" it frequently focuses on the salesman's understanding of promotable features, rather than adding to his basic technical knowledge. Some companies, however, arrange for a portion of each sales meeting to be devoted to some technical subject, often bringing in technical personnel for this purpose.

> A division of a large oil company holds day-long sales meetings every month at the regional level. The bulk of each meeting is devoted to a special topic—usually, but not always, a technical one—although each meeting does include presentation of information on the supply situation, markets, competitive activity, and similar matters of immediate interest to the salesmen.

> A division of a large chemical company holds quarterly sales meetings. Primary emphasis is on technical information on the company's products, although nontechnical topics may be selected if the regional sales manager believes that such presentations are more needed by the sales force under his direction at a particular time.

At most sales meetings, if technical information is presented at all, it is almost always in the form of information on company products.

Sales meetings may be an excellent vehicle to transmit to the salesmen the results of operations, especially the successful application of new methods or the solution of new customer problems having more than unique interest. They are also a useful means of passing on new or modified ideas about customer industries and customer behavior. The ability to make such meetings interactive and to reach large numbers of salesmen simultaneously may make group meetings more suitable than either issued materials or individual coaching for the communication of new nontechnical concepts and knowledge.

Discussions within peer groups are often useful learning experiences for all participants in such areas as customer problem solving and dealing with problems of selling in the field. Such "shop talk" is likely to enjoy high credibility and high relevance and thus may provide a useful form of learning experience. Indeed, at large sales meetings, conferences, and conventions, experienced salesmen may learn as much or more from such informal peer-group activity as from the formal program. Proper timing and physical arrangements can encourage such interchanges.[8]

Issued Materials

Sales letters, bulletins, and other printed material are commonly distributed to salesmen—perhaps directed *at* salesmen would be more appropriate terminology. Information to add to salesmen's knowledge of company products may be presented in the form of technical bulletins, sales newsletters, reprints of periodical articles, or tear sheets of company advertisements. In order to reduce the flood of papers issued to salesmen, newsletter-type materials may be put out in cartridge tape form to which the salesman listens at his convenience.[9] In a few companies, material transmission activity has been extended to programmed instruction courses and videotaped leotures.

While such distributed materials may be useful in advising the salesman of successful new applications and providing a file of new product information, their value in updating the man's own competence would seem to be quite limited. Unless a piece of literature happens to reach a salesman at the particular moment that the information it contains has special relevance, he is unlikely to be motivated to exert much effort to master the contents. Its main function is, consequently, to update the salesman's reference files rather than the man himself.

The development of programmed instruction courses and videotaped materials affords the opportunity to extend not only the form of issued materials but their role in maintaining salesman competence. The techniques exist for the dissemination of technical study materials which, given proper motivation, salesmen could use to arrest the decay of their competence. To date, such usage has been extremely limited, if it exists at all. In part this may reflect the lack of suitable material, most standard training films being largely concerned with techniques and interpersonal matters rather than with

---

[8] The guidelines for the conduct of sales meetings used by one company with an effective training department are shown in the appendix to this chapter.

[9] "Spreading the Message with Tape," *Business Week,* July 9, 1966, p. 87 and "Taped Newsletters Sound Off," *Business Week,* July 26, 1969, p. 58.

technical advance in the fields.[10] A more serious problem is the difficulty of obtaining motivation for this, or any, kind of home study for which the salesman is unlikely to perceive a short-term payoff.

Individual Feedback Reports

The maintenance of a salesman's competence requires that he know the outcome of his activities and that he be kept current on developments in his territory. Because such information pertains directly to the individual man, it is best provided by an internal communication system which feeds back to the salesman relevant information obtained from his reports and, after appropriate summarization and analysis, information from other territories which has relevance for him. This may be accomplished through routine reporting-to-the-salesman forms and probably should not be held over for formal meetings. The contents of individualized reports *for the salesmen* (not *directed at* the salesman) if stringently edited are likely to enjoy high relevance.

Joint Calls with Technical Personnel

Joint calls with technical personnel provide some updating of the salesman, although their primary purpose usually is to strengthen the technical presentation to the customer. Where the salesman has primary responsibility for communicating with customer technical personnel and can call in technical aid from his own company, it is to be expected that the salesman will be motivated to grasp what he can through observation and conversation with the technical personnel. On the other hand, in the situation in which technical personnel have the communication responsibility—for example, where they go into the field in connection with the introduction of new products—the expectation that the salesman will be motivated to pick up enough information through these means to properly service the customer in the future seems more questionable. In any case, such updating as occurs is likely to be quite specific to the problem or product at hand and does little to provide a general updating of the salesman's technical competence.

Individual Salesman-Supervisor Interaction

Coaching on the job is useful in maintaining the competence of experienced salesmen as well as in training recruits. If furnished in a problem-solving rather than a teacher-student context, it enables

[10] This lack may, in turn, reflect the general lack of the use of modern visual aid and related techniques in universities which are the ultimate source of much of the new knowledge.

the supervisor to appraise the skills and work habits of each of his men and to attempt to improve them through coaching.

Salesmen's discussions with their supervisors in the supervisor's office can also perform a training function if undertaken in such a context.

Refresher Courses

Regular refresher courses seek to deal specifically with the problem of knowledge obsolescence. To minimize the interruption of field operations such courses are frequently a week or less. Such courses, usually conducted by company personnel, are becoming increasingly popular, especially in larger companies and in companies where the technical aspects of the salesman's responsibility are significant. Fuss found, for example, that four out of five chemical marketing organizations had some sort of in-house technical refresher activity. Unfortunately, such programs tend to be inward-looking and quite limited in scope and sophistication. Too often, they consist of presentations by technical personnel from the product development laboratories or engineering departments devoted to subjects such as "What the salesman needs to know about Product X."

> One chemical company proposes to use the refresher course technique in combination with its regular practice of sending printed materials to salesmen as new products are introduced. Each salesman will be issued a manual. At intervals of perhaps three or four years the salesman will attend a refresher program which is built largely around the manual changes which have occurred since his original training or last refresher. Thus the program at any time will be built around developments which have occurred since the last training period and not confined merely to hot items of immediate interest. The course will thus serve as a review of new information which has been sent to the salesman and promote its integration into his overall knowledge.

For high technology firms, more frequent interaction between salesmen and inside technical personnel may be required.

> Hewlett-Packard salesmen attend a week-long seminar at least once a year at one of the company's 12 plants. In addition, they visit each of the other plants at least once each year. To make updating an almost continuous activity, roving instructors visit each territory once a month for one-day refresher courses.[11]

Whereas a continuing series of regular refresher courses may be adequate to deal with evolutionary changes, special event courses

[11] *How They Sell* (New York: Dow Jones & Company, Inc., 1965). Reprinted in James H. Bearden, *Personal Selling: Behavioral Science Readings and Cases* (New York: John Wiley & Sons, Inc., 1967), pp. 34–35.

may be required on the occasion of a revolutionary event such as the entry into a new market, the introduction of a radically different product line, merger of sales forces as part of a reorganization of the sales force, or as a result of corporate merger or acquisition. Such courses are aimed at removing the knowledge deficiencies of some or all of the personnel and bringing them at least to a minimum level so they can operate effectively in the new situation.

Firms with large sales forces generally can afford an in-house capability to offer both regular refresher and such special programs as may be needed. It is not uncommon, however, for such firms to seek to enrich their programs through the use of consultants to provide a variety of insights and perspectives. Firms with smaller sales organizations may find the periodic use of consultants more effective and less costly than maintaining an in-house staff.

Refresher programs, especially those conducted by in-house personnel, tend to concentrate on the company's offerings. Unfortunately, they rarely, if ever, are directed at improving the salesman's grasp of his customer's problems or the changes that are taking place or are in prospect for customer markets.

Refresher courses can, however, be participative and problem oriented.

> A large industrial firm sends salesmen in small groups to its application engineering facility for a one-week refresher program. A one-to-one student-teacher ratio is maintained with heavy emphasis on participation. The program is problem oriented and covers such topics as how to deal with certain kinds of problems and where certain products should be employed. During one or more evenings, the students meet in small groups in a motel room with young applications technicians. In these informal meetings salesmen ask many questions which they are reluctant to ask in formal classes or in the presence of seniors.

Outside Seminars and University Courses

Outside seminars and university courses present an opportunity to expose the salesmen to current developments outside of their own company and to the thrust of research which may be affecting their customer groups. Unfortunately, the immediate relevance of such programs is not always evident to either salesmen or management. Their use, thus far, has been extremely limited.

Companies having tuition aid programs for the purpose of encouraging their employees to further their education usually extend these benefits to sales-force personnel. However, participation in these programs by sales-force personnel is frequently quite small. Lack of participation in such programs on the part of sales-force personnel may be attributed in large part to the requirements of the sales job (for example, irregular hours, extensive travel) which make it difficult for salesmen to attend classes regularly.

NURTURING OF PROFFESSIONAL SKILLS

Not all of the problems of maintaining the competence of a sales force fall in the area of new knowledge. Sales techniques and work habits are also subject to decay and to a failure to make full use of new knowledge as to the best means to develop relationships and deal with problems. Even more important, true professional growth requires that the salesman improve his own diagnostic capability not only in understanding his customers' behavior and their problems but in his understanding of himself and his perception and utilization of data. Even in nontechnical fields, the able salesman must continually improve his ability to make meaningful data-to-information and information-to-intelligence transformations both for his own use and in the discharge of his intelligence responsibilities to his firm.[12]

Some of the techniques which have been mentioned above can be employed to improve work habits and to develop motivation within the sales force. Sales meetings may be devoted to demonstration of factors which comprise good work habits such as recommended call or demonstration procedures and reporting systems. Inspirational messages which add to the salesman's confidence and self-esteem may serve to soften the effect of the hard knocks encountered on the road. Courses in professional selling skills may help the salesman to improve his communicative performance.

Group discussions may be particularly effective in aiding experienced salesmen to solve problems and develop their own problem-solving skills. Group sessions in which different salesmen detail how they deal with a problem which is common to many men are often effective, at least in part because of their peer-group origin which makes the related experience appear more relevant.

Groups may also be effective in developing solutions to supervisory, operational, or performance problems. For example, a sales manager confronted with a performance problem common to many men is likely to find that a lecture to them about the problem and his recommendations for solution will be less effective than presenting the evidence of the problem to the assembled group and letting the group develop its own diagnosis and prescription.[13]

Coaching on the job may be an important tool in the improve-

---

[12] See Chapter 9.

[13] For an example of an experiment in group decision making directed towards behavior of members of the group, see Jacob Levine and John Butler "Lecture vs. Group Decision in Changing Behavior," *Journal of Applied Psychology,* XXXVI (1952), pp. 29–33.

ment of work habits, especially in dealing with the newer and younger men. Interpersonal relationships between the sales supervisor and his men play a major role in determining their receptiveness to suggestions for improvement.

EVALUATION OF COMPETENCE MAINTENANCE ACTIVITIES

Measures to maintain salesman competence are costly. Their functioning may often be critical to the organization's survival. Unfortunately, their effects are often taken on faith. Although the problems of measuring effects are difficult, the various means suggested in the previous chapter for measuring and appraising the results of initial training are fully applicable to activities to maintain the competence of the sales force.

SUMMARY

The problem of maintaining the competence of a sales force is a continuing and growing one. The rapid pace of change throughout the economy results in a substantial decay rate of the salesman's knowledge of his products, of the processes and problems of his customer group, and of the most effective ways to handle customer relationships. This decay is not confined to salesman selling so-called technologically advanced products but touches a wide variety of sales situations as changes permeate through the economy and affect the operating methods, products used, and competitive positions of firms and industries.

When new knowledge was developed slowly and its transformation into industrial practice was sluggish, knowledge obsolescence in the sales force could be met through normal attrition. Today the half-life of a salesman's knowledge is much shorter—possibly as little as a half-dozen years in some technologically oriented industries. As a result, normal turnover of older men and their replacement by up-to-date but inexperienced young men is of little help.

In a production-oriented world, deficiencies in the salesman could be overcome by defining their responsibility narrowly and assigning the technical responsiblities of the selling job to home office product specialists. With a growing market orientation and recognition of the salesman as problem discoverer and resolver for his clients, this solution is becoming increasingly more unrealistic. Moreover, the growing need to rely on the market as a source of ideas for development requires that the salesman, and not merely a person to whom he can refer, have the capability to recognize significant events and opportunities in the customer's situation. Lacking such capability he cannot effectively perform the all-important intelligence function.

Sales management must meet the problem of man obsolescence head-on. Market orientation dictates that the salesman assume increasing responsibility for technical communication and offers less opportunity to divide responsibility in such a manner that only home office technicians need to be qualified.

The techniques for offsetting man obsolescence are not far advanced. Sales meetings, issued materials, and refresher courses are used but the results are rarely measured so that their effects are largely unknown. An examination of the programs in one industry, chemicals, suggests that such programs are largely devoted to maintaining knowledge of the company's products and to providing some modest additions to the salesman's knowledge of sales techniques.

In a world which is becoming increasingly market oriented, such programs appear to fall far short of needs. The maintenance of high quality intercommunicative relationships requires that the salesman understand what is going on in the using industries as much as, and perhaps even more than, he understands what is happening in his own.

As the organizational factors which have thus far minimized the problem become less effective, managements will become more motivated to develop programs to offset obsolescence. Steps will need to be taken to insure that the salesman is motivated as well. For the salesman, self-improvement programs, whatever their long-term benefits, rarely promise short-term results commensurate with the time and effort which must be devoted to them. Thus management must insure that salesmen are motivated to maintain their competence, especially in areas beyond company product knowledge and matters of relevance to their current daily work.

Much bolder, broader programs appear to be called for if sales-force competence, especially in industrial sales work, is to be matched with the need for it. Programs to forestall and overcome man obsolescence should give important consideration to developments *outside the firm* which are having and will have impact on present and prospective customer groups. Both industrial and consumer goods managements which continue to look primarily inward in the future well may find their sales forces poorly prepared to compete in the customer problem-solving arena of the marketplace.

APPENDIX TO CHAPTER 8

THE CONDUCT OF SUCCESSFUL SALES MEETINGS[14]

I.   Advance preparation
    A.   Decide on basic objective
        1.   What do you want the salesmen to *know* as a result of this sales meeting that they wouldn't know otherwise?

[14] Prepared by James M. Alexander.

   2.   What do you want them to *believe* as a result of this
        meeting that they might not believe otherwise?
   3.   What do you want them to *do* as a result of this meeting?

B.   Prepare a detailed plan
   1.   Adequate Pre-planning is a *Must*
   2.   Select Topics in Keeping with Basic Objective
   3.   Outline Your Plan in Terms of the Salesmen

      a.   How can I clearly show the salesmen why it is to
           their advantage to do what I suggest?
      b.   In specific terms, why is the meeting important to
           them?
      c.   What will the sales meeting do for them?

C.   How long a meeting?
   1.   Impossible to generalize in terms of time-length
   2.   Meeting must be long enough for objective to be reached

D.   Best time for meeting?
   1.   Internal and uncontrollable factors—customer traffic,
        and so on—may prove a limiting factor
   2.   Most acceptable time: early morning, early part of week

E.   Maintain a positive tone
   1.   In meetings, salesmen should be encouraged rather than
        reprimanded
   2.   Emphasize successes of today and plans for tomorrow,
        not yesterday's failures

II.   Content And Methods

A.   Content
   1.   Policies and procedures

      a.   At least part of one sales meeting per year for review
      b.   Special meetings for major changes

   2.   Selling fundamentals—"how to sell"—analysis of "the
        sale"

      a.   *The Pre-Approach*—obtaining as much information
           about the individual to be sold, prior and during the
           call, as is pertinent
      b.   *The Approach*—begins with the initial contact with
           the prospect and terminates when the salesman be-
           gins his product presentation. It includes dealing
           with receptionists, various assistants, and so on,
           and the opening remarks made by the salesman to
           the prospect

    c.   *The Presentation*—that portion of the sales interview in which the salesman relates the features of the proposition to the buying motives of the prospect *and* supports the verbal claims with tangible evidence

    d.   *Objections*—any reason why a prospect refuses to buy

    e.   *The Close*—any direct attempt on the part of the salesman to consummate the sale

3.   Product knowledge

    a.   Teach product knowledge from the customer's viewpoint—"What's in it for me?"

    b.   Salesmen should always *sell the benefits.* A *benefit* is a tangible gain which the customer derives from using the product. Included as benefits are all the advantages that the product features make possible for the customer.

4.   Knowledge of work habits and attitudes

    a.   Proper planning—yearly sales goals, weekly and daily planning, and individual call planning

    b.   Proper use of time—increasing actual selling time, territorial coverage

    c.   Enthusiasm and morale help your salesmen re-sell themselves on your company, your products, and their role as truly professional salesmen

B.   Methods—how to teach

   1.   The Lecture

    a.   Must be adequately planned—competent speaker needed

    b.   Use blackboard, flannel-board, visual sheets and pass-out summary of key points.

   2.   The demonstration—performance

    a.   Method best adapted to teaching manual skills involved in selling

    b.   Make certain that each salesman practices the process or technique involved

   3.   The group discussion

    a.   Essential feature is the exchange of experience among the salesmen

    b.   A method for promoting thinking rather than imitation

        4.   Role playing

           a.   The best method to simulate real-life sales situations

           b.   Salesmen get actual selling practice, followed by analysis and discussion of the results

III.   Evaluating results

    A.   Obtain opinions from salesmen and management

        1.   Advantage—forces a review of meeting content

        2.   Disadvantage—biased opinions in your favor

    B.   Utilize Reports

    C.   Observe Performance of Salesmen

        1.   Examine sales and other records for evidence of use of information

        2.   Use field sales supervision as "follow-through"

9 Inward Information Flow: the sales force as an intelligence system

An important function of the sales force in nearly all marketing organizations is the collection, initial evaluation, and transmittal of information about developments in the environment which affect the company's opportunities and performance. Where there is no formal marketing research or marketing intelligence department, the collection of intelligence may fall entirely on the salesman. Even in firms having formal intelligence systems, a major portion of the responsibility for the gathering of many types of information and its transformation into intelligence is likely to fall to the salesman as the individual in the field in the best position to do this.

THE INTELLIGENCE PROCESS

Marketing intelligence is information which is selected, evaluated, interpreted, expressed and disseminated in such a way that its application to a marketing problem, present or potential, is clear.[1]

[1] Edward L. Brink, *Marketing Intelligence and Intelligent Marketing* (forthcoming).

Figure 9-1 depicts the marketing intelligence process. In examining Figure 9-1, the reader should note that an intelligence system does not just scoop up all kinds of data for its own sake. Data are collected which will provide information and, eventually, intelligence, which is relevant to decisions which will need to be made. An important portion of the intelligence process is the determination of the information which should be sought.

Data gathering represents but a small portion of the total intelligence process. It has been noted earlier (Chapter 2) that raw data become information only when they have relevance to the recipient and that data which lack such relevance, even if perceived, are likely to be discarded by the receiver rather than being drawn into his "information bank."

Information, in turn, is transformed into intelligence through the process of evaluation which considers both the credibility of the source and the believability of the information itself.

The recipient of information finds it necessary to *evaluate the source* as to its reliability (for example, is the reporter a good observer?), integrity (for example, has the source selected examples out of context in order to "prove his point?"), and judgment (for example, does the source exercise good judgment in his screening decisions as to what information is significant for transmittal?). The sum of such evaluations constitutes the *credibility* of the source, as seen by the receiver of the information.

Information even from credible sources may have low *believability*. The data themselves may be unconvincing because they are based on too few observations (for example, indictment of a product on the basis of a single report by one customer) or are inconsistent with other data or with supportable hypotheses about relationships. Thus the recipient may accept the legitimacy of the evidence placed before him by the source but still assign a low believability to its substance.[2]

SALES MANAGEMENT PROBLEMS IN DEVELOPING AN EFFECTIVE SALES-FORCE INTELLIGENCE SYSTEM

The development and maintenance of the sales force as an effective system for the provision of market intelligence requires

[2] In military intelligence work, letter grades are used to denote the evaluator's appraisal of both the credibility of the source and the believability of the information. The use of such a grading system requires the prior definition of the criteria to be used for the assignment of each grade. Such a system well might be developed for marketing intelligence.

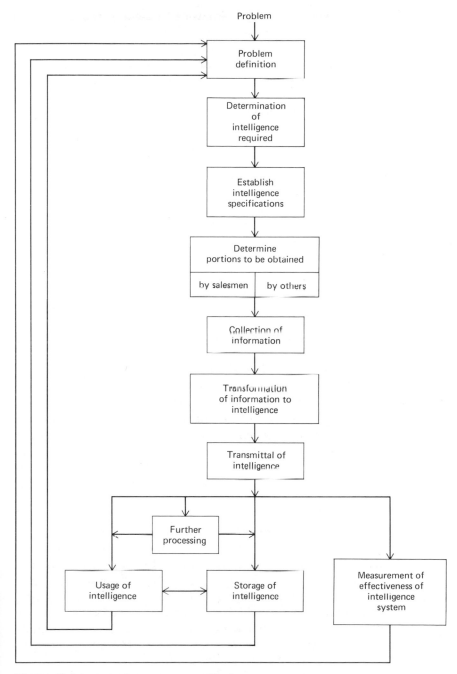

Figure 9-1
A MODEL OF THE INTELLIGENCE PROCESS

the manager to develop workable answers to several types of questions:

What do we need to know about the environment? about specific customer problems? about response functions? about customer's people and organizations?

Which parts of the required intelligence should be obtained by the salesmen?

How can salesmen learn to perceive which data contain information?

How can salesmen's capabilities in interpreting and filtering information be developed?

How should information and intelligence be recorded, transmitted and stored?

How can decision centers best obtain intelligence once it is in the system?

How can the performance of the intelligence system be evaluated so that needs for modifications can be detected? How can modifications be developed and made effective?

This chapter will examine these questions.

ESTABLISHING THE INTELLIGENCE SPECIFICATION

The intelligence specification is primarily, although not solely, a user concern. The concepts which apply to the determination of the desirable attributes of a product in the process of being designed apply to specifications of intelligence needs as well. First, the nature of the problem to be resolved through the use of the product (in this case, the intelligence) must be identified. A sufficiently clear understanding of the problem must be secured to enable the designer (whether of a product or of an intelligence system) to determine the attributes which will offer a better solution to the problem. From the ideal set of attributes thus formulated, the designer then introduces questions of feasibility, including cost and the cost/value relationships which alternative solutions might afford. In short, a clear understanding of the use to which the intelligence is to be put is the *sine qua non* of a sound specification. Such an understanding is not provided merely by lists of things which it would be nice to know or which would be helpful in a particular decision situation. Rather, it entails specifying in the greatest feasible detail the information needed in terms of the problem to which it will be applied.

For example, it is quite inadequate to specify that the system should provide intelligence "about competition" or "about competitive activities" or "whether a competitor's new product is selling."

What the marketing decision maker needs to know if he is to evaluate alternative responses properly is more likely to take the form of answers to such questions as "In what applications have customers switched from our product Z to competitor's product Y?" "What attributes of Y, or of the service package accompanying it, led customers to switch?" "What attributes not provided by the competitive products would represent added value to this market segment?" "How much of the attribute is needed to be meaningful?" "How large a market would a product tailored in this way attract?"

Similarly, it is insufficient merely to specify that the intelligence system should keep the firm's executives advised on changes in customers' problems. The decision maker is more likely to require well-digested intelligence on:

1. changes in the attitudes and perspectives of personnel in positions of influence in the using industries;
2. changes in the problems of using industries because of technological changes or changes in their own markets;
3. changes in the ways problems are being recognized by different functionaries in the using industries;
4. probable consequences of such changes in problems and attitude towards them on the operations and purchasing practices of customer industries;
5. probable responses of other suppliers and prospective suppliers to these developments.

In short, the development of a plan for gathering intelligence about the market starts with a detailed specification of the intelligence which is to be sought.

The intelligence specification must, of course, weigh the value of the information against the cost of obtaining it. Such costs include not only the explicit out-of-pocket costs of obtaining data, extracting information from it, and transforming the information into intelligence, but also the opportunity costs which occur because the securing of some information diverts resources from securing other information or devoting time to other activities, for example, sales.

The specific needs of a particular decision or operating activity will vary with its responsibilities and with the other information sources upon which it may draw. Nevertheless, some generalizations can be made about the kinds of intelligence which are generally useful to salesmen, analysts, and executives.

Intelligence about the Environment

The identification and evaluation of market opportunities is required by executives who are charged with planning and revising the elements of the marketing mix. In particular, central-office personnel need to know how the makeup of the customer and prospect group is changing and how company and competitive products are being received by the various market segments.

INTELLIGENCE ON CUSTOMER AND PROSPECT OPPORTUNITY

The salesman is the most likely source for such information as the location and relocation of prospects, changes in operating methods, practices or rates of customer firms, changes in attitudes and perspectives of personnel in using firms, and a host of other matters which can be detected more promptly by the field salesman than by more formal research methods. In particular, the salesman in the field can provide an early-warning system sensitive to new developments in customer industries. The increased pace of technological change and the increasingly rapid adaptation of customers and competitors to both technological and market developments places a premium on the ability not only to detect onrushing developments but to perceive their significance.

In terms of the intelligence process, salesmen often have time and source advantages over other means of obtaining this type of data. Perhaps more importantly they are often, despite the hazards of bias, in a superior information position to perform the initial evaluation activity. The questions of securing transmittal and the importance of first-level supervision grasping the significance of small events will be examined later in this chapter.

The salesman is often the preferred source for information of this type because he is in a better position than a more remote analyst to sense the substance of what he observes. In the marketplace facts rarely speak for themselves. While hard, factual information can tell management what happened in terms of some observed result, the really important concerns commonly lie in the area of *why?*—an area in which perception, understanding, and feel contribute importantly to data evaluation.

Much of the data about the environment which the salesman perceives is only of value to the salesman himself as an aid to planning and carrying out his own work. Important parts of it, however, are required by peer and higher echelons: those involved in other relationships with customers and prospects (from direct mail contacts to those who must meet customer product, delivery, and service needs); those charged with planning changes in various marketing mix elements; and those concerned with evaluating feedback from company and competitive actions.

Because of their superior information position in regard to customer intentions and plans, some companies ask salesmen to prepare sales forecasts for their territories. In the case of capital goods involving long periods of discussion and/or negotiation and where knowledge of specific customers' plans is the most significant evidence of probable purchase volume, the salesman may be in the best position to estimate customer takings within a forthcoming and not-too-remote time period. Salesmen working with utilities, for example, may have insight into the growth and expansion plans of each of their customers which may be superior to estimates which could be derived by the examination of "objective" factual data about the area in which the utility operates and the recent history of its purchases. The preparation of sales forecasts by salesmen is most often found in firms selling industrial products. However, some consumer goods companies whose salesmen maintain continuing relationships with wholesalers, chain-store buyers, and other trade accounts also place considerable faith in salesmen's forecasts for their territories. Rarely, if ever, are salesmen's forecasts used as the sole forecasting device; generally other forecasting techniques are used as well.

When salesmen are asked to make forecasts, it is important that the ground rules and assumptions about the business environment be specifically laid out so that the various salesmen can proceed from the same premises about the external factors. More importantly, failure to establish such ground rules *ex ante,* thus requiring each salesman to make his own assumptions about such matters as interest rates, business conditions, and strikes, impairs the capability of the sales manager or staff analyst to interpret the reported forecast or to adjust it for changed conditions simply because he does not know the premises on which the base forecasts were made. However, where premises, assumptions, and the methodology to be used are clearly set forth beforehand, the salesmen may provide good forecasts of the behavior of their own customers.

If sales forecasts are used as quotas or otherwise become the yardstick for evaluating the salesmen's performance, the forecasting system must be sterilized so that forecasts are not manipulated to further personal goals.[3]

The closeness of salesmen to market situations and their rapport with buyers suggest to some companies that salesmen would also be desirable field interviewers for more formal marketing research studies. It is sometimes argued that salesmen benefit from the information obtained through such experiences and that they are well motivated for research field work because they see its utility. However, the use of salesmen in such projects comingles the formal and

[3] The biases involved in estimating by subordinate managers and suggestions to deal with the problem are discussed in Donald H. Woods, "Improving Estimates that Involve Uncertainty," *Harvard Business Review,* July-August 1966, pp. 91–98.

essentially staff information-gathering activity of the home office with the line intelligence gathering system which is intended for quite another purpose. This is not to suggest that salesmen do not do "research" but rather that both their talents and their positions make it undesirable to involve them in more formal types of data gathering and hypothesis testing where different standards—including the desirability of neutrality and objectivity about the hypothesis—are appropriate. The use of salesmen as part of a formal marketing research data collection team is open to a number of additional objections:

1. such duties are an inappropriate use of salesmen's time;
2. questions designed for research purposes may adversely affect salesman-customer relations or the salesman may consider that a question might do so;
3. controls over field interviewers who consist of salesmen are likely to be more difficult to establish than with other types of interviewers;
4. some studies are appropriately undertaken with a specific need for independence from the line sales organization.

Nevertheless, where the research problem involves intensive study of users or their problems, the salesman may work with the researcher by providing contacts and assisting in assessing the credibility of respondents.

One company which views its salesmen and district managers as territory managers uses the salesman-researcher team to avoid any appearance of outside intervention in a territory. The management believes that in addition to the salesman's contribution in opening doors and aiding in credibility assessment, the procedure provides some desirable side effects in flattering the account ("A man from our home office would like to come out to talk with you next week") and building up the salesman's status with the account.

COMPETITIVE ACTIVITIES

The salesman is likely to be in a good position to observe such competitive activities as product innovations, price changes, and in-store promotional programs and new arrangements offered to dealers.

A parts manufacturer in a highly competitive industry requires its salesmen to report all competitive price moves to the sales contract manager. The same salesmen are required to report distributor deals, promotions, and all other developments on the distribution front to district managers.

The salesman is often in a better position than central office personnel in estimating the probable response of customers to such competitive moves and the prospective inroads of competitive products.

Intelligence about Specific Customer Problems

For his own purposes the salesman needs substantial information about customers' specific needs and problems in order to diagnose the needs correctly, to prescribe for the customer properly, and to draw effectively on the resources which his own service and technical departments can provide.

The need for specific knowledge about customers' problems is not confined to situations in which the firm is offering a made-to-order or tailored-to-order product. Even where the offering is limited to a standard line, the salesman needs substantial information about customers' needs and problems to be able to select the proper items to best meet the customers' needs.

The extent of detail about customer problems which is needed by other individuals in the salesman's firm for the performance of their duties varies. To the extent that the salesman serves chiefly as a contact man and problem definer for specialists in his company who prepare technical proposals, his major activity may revolve around the quality and completeness of the information which he provides to his inside associates. These associates rely almost entirely on the salesman for information about the customer's problem, the constraints imposed on possible solutions, and the competitive milieu in which company proposals will be received. In some cases, the information will be received in terms of performance or product specifications; in others, it will be framed in terms of the problems to be resolved and the constraints on the solution imposed by the customer and various environmentals, including probable actions of competitors.

More generally, the salesman and many echelons in the firm which employs him need competent insights into customer problems and, in particular, into the application of products, if they are to develop improved products or new ones which can offer meaningful benefits to users. An important problem for the sales-force communication system is to collect, interpret, and transmit relevant information for this purpose to levels at which it can best be utilized within the salesman's firm. This task is not always performed well. "Some homebuilders complain that manufacturers lack understanding of conditions in the field."[4]

---

[4] Reavis Cox, Charles S. Goodman and Franklin R. Root, *The Supply Support Requirements of Homebuilders* (Washington: The Producers' Council, Inc., 1962), p. 87.

A manufacturer of a precisely engineered air-contamination treating innovation traced the difficulties on many early installations to the failure of the installing contractor to follow instructions precisely. He solved the problem only when he recognized the need to adapt his product to the installers' methods of work. Initially, this meant confining sales to projects which could be undertaken by a few selected installers. For the longer term, it meant modifying his products, selecting his applications, and preparing installation instructions to make them "goofproof" in recognition of the imprecise installation procedures which were to be expected.

Intelligence about Response Functions

In the course of their daily work salesmen have the opportunity to accumulate a substantial amount of information about the response of customers and prospects to various sales approaches and to changes in such other marketing-mix elements as those involving products, prices, delivery, and maintenance services. Much of this information, after collection and processing, could be of great significance to executives with responsibilities for product development, pricing, distribution, and the level of service to customers. Sales management must determine which information should be brought into the firm's intelligence system.

In planning his own work, the salesman needs information on such details of customer responses as responses to different approaches, reactions to calls on different days of the week or times of the day, the attitude of customers towards free lunches, customers' responses to offered deals or to displays, and customers' responses to new items. Some presentations are effective; others fall flat. Certain days and times may be highly desirable for calling; other days or times will produce unfavorable responses. Some customers will be highly receptive to promotional deals; others have no interest in them.

Sales management is more interested in aggregated intelligence, such as the reception being accorded a new display or deal, customer responses to changes in mix elements, and customer reactions to activities directed beyond them—for example, an advertising campaign directed at end users who buy customers' products. Sales management may also be interested in more detailed matters such as the response of customers to changes in call frequencies or the response of a particular bellwether account to a price or product change.

Intelligence may also be sought on the response of competitors to changes in policies or practices of his (the salesman's) firm. For example, has a package change by the salesman's firm induced price shading, although not a published price reduction, on the part of some competitor?

Intelligence about Customers' People and Organizations

Much intelligence about customers' people and organizations is required for the daily work of the salesman. He needs information on the names of people in prospect and customer organizations who are likely influences on purchasing decisions and on their interests, both business and personal, as well as on the relationships operating within the customer firm. Of particular interest is the de facto information handling system of the buying firm. For example, despite what the organization chart says, to whom does the designer turn to get certain information about a product or problem? To whom does the buyer turn to get "the truth" about supplier performance? Upon whom does the shop manager rely to maintain stores at appropriate levels and perhaps to review possible item substitutions?

Intelligence of this type is primarily of interest to the salesman himself and may not go beyond his own written or unwritten data bank. However, some information in this category is of interest to those in the salesman's firm who design its "product." In the sale of services such as those provided by advertising agencies, insurance agencies, law firms, and other professional personnel, the personal preferences of executives may play an important role.

THE SALES FORCE AS AN INTELLIGENCE SOURCE

Given that certain intelligence should be obtained, to what extent should the sales force be the means of gathering the data? Of transforming it into intelligence? A trite rule often cited is that salesmen should not be used to gather input information which can be obtained by some other means at a lower cost. Provided adequate weight is given to the opportunity costs involved when salesmen are used for data-gathering work, such a rule can provide a useful guideline in those cases *where the only requirement is the collection of raw data.* In such situations, cost to collect is a meaningful criterion for choice of means. Canvassing an area or local source materials in each territory to establish route or prospect lists and tabulation of dealers' inventories are examples of pure data-collection tasks to which a cost criterion might in some circumstances apply.

The case for the use of salesmen as parts of the intelligence network does not in most cases, however, rest on their capability as economical collectors of raw data but rather on their ability to contribute to the data-to-information and information-to-intelligence transformations in a unique manner. The salesman as a field scout provides perceptive capability in the selection of data which have information value to his firm. He may be more able than an observer outside of the supplier-customer interactive process to perceive that certain data which he encounters contain information of possible value.

The salesman, for example, may be in a superior position to sense changes in customer attitudes towards the firm or its products, or to appraise the likely significance for his firm of changes in customer personnel, plans, or policies.

In addition to his role in the data-to-information transformation, the salesman is often a more timely data source on fast breaking or current events than a more formal periodic or intermittent data collection system. Moreover, sales-force-gathered information may provide a continuity on such matters as current business conditions in various customers' trades; demand, supply, and inventory situations in various markets; buyers' attitudes toward company and competitor policies; and competitors' activities which periodic surveys can provide only with difficulty, if at all. Thus the salesmen are employed as the scouting force on the firing line not so much because they are economical data collectors but because the information produced is likely to have attributes of quality which other sources cannot provide.

A by-product of active salesman participation in the intelligence process is its possible therapeutic value to the salesman. A truck manufacturer notes that giving salesmen increased intelligence responsibilities increased their sense of importance and perceived responsibility.[5]

Having determined that the salesmen should provide certain inputs to the company's intelligence system, the sales manager must now develop arrangements which will bring the required information into the system, properly evaluate it, and forward it in a timely manner to the proper points. To accomplish this, he must find ways to develop the salesman's abilities to seek out and perceive data which contain information of intelligence value, to develop the salesman's interpretive skills, and to provide procedures for the transmittal, storage, and retrieval of the intelligence in the system.

DEVELOPING THE SALESMAN AS AN INTELLIGENCE PROVIDER

While the foregoing discussion shows why salesmen are used as information providers, it leaves untreated the portion of the salesman's role in the intelligence system which may pose the greatest problems for the sales manager—the development of the salesman as an information gatherer and intelligence provider.

Not only does the salesman often have sole responsibility for determining what observations represent information (the data-to-information transformation), but he is also frequently charged, though often only implicitly, with the initial evaluation of data. Whereas the data-to-information transformation deals with the significance of what

[5] J. N. Bauman, "The Rebirth of the Salesman," *Dun's Review,* March 1968, p. 100.

he has observed, his evaluation activity is concerned with the believability of the data and the credibility of the particular source from which it came. In the performance of this activity, the salesman enjoys a particular advantage. Because he has had prior, and often frequent, contact with many data sources, he is in a position to evaluate their credibility as sources of information as well as to pass judgement on whether the data themselves are believable.

It does not follow, however, that the salesman by mere virtue of his job as salesman will do these jobs well. A problem of concern to the sales manager is the development of a high level of capability for both data-to-information and information-to-intelligence transformations by his salesmen.

The salesman is exposed to much data in the course of his interviews with customers and prospects and through observation in the communities and facilities which he visits. More data can be obtained if he knows what questions to ask and what to look for in the course of meetings with customers. The central managerial problem is the development within the salesman of perceptive skills so that he will (a) recognize data which contains information, (b) make effective information-to-intelligence transformations, and (c) make sound decisions as to what intelligence should be forwarded upstream and to peers and what intelligence should be filtered out at his level.

A major sales-management responsibility is to inaugurate the training and provide the incentive necessary to enable and induce the salesman to undertake and conduct intelligence activities in a responsible and productive way.

Both knowledge of what will be useful and skills in perceiving data which contains information must be developed. For information which the salesman will use himself, such as that about the people on whom he calls and their organizational and internal-information relationships, motivational problems are not likely to be difficult as the salesman is quite likely to perceive the value of this type of information to himself. Even here, however, management, through training, must assist the salesman in developing the means to gather and understand this type of information and to maintain it in forms in which it will be useful to him.

For intelligence to be used by others, the salesman needs to be as familiar as is feasible with the users' needs. Some exposure to operations within intelligence-using departments may appropriately be a part of the salesman's training.

Although intelligence users' needs can never be fully specified, success in making intelligence needs clear to the salesman is likely to improve the likelihood of having the right types of information reported.

A manufacturer of packaged products requires each salesman to regularly complete a questionnaire on competitive activity as it involves each account. Thus the salesman knows what is wanted. This data is fed directly to the computer to insure its input to the firm's marketing information system.

Information about specific customer problems is derived largely from the sales interview. The information elicited in an interview will, however, depend in large part on how well the salesman can communicate with the prospective buyer, particularly how well he can perceive the buyer's problems and draw from him information about the problems and their substance. The astute salesman develops an ability to separate the substance of customer problems from the often superficial apparent need or demand. As has been suggested elsewhere, even minimal performance demands that the salesman understand the problem which the customer is trying to communicate. Often this requires considerable insight into the buyer's industrial or household operations in order that the problem can be seen in full context.

An able salesman does not stand aside until customers and prospects identify problems so that he can provide solutions for them. Rather, he perceives problems before they have been articulated by the prospect, perhaps even before the person being interviewed recognizes that he has a problem.

A sales representative of a firm selling equipment to control dirt, smoke, and odors in air streams called on an executive of a publishing company. The executive assured him that the firm had no dirt problems in its photoengraving operation. The salesman asked to visit the shop where these operations were performed and requested that the executive accompany him. Upon entering, the executive asked the man in charge: "Do you have any problems in this operation?" The immediate reply: "Dirt and dust in the air! We should follow the model "Cleanliness is next to godliness'."

In the operation covered by this illustration and in many similar operations, dirt particles have been problems for years, especially in shops in which a high quality product is desired. However, as all dirt which was not controlled or removed by the normal air-conditioning system was regarded as a necessary evil, persons in charge at the shop level had not proposed remedial action to management and management did not know that a problem even existed. The alert salesman ferrets out such problems.

In the foregoing example the problem had in fact been recognized even though it was not known to purchasing personnel or the senior executives of the company. In many situations, in contrast, the prospective buyer has not perceived that a problem exists. Thus, it remains for the salesman not only to show the way to a solution but to perceive that a problem exists and to show the interviewee that there is a problem and that the salesman's firm can resolve or ameliorate it.

The really able salesman does much more than this. Through his grasp of relevant aspects of the customer's operations, he anticipates problems before they arise and is thus in a position both to prescribe preventive action and to aid his company in developing products for the expected new solutions.

These relationships between a salesman and his account have been noted earlier. They are raised at this point because an important intelligence function of the salesman is not only to observe and perceive for the purpose of making a sale, but equally important, *to transmit information about customers' problems to others in his company who need to know.*

This activity is most obvious when the seller is tailoring a product to the specific needs of the buyer. Here the salesman serves both as an information pipeline—for example, taking off the specifications from a set of plans and sending them to the shop technical personnel for the preparation of a proposal—and as a broker among the information-possessing and information-seeking personnel of the two firms. His intelligence function here may often be to determine the customer's problem with sufficient detail that he knows which personnel in his organization should receive the information and take appropriate action to develop further relationships.

The perception, screening, and forwarding of information about customer needs is by no means confined to the tailored-to-order product situation. An effective information system must provide meaningful information about present and developing general customer needs and the attributes which might appropriately be put into products to meet such needs.

From a product development and product improvement perspective, the need is to get the salesman to concentrate on customer problems, especially those for which fully satisfactory solutions are not presently available either from the company or from others.

> Hewlett-Packard Co. encourages its salesmen to become new product idea men by a policy of encouraging the salesman to take the customer's side on any issue involving the performance or adequacy of an HP product. Thus by pointing up inadequacies the salesmen serve as a force for product modification oriented to customer needs.[6]

[6] "Hewlett-Packard: We don't sell hardware. We sell solutions . . . " in *How They Sell* (New York: Dow-Jones & Company, Inc., 1965), pp. 3–17. Also reprinted in James H. Bearden, *Personal Selling: Behavioral Science Readings and Cases* (New York: John Wiley & Sons, Inc., 1967, pp. 33–37).

The nature of formal reporting forms is only incidental to the development of appropriate skills and judgement in the salesman. In the end, it will be the salesman's ability to understand the nature of customers' and prospects' problems and their implications for his company and his understanding of what information his peers and associates need that will determine how effectively information will be collected, screened, and forwarded to those who need it.

This is more than a matter of formal training and the furnishing of lists of information wanted to the salesman. If his motivation to seek out and provide intelligence is to be maintained, the salesman must believe that what he provides is useful and used by those who receive it.

> In one industrial organization, so much of the intelligence provided by salesmen was filtered out by the line sales organization that little reached the headquarters organization. Receiving no feedback that the intelligence was useful, the salesmen stopped providing it.

The salesman must not only report; he must evaluate. As the individual in closest contact with the prospective buyer and presumably the individual in his firm most knowledgeable about the customer's problems and situations, he is in the best position to evaluate the credibility of statements made to him by customers and prospects. In most situations the salesman on the account is the only individual in any position to evaluate the credibility of the statements made to him by those with whom he talks in the customer organization.

Unfortunately, because he is directly involved in producing the response functions, the salesman may not be an astute, detached observer of prospect and customer behavior. He may give excessive credence to claimed reasons for behavior or may improperly infer causation. Even worse, he may distort or even eliminate information which he feels would adversely depict his performance.

The involvement of the salesman in inducing responses and the resulting lack of detachment in reporting the results of these efforts leads peers and superiors to assign relatively low credibility to salesmen's reports about customers' responses, especially as they apply to lost business. Where credibility problems are severe and the need for accurate intelligence is great, collateral information from independent sources (for example, marketing research, extra-channel communications with customer personnel) may be employed to refute or reinforce the information obtained from sales personnel. Despite the many difficulties, however, the sales force remains as the principal, often the only, source of information on many environmental developments and many types of customer responses. He is often the only individual in the selling firm in a position to gain insight into customer problems. Hence, the sales manager stands to benefit to the extent that he can improve his salesmen's capabilities as observers and as evaluators.

In addition to this possible lack of objectivity, salesmen may not be fully effective in determining which information about customer responses should be passed upstream. As a consequence, other individuals in the firm may fail to receive information of significance to them. Such events can be minimized only by programs to insure that salesmen understand what should be passed on and the uses to which the information will be put. Such an understanding must be precise, for the salesman must serve as a filter and evaluator; he can't and shouldn't put every bit of information he encounters into the system. The salesman's understanding of upstream information needs is enhanced if he is well informed on the projects which the company is undertaking and the directions in which its efforts are moving. Security policies which keep the field sales force uninformed on such matters may, whatever their other merits, be counterproductive in their effect on information acquisition and transmittal.

The entire evaluation process does not, of course, take place at the field level. Further evaluation of information into intelligence will take place at subsequent echelons. But the process starts at the field level where the salesman must determine what information in his possession is sufficiently significant, credible, and believable to place in his own information storage bank and to pass on to other echelons. Errors of omission at this point cannot be corrected in the course of later review. At the other extreme, transmittal of excessive information clogs the system and impairs its effectiveness. Hence, the calibre of performance by the salesman is critical.

THE TRANSMITTAL AND STORAGE OF INTELLIGENCE

The collection of information by the salesman and its initial transformation into intelligence by him is only a step, albeit a critical one, in the intelligence process. To be of value, intelligence must reach the appropriate users at relevant times. In short, this means that the right intelligence must flow to the decision maker at the time he requires it for his decision. This requires provision for the (1) internal transmission of new intelligence, (2) further processing, (3) storage, (4) updating, and (5) dissemination of intelligence to users.

Internal Transmission of New Intelligence

Internal transmission of new intelligence is most commonly provided by reports from salesmen and from various supervisory echelons of the organization.

Although the bulk of material transmitted in reporting systems is in the form of routine, short-answer types of reports, narrative reports and even oral reports may be of considerable value on matters of import. While oral reporting has the advantage of speed and contributes to timeliness and to more meaningful two-way communication between reporter and recipient, such reports should be reduced to writing in some form for future reference and to minimize the risk of misunderstanding.

Salesmen's activity reports often form a major (in some cases, unfortunately, *the* major) means of initial transmission. While such reports are generally adequate for transmitting information about the salesman's activities and some fairly perfunctory information about the people and organizations called upon, most such reports do not provide good vehicles for transmitting *intelligence* about the environment, about customers' problems, about response functions (although raw information about customers' responses may be developed from activity reports), or about customers, as they rarely give sufficient emphasis to the conversion of information into intelligence by the salesman. Although some special types of reports (for example, lost-business reports, reports of complaints) do provide some vehicle for the transmission of intelligence, most intelligence in these areas must be drawn from the salesman in other ways if it is to reach others in the organization. Because few companies, if any, have been able thus far to devise formal systems for drawing this type of intelligence out of the salesman's data bank, it commonly remains internalized within the salesman. The salesman "knows" but his superiors and peers who need to know do not get the word. The developing use of portable recording devices may make it possible for organizations to get more subjectively evaluated material from the salesman's head into the firm's formal information system. At the present time, however, much of this intelligence moves from the salesman only through meetings with peers and supervisors. It then enters the system in unstructured form, often as part of the "experience" of the recipient in the performance of his work.

The introduction of intelligence in such unstructured forms is hazardous because of the operation of the exception principle. Normal events tend to be unnoted and not commented on while unusual ones receive comment and attention which may be out of proportion to their true significance. Hence the recipient may obtain a warped view of the state of affairs.

Most customer complaints in a large department store are handled in the selling department. In a small percentage of cases the customer wishes to return merchandise or obtain an adjustment which the department head does not wish to grant or which is beyond his authority. Such cases are commonly handled at an "adjustment" window. In a few cases the customer's demand goes beyond what even the employees at that activity deem reasonable, or which involves conditions which they are not authorized to grant. These few cases will reach the desk of the responsible store executive. Although they represent only a tiny fraction of the adjustment requests which customers make, they are the only ones which reach his desk.

Unless conscious measures are taken to bring the numbers into focus, the executive may develop a very jaundiced view of the behavior of the store's customers and the nature and reasonableness of their demands.

Even in the transmission of factual information, salesmen complain, often with considerable justification, that they are being asked to devote time and effort to the preparation of reports of no real utility to the recipient. Periodic review, not only of reporting forms and procedures themselves but of the *uses* to which the information is in fact put, provides a means to eliminate the collection and transmittal of information which is not being utilized or for which the cost, including the opportunity cost of the salesman's time, outweighs its value to the receiver.

Both in providing information about his own work and in furnishing various types of evaluated information (intelligence), the salesman is more likely to provide complete, accurate, timely, well-evaluated information if he fully understands and appreciates the use to which it will be put. A well-designed and frequently-reviewed report system encourages a higher level of cooperation from the sales force.

Ideally, report systems should be developed from the perspective of what recipients need to know rather than from standing traditions that certain things should be reported or that certain types of reports are desirable. While the traditional listing of types of reports from the field—itineraries, call reports, sales reports, sales forecasts, new-account reports, lost-business reports, complaint reports, expense reports, and so on—may provide a useful checklist, merely aping tradition by providing for the submission of such reports is likely to burden the salesmen with requirements to provide information which is not really needed and to impede, rather than develop, the furnishing of information from the field which is of the greatest value and in the most valuable form. Reporting systems oriented around user needs have the additional advantage of making it easier to make clear to the reporter that the information is needed and that it will be used. The demonstration of the actual use of salesman-furnished information is perhaps the strongest motivation available to induce careful, complete reporting from the field.

Different users of even the same information may require it in different forms. For example, an immediate supervisor needs detail about a salesman's work and problems which others may need only in so far as it is reflected in summaries and aggregates. Similarly, the information provided by routine reporting and accounting systems may be based on the data which a research analyst needs but may exist in the company's information system in a form which does not yield the desired intelligence. For example, the sales summaries provided by the records may not yield customer or geographic identification data of interest to the analyst of a particular problem because the primary users of the summaries have no interest in the particular detail.

A major problem in most organizations, and especially in large ones, is that the collectors and possessors of information do not know what information is useful and to whom the information has value. Hence, unless solicited by a formal reporting system or an inquiry, such information which could be brought into and processed within the firm's information system is either not collected or, if collected, is filtered out or misrouted so that much or all of its value is lost. ("I didn't know you wanted to be bothered with *that*".) Even where a type of information is called for by a reporting system, the quantity and quality of information received is likely to be directly related to how clearly the information specification is drawn and to how well the information provider understands the use to which it will be put.

On the other side, individuals who could use information may fail to request it simply because they do not know that it exists or that it could be readily obtained. Albaum has noted that unsolicited information will flow to the extent that its possessors know who the potential users are but that in most companies of any size possessors and potential users know relatively little about each other's information needs and capabilities.[7] Moreover, the formal reporting system, unless carefully developed with these needs and capabilities in mind, may do little to get meaningful, properly filtered, and evaluated data into the system.

Further Processing

The salesman performs only the initial transformation of information into intelligence. While the resulting product is intelligence to him, what he transmits to others is intelligence information which has received some evaluation. This information will receive additional evaluation by recipients. To begin with, each recipient may wish to assign his own values of credibility and believability to the information which reaches him from the salesman. In the process of evalu-

[7] Gerald Albaum, "Horizontal Information Flow: An Exploratory Study," *Academy of Management Journal,* Vol. 7, No. 1 (March 1964), p. 22.

ating the information, the recipient will combine it with information from other sources or in other forms, not only to aid in evaluating the believability of individual bits of information which arrive from the field but, more importantly, to summarize and combine bits of information of many types into a composite useful for the decisions which he will have to make. Indeed, many bits of information which come in from field observers are themselves quite meaningless; it is only when such bits have been aggregated and compared that a picture about an environmental factor, a response function, or a customer situation emerges. At the user level, even this summarized and combined information needs to be related to the decision problem at hand before it can be properly considered fully developed intelligence.

Generally, as information moves up through the organization it is filtered and summarized so as to make it more useful to recipients. At the lower levels, information which is not worth passing on is screened out while other information is combined into summaries to make it more useful to the receiving individual or activity. At intermediate and higher levels, the emphasis shifts to interpretation of information and its significance for problem solving. Stated differently, we could say that at the lower administrative levels, the filtering process is largely one of removing what the processor conceives to be insignificant information and consolidating the significant information into summaries of various sorts for transmittal in forms usable by receivers. At higher levels, the principal concern is with the information-to-intelligence transformation.

An important responsibility of the various echelons of supervision from the salesman's immediate field supervisor to the senior marketing executive of the firm is to grasp the significance of separately reported, and perhaps individually small, incidents. While summarizing systems and other data processing devices can process the incoming data, *the perception of significance which is so central to its conversion to intelligence is basically a human activity.* The record of even able managers of business and world affairs in this respect is not an enviable one.

Storage

Although some of the intelligence which the salesman secures will be retained in his head for subsequent use, much of it needs to be recorded both for the salesman's own future reference and because many bits of intelligence information will have maximum value only when summarized and combined with other bits of intelligence information. Intelligence for the salesman's own use is commonly retained by the salesman in his own files. However, because it is of interest to successors should a different individual assume a particular sales responsiblity, some sales managers prefer to see such information recorded and brought within the firm's information system so that it can be available to others should the need arise. Detailed account histories may provide intelligence of this type, although such histories are rarely, if ever, likely to include all of the information on interpersonal relations which a successor would find useful. Unless effective procedures to incorporate information *evaluation* have been in force for some time, much historical information in company records and files is likely to be little more than raw data and thus of only limited value.

Salesmen can be encouraged to furnish accurate, complete, evaluated information to an account history or territorial history data bank by assuring that the salesman will benefit from withdrawals from the bank as well as provide deposits of information into it. This may be accomplished by feeding back to the salesman, at appropriate times, information which he has deposited, together with information from other sources, which is relevant for his work.

One large chemical company, for example, abstracted salesmen's call report information onto account histories and then fed pertinent information back to the salesman at the time he was about to plan his next call on the account. By submitting accurate reports on his activities, the salesman was thus putting information into a system which would help *him* at some future time. He thus had a motive for considering this activity a useful one rather than a mere administrative chore. Some of the kinds of information recorded were persons met, personnel changes, products used, their applications and sources, literature requested, prospective customer capital, product and personnel changes, and promises and offers made.

As the abstracters both filtered and interpreted, the quality of output of a system of this sort rests heavily on the capability of those doing the abstracting. Poor abstracting by clerical personnel would render the system worthless. The example company used sales trainees.

To the extent that account histories can be developed which contain meaningful intelligence and to the extent that such histories can be kept current, the sales manager has both a data file should it be needed by a successor on the account, and a data source of account information for special analyses should they be needed by the sales manager, by a sales force analyst, or by others in the organization.

Traditionally, information from the field has been summarized, the summaries rather than the original data then being kept in file. Some firms have used account history systems and similar means of keeping information in available, manageable form. Unfortunately, such largely paper record systems do not lend themselves to economical machine analysis of the information contained therein. We

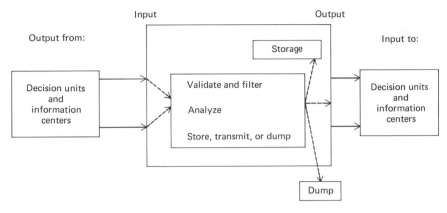

(a) Information center processing information

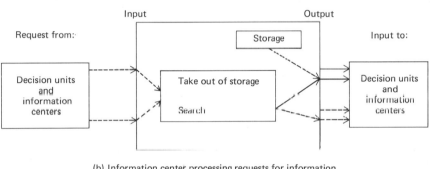

(b) Information center processing requests for information

Figure 9-2

FLOW DIAGRAM OF PROCESSING BY INFORMATION CENTER

SOURCE: Gerald Albaum, "Information Flow and Decentralized Decision Making in Marketing." © 1967 by The Regents of the University of California. Reprinted from *California Management Review*, Vol. IX, No. 4, p. 65, by permission of The Regents.

may therefore expect to see data banks in tape or other forms suitable for computer input, processing, and readout.

Albaum advocates a centralized company information system consisting of specialized information centers located at various parts in the company. Information and requests for information would be fed into the system; the system would put out information and requests for information. The staff of such an operation would, it is hypothesized, acquire the knowledge of who can use what information and develop direct communication links to minimize message distortion.[8] Albaum shows the flows of information and requests in chart form in the manner shown in Figure 9-2.

[8] Albaum, pp. 31–33.

The reader may recognize that a system such as that just described represents a formalized, internal application of the information storage and brokerage function which is performed by many technical salesmen. Another less formal example is the case of a liaison officer in military aviation research and development work who acts as a centralized source of information on problems which research activities have encountered in their work and the nature and success of their efforts to resolve them. A firm faced with a problem in military aviation R & D work can determine, by referring to this individual, if another contractor has faced a similar technical problem and what steps were taken to research it.

While a centralized information system could provide for the orderly handling of information, given the specifications, it remains to be seen if it would assist or impede information-to-intelligence transformations. It seems doubtful that information-center staff personnel could define all problems of all users in sufficient precision to accurately identify all the information of intelligence value for each problem.[9]

Much information of possible intelligence value that is not reported by the salesman because he does not believe others have a use for it is stored in the salesman's head, most commonly as part of his unstructured experience. For information for which a need elsewhere in the organization has not been established this is not necessarily undesirable. A small proportion of such information may be needed at some time. It can be retrieved by appropriate inquiry — if the individual needing the information knows where to look.

> A manufacturer selling nationally through supermarkets made a one-time inquiry of its field personnel to ascertain which promotional tactics were most effective in their respective areas and which were taboo.

Updating

Stored information, to be fully useful, must be kept current through appropriate updating procedures. Computerized information systems possess advantages over paper systems in this respect in that they can be programmed to constantly update their information store as new information comes in. The most common example of this type of automatic updating is found in systems that are programmed to discard the oldest bit of data in a classification whenever a new

---

[9] The hazards inherent in the so-called total information systems concept are noted by Adrian McDonough in "Information Systems as a Context for Market Segmentation," in Reed Moyer, *Changing Marketing Systems* (Chicago: American Marketing Association, 1968) (Proceedings Series #26; Winter, 1967), pp. 72–75.

bit is added. This type of updating is especially prevalent where moving averages, regression lines, and similar types of information are computed regularly for use in planning and projection work.

This type of chronological updating is, at best, a first step toward the ideal of limiting the fund of stored information to that which has possible intelligence value—that is, applicability to a problem. A system can, in theory, be developed to maintain the fund of information in such a state that all of it has potential applicability to a current or continually recurring problem by precisely and fully defining the problems and the information needed to handle them, then limiting the information placed in the fund to only those classifications so identified. An example of a system of this type might be an accounting information system where the problems are recurring ones (calculation of depreciation charges, making up payroll checks) and the information requirements are well known.

But it is the nature of most management problems to change. Old ones are solved, new ones are discovered. And as the problems change, so do the types of information that have possible intelligence value. No one has yet devised a way of determining what management's future problems will be or what information will be required to solve them so that the intelligence system can gather the needed information in advance of the problem. About the best that can be expected of an intelligence system is that its fund of information follow closely the changes in management's information requirements.

Even this is a momentous task. It requires close liaison between management and the intelligence system to determine on a continuing basis just what the information needs of management are, continual modification of the intelligence system to gather it, and constant revision of the information fund to keep it pertinent. Such a process cannot be programmed. It requires the constant attention of highly skilled personnel throughout the intelligence system.

DISSEMINATION OF INTELLIGENCE TO USERS

Effective dissemination of intelligence requires the ability to retrieve information on file at the appropriate time and to route it to the decision center or individual who can benefit from the intelligence. The transmission process should be appropriate (to the right parties), timely, and as noise-free as possible. To attain the latter, information which is *not* needed must be kept from transmission. Unless this can be accomplished, the communication system will become overloaded and the recipient will be swamped with information, most of it irrelevant to his immediate problem.

Although the concept of separating noise from information is straightforward, its application is difficult. Since the user's problem and needs are never *fully* specified, there will always be some difference in understanding between the user and the information supplier, whether the latter be an originator or an information switcher. Indeed, it is likely that the information user himself will not classify the same type of data as "information" or "noise" with complete consistency over time as *his* problems and perceptions of them change. Thus dissemination programs are subject to the same difficulties noted earlier in connection with the transmission of new intelligence. While a useful rule of thumb would appear to be "If in doubt, disseminate," such a rule could rapidly overload any communication system if applied indiscriminately.

Among the users to whom intelligence must be fed back are the salesmen themselves. Appropriate feedback to salesmen assists them in self-evaluation of their performance over time as well as providing a data base for planning their own activities. Feedback of summarized information can also be employed to inform salesmen of what is going on in the field outside of their immediate territories.

EVALUATING THE PERFORMANCE OF THE INFLOW INTELLIGENCE SYSTEM

In this section, suggestions are made as to how a message system can be evaluated. The reader should be cautioned at the outset, however, that there is no direct method for accurately measuring the effectiveness of a system of gathering information and processing it into intelligence.

Appraisal of Reporting Systems

As suggested earlier, reporting systems should be subjected to periodic review so that they can be modified to keep them in line with the needs of the organization and with input materials which are available. Phelps and Westing suggest the following checklist of criteria which can be applied in appraising a reporting system:

1. Is the reporting system in alignment with the overall control system?
2. Is there an important use for the information requested or furnished? Is it so used, and do those who furnish the information know how it is used?
3. Could the information be secured from any source other than the salesmen or the field selling offices?
4. Does the reporting system provide for a reasonable work load for the salesmen and field offices?
5. Has the need for a two-way exchange of information been given proper attention? Is there nice balance between incoming and outgoing information?

6. Have the mechanics of reporting been handled effectively?
7. Does the reporting system have the approval of all parties concerned—home-office executives, field executives, and salesmen?[10]

While this and similar checklists provide guidance in reviewing existing reports and their usage may help thin out "the paperwork jungle," they serve mainly to locate sins of commission. They fail to come to grips with such questions as:

1. What information not called for by the reporting system should have been obtained and reported on?
2. How perceptive are the information gatherers? (That is, how good is the process of recognizing raw data as containing information?)
3. How good are the filtering decisions at various echelons? Is unimportant information passed through the system? Important information filtered out?
4. How sound are the information-to-intelligence transformations at the originating (salesman) level? At higher levels?
5. Have the relevant parts of the intelligence system been regularly reviewed and modified to reflect the changing needs of marketing management, sales management, salesmen, planners and other users? To reflect new sources of materials, developments in intelligence processing, and cost/benefit relationships?

Such reviews may provide an operational means of culling out and modifying portions of the existing system. They do not, however, measure the performance of the system itself.

Flow Tests

In a flow test, data is exposed to the information gatherers and observations are made as to its collection, evaluation, and transmittal through the system. Such a test thus measures whether the system senses the data and conducts correct data-to-information and information-to-intelligence transformations.

In an exploratory study of one company's intelligence system, Albaum used six items of data which had been selected by the com-

---

[10] D. Maynard Phelps and J. Howard Westing, *Marketing Management* (3d. ed.) (Homewood, Ill.: Richard D. Irwin, Inc., 1968), pp. 781–782.

pany's management as being of considerable interest and importance. Each of these items was planted with a cooperating purchasing agent who let it pass as raw data to the salesman. After an appropriate time lapse, a questionnaire was administered to everyone who might have been involved in the intelligence gathering process to determine how the six items had been handled.

The results showed that four of the six items had been completely lost. The salesmen with whom they had been planted did not remember having received them. Thus they had been screened out at the very first step because the salesmen had not recognized the data as containing information.

Of the remaining two items, one was reported routinely through the channel to the wrong person and in such distorted form that management would have been misled.

The only item that was reported in usable form to the proper person did not go through the established intelligence system at all. The salesman who had received it was a personal friend of the manager concerned and had prior experience in the area to which the information had pertinence. He reported it directly to the manager in a personal memo.[11]

Flow tests are difficult to control and expensive to conduct. But where they are used they can produce valuable insights into the way an intelligence system actually operates.

Other Pathological Symptoms

The flow test provides one method of identifying a pathological state. Other indications that the intelligence system is not fully effective include:

1. nonperformance of intelligence duties by salesmen (a steel company noted some salesmen who *never* reported information on developments in customer industries);
2. improper filtering in the line organization (a field sales manager of an equipment company complained that salesmen were reporting too much information);
3. failure of decision makers to "get the word" when the information was already in the system;
4. erroneous evaluation;
5. conflicting information reaching different decision makers.

SUMMARY

An important function of the sales force is the recognition of data which has information significance to the firm and at least the

[11] Albaum, pp. 23–31.

initial stages of its transformation into intelligence useful for decisions. This involves evaluating the credibility and believability of
bits of information as well as perceiving their significance to diverse
potential intelligence users.

Many kinds of intelligence are required: about the environment,
about specific customer's problems, about response functions, and
about customers' people and organizations. Some information for
intelligence can be derived from internal records, market studies,
or other sources. Much can come only from the salesman. Other intelligence will be more timely and, in some cases, more cogently
evaluated if secured by the salesman.

Much intelligence is primarily for the salesman's own use.
Other intelligence must be processed and transmitted so that it may
be of maximum value to others in the organization whose decisions
are based upon it.

If the salesman is to be a fruitful source of intelligence, he must
be provided with an understanding not only of the data collection,
screening, evaluating, and transmittal processes, but also of the intelligence needs of various individuals in the firm. He must develop
competence to (a) recognize data which contains information, (b)
make effective information-to-intelligence transformations, and (c)
make sound decisions as to what intelligence should be forwarded
upstream and to peers and what intelligence should be filtered out
at his level.

Failure in the performance of any of these activities represents
a malfunction of the intelligence system. If the salesman fails to recognize data as encompassing information of intelligence value, that
information is lost to the system. If he grasps the information but
fails to evaluate correctly its significance and credibility, the information may fail to reach the proper party in his organization or, even
worse, may contain the wrong message. Finally, if he filters out information which he believes to be of no interest but which in fact
others need, the organization is deprived of the benefits of information
which has been brought in and processed.

The avoidance of malfunctions of these sorts depends very
largely on the ability of the sales organization, through training and
instructions, to grasp what will be of value and to report it in a properly evaluated and timely manner. This can rarely, if ever, be accomplished merely by providing for the "right" system of reports. *It requires, rather, that the salesmen understand quite precisely what is
wanted and for what purpose. Without such an understanding the
salesman is not likely to be in a position either to choose properly
what information should be transmitted nor how the information
should be evaluated for maximum value to the recipient.* The communication, supervisory, and training systems for salesmen must develop

both the capability and the machinery for carrying out these responsibilities.

Because of the growing role of the intelligence function, sales management needs to evaluate its performance on a regular basis.

SELECTED READINGS

Kelley, W. T., *Marketing Intelligence.* London: Staples Press, 1968. The nature and implementation of marketing information systems.

McDonough, Adrian, "Information Systems as a Context for Market Segmentation" in Reed Moyer (ed.) *Changing Marketing Systems.* Chicago: American Marketing Association, 1968. Proceedings series #26, Winter, 1967, pp. 72–75. The possibilities and limitations of information systems in an information-oriented society.

Platt, Washington, *Strategic Intelligence Production.* New York: F. A. Praeger, 1957. The nature and production of intelligence.

Part III

Operating the Field Sales Organization

10 Salesman Support

The salesman's role as the primary intercommunicative interface between a firm and its market has already been noted. The salesman is not only the central figure in the communications interaction with customers; he is also the center of decision making in the field in dealing with customers and prospects. In the execution of these responsibilities, he requires four kinds of support from his firm: (1) support intelligence, (2) support facilities, (3) technical and service support, and (4) funding of his activities. Each of these will be examined in the present chapter.

PROVISION OF SUPPORT INTELLIGENCE

In Chapter 9, the role of the salesman as a *provider* of intelligence was examined. The salesman is also a major *user* of intelligence. A significant problem in providing such intelligence to him involves the orientation of the firm's information and control system so that it *serves* the selling organization rather than *dominates* it.

The Nature of Salesman-Support Intelligence Systems

The concept of the salesman as an intercommunicator with personnel in the buying system and as communicative link between the buying and selling systems places the salesman in the role of a *decision maker,* not merely an executor of decisions made by others. This role demands a *salesman-centered* information system which will provide him with the information which he needs for his work with customers. This requires much more than the provision of information useful in making presentations *to* customers. It involves, also, information which he needs to assist him in gathering information from customers and the marketplace and in making decisions about his own tactics and behavior.

The concept of a salesman-centered information system is not widely held because many firms cling to hierarchical, as contrasted with participative, concepts of the management process and thus view the salesman as a mere executor of decisions reached at higher levels. Moreover, it is unlikely to secure wide acceptance where marketing is still regarded as a disposal, rather than a supply, system.

On the other hand, the firm which is oriented towards serving and supporting its customers and which recognizes the centrality of the salesman's role in the intercommunicative process can be expected to recognize the importance of the salesman as a decision center. It may thus logically design its information system with important emphasis on support of the salesman rather than primary concern with providing information to managers at various levels, doling out to salesmen only what managers believe the salesman ought to have.

Figure 10-1 illustrates a support information system for salesmen. Salesmen draw information about opportunity, constraints, and other factors in the environment from their own observations and from interactions with the persons upon whom they call. In addition, they secure information about the environment from various managerial echelons. These echelons (collectively denominated "sales management" in Figure 10-1) obtain information through formal marketing research, their own observations and experiences, and customer interactions with persons in the organization other than salesmen. This information is processed into useful intelligence through evaluation, filtering, analysis, and synthesis. Then it is forwarded to the salesmen through some appropriate channel such as the line of supervision, the salesman's support staff if one exists, or through materials issued to the salesman or other competence-maintenance means discussed in Chapter 8.

In addition to information about the environment, sales man-

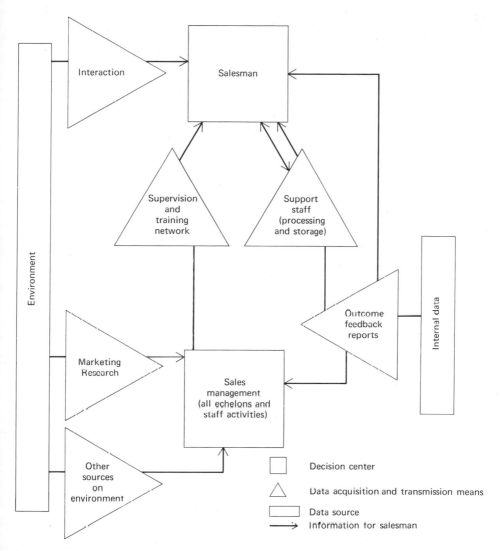

Figure 10-1
SUPPORT INFORMATION SYSTEM FOR SALESMEN

agement echelons also secure feedback information on the outcomes of salesman activities in the form of various reports and analyses which they may prepare themselves or secure from the firm's accounting and controllership activity. Examples of the kinds of feedback information which may be obtained are sales results, analysis of sales by products, customers or territories, distribution cost analyses, degree of quota attainment, and comparison of actual results with revenue and expense budgets. Some of this information may flow directly to the salesman. Much of it will be processed at managerial echelons before being furnished to the salesman in forms useful to him.

The measure of success of a salesman information system lies in its utility to the salesman. Generally, this means that the data obtained from various sources—both the salesman's own and those provided by his organization—are integrated and directed towards his intelligence needs—that is, towards improving his own competence in his intercommunicative role. These needs, in turn, depend on his grasp of organizational goals and his perception of the intelligence value of various types of information which might reach him. These needs are not static. The environment changes. Feedback information reveals new developments in customer behavior which raise new and often different questions about causation. The salesman himself is undergoing a learning process so that what is relevant and important to him will be undergoing change. Thus the salesman as an intelligence-using decision maker has intelligence needs which themselves are likely to undergo substantial changes over time, even in what is nominally the same sales environment.

Elements of a Salesman-Support Intelligence System

As Figure 10-1 shows, the salesman may draw information from a number of sources: his work in the field, his support staff (if one exists), the supervisory and training systems, and (in some cases) directly from the firm's accounting and controllership activity.

WORK IN THE FIELD AS AN INTELLIGENCE SOURCE

Much of the information which the salesman needs to support his work will be provided by the salesman himself as a direct result of his work in the field. Its adequacy will depend not only on the extent to which it provides subject coverage appropriate to the salesman's needs but also by his abilities in data-to-information and especially information-to-intelligence transformations.

Many salesmen need to be taught the value to themselves of obtaining certain types of information and of promptly recording the events in each interview and information about the interactive situation which is developed from or can be inferred from the interview experience. Training can assist the salesman in improving his perceptive skills, in seeing the significance of bits of data to which he is exposed and in making more meaningful information-to-intelligence transformations.

How would you develop these skills in salesmen?

STAFF SUPPORT FOR SALESMEN

One way to assist the salesman in maintaining an information bank is to provide him with staff assistance at the local office. An in-house assistant, who may serve more than one salesman, obtains information from the salesman's reports, from sales management, and from the accounting and controllership activity which is banked and, where appropriate, processed for the salesman's subsequent use. In addition to the salesman's most recent reports on a customer, the file on an account might, for example, contain information on orders received from the customer, an analysis of those orders, information about the customer obtained from marketing research or other nonsalesman sources, and relevant information furnished by other salesmen of note to the salesman handling the account. Office staff may also screen reference sources for information of possible value to the salesman.

> A manufacturer of windows and other metal products used in nonresidential construction has office personnel screen Dodge reports for leads which are forwarded to the salesman in the territory.

The same support staff which feeds information to the salesman could act as an in-house service aide to assist the salesman's accounts (for example, following up on an order) when the salesman is on the road or otherwise not available.

Although not currently a common practice, the use of a support staff affords a means of relieving the salesmen of the detail of building and maintaining a data bank while at the same time providing him with the information which he needs at the time when it is required; for example, when he is preparing to make a call on an account. If staff assistants are to be effective in meeting the salesman's intelligence support needs, they must function in a manner which makes clear to the salesman that the staff member is working for the salesman, not as part of a hierarchical system to control his activity.

THE SUPERVISORY AND TRAINING SYSTEM AS INTELLIGENCE SOURCES

The supervisory and training system represents a major source of information for the salesman. Information about the environment, about company operations and plans, about customer response experience in other territories, and about the sales and other results of the salesman's own work in the field commonly reach the salesman through the sales management structure.

The quality of intelligence support which is provided by the supervisory and training systems is likely to depend very heavily on how well managers, supervisors, and trainers understand the salesman's intelligence needs at the time they are obtaining, processing, and forwarding information. It was noted in connection with the gathering of intelligence in the field by salesmen (Chapter 9) that the effectiveness of intelligence work is limited by the salesman's often limited understanding of the information needs of others in his organization—the intelligence users. In the same way, the quality of information furnished to the salesman is limited by management's understanding of what is really useful out in the field. One argument for requiring experience in the field as a prerequisite for certain sales management jobs is the need for an understanding of field needs by those controlling the information going out to the salesmen.

Unfortunately, field conditions and information needs change, often drastically, so that the information needs which are perceived by managers may have little relevance to those which would be most useful in improving the competence of a particular salesman in the field at a particular time. If the supervisory and training systems are to serve effectively in support of the salesman's intelligence needs, it is imperative that the supervisors and trainers be perceptive listeners in their interactions with the salesmen and that they seek out ideas on the kinds of information which the salesman would find useful in carrying out his work.

ACCOUNTING AND CONTROLLERSHIP ACTIVITIES AS SOURCES OF INFORMATION FOR INTELLIGENCE[1]

The firm's accounting-controllership activity can be a useful data source for information on what the salesman's customers are actually ordering and, if related to inputs, can provide bases for estimating response functions. Unfortunately, most accounting-controllership data is prepared from perspectives somewhat different than that of the salesman involved in planning his tactics for the next calls. Hence, such data may need to be converted to relevant information (for example, by sales analyses) and then placed in the context of the salesman's decision-making process before their full utility can be obtained. Such data may need to be both interpreted (analyzed) by sales management and placed in their problem-solving context by the salesman himself. Training may be needed to enable the salesman to perceive the significance and utility of data furnished him.

[1] Accounting-controllership activities are not necessarily performed in accounting or controllership departments. Sales and cost analyses, for example, are often undertaken by marketing research departments. The concern here is with the provision of feedback to the salesman; the organizational location of the data processing activity is not an issue here.

PROVISION OF SUPPORT FACILITIES

In addition to the provision of such housekeeping facilities as office space and secretarial and clerical assistance where appropriate, the salesman needs reference materials for his own use and sales aids to assist him in communicating with prospects and customers.

The needed reference materials may consist of no more than the merchandise itself or simple manuals, catalogues or other descriptive materials. On the other hand, detailed manuals may be required to assist the salesmen in dealing with the customer's problem. As salesmen increasingly become problem solvers for their customers, reference libraries may become desirable.

To assist him in identifying the customer's problem and preparing a specification or proposal to resolve it, the salesman may need measuring devices (for example, perhaps no more than a tape measure for a floor covering), problem analysis forms and estimating sheets (for example, to determine the benefits which might be achieved by the use of a device to improve the efficiency of a heating system), and in some cases a variety of manuals to calculate the costs of various elements in the specification (for example, the reference manuals of life insurance salesmen and those selling customized homes). These are literally the tools of the salesman's trade. They need to be provided in the forms and formats which are most useful to the salesman in the course of his work. The question for management is: Can a more useful set of tools be provided to the salesman?

Where products and concepts are well understood and the salesman's task is largely one of matching goods to particular needs, samples of merchandise and catalogues or other descriptive materials may be all that the salesman requires in dealing with customers. In much selling to the trade in which the salesman's role is to present new lines and to aid the merchant in selecting items to fill out and strengthen his assortments, the traditional salesman's sample case and catalogue probably continue to be adequate. For less well-understood products, slides, motion pictures, and other visual aids may be useful in conveying understanding of a new idea or establishing an image of a poorly understood product. In other situations, application of the actual product in the prospect's plant, home, or office is highly desirable to demonstrate product merit and performance. Such demonstrations can be highly powerful if they can be applied to the solution of a problem which is either recognized or can be highlighted and dramatized by the salesman's presentation of what the product actually can accomplish.

In addition to sales aids, the salesman may be provided with an array of promotional materials either for his own use or, more commonly, to leave with the prospect for reference and to show to others involved in the decision-making process in the buying system. Where the salesman is calling on resellers, reference and promotional material may also be provided for the buyer's use in selling to his customers.

Sales aids and promotional materials are likely to be of special value in sales to the trade and in the offering of new products, especially innovative products where the salesman has something of real interest to show or demonstrate to the prospect. Their utility thus depends very largely on whether they can convey something that is meaningful in the context of the buyer's situation—that is, whether they have something that is worthwhile for the listener to hear. Unfortunately, many sales aids and promotional materials fall short on this point. Often they are no more than unidirectional promotional materials which have no role in the interactive process and are better distributed through appropriate unidirectional channels. It is little wonder that much of the material provided some salesmen lies unused by the salesmen or is distributed by them only to be discarded by the recipients.

The utility of the use of demonstration and promotional materials is not difficult to test. Observational or experimental studies can determine whether the use of the materials affects sales volume and, if so, if the effects warrant the cost.

Table 10-1 shows an observational study by a distributor of proprietary drug products which revealed that the percentage of mentioned items sold varied with the materials used.

Table 10-1

MATERIALS USED	PERCENTAGE SOLD
Samples	22.8%
Printed matter	20.0
Samples and printed matter combined	34.3
No materials	23.0

SOURCE: "Weco Products Company" in Harry R. Tosdal, *Introduction to Sales Management* (New York: McGraw-Hill, Inc., 1957), p. 674.

The use of samples and printed matter in combination would appear to result in the greatest sales response in this instance. However, the use of these materials consumed more interview time than verbal presentations without these aids so that sales volume per selling minute was greater without them, as seen in Table 10-2.

In these circumstances it would appear that although the use of both samples and printed matter in combination was the most effective way of presenting the particular products, verbal presentations alone represented a more productive use of the salesman's time. If the time freed by the shorter presentations per item could be used for the presentation of additional items—a condition commonly found in sales to the trade—it would, thus, be preferable for the salesman to forego the use of the props in the interest of greater item coverage.

Table 10-2

MATERIALS USED	SALES PER SELLING MINUTE ($)
Samples	$1.16
Printed matter	1.08
Samples and printed matter combined	2.55
No materials	2.82

SOURCE: Same as Table 10-1.

The foregoing example, being derived from an observational study did not hold constant the items being sold. As the benefits to be derived from the use of various sales aids is likely to be substantially affected by the item involved and the buyer's information state and predisposition toward it, a more precise evaluation of the merit of particular sales tools would require an experiment in which the products being sold and the customers' relation to each product were held constant as various sales methods are tested experimentally. With available experimental and observational methods, there is no need to employ various sales aids solely on the basis of intuitive judgment and faith in their efficacy.

How would you design an experiment to determine if use of a particular sales aid (for example, a portfolio of testimonial letters; a working model) was worthwhile?

PROVISION OF TECHNICAL AND SERVICE SUPPORT

In addition to the materials for his own use, many salesmen require the support of technical and service personnel in (a) assisting in the diagnosis of customer problems, (b) preparing proposals or otherwise assisting in prescribing solutions for customer problems, and (c) installing, demonstrating, and servicing the products sold so that the intended level of performance is, in fact, provided.

The manner in which technical and service support is provided is likely to have important effects on the kind of relationship which the salesman is able to maintain with members of the buying organization. Yet, many of the technical and service personnel are organizationally distant from the salesman and may have their own perspectives. They are experts and technicians in their own fields and concerned with their own responsibilities. Some will become involved in face-to-face interactions with members of the buying system; many, however, will develop their perceptions of the buying system and its problems and people only secondhand.

It has been noted earlier that an important role of the salesman is to act as communications link between technical personnel in the buying and selling organizations. Organizational arrangements within the salesman's firm must be such as to support the salesman's needs in his work at the buyer-seller interface. Because technical and other service units may not always understand what is important to customers, it is relatively easy for them to become inward-looking and to see their own operating problems (for example, as to scheduling) rather than the needs at the buyer-seller interface. Possible and not infrequent consequences are buyer beliefs that (a) suppliers do not understand user problems, and (b) the salesman lacks interest and/ or ability to accomplish follow-up activities important to the customer. Often affirmative action by sales management or higher echelons is required to maintain a service-to-the-account perspective in such parts of the organization. Yet the salesman, as the focal point of the relationships with the customers, must have this support.

In these and in other, less technical, situations the salesman may also benefit from in-house staff support. In addition to acting as intelligence sources for the salesmen, such inside aides can work out complaints, follow up on the progress of orders, expedite status reports to both customer and salesman, and in many ways both serve the customer and free the salesman from many time-consuming duties.

> A small steel company has an inside man in each district office to relieve the salesmen of routine tasks. These aides spend about 80 percent of their time on the telephone with customers, plants, and salesmen on the road.

FUNDING THE SALESMAN'S FIELD ACTIVITIES

Keeping salesmen in the field entails expenses of many types. Many of these expenses, such as the salesman's compensation; the provision of his reference, sales aid, and promotional materials; and the costs of managing the sales force can be readily administered in the offices of the company. Other expenses must, however, be incurred by the men as they go about their work in the field. The salesman himself must arrange for much of his travel, lodging, and maintenance and for the wise expenditure of company resources for these purposes and for entertainment or special services to customers. Because the amounts involved are often large, amounting to as much

as $10,000 per man per year in some situations, these resource alloca-
tions by salesmen may significantly affect the profitability of operations.

Clearly, the company has the responsibility of providing funds
for expenditures incurred in carrying out work in its behalf. At the
same time, the salesman, as agent of the company, has the responsibility to use the allotted funds toward the attainment of common
goals—that is, in the furtherance of the company's, as well as
the salesman's, interest. These mutual responsibilities exist whether
the funds are provided to the salesman in advance of expenditure
or later on in the form of reimbursements.

Two kinds of problems exist in the administration and control
of salesmen's expenses in the field. One is the need to insure that
expenses charged to the firm are legitimate costs of the firm. This
requires a clear distinction between the reimbursement of salesmen
for expenses incurred on the company's behalf and his personal
compensation. A commonsense rule is that the company should pay
for those expenses which the salesman would not incur were he not
engaged in the field on company business. Although the application
of this rule may involve difficulties in borderline cases—for example,
whether laundry service is reimbursable while the man is away from
home—the overall principle can be applied quite generally. Unless
the principle is generally accepted and clearly understood, problems
are likely to arise in the form of padded expense accounts. Some
managers have been known to blur the distinction between compensation for services and reimbursement of expenses made on the
company's behalf in the belief that such blurring pleases the salesmen
by assisting them in understating their incomes for tax purposes.
Aside from the very substantial moral and ethical issues which such
falsified accounting behavior involves, the management following
such a practice may soon find that cheating begets more cheating and
that those who succeed in cheating the tax collector may next turn
to cheating the customer and the company. Over the long term, a firm
is generally well advised to maintain the integrity of its own expense
classifications by insisting on as tight a line as is feasible between
compensation and expense reimbursement.

In addition to the problem of legitimacy, there is the need to
insure that company resources are used wisely. This is not so much
a matter of keeping costs down as of assuring that the salesmen are
making sound judgements in the allocation and use of company
resources. In the case of the use of expense monies, as in the case
of the use of the salesman's time and other resources, the salesman
must be provided with bases for evaluating the probable payoffs
to be expected from certain types of expenditures and with an understanding that expenses are incurred with organizational purposes

and goals in mind. In both areas training can assist the salesman in determining what is prudent and desirable in the overall interest of the firm.

If a common understanding on these general principles can be achieved, salesmen are unlikely to make unreasonable requests, and many of the problems of dealing with salesmen's expenses can be kept under control.

Funding Methods

Companies employ a wide variety of arrangements to deal with salesmen's expenses in the field. Some provide the facilities themselves (for example, a company car) or a means of securing facilities without outlays (for example, a credit card). Although providing some measure of control, this practice in itself neither prevents illegitimate use (for example, use of company credit card for family dining and company car for family travel) nor provides the salesman with wisdom in the use of these resources.

At the other extreme some firms, generally those compensating salesmen largely or entirely on a straight commission basis, make no separate provision for expense reimbursement. The salesman pays all his expenses from his commission, the rates of which have presumably been set to allow for expenses. Expenses of such salesmen are thus treated as those of an independent contractor rather than as an agent expending funds on behalf of the firm. Under these conditions, management can expect to exercise little control over the manner in which the salesman employs his resources—even his own time. Even so, training may help the salesman understand the benefits of wise use of his time and money resources to the ultimate gain of both salesman and company.

The more common practice is to provide expense monies to reimburse the salesman for expenses incurred in the firm's behalf. Usually, this is accomplished by a straightforward reimbursement-upon-accounting procedure although some firms may modify this by providing advances or an expense fund against which the salesman may draw. Others seek to avoid the necessity for accounting by providing a flat per diem allowance for travel. While such arrangements may be suitable where outside travel is relatively infrequent so that any gain or loss is small in relationship to the salesman's total income, it can create problems where large amounts of travel are involved unless the per diem rates established make due allowance for differences in the costs of meals and lodging in different areas —especially between the high cost major metropolitan centers and smaller communities. Even where per diem is used for maintenance expenses, the practice is generally to reimburse for travel on the basis of actual cost, when public facilities are used, and an auto-mobile allowance when the salesman uses his car.

Automobile Expenses

Reimbursement for use of the salesman's car is most commonly on the basis of a flat rate per mile although some firms attempt to allow for the spreading of fixed costs by a graduated scale which provides lower rates for greater mileages. Even such arrangements do not take into account differences in operating costs in different areas or for different makes of cars. These differences can be pro-vided for by more complex plans.[2] If the sales manager selects a mileage reimbursement basis which is viewed as reasonable or even slightly liberal by the salesman, minor differences in operating costs among areas are not likely to be troublesome. This is especially true if the salesman considers that he would have the car in any event. In such cases an allowance which liberally covers operating costs is likely to be acceptable even if fixed costs are only approximately covered. Differentials may still be needed where costs are sub-stantially higher (for example, outside the contiguous states) or where a more costly vehicle is required to meet company needs. Where the salesman elects a more costly car than is required for the performance of his duties, it is by no means clear that these excess costs should be reimbursable.

Although the goal of reimbursing the salesman precisely for his outlay for automobile usage is a desirable one, precision on this point may be less important than the need to have the salesman feel that he has been fairly treated. For this reason, it may be useful to use a generally accepted reimbursement rule in lieu of precise cost figures. For example, a firm might use the standard allowance granted by the Internal Revenue Service for use by individual taxpayers using their automobiles for business purposes. For the year 1969 this was 10 cents per mile for the first 15,000 miles of business use plus 7 cents per mile for additional business use.

Expense Account Control

Expense accounts which are niggardly not only create morale problems but may discourage the salesman from incurring expenses which would be in the interest of the company, such as travel to a remote account or conducting business over dinner with an important client. At the same time, expense funding which encourages extrav-agance and indulgence is likely to divert the salesman from the

---

[2] Automotive expense analysts such as Runzheimer & Company, Rochester, Wisconsin offer detailed plans for various situations.

pursuit of the common good, and convert the expense account into a "swindle sheet"; the company may pay more and actually get less in return.

Some firms attempt to deal with the overall problems of expense control by the establishment of limits and by sets of rigid rules as to reimbursability. While such procedures have their uses, they can easily be counterproductive if they create an adversary atmosphere between salesmen and management. In the final analysis, the real control over expenditures entrusted to the salesman must be agreement on common goals and training in means for achieving them, rather than in operating controls which deal with means and symptoms.

SUMMARY

The salesman as a major user of intelligence requires a support system which will acquire, store, process, and feed intelligence to him so as to improve his competence in his interactions with customers. He must also develop ability to perceive the significance and utility of data of possible intelligence value to him.

Much of the intelligence which a salesman needs will be gathered, processed, and held by the salesman himself. A support staff can assist the salesman by storing information and by obtaining data from other sources for the salesman's use.

The firm's accounting and controllership activity and various managerial and staff activities constitute additional data resources for the salesman. Although some information from these sources will flow to the salesman directly, most of it reaches him through the supervisory and training network. The quality of the intelligence information provided depends heavily on how well the managers, supervisors, and trainers comprehend the salesman's intelligence needs at a particular time.

In addition to housekeeping support, the salesman needs reference materials and, often, sales aids to assist him in his work with customers. The utility of various aids can be measured.

Many salesmen require technical and service support in assisting in the diagnosis of customer problems, in preparing proposals, and in assuring that the customer receives the level of performance to which he is entitled. Affirmative action by management is often required to provide effective support for the salesman and to maintain service-to-the-account perspective in diverse parts of the organization.

Two kinds of problems are involved in funding the salesman's activities. The problem of legitimacy can be dealt with by trying to maintain as tight a line as possible between compensation and reimbursement for expenses incurred on the company's behalf.

A more difficult problem is to develop the salesman's capability to make sound judgments in the use of company resources so that they are used wisely.

11 Macro-Direction of the Sales Force

In addition to formulating plans and providing competent manpower, sales management must develop viable systems to translate plans into actions.

In this chapter the principal macro-directional problem areas with which the sales manager must deal are examined: (1) routing the salesman so as to make most effective use of his time; (2) the establishment and administration of performance standards, including quotas; and (3) the development and operation of the feedback system through which sales management can ascertain those changes in direction or execution which are desirable. The micro-directional problem of guiding and motivating the individual salesman, largely through supervision, is treated separately in Chapter 12.

ROUTING AND SCHEDULING

Routing and scheduling are the managerial activities through which the territorial plan and the rules selected for the allocation of effort are carried into effect. Three types of questions must be re-solved:

How shall the responsibilities for routing and scheduling be allotted as between central management, field management, and the individual salesman?

To what extent should routing and scheduling be planned as opposed to having the salesman play by ear?

How can routes best be laid out for economical coverage?

Roles of Salesmen and Managers in Routing and Scheduling

In some organizations, routing and scheduling are considered managerial responsibilities with the actual work being performed by staff assistants to line managers. More commonly, the development of his itinerary is left to the individual salesman as part of his own responsibilities for self-management. It is his duty to plan the use of his time wisely in the management of the territory for which he has accepted responsibility. Such firms operate on the premise that the salesman is likely to have a better feel than management for the timing of calls and that, since he seeks maximum sales, he will be motivated to schedule and route himself to best advantage. Management's role is to support him in these activities.

Several objections may be raised to these premises. First, the best routing plan is not easily discerned. Even management with the information and analytical tools at its disposal is limited in its ability to select the best route and schedule. Can the salesman left to his own devices be expected to do so?

Secondly, the pattern perceived as optimal by the salesman may not be the optimal pattern for the firm. In fact because of per-ceptual error, it may not even be the pattern which best fits the sales-man's own goals. Some salesmen tend to prefer "spoke" travel plans enabling them to return home each evening even though the resulting driving time represents, though perhaps unrecognized, an uneconomic use of the salesman's time.

Thirdly, it is argued that routing activities are specialized duties that need not take the salesman's time and can best be performed by technical specialists on the staff.

Finally, it is noted that salesman self-routing can lead to rout-ing habits which are insufficiently sensitive to new needs and new information—that is, the salesman's route becomes so routinized that it adjusts inadequately, if at all, to changes in opportunity. Moreover, such routing can easily become intuitive and perhaps even lazy. The salesman can, it is alleged, too easily tend to confine his calls to places where he is comfortable with those with whom he comes in contact.

The complaint that some salesmen seem to concern themselves solely with their old accounts is, perhaps, recognition of this symptom.

Where the sales job calls for regular, extensive coverage of an extended market, the development of routes, and perhaps even schedules, by management offers the opportunity to apply available quantitative tools to lay out routes which will both assure adequate market coverage and minimize travel time and costs. Such managerial planning is particularly suitable for calls on the trade by manufacturer and wholesaler salesmen and to other situations in which a fairly regularized call pattern meets the needs of the buyer-seller relationship. It requires that the planner have available detailed information on numbers, types, locations, and approximate call values (pV) for those upon whom calls will be made, appropriate call frequency rates, and necessary transportation data.

In other types of sales jobs, flexibility, rather than regularity, is paramount. Many industrial salesmen must schedule their calls to meet the particular needs of the moment. The salesman must call when he is needed by the buyer or when indicated by the unfolding of events in the sales process (for example, a proposal or idea ready for presentation to the buyer; need to interact with buyer personnel to aid the salesman's insight into some problem of mutual interest).

In other situations, the market is not sufficiently well defined or understood to enable headquarters routing. Sales organizations sometimes find themselves in the exploratory phase of market development. The staff planner has little information with which to formulate routes; indeed the salesman on the spot may have but little more. But as an explorer, he must seek out opportunities; he must be given sufficient freedom to discharge that duty.

In still other situations, the great variances in the length of particular calls, the need to see certain individuals who are best reached at certain times, and other constraints imposed by buyers make scheduling and routing more an art than a science. This art is often best mastered by the salesman with a feel for the particular situation. Moreover, in many types of selling, the salesman is the individual most likely to have the kinds of current information of greatest relevance to the practice of this art.

A device used by some organizations to provide direction while at the same time encouraging the salesman to plan his own route is the supervisor-salesman meeting for planning the salesman's work for the ensuing period. Where this would provide insufficient flexibility, joint salesman-supervisor planning may be confined to call frequency goals, actual routing and scheduling being left to the salesman. Further flexibility to adapt to conditions as they develop can be provided by working out call frequencies for accounts which must be serviced and permitting the salesman to employ any remaining time on an opportunistic basis.

> In planning call frequencies for its detail men, a drug manufacturer works out minimum call frequencies for physicians who write significant prescription volume. All other physicians are treated as "targets of opportunity" and will be called on if and when the salesman's time in the particular area permits.

Where both routing and scheduling are the salesmen's responsibilities, management must demonstrate the benefits of planned coverage and effective routing to the salesmen. Sales time made available through more effective routing is often substantial; examples of gains in sales time through more efficient routing may be useful in helping the salesmen to recognize the contribution which good routing can make to increasing the time available for face-to-face interactions. In addition, management can provide useful formats and planning tools to assist the salesman in formulating his own route plans and can assist his planning work by providing him with an understanding of relevant routing principles and considerations. Given these aids and an understanding of the benefits, able salesmen can become motivated to plan effectively. Personal review of plans and ex post review of travel and call patterns by supervisors are also useful in improving the salesman's routing performance.

Whether routing is centralized or performed by the individual salesman, it should seek to apply the scarce resources committed to personal selling to the most efficient use. The following section is concerned with formulating routing plans to this end.

Minimizing Access Costs

Chapters 3 and 4 examined (1) what the salesman should do, (2) to which accounts and prospects he should direct his efforts, and (3) how much time or effort he should devote to each account and prospect. The rules for allocation of effort suggested there considered only the costs of the salesman's time *with* the prospect or customer. They did not deal with the question of how the salesman is to *reach* the persons to be called on or the costs of reaching them. By omitting the costs of securing access to the persons interviewed, these chapters, in effect, treated access costs as if they did not exist. This is by no means a vacuous case; access costs for the personal salesman will be zero where the buyer comes to the salesman who merely awaits the arrival of buyers—for example, in retail stores, manufacturers' and distributors' sales rooms, and booths at trade shows and conventions. In these situations, effort may properly be allocated to maximize expected return, pV, although often allocation is the result of customer behavior rather than seller choice. On the other hand, where the salesman calls upon the customer, the costs of access are a necessary consideration in the formulation of optimal call patterns. If resources are to be soundly allocated, sales call planning, whether done formally or intuitively and whether undertaken by management or by the salesman himself, must consider not only the salesman's time in making the sales effort but also the costs of positioning him spatially to do so.

The time, and thus the costs, of getting to the person to be interviewed is by no means trivial. Salesmen in the field normally spend substantially more time in gaining access than in actually speaking with the persons with whom they interact.

> In the example of time study using random alarm devices given in Chapter 3, the average salesman spent more than twice as much time in travel to make his calls as he did in face-to-face meetings. Total travel and waiting consumed four times as much of the salesman's time as did actual interviews. And these data did not include homeward-bound travel time.

THE NATURE OF ACCESS COSTS

Access costs are of three types. *Travel costs* are largely within the control of the selling organization, given the existing transportation system and the structure of charges. Travel costs include (a) the costs of transportation, (b) the costs of the salesman's time and (c) the costs of maintaining the salesman on the road, such as the costs of food and lodging. The first two of these costs generally vary with distance, but rarely in a proportionate manner. Maintenance costs are likely to be a step-function, depending upon the need to remain on the road overnight or over weekends. Some substitutability is possible—for example, an overnight stay versus a drive home. Because they are relatively controllable and relatively easy to measure, it is tempting to treat travel costs as the only cost of access in the layout of a routing plan.

Waiting time costs are largely beyond the control of the salesman. In planning, they may be treated as a constant cost of "overhead" time associated with each sales call. Some control over waiting costs can, however, be achieved through calling ahead for appointments and by planning arrival times to avoid interviewees' peak work loads.

Slack time costs occur because many possible arrival times are unacceptable to interviewees—for example, after 5 P.M., between 12:00 noon and 2:00 P.M., on the afternoon the buyer plays golf each week, on the buyer's religious holiday. Such interviewee-imposed constraints may drastically limit the ability of the salesman to call at the time which an itinerary based solely on costs of travel would suggest. In some lines of business such constraints can be significant. Certain times of the day, days of the week, or times of the year are taboo (for example, food stores on Friday afternoon, department stores in mid-December). In some trades, wholesale and chain store buying offices have established hours at which salesmen will be seen —for example, Tuesday, Wednesday, and Thursday from 9:30 A.M. to 12:30 P.M.

The constraints upon access which are imposed by buyers' preferences are reflected in waiting time and slack time costs. They prevent total access costs from being linear, even if travel costs do take that form. They also make costs specific-time dependent.

Because of the limitations of present tools, most routing plans either consider the waiting and slack factors as scheduling matters and thus outside the scope of the routing problem or treat them as factors to be considered in modifying a mathematically calculated routing plan. These factors are thus generally not included in formal routing analyses.

THE CASE OF EQUAL, OR SUBSTANTIALLY EQUAL, ACCESS COSTS

Where access costs are nonzero but equal for all calls, regardless of the sequence in which calls are made, access costs may be treated as a fixed charge per call. By definition, such situations do not have routing problems; the sequence of calling does not matter. The addition of a fixed charge per call will, however, affect the relative value of "more time on an existing call" versus "more calls." In terms of the symbols used in Chapter 4, instead of being a constant unit for all calls—that is, the call (which presumes calls all of same length) or a man-hour unit directly proportionate to call length E (effort) will be a function embracing both a fixed term (access cost per call) and a variable term (man-hour cost of call time).

ACCESS COSTS NOT EQUAL FOR ALL CALLS

In the more common situation, access costs per call are not the same for all calls and do not remain unaffected by the sequence in which calls are made. Some accounts and prospects will be more remote than others. More significantly, if, as is generally the case, the salesman makes more than one call on each trip from his base (home or office), the cost of reaching any particular customer depends on the salesman's location at the conclusion of his previous call. For a series of calls, access cost is thus a function of the sequence in which calls are made. This sequence is called the salesman's *route*. Effective routing seeks to deploy the salesman so as to make the most profitable use of the salesman's time. Given a set of calls to be made, such routing seeks to minimize the cost of covering the route.

SIMILAR VALUE (PV) FOR ALL CALLS   The simplest form of the routing problem occurs when the expected value of the call effect, pV, is similar for all those to be called upon. Figure 11-1 illustrates this situation. The goal is to find the route which will minimize the access costs for a once-around trip. This once-around trip may be a single continuous trip from the base point through the territory and returning to the base point. More commonly, operating constraints— for example, the requirement that men be scheduled to return home each Friday or that they be at the base point to handle mail or attend meetings at certain times—result in a route which consists of several loops into the territory and returns to base, as illustrated by Figure 11-2.

The cost-minimization problem can be readily formulated as a linear programming problem in which the maximum feasible number of calls per trip and the required call frequencies are treated as constraints. Mileage is generally taken as the objective function to be minimized, on the assumption that it represents the basic cost factor and is a suitable surrogate for the other costs.[1]

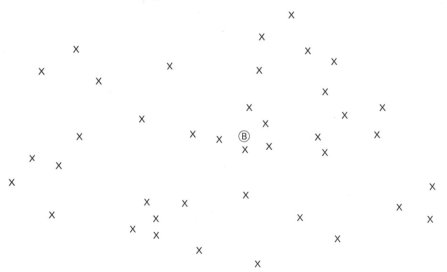

Figure 11-1
ROUTING PROBLEM: EQUAL VALUE OF ALL CALLS

[1] For example procedures, see S. Vajda. *Mathematical Programming* (Reading, Mass.: Addison-Wesley, 1961), pp. 191–92; and John D. C. Little, Katta G. Murty, Dura W. Sweeney, and Caroline Karel, "An Algorithm for the Traveling Salesman Problem," *Operations Research,* XI (November–December, 1963), pp. 972–989.

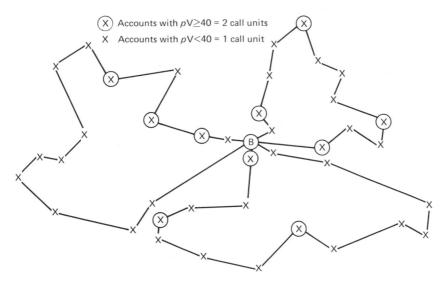

Figure 11-2
ROUTING WITH MAXIMUM TRIP-LENGTH CONSTRAINT

Under modern conditions, it is often more appropriate to treat the salesman's *time,* rather than his *mileage,* as the factor to be economized. This is particularly true in metropolitan areas. The routing plan thus seeks routes which minimize total travel time. This has the additional benefit of enabling refinement of the model to incorporate elements of waiting time and slack time, if these elements are sensitive to the route—that is, if they are affected by the time of arrival of the salesman—and if reasonable estimates of these effects can be obtained.

DIFFERENT VALUES (PV) FOR DIFFERENT CALLS   In many situations, pV will differ substantially among various calls. Important accounts may expect call frequencies to which they feel their volume of business entitles them. Protection from competitive inroads into present accounts and the prospective reward for landing an important new account may also suggest a high value of V, and thus of pV. Other accounts may be judged to represent only a modest V but the relationship between buyer and seller at a particular time leads the salesman to believe that his calls are likely to have a substantial influence on buyer behavior—that is, that ps are larger than normal for such calls. Still other accounts are believed to have modest values of both p and V. The planner's map looks something like Figure 11-3.

In these circumstances the planner is unlikely to accept the premise that all calls have even roughly equal value (roughly equal pV). Hence, he must seek a routing plan which considers both access costs and the value (pV) of securing that access. No generalized algorithm is available for this problem, but some rules of thumb are employed to divide the accounts into groups for calling purposes.

Where salesman's response to differences in pV is limited to providing *more time* per call on the accounts with higher call values, but does *not* entail more frequent calls on such accounts, routing sequences may remain the same. The greater time needed to cover the route can be provided for by defining a route length constraint in terms of call units with calls of various length counting as different numbers of units. For example, in Figure 11-2, calls on high pV accounts count as two call units; others as one call unit. Trips are limited to 18 call units.

In many situations, high pV accounts warrant more frequent calls.[2] In such cases, customers may be classified by their pV values and each assigned either to a complete, or "slow," route in which all accounts are called upon or to an "express," or "fast," route in which

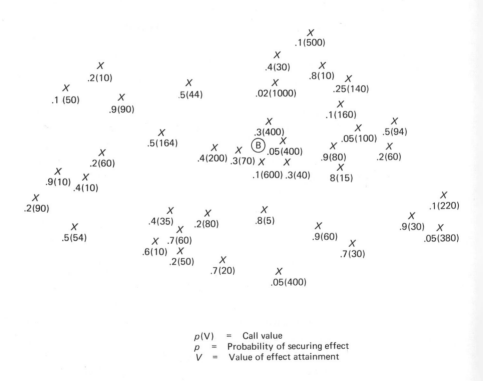

p(V) = Call value
p = Probability of securing effect
V = Value of effect attainment

Figure 11-3
ROUTING PROBLEM: UNEQUAL VALUE OF CALLS

[2] See Chapter 4.

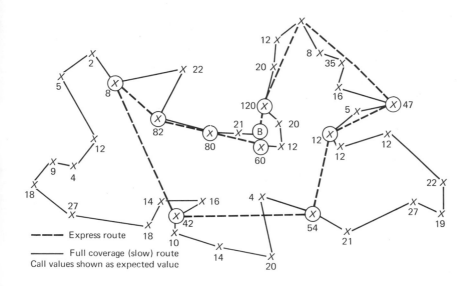

Figure 11-4
USE OF FAST AND SLOW ROUTES TO RECOGNIZE UNEQUAL CALL VALUES

only selected accounts are reached. The salesman may, for example, employ a complete (slow) route similar to Figure 11-4 which takes him to each account once each quarter and an express route which takes him to the high pV accounts one or more times in the intervening months.

One problem with the slow and fast route concept is that each locale may contain one or two major accounts which would warrant fast route treatment and a number of prospects with small pV values. A fast route over such accounts would entail substantial travel time between calls. In such situations, access cost considerations may suggest a series of parallel routes each of which will incorporate all of the major accounts and a portion of the minor accounts in each locale. This arrangement offers some additional advantages: (a) more uniform call intervals on major accounts, since each route is about the same length and takes about the same amount of time; (b) greater opportunity to avoid excessive "slack time" arising from arrival too late in the day for calls, and (c) added flexibility as smaller accounts may be used as fill-ins either before or after their scheduled turn.

While slack time is likely to be lower under the parallel routes plan, which treatment provides the lowest travel costs will depend on the pattern of calls required by a particular sales force. In general, the parallel routes plan is likely to minimize travel if most of the low pV calls are to be made at places near high pV calls—for example, small dealers in the same communities as large ones. On the other hand, if the low pV calls are geographically remote from high pV accounts— for example, in rural locations as contrasted with those in major metropolitan areas—the express route (slow/fast) system is likely to yield the lowest travel costs.

In many sales situations, especially in industrial selling, the best estimate of the call value, pV, of a call on a particular account, rather than being constant for that account, will range widely depending on such considerations as the status of the relationship following the most recent call (for example, account wavering on matter of changing supplier), developments since the last call (for example, competitive activity or service needs which make a call urgent to protect a position against intrusion), or events external to the selling organization which may affect buyer needs (for example, information that buyer is likely to receive a large contract). Situations of this kind suggest that the salesman may wish to formulate his route in a somewhat opportunistic fashion to reflect the changing perceived values of pV.

A heuristic approach to the routing-scheduling problem along the lines proposed by Cloonan may be useful. In such a procedure, an optimal route without regard to pV is first selected as the salesman's basic route. Rather than cover this predetermined route for all trips, the salesman employs a heuristic routine in planning each trip. He starts by appraising the probable effects of calling on the first account on the tour at this time, as opposed to passing over it until a later tour. This appraisal involves examination of the relationship with the account and the probable effects on the relationship of calling on this trip. This pV value for a call now is then related to the incremental cost, C, of making the call. The latter is measured as the amount of delay in reaching the next call which making this call will entail. This cost thus includes interview and service time, waiting and slack time, and travel time in excess of that which would be incurred if the call were by-passed. If the benefit/cost ratio, pV/C, exceeds the management-established minimum, or "go" ratio, the call is made. If not, it is omitted from the current trip. This procedure is continued until the number of calls which the salesman can make during the trip period has been scheduled.[3]

[3] The basic idea set forth here is derived from James B. Cloonan, "A Heuristic Approach to Some Sales Territory Problems" in John D. C. Little, ed., *Proceedings of the Fourth International Conference on Operations Research*, 1966, pp. 81–84. Cloonan suggests the value of a call as a quadratic function of "time since previous call" multiplied by maximum sales volume. This enables him to simulate the effects of call patterns thus generated for compari-

If management has determined the critical benefit/cost ratio correctly *and* if areas of customer responsibility have been assigned to provide just the right work loads, this procedure should result in adequate but not excessive coverage of all accounts over a number of tours. To the extent that these rather rigorous conditions do not hold, the procedure described could lead to suboptimization. On the one hand, a salesman might find so many accounts which meet the standard "go" criterion that accounts near the end of the route may never be reached even though they might have benefit/cost ratios substantially above those of prospects more favorably located along the route. That this condition suggests that the territory is understaffed (that is, that the salesman has too large an area of responsibility), while relevant to staffing and territorial design questions, does not avoid the difficulty that, given the assignment, the salesman is not making the best use of his time. On the other hand, the application of a fixed "go" rule might result in the salesman making fewer calls than his time permitted, simply because several possible calls each fell below the "go" level, and then returning home early. The stated benefit/cost coefficient has, for the moment at least, overvalued the salesman's time and idle-time results.

The latter difficulty can be remedied rather easily by providing a feedback loop in the planning procedure. If the planned tour fails to exhaust the available time, the planning procedure is repeated using a slightly lower "go" value.

The problem of inadequate treatment of accounts near the end of a long route is somewhat more difficult. One possibility is to require the salesman to continue his estimating of benefit/cost values to cover the entire route. If this calls for too many calls, the "go" value is then raised to bring the salesman's plan within the time constraint. A somewhat less formal procedure which might produce acceptable results would be to require the salesman to reverse the direction of travel in *planning* alternate trips. In this way, accounts so located as not to be considered on one trip have a high probability of consideration when the next trip is planned. Such a procedure would not require that the direction of *actual travel* be reversed. On the contrary, considerations of call interval on high call-frequency accounts may require that the direction of travel should be consistent. The alternative-starting-point

---

son with those generated by other decision rules. His procedure is summarized in Philip Kotler, *Marketing Decision Making* (New York: Holt, Rinehart, and Winston, Inc., 1971).

The present author prefers to have the salesman assess call values on the occasion of each planning period, for example, when he is planning his itinerary for the week. This gives maximum effect to the salesman's *current* appraisal of the situation as it pertains to each possible call.

planning procedure is likely to be most useful where the basic heuristic plan takes the salesman not more than two-thirds over the route on a given trip.

Management science has developed programs to select salesmen's routes which will minimize the travel required to reach all assigned accounts. With such tools available to management, why should the salesman select his own route?

Upon receipt of the marketing research department's annual estimates of the potential of each account, a salesman laid out his route and schedule to cover his territory over a two-month period. Eight weeks later, in planning his second round, the salesman used the same data on potential but developed a different route. Is his behavior consistent with sound routing and scheduling principles?

ESTABLISHMENT OF PERFORMANCE STANDARDS

Performance standards assist in providing direction to the salesman and in encouraging the salesman to become motivated toward attaining these standards. Such standards also provide the salesman with a measure of his own progress and provide some measures useful in the evaluation of his performance. Because most salesmen work independently, performance standards of some kind may be more necessary than for workers who work and are supervised at a fixed location. Both output and input standards may be useful.

Output Standards or Quotas

Sales quotas are short-term goals established for marketing units such as divisions, districts, and individual salesmen.

THE NATURE OF QUOTAS

Strictly speaking, the term "quota" denotes a share. Thus a quota for a unit could be that unit's share of the firm's potential, its share of expected sales, or its assigned share of the overall responsibility for attaining a particular goal. That is, one could divide up either the company's total opportunity, its total expectation, or its total sales objective into shares or quotas for each unit and subunit. In practice, quotas refer to objectives. They are expressed as dollar or unit amounts rather than as ratios.

It is well to recall at this point the distinction among sales potential, sales forecast, and sales quota.

Potential is a measure of opportunity.
Forecast is a measure of expectation
Quota is a statement of objective or goal.

Hypothetically, one set of numbers could represent all of these things. Thus a company might expect that full potential was achievable in every territory and that it would therefore represent an attainable and desirable goal for each salesman. At this same time, it would fully expect such potential to be achieved so that the forecast would again be represented by the same dollar amounts.

In the normal situation, however, intervening factors suggest that different values are appropriate for opportunity, for expectation, and as objectives. Forecasts will be distinguished from potentials by allowance for the levels of efforts which are to be applied and the response functions which are expected to result from those efforts. As response functions will differ among territories, expected results (forecasts) will represent different percentages of potential in the various areas.

Goals for individuals and units, although ultimately based on the estimated size of opportunities (potentials) and the difficulties of attainment, must also reflect behavioral considerations. As the establishment of these goals is basically a tool for managing people, the effects of the quotas on the salesman's behavior are paramount. In particular, quotas must be perceived as equitable by those to whom they apply, consistent with the individual's personal goals and attainable with reasonable effort. We may thus appropriately have, for each unit, an expression of its potential, a goal figure for its operations (quota), and an expectation of what will, in fact, be achieved (the sales forecast).

Although there is general agreement that goals should be "attainable," there is wide divergence of views as to the interpretation of that term.

Some advocate "hard" quotas—goals that are somewhat above what most salesman are likely to achieve but which are possible for all and will be attained by a few. Supporters of this view maintain that such quotas induce motivation and provide incentive. In addition, if salesmen participate in quota-setting, it is argued, such high standards tend to offset any tendency of the salesman to set a relatively low goal for himself—that is, two questionable estimating procedures will offset each other.

This practice is exemplified by companies that assign quotas to individual units, the sum total of which substantially exceeds forecast sales results. It may also be observed in divisions and departments in which the quotas assigned to subunits or individual men exceed, in the aggregate, the division's or unit's own quota.

> A highly successful district manager for a large information systems organization explains his success in regularly reaching or exceeding his own quota over many years on the fact that the quotas which he assigns to his men regularly total 120 percent of his quota.

Some executives take an opposing view. They maintain that goals should be modest in order to (1) increase the likelihood that they will be perceived as attainable, and (2) secure the motivation which results from the salesman's having reached his goal. Incentive for attainment of quota and for performance beyond it is provided through financial rewards, such as the so-called salary-quota-bonus system in which the salesman receives a bonus if he reaches his quota and on sales made beyond quota. Similar considerations suggest relatively "easy" quotas wherever compensation is importantly affected by the fact of quota attainment—for example, where the commission rate is stepped up when quota is reached.

A third view accepts potentials and forecasts as inputs to the quota-setting process, but adds subjective considerations to take account of the individual differences among salesmen. Because of these differences, individual salesmen may be expected to have diverse responses to any particular quota tactic. Thus a 40 percent increase in quota over last year may be regarded by salesman A as a challenge; salesman B may consider such an increase as an unreasonable, unattainable imposition regardless of the evidence of potential which the manager may have offered. Advocates of flexibility argue that the establishment of quotas, like other goal-setting activities, is an art which must take due account of expected response profiles of each salesman. Without denying the merits of this contention, it should be clear that such individualistic quota setting may be hard to defend objectively to other salesmen and may thus create problems of its own.

A fourth view considers the forecast itself as an appropriate goal for the firm as a whole. Quota setting and forecasting are intertwined with each territorial quota being, in effect, a forecast for that territory. One may object that the use of forecasts to determine goals reverses presumed causation by fatalistically assuming that "what will be, will be" and that sales will not be affected by the amount of effort; hence, goals should be set to conform to this "reality." The stage is thus set for the self-fulfilling prophecy.

There are, however, situations in which the use of territorial forecasts as sales quotas is not too seriously inappropriate. For example, where the forecast itself is built up from carefully appraised estimates of expected results in each territory, the forecast may, in fact, be quite close to what those in the territory consider realizable goals.

DETERMINATION OF QUOTAS

The development of sales quotas logically starts with determination of the opportunity for the company—that is, sales potential—for each territory. This may be accomplished by any of the methods described in Chapter 5.

Secondly, consideration must be given to the possibilities of attaining various proportions of sales potential with due regard to the salesman's and company's position in each territory. For example, a territory not previously cultivated or one in which competitors are exceptionally strong may not be expected to attain as large a share of its potential as one in which the company has an established position and reputation and in which competitors are relatively weak. Thirdly, allowance must be made for the effort which can be devoted to that territory. In the case of a newly opened territory, for example, it may be possible to conduct only exploratory interviews and approach perhaps only a few key prospects with the resources which can be applied to that territory at a particular time. Finally, the firm must study, or at least estimate, the effects which the goals themselves will have on the sales personnel in order to determine the appropriate level for the quotas—for example, to provide quotas which are challenging but perceived to be attainable.

Two kinds of quota establishment will be examined here. In the first type, personnel management effects and the consequences of uncertainty are ignored; quotas are based on potential and possibilities of attainment. In the second, consideration is given to the personnel management effects and the uncertainties which surround sales forecasts.

QUOTAS TIED TO FORECASTS   When quota determination is tied to forecasts, the company total sales quota is, by definition, the company total sales forecast. The same tools which were used to make the forecast are used to determine quotas. If forecasts are made through the field-force composite or any other territorial building-block method, the final forecasts become the quotas for that unit. If the overall forecast is made by means of projections of external data, the resulting company forecast is then broken into territorial units by some dividing procedure to determine the fair share of that company quota which should be contributed by each unit. The formula used for this division is called an *index*. (See Chapter 5).

Because forecast-quotas must take account of factors in each territory which affect attainability as well as potential of that territory, the index which is appropriate for determining potential in various territories is generally not appropriate for determining forecasts or quotas. Potential is a measure of opportunity. It tells us where we want to go. But it does not tell us where we are or how rough is the road over which we must pass.

Conversely, past sales tell us where we have been but tell nothing of untapped opportunity or where we want to go. Hence, such sales are inappropriate as an index to divide a total forecast or quota among units. Flat percentage changes from past sales are naive, if not dangerous, as either quotas or forecasts.

For these reasons quotas tied to forecasts require that the forecasting procedure recognize both opportunity and difficulties of attainment and that these recognitions must be considered individually for each territory and not merely on an overall basis.

> One company, for example, uses an index to distribute the company total forecast which is based 50 percent on estimates of potential, territory by territory, and 50 percent on past sales in that territory. Although there is nothing particularly sacrosanct about these particular percentages, the company in this way tries to recognize both where it has the opportunity to go, as measured by estimates of opportunity, and where it is now, as measured by its most recent sales experience in a territory. It thus neither perpetuates keeping weak territories weak nor commits its resources without regard for its own current strengths and weaknesses.[4]

QUOTAS DIFFERENT FROM FORECASTS   In order to take behavioral considerations into account, the manager may wish to employ quotas which are larger or smaller than forecast sales. This could be accomplished by taking a percentage of the forecast for each territory as the quota for that territory. Thus quotas could be uniformly set at, say, 80 percent or 110 percent of expected sales.

Often, however, it will be more appropriate to consider quotas involving different percentages of potential or forecast in order to deal with what the manager believes to be the response functions of the individual salesman. In particular, salesmen whose performance has been far below territorial potential may be assigned quotas which gradually close the gap between recent performance and what might be termed a reasonable expectancy for the territory by a series of upward revisions over a period of three to five years.[5]

---

[4] See D. M. Phelps and J. Howard Westing, *Marketing Management* (3rd. ed.) (Homewood, Illinois: Richard D. Irwin, Inc., 1969), pp. 739–753 for this and other examples of quota determination.

[5] National Industrial Conference Board, *Measuring Salesmen's Performance* (Studies in Business Policy, No. 114) (New York: 1965), p. 20.

When a firm is operating in territories with which it has vastly different experience or which are in varying states of market development, it may find substantial variation in its confidence in its forecasts. It might, for example, feel that its sales in established markets are highly unlikely to deviate by more than 5 or 10 percent from those forecast. On the other hand, forecasting information for proposed new uses or in new areas may be imprecise at best. As a result, the company is prepared for the likelihood that actual sales may run from a small fraction to several times those forecast for the new market. In such circumstances, the company may wish to set goals for its salesmen in the new areas somewhat optimistically but temper this optimism for revenue planning by a conservative sales forecast. In other situations, a similarly situated company may make a liberal forecast in order to be able to meet demands if they materialize but may realize that the market may not materialize as rapidly as expected and that the forecast might be viewed as an unattainable goal by the salesman. These and similar situations can be dealt with by developing potential for each territory from objective factors and then deriving two sets of values to reflect expected attainment; one set is used for goal setting (quotas) and the other for revenue expectations (sales forecast).

This procedure may be illustrated by an example using three territories within the responsibility of a regional manager. The estimates for the first and third columns of Table 11-1 were prepared for

Table 11-1

QUOTA FORMULATION WORK SHEET, 1972
(THOUSANDS OF DOLLARS)

	1971		1972	
Territory	Potential	Actual*	Potential	Comments
27	100	90	125	Well-developed territory in which we have strong position and excellent distribution. Approaching maximum market share which our offering can reasonably secure.
28	200	90	250	Heavily competitive area in which leading competitor has strong salesman, excellent distribution, and a major plant. Have less than half the market share which our offerings warrant because of competitive strength.
29	150	15	180	New area first covered by our men in 1971.

*January 1 to November 15 from accounting department; November 16 to December 31 estimated by sales manager.

his use by the market research department. Comments were added by the manager.

The manager noted that in 1971 the company had attained 90 percent of its sales potential in Territory 27, 45 percent in Territory 28 and 10 percent in Territory 29. Upon review of prospects with the individuals involved, he felt that the company well might seek to attain 94 percent of its potential in Territory 27, a strong area, or $117,500. In Territory 28, his goal is to secure one-half of the new company potential in the area. His estimate of $115,000 represents 46 percent of company sales potential in this area of difficult penetration. As the effects of initial cultivation efforts and new distribution secured in 1971 take hold, penetration of Territory 29 should grow to one-fourth the company potential in 1972 and, hopefully, to one-half or more the following year. As Territory 29 is the slowest growing territory in terms of potential for the class of product, serious new thrusts by competitors are deemed less likely than in the more rapidly growing markets. The manager summarized his goals for these territories in Table 11-2. This table also shows his sales expectations for these territories which will be used for financial planning. These expectations, or forecasts, are somewhat more conservative than the goals set for the sales force.

SALESMAN PARTICIPATION IN QUOTA PREPARATION

Regardless of the method of original calculation, each quota should be regarded as tentative until it is reviewed with the salesman or manager to whom it will apply. In part, this is to give the salesman or subordinate manager a sense of participation in the quota-setting process in the belief that he will be more favorably disposed towards a goal which he has helped to establish. In addition, the salesmen and subordinate managers are often able to provide additional information which suggests revision of some of the values used in estimating attainability; at times they may have additional or updated information dealing with potential itself. For these reasons, it is desirable to bring them into the quota-setting process.

Table 11-2

TERRITORIAL QUOTAS, 1972

Territory	Sales Potential (thousands of dollars)	Quota		Sales Forecast (thousands of dollars)
		thousands of dollars	percent of potential	
27	125	117.5	94%	115
28	250	115	46%	110
29	180	45	25%	30

In some cases, the salesman may be asked to make the initial quota estimate. In such cases the salesman should be given the estimates of potential prepared by the marketing research department or similar activity, as a basis for his planning. In addition, estimates of the expected economic environment and other uncontrollable factors should be provided. Such data is needed if the salesman is to establish valid plans and a relevant quota and so that users of the quota can understand the context in which it was formulated. The salesman can then apply his knowledge of attainability in various parts of the market and prepare his own goal (quota) for the forthcoming period. Management participates in such goal setting through review of his plans and estimates with each salesman. Undue optimism or pessimism can thus be tempered. Salesman-proposed quotas are most suitable for more professional sales forces and where attainment of quota itself is not the critical factor in compensation. In these circumstances the salesman is not under pressure to establish a low quota in order to assure its attainment.

Whether quota preparation should be initiated in the field or in the home office depends on the relative information positions of the individuals involved. Unless more accurate forecasts can be made by the salesman, conservation of the salesman's time suggests that he be spared this essentially administrative activity. One company which for several years built its forecasts from estimates made in the field ran a six-quarter test in which both field-developed and home-office-generated forecasts were made. As the forecasts did not differ significantly, the company shifted the forecasting responsiblity to members of the sales manager's staff.[6] Despite the quantitative record, however, it is probably desirable for personnnel management reasons to at least consult with salesmen before final quotas are fixed.

PRODUCT-LINE AND PRODUCT QUOTAS

In addition to establishing overall volume quotas, some companies assign quotas for product lines and even for the sale of individual products. The rationale of such quotas is to encourage the sale of more profitable items, to overcome any tendency for the salesman to stick to "old standbys," and to encourage so-called balanced selling. Some go so far as to establish quotas in terms of gross margin on the not always justified premise that the sale of high margin items is more profitable and should be encouraged.[7]

The use of product-line or product quotas may be an effective way to induce the salesmen to solicit prospective users of new prod-

[6] Phelps and Westing, *Marketing Management*, pp. 748–49.
[7] For example, John U. Farley, "Optimal Plan for Salesmen's Compensation," *Journal of Marketing Research*, I (May 1964), pp. 39–43.

ucts or to give appropriate attention to certain items in the company's line. It can thus serve to offset the tendency of natural segregation in which the salesman tends to promote his particular favorites—often those products with which he finds himself most comfortable and effective.

> A parts manufacturer has many customers who buy a range of items within the company's broad product line. As all the large customers consider single sourcing to be hazardous, each customer's purchases tend to be divided between two or more suppliers. In this situation, the salesman knows that he cannot obtain the exclusive business of the account. He may thus tend to be indifferent as to the items purchased, so long as he obtains as large a total share of the business as he deems feasible.
>
> The marketing department is far from indifferent, however, as there are great divergencies in the profitability of different items. It wants to induce the salesmen to take their business share in the items most profitable to the firm rather than "potluck." Because of production scheduling at various plants, changes in import competition, and other factors, the list of items which are most advantageous to sell does not remain the same for long.
>
> Product-line quotas are developed in the marketing department on the basis of salesmen's and district managers' estimates of usages and market shares, account by account. In evaluating salesmen for bonus purposes, the percentage of product lines on which quota was met is taken into account.

Product quotas, like other devices to promote the sale of particular items, should be used with considerable care. It is one thing to induce the salesman to draw on the entire product repertoire in serving his customers. It is quite another to induce him to push those items which are more profitable to the seller even though they represent less good buys for the customer.

Unless they are carefully controlled, item incentives, including product quotas, may subvert the salesman's responsibility to recommend to the customer that which is best for that customer. If, as is often true, large numbers of salesmen are giving insufficient attention to parts—perhaps the most profitable parts—of the line, management might be well advised to diagnose the causes of such salesman behavior rather than to prescribe incentives as solutions. As noted in Chapter 8, such behavior may reflect limitations in the salesman's competence, or self-perceived competence, which can best be overcome through training. In some cases, the salesmen may be correct in their action because the items most profitable to the seller are not, in fact, the best solution to customer's problems.

PROFITABILITY TYPE QUOTAS

Some firms employ quotas expressed in terms of gross margin or net profit dollars in order to emphasize the importance of selling the most profitable items.

Gross margin quotas proceed from the premise that the items carrying the largest gross margins are the more profitable to sell. This premise may be valid where profit contributions are roughly in proportion to gross margins or where competitive conditions necessitate selling commodity-type products at low margins while more distinctive or innovative products carry wider margins. In many other circumstances, however, high gross margins may reflect other factors such as high order-filling costs (for example, on small orders on which a customer did not receive quantity discount), high handling costs (for example, highly perishable products or those requiring special packing or handling), or special services (for example, special-order merchandise which carries good margins but requires substantial administrative work and possibly set-up costs). It is at best a dubious practice to tie quotas to gross margins unless the reasons for the different gross margins are fully recognized.

In an attempt to avoid some of these difficulties, it is sometimes suggested that net profit or return on investment be the criterion. The difficulties inherent in this practice, including the fact that many factors affecting net profit, even if measurable, are beyond the control of the salesman, are examined in connection with performance evaluation in Chapter 13.

Like product quotas, devices to encourage the salesman to push certain items may subvert the salesman's responsibility to his customer.

Input Standards or Activity Quotas

Activity or input quotas can provide standards on such input matters as number of calls per day, number of demonstrations per week, number of calls made on nonaccounts, retail stores visited, displays set up, or the performance of other selling or nonselling duties.

Activity quotas can be a usefull tool to keep the salesman on the job all of the time and to encourage him to use his time wisely. They serve to provide a performance standard where the relationships developed by the salesman with prospective users or buying influences do not appear in immediate sales results but only over an extended period of time. This kind of situation exists in much missionary work in retail outlets and in calls made on architects, physicians, and other professional men to acquaint them with new products and applications.

Injudicious use of activity quotas can lead to a misdirection of efforts, an undue emphasis on particular input activities, and excessive attention to the quantity, rather than the quality, of input efforts. Calls may be made for calls' sake and demonstrations for demonstrations' sake, without consideration of the relationship of those inputs to the outputs desired. Demonstrations may be given to those upon whom it is a waste of both prospect and salesman time in order to help the salesman make his "demo quota." Calls can be terminated too early, in order to enable making a call quota. To consider an extreme example:

A New York shopper, contemplating longer-than-normally as she prepares to make a purchase, is told by a clerk "We can't allow people to stay here this long if they don't buy something. . . ."[8]

Judiciously employed, both input and output standards can be useful in providing direction to the sales force.

FEEDBACK SYSTEMS FOR REDIRECTION
In Chapter 10 the system for providing intelligence support to the salesman was examined. For that system, which was described in Figure 10-1, it was appropriate to view the salesman as the decision maker being served by the intelligence system. Now it is necessary to view the internal intelligence system from a somewhat different perspective—that of serving the needs of those in sales management who must ascertain whether changes are needed in the goals of various programs, in the means being employed to attain those goals, or in the execution of parts or all of the sales program. These needs embrace information about the environment, including particularly changes in opportunities, and feedback on the outcomes of sales efforts being undertaken. One particular facet of feedback—the evaluation of the performance of individual salesmen—is treated separately in Chapter 13. The more general problem of feedback for redirection will be examined here because it lies at the heart of the administrative process.

Much of the same network which serves the salesman as described in Figure 10-1 provides intelligence to sales management for its redirection decisions. However, the intelligence user (in this case, sales management) is different so that the direction of some flows is altered. More importantly, the function of the intelligence system is different. In the salesman-support information system the salesman is the decision center. The function of the system is to support his interaction with the outside world and his decisions as

[8] *Home Furnishings Daily,* October 14, 1969, p. 31.

to the conduct of his activities. In the redirection information system, in contrast, sales executives (referred to collectively as "Sales Management" in the charts) are the decision centers. The function of the system is to provide intelligence for redirection decisions. In Figure 11-5, Figure 10-1 has been expanded to show information flows to sales managerial decision centers.

The role of the salesman as a source of information on the environment, on specific customer problems, and on response func-

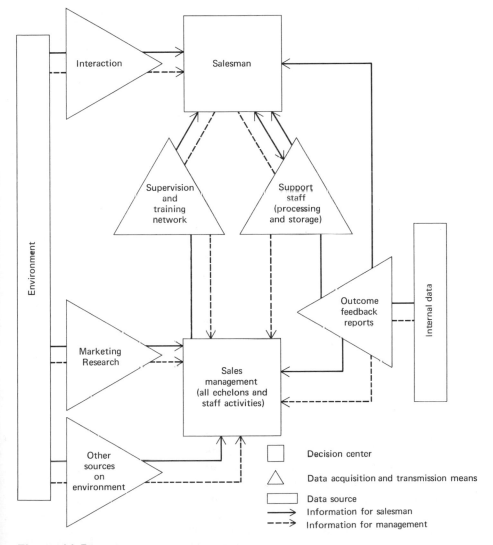

Figure 11-5
REDIRECTION INFORMATION SYSTEM

tions and his participation in processing that information into intelligence has already been examined in Chapter 9. Much information on the environment and some intelligence on response functions will reach the sales managers through salesmen in the field. Other information about the environment and changes occurring in it will come from formal intelligence-gathering activity (market research) and through less formal means such as observation, reading, customer correspondence and complaints, and similar sources.

Most importantly for appraising the need for redirection is the feedback of outcomes of actions taken by the sales force. These feedbacks reach the decision centers in the form of reports from salesmen, observations in the field, and, most importantly, reports from the firm's accounting-controllership activity. These latter are more useful to decision makers after they have been analyzed either in the accounting-controllership activity or by a management staff activity such as a marketing research or sales research department. Accounting-controllership reports are sometimes referred to as "controls" and the actions taken by executives to insure conformity to plans as a controlling activity. Reports do not, of course, "control" anything. Such control as takes place results from the actions taken by decision centers at least partially in response to the intelligence obtained from the reports.

So-called control systems in sales management are invariably of the open-loop variety. That is, deviations from programmed performance lead not to automatic, servo-mechanistic, correction but to a decision to take some action to modify future conduct. As noted in Chapter 1, what is commonly called controlling is largely a matter of determining what has been accomplished so that better plans, directions, and methods can be employed in the future.

In this context, the function of the redirection information system is to provide the decision centers (chiefly sales managers at various levels) with intelligence to enable them to make better and more current decisions on goals and the means to attain them. The performance feedback system must thus be oriented to its central use—*the provision of intelligence for redirection.*

The Nature of Feedback-for-Redirection Systems

Redefinition of goals and redirection of efforts take place through the information and control communications system of the organization. This system feeds intelligence information to the decision centers which act upon it. The role of the communications system is not to make various individuals in the system behave themselves but rather to make their goals converge and to provide a system of behavior rules through which the various individuals in the system can accomodate such differences as they may have.

Such a control system is needed in an organization because, even in the most informed organizations, the different parts do not, and from the very nature of things, cannot, know everything about all of the other parts. These uncertainties are compounded by uncertain knowledge about the environment and about response functions of others both within and outside the organization. The information system provides the means to reduce these uncertainties and deal with those that remain. It does not actively "control" the behavior of the components of the system. But if the system works effectively, the result will be control in the sense that the parts work compatibly.

"The (ideal) information and control system is one which enables each member to utilize his actual competence while compensating for his inabilities whether physical or conceptual."[9] If the system functions well it will have a synergistic effect on the behavior of various individuals in the organization. The competence of each party in the performance of his work will be improved as a result of the communications among them. Such a system will also be adaptive. That is, it will recognize that as a result of the learning process, as well as changes in the environment, the information needs of the various parties will change.

A number of pathological conditions are not uncommon in the information and control systems of sales organizations. Some systems are unable to utilize important inputs. For example, significant data obtained at the field level fails to reach decision centers or is improperly downgraded as to credibility or relevance. Another example occurs when managers fail to understand the nature or import of accounting or research reports or analyses and, as a consequence, fail to utilize fully the significant content thereof.

Some systems provide not too little but too late. A quarterly analysis which reaches the executive responsible for performance 20 days after the end of each quarter may be three months too late for meaningful redirection. Computerized data processing systems now enable firms to maintain information of intelligence value on a current basis, especially if sales and salesmen's data are entered daily. It remains, however, to furnish the intelligence itself to executives in forms and at times meaningful to them. Automatized flagging processes based on control limits and the exception principle may prove useful here.

[9] Robinson and Stidsen, p. 267.

A related problem is one of information economics. As the collection, processing, storage and transmittal of information is costly, it is important that information systems take due account of both the cost and value of furnishing particular information to particular decision centers.

Other systems develop rigor mortis. The system of reports tends to become sacrosanct with little or no attention to the utility of the information to those who will use it. Organizational drift may also lead the system towards an input orientation. Thus the system tends to concentrate on information of which the acquirer is aware or believes should be useful rather than information actually most valuable or perceived as valuable at a particular decision center.

A companion difficulty sometimes found in sales organizations lies in the salesman's desire to attain or conform to standards or to please his superiors rather than striving towards common goals. Thus he acts in a certain way so as to adapt to what he perceives his superior wants rather than in the way which he personally perceives as optimal vis-à-vis the environment—that is, what he believes is best for both himself and the company over the long term. He might, for example, consider as his primary goal the attainment of quota rather than the development of the relationship with accounts which he would consider best for the long pull. Even worse, he might make his overriding goals the achievement of the standard product mix (balanced selling), the standard expense ratio, the standard order-call ratio, and the standard number of calls, all marks of a hierarchical, rather than a cooperative, relationship. He might even seek to help his superior by proving the accuracy of his superior's forecast through attaining it exactly.

Some Useful Feedback Tools

Every firm requires an information and control system to provide a continuing intelligence base for decisions on the possible redefinition of goals and/or redirection of efforts. For this purpose, the system must continually provide answers to four different types of questions:

1. How well are the planned goals actually being achieved?
2. How closely are inputs being provided in accordance with plans?
3. How do customer response functions appear to differ from those expected?
4. How do actual input-output relationships differ from those expected in each area?

Answers to these questions can be sought in a number of ways.

Rarely, if ever, will the answers reveal that for every part of the organization down to the smallest territory all inputs precisely match plans; response functions are exactly those anticipated by the plans; and goals are being attained exactly. Instead, the feedback information reveals deviations from expectancy at many points and in diverse ways. The points thus identified can then become the locus of further probing to ascertain causes. Only then is the analyst or manager in a sound position to suggest either a change of course or remedial action to restore the previously selected course.

COMPARISONS OF ACTUAL AND PLANNED RESULTS

The most general measure of plan accomplishment is a comparison of actual sales for the firm or any marketing unit, with a sales budget or company quota. Similar analyses can be made for product line or customer group goals, and to determine whether goals other than sales volume (for example, number of new outlets secured; number of high profit units sold) have been attained. Examination of the performance of subunits will indicate the areas which have fallen short and those which have exceeded expectations.

Measures of attainment do not reveal the causes of attainment or nonattainment. Alone, they are thus of limited use in the decision process. However, such revenue and other analyses provide a useful starting point in understanding what has occurred and where the deviations are located.

COMPARISONS OF ACTUAL AND PLANNED INPUTS

The most general comparison of planned and actual inputs is the comparison of budgeted expenses with those actually incurred. Expenses, however, constitute the cost of inputs rather than the real inputs themselves. Hence, it is preferable to establish standards in terms of real input units such as sales calls, demonstrations, and accounts serviced. Comparison of actual inputs with the standard inputs can then reveal whether the inputs originally planned and authorized were in fact put in. For example, did the company actually accomplish the 250,000 sales calls and make the 10,000 demonstrations called for in the sales plan for the year?

Many companies have a wealth of data on inputs from call and activity reports. Often little use is made of this data beyond its immediate use in verifying that the salesman is at work and in validating his expense account. Such data can provide a veritable mine of information not only on the salesman's inputs but also on their relationship to results. Once programs are prepared, modern data processing facilities permit examination of these various relationships at modest cost.

It is also meaningful to determine if unit input costs have conformed to plans. Thus the analyst may wish to determine not only how many calls were made but whether cost per call was in accord with expectations. In the event it is not, reasons must be sought. Perhaps efforts were poorly planned (for example, poor routing) or poorly executed (for example, excessive interview time on general conversation, insufficient cost consciousness in securing services, such as those for auto rentals, lodging, or communications). In such cases, corrective action may be called for to bring unit costs into line. In other situations, it may appear that the costs actually incurred in the most recent period represent a more realistic estimate of unit costs than those employed in the preparation of the sales operating plan for the period. In such a case, the standard cost may need to be revised. Future plans will need to be made in the light of the new information about the structure of unit costs. This new structure might suggest a greater or lesser level of a particular activity, for example, calls on nonaccounts, in view of the fact that the cost per input is different from that envisioned when earlier plans were formulated.

VALIDATION OF EXPECTED RESPONSE FUNCTIONS

Even under experimental conditions, response functions are not easily identified. Yet efforts cannot be even reasonably well allocated without tolerable measures of the true shape of the response functions.[10] An important feedback in any sales organization, therefore, should be an attempt continually to improve knowledge of response functions of particular customers and prospect groups.

Much of the evidence on response functions reaches the manager, either semistructured or unstructured, in the form of the salesman's experience in the field as expressed in his written reports and his discussions with supervisors. Evidence in more structured form appears in the records of purchases by customers, *to the extent that those purchases can be related to effort inputs.* Routine sales analysis cannot provide this information. What is required is an analysis of the association between changes in sales and such input as sales calls or time spent with customers, or particular services performed. To date such analyses have been sparsely used; however, the possibilities of rapid and economical data processing now appear to make such analyses feasible as well as desirable.

Simple sales analyses by customer groups, market segments,

[10] See Chapter 4 for the nature of response functions.

account size, territory, salesman, and so on, have some valuable, if limited, uses. For one thing, they can identify responsive segments— that is, those groups which have made purchases or who constitute the major source of revenues. These groups can be distinguished from those who have made only minor purchases. Thus sales analysis may show that forty large accounts contribute 80 percent of sales, or that segment *G* provides 32 percent of sales volume while market segment *H* provides only 3 percent. Unfortunately, it provides no information as to the amounts of effort that were devoted to securing this business, nor does it relate the business obtained to the business potentially available. Nothing in this paragraph, for example, is inconsistent with the hypothesis that market segment *H* is the firm's largest market and did surprisingly well in providing 3 percent of volume since only 1 percent of sales effort was devoted to it.

Secondly, sales analyses may be useful in spotting changes in customer purchasing patterns that may alert management to changes which are occurring in the market or in the environment in which customers are operating. Marked changes in either direction in the purchases of any customer group or market segment serve as flags. Something must have occurred to cause such changes. Once flagged, the analyst can seek out whether the causes lie in controllable actions of the company or in uncontrollables in the environment which the firm should take into account in future plans.

Finally, analysis of the sales obtained in a territory or district may suggest that efforts in that territory or district are being directed in a certain way. Thus, for example, a district product mix pattern different from that found in other districts with similar market characteristics might suggest that the salesmen in that district were dividing their efforts among products somewhat differently than in other areas. It should be noted that sales analysis can only *suggest possible* causation and may not even do that. Further investigation will be needed to determine if the cause, in fact, lies in the behavior of the salesman or, on the other hand, is the result of some characteristics of the users in the area. Even if the observed pattern is finally traced to behavior of the salesmen, the finding is distinctly neutral as to whether this is desirable or undesirable. The observed mix may reflect failure of the salesman to promote some items. On the other hand, it well may be that the salesman in question has found a way to present and sell a highly profitable item and that this experience well might be applied to operations in other areas.

In summary, sales analysis is an incomplete measure of response functions because it ignores sales-effort inputs. Nevertheless, it is an important feedback tool because it identifies events which warrant more careful examination and probing. The latter, in turn, may provide the insights on causal relationships which are so necessary for intelligent managerial response.

MEASURES OF INPUT-OUTPUT RELATIONSHIPS

Measurements which reflect both outputs and the inputs used to achieve them are generally more useful than measures of either inputs or results alone.

MEASURES OF RELATIVE PERFORMANCE   Scatter diagrams provide a relatively simple technique for relating deviations from planned inputs and deviations from planned results. Figure 11-6 plots deviations above and below quota against deviations above and below planned expenses for different regions. Deviations from expense budgets can thus be viewed in the context of the resultant sales achievement. In addition to situations in which both expenses and sales conform closely to plans, four types of situations may be distinguished:

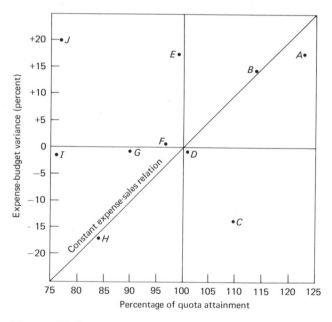

Figure 11-6
COMPARISON OF EXPENSE AND REVENUE
DEVIATIONS
UNITED STATES
BY REGION

Adapted from D. M. Phelps and J. H. Westing. *Marketing Management* (3rd. ed.) (Homewood, Ill.: Richard D. Irwin, Inc., 1968), pp. 754–755.

sales and expenditures both in excess of plans (Quadrant I); sales below quota but expenditures greater than budget (Quadrant II); sales and expenses both below plans (Quadrant III); and sales above quota but expenses below budget (Quadrant IV).

Large deviations from the axes, especially those in Quadrants II and IV are of interest to the analyst. Expenses in excess of budget with returns less than quota suggest difficulties which at least must be isolated and are likely to warrant careful investigation and quite possibly some corrective action. To further isolate the location of the problem a similar chart such as Figure 11-7 is prepared for each unit within the problem region. Figure 11-7 shows such a chart for region *J*. The chart suggests that District 11 should receive first attention, since its expenses were extremely high and its attainment very low. Districts 6, 5 and 2 also had high expenses. In the latter district, however, sales results were so good that despite expenses 38 percent above budget, expense as a percent of sales was only slightly above the standard.

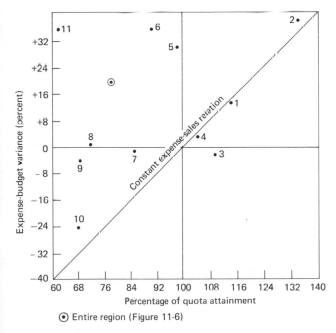

⊙ Entire region (Figure 11-6)

Figure 11-7
    COMPARISON OF EXPENSE AND REVENUE
    DEVIATIONS
    REGION J
    BY DISTRICTS

    SOURCE: Same as Figure 11-6.

How would you characterize the results in District 10? 9? 3?

The process can be extended down to individual territories or the smallest units for which budgets and quotas are prepared. Those districts or territories requiring attention, rather than the entire United States, may then be subjected to intensive examination.

Results in excess of expectations, especially when accompanied by below-budget expenses also warrant investigation. Perhaps fortuitous events accounted for unexpected sales. On the other hand, inquiry may reveal that techniques used in a particular region have been notably effective or that the salesman has uncovered a previously unrecognized segment of opportunity. Techniques thus revealed as effective may be used elsewhere. Segments discovered may be explored further.

Relationships in all quadrants may be interpreted in reference to the expense-sales relation line. Observations on, or close to, the line represent cases in which sales and expenses differ from plans to roughly the same degree so that expenses as a percentage of sales remain close to those planned. Substantial deviations above this line indicate the units in which the expense variance exceeds budget by more than the sales variance, while cases below this line reveal units in which the sales overage was greater than the overage in expenses.

PROFITABILITY ANALYSIS   The growth of mechanized accounting and the development of data processing activities have made it increasingly feasible to match items of cost with the corresponding units of revenue. Thus the profit contribution of various market segments, product lines, or territorial units can be determined. It is not unusual for such studies to reveal that certain segments are unprofitable because the cost of serving them is high or because their purchases consist primarily of items with margins too low to sustain the servicing costs. In some cases, such segments would continue to be unprofitable even if substantial increases in sales could be obtained. At the same time, other segments may be found to be sufficiently profitable to suggest that increased efforts be devoted to them.

In any costing procedure for managerial purpose, it is important to distinguish charges which may be *assigned* to a unit from those which are *allocated* to it. Costs which are directly attributable to the unit being analyzed and which would therefore be avoided if the unit were eliminated are *direct* charges and are *assigned* to that unit. The unit's contribution to overhead and profit is determined by substracting all assigned costs from the revenues derived.

In contrast to direct charges, overhead charges are incurred on behalf of more than one unit and would not be significantly affected if the unit were dropped. If full costing is used, various overhead charges are *allocated* to the various units which benefit from them on some equitable basis, called a service unit. The deduction of these allocated charges from the net contribution yields the net profit.

Whether a particular expenditure is a direct (assignable) charge or an overhead item which must be allocated depends on the object of analysis. For example, consider a salesman traveling to a remote prospect to offer him a line of several products. The cost of the salesman's travel is clearly a direct charge in analyzing the profit contribution of the customer, the customer group to which he belongs, and the territory. But in making a profitability analysis of products, no cost is assignable to any one product. If any product were dropped the travel cost would in no way be changed. The total cost of the trip could be *allocated* in some way, for example, on the basis of the time spent by the salesman in presenting each product.

For most managerial purposes, net contribution margins (revenues less all assignable costs but before deducting allocated charges) are the more relevant. For decisions affecting a unit, it is only those charges which will be affected by the decision that matter. The unit's allocated share of the president's salary, for example, is irrelevant. The use of net contribution margin rather than net profit after allocated charges has the additional merit of freeing the decision and sales administration process from the consequences of allocation rules which are often necessarily debatable (as to what basis of allocation is appropriate). In discussing problems with subordinate managers, attention on matters clearly beyond the control of the manager and which cannot be affected by the decisions under consideration is thus avoided.

The utility of profitability analysis is by no means limited to determination of which units are profitable or the relative profitability of different units. Its greatest value may often lie in isolating the sources of costs and thereby broadening the range of possible corrective action.

Tables 11-3 and 11-4 illustrate customer profitability analysis for a distributor. The activity of some example accounts is shown in Table 11-3. Gross margin averaged 17.9 percent for the firm. The actual gross margin obtained on sales to each customer varied depending on the product assortment purchased and the extent to which the customer was entitled to "full case" or other quantity discounts. Gross margin by customer is shown in Table 11-4, column two. The following columns show the three costs which are directly assignable to particular accounts:

1. The cost of each sales call which was $6.
2. The cost of selecting the item from stock in the warehouse, which amounted to 50¢ per line item.
3. The cost of delivering each order to the customer which was $2.50—the amount charged by the contract trucker for each delivery stop in the metropolitan area.

Column seven shows the net contribution to overhead and profit obtained from each customer after these direct costs have been deducted from the earned gross margin. Net profit on a "full cost" basis is shown in column nine after deduction of an overhead allocation of 5 percent of sales.

Table 11-3

PURCHASE RECORD OF SELECTED CUSTOMERS

Customer	Purchases (dollars)	Sales Calls (number)	Orders (number)	Line Items (number)
A	$ 200	6	4	20
B	300	6	2	10
C	800	6	4	20
D	1100	12	12	80
E	2000	20	50	250
F	3500	20	30	200
G	5000	20	32	250

Overhead for customer analysis purposes includes all expenses which are not directly attributable to an individual customer. It includes such costs as those for buying, sales administration, inventory management, warehouse supervision and administrative expenses of the firm.

Table 11-4 shows that all but two of the listed accounts contribute positively to the company's net profit. Why do B and D contribute to profits?

More importantly, Table 11-4 shows that the reasons for lack of profitability differ among the customers. Customer A clearly does not generate enough volume to warrant six calls by the salesman. In the case of E, in contrast, the problem seems to lie in frequent ordering of small quantities. Customer E not only required the processing and shipment of fifty different orders, he purchased small quantities of each item on the orders so that order selection costs were high. The average line extension (dollars of purchases per item purchased) was only $8 for E compared with $40 for C and $17.50 for F. Thus E's purchasing practices made his business unprofitable even though the total volume was adequate.

Table 11-4

PROFITABILITY ANALYSIS OF SELECTED CUSTOMERS

| Customer | Gross Margin | Order Filling Cost | | | Total Assigned Costs | Contribution | Overhead Allocated | Net Profit |
		Call Cost	Warehouse Cost	Delivery Cost				
A	$ 36	$ 36	$ 10	$ 10	$ 56	(20)	10	(30)
B	57	36	5	5	46	11	15	(4)
C	150	36	10	10	56	94	40	54
D	188	72	40	30	142	46	55	(9)
E	300	120	125	125	370	(70)	100	(170)
F	600	120	100	75	295	305	175	130
G	850	120	125	80	325	525	250	275

Should any of these customers be dropped? What alternatives would you consider in the case of A? B? D? E? Do the data suggest that some sales administration policies might be reconsidered?

SUMMARY

Macro-direction of the sales force involves the establishment of routes and schedules to make the most effective use of the salesman's time, the formulation of performance standards for the salesman's work, and the development of feedback systems through which managers can ascertain desirable directions for changes in goals or means for their attainment.

Routing

Sound routing principles are necessary to make the most effective use of the salesman's time. Routing plans can be developed by sales management, often with the aid of mathematical tools. Relatively straighforward time- or distance-minimization plans may be useful where all calls have similar value. Where call values differ, slow-fast or parallel-route schemes may provide more effective application of salesman resources to opportunity.

Where the desirability of salesman contact with accounts is affected in only a minor way, or not at all, by changing current relationships with them, management-prepared routes and schedules may enable full use of managerial tools while relieving the salesman of a time-consuming activity.

Especially in nonroutine types of selling, the art of call timing and thus of scheduling and routing can be undertaken more effectively by the salesman as the individual most likely to have the kinds of current information and feel for current relationships needed for effective call planning. In these circumstances, management's job is to demonstrate the advantages of good routing and scheduling and to develop the salesman's competence in applying sound routing and scheduling principles.

Performance Standards

Performance standards assist in providing direction to the sales force and in encouraging the salesman to become motivated in the directions indicated by the standards.

Input, or activity, standards are useful in indicating to the salesman what is expected of him in terms of the various duties and responsibilities which he is asked to assume.

Output, standards, or quotas, provide goals towards which the salesman may strive and against which both the salesman and his superiors can measure his attainment. The establishment of performance standards should take into account the three factors of opportunity (sales potential), expectation (sales forecasts), and the personnel management effects to be expected from the establishment of different goals.

The participation of the salesman concerned in goal establishment is desirable. At the least, tentative goals should be reviewed with the men. When the salesman's information position permits, more active participation is feasible, even in some cases to the extent of having each salesman establish his own goals with only minimal participation by management.

Feedback Systems

Information and control systems which provide feedback to managers and salesmen are indispensable to sound planning and constructive redirection of sales-force activities.

They should be cast, however, not in the context of devices to implement a top-down hierarchical system but rather as an essential element of a mutually supportive sales-management system. It is this system which defines opportunities and applies the resources to capitalize on them and which redirects both its posture to the outside world and its internal relationships as new situations are revealed.

The sales manager has a number of measuring tools to determine the outcome of plans previously made. These enable him to determine how closely the inputs which were provided corresponded with plans, how well customer response functions agreed with those which had been envisaged, and how well planned goals were, in fact, achieved. The thrust of these tools is to identify areas of deviation from goals or other standards and then, through more detailed and complementary analyses, to seek to ascertain causes so that changes can be made in either the goals themselves or in the activities which are carried out to attain them. Thus the executive is supplied with a continuing flow of new intelligence about the environment and about relationships between his firm and that environment. It remains for him, however, to utilize that intelligence to make the decisions which are the substance of any control or redirection system.

Despite their rather clear utility in feeding back to management intelligence of considerable import for decision making, many companies still make only modest use of the analytical tools described. Some go no further than to compare sales results with some not always very sophisticated standard. The cost of obtaining data and of processing it by manual methods has sometimes been offered as a primary reason for the failure of these tools to be more widely used.

With the advent of data processing systems and access to computing facilities by even small firms, a major impediment to more thorough analysis has been removed. Some firms will go as far as the utilization of "real time" systems in which salesmen's activity reports, intelligence from the field, and data from the firm's accounting-controllership activity are constantly used to update the firm's data bank. As only standard analytical programs are required, various types of analysis can be made available to the sales manager without great cost and while the data are still current. A substantial increase in the use of the available tools to provide more analytical and relevant feedback to decision centers, therefore, seems inevitable.

12 Micro-Direction of the Individual Salesman

Productive sales effort results from a climate which encourages and rewards self-development.[1] Sales organizations become and remain viable in the same way—by the maintenance of a climate which encourages and rewards self-development.

Individual salesman development has both long-term and short-term aspects. For the long term, means and incentives must be provided for the professional growth of each man whether this growth leads to a managerial area, to some other role in the firm, or to a career as a salesman. For the short term, the problem is largely one of making the goals of the salesman compatible with the goals of the firm so that efforts to achieve them will be mutually supporting.

[1] John M. Rathmell, *Managing the Marketing Function* (New York: John Wiley & Sons, Inc., 1969), p. 257.

LONG-TERM DEVELOPMENT OF THE INDIVIDUAL SALESMAN

Development of the individual salesman does not just happen. It occurs only as the result of conscious management policy and specific activities to bring it about.

THE LONG-TERM DEVELOPMENT PROBLEM

Many firms find themselves with a chronic shortage of really qualified salesmen and sales executives. Others find that although men with excellent potential are recruited, many of the best men leave the firm before reaching positions of important responsibility.

A not uncommon situation in many companies is that of a large number of salesmen performing "adequately" but not growing with the job. Thus, they do not become more valuable to the customer, to the firm, or to themselves, despite their added years of tenure.

One reason for the loss of good men is the failure to move them ahead as fast as their capabilities, experience, and performance warrant. Sometimes this failure is a result of excessive emphasis on seniority in promotion, compensation, and recognition of status and an unwillingness to separate or transfer weak personnel at various echelons. A result is a loss of incentive for the more able and ambitious. Good men can also be lost because they do not correctly perceive the opportunities which lie ahead and the rate of advancement which is possible.

Even more serious than the loss of men is the failure to fully develop the potential of each man in the organization. Under modern competitive conditions, few firms can afford the luxury of failure to utilize fully the human resources which it has available, nor can society as a whole, Thus, both a firm's self-interest and social needs require that human resources be fully and effectively utilized.

The problem is made more difficult by the need to maintain motivation. As a man masters a job, its ability to challenge him declines.[2] Concurrently, job accomplishment contributes less to fulfilling the man's psychological needs for achievement. Consequently, these motivations become less potent. Thus the firm needs to provide opportunities for individual growth not only because some people want to grow but because men generally are subject to a fundamental phenomenon of living things—they must grow and adapt or they tend to wither and die.

An oil company executive noted that the loss of experienced men was heaviest among those who seemed to be most highly achievement-

[2] Saul W. Gellerman, *Management by Motivation* (New York: American Management Association, 1968), p. 84.

oriented. Yet these men rarely left the company for higher-paying jobs elsewhere.

A particularly difficult problem is motivating the man who has reached his level and has begun to realize this.

> A power equipment manufacturer had a technical sales force most of whom had been with the company about 20 years. As each man began to realize that he would probably not become a manager, motivational problems grew. In some cases, the symptoms took the form of declines in enthusiasm and effort; in others they extended to off-the-job behavior—drinking, family difficulties, and so on.

A related problem is fully utilizing men who are overvalued in terms of their present capabilities. Such overvaluation may occur because of (1) errors in the selection of men for promotion, (2) a man's failure to change with the changing requirements of the job, or (3) some external event (for example, heart attack; neurosis) which impairs the man's suitability for his present job but is not so serious as to require retirement for medical reasons.

> A manufacturer of packaged products seeks to meet its ethical and social responsibilities in such cases by transferring the men to less arduous and sensitive positions in the home-office organization. If the cases occur in the headquarters area and are not too numerous, the impact on both the men and the organization may be acceptable. The number of openings to which such men might be assigned in the field offices is so limited, however, that it does not provide a ready solution for cases arising in the field.

If a firm is to develop its manpower, it must both nurture professional growth and make clear to its men that professional growth will be properly rewarded.

PROFESSIONAL DEVELOPEMENT AND CAREER PATHS

Successful development of personnel entails both the encouragement of personal development by each individual and provision of the means through which that development may be aided. The former requires that each salesman perceive goals which he deems to be both worthwhile and attainable. Management can assist in this perception by making explicit the kinds of career opportunities which are available and the career path which the salesman may be expected to follow either within the field of personal selling itself or through the personal selling echelons into some management position. To be effective as motivators, the attainment of these goals must be realizable within credible and acceptable time periods. We have long passed the time when the delivery boy would work for small wages in the hope that in forty years he might become the owner of the store.

The need for prompt recognition or reward is common to all fields. It has particular application to careers in which the achievers tend to seek excellence, *per se.* Sales work is an example. One writer alleges that early recognition in life is a primary motivator in the selection of a sales career.[3] A company in which an able man must wait five years for his first promotion and cannot reasonably expect a position of real responsibility for 20 years is likely to have little appeal as a recruiter or in retaining the best achievement-oriented men from those who do join it.

If the promise of advancement for accomplishment is to be credible and meaningful, opportunities for advancement must be kept open. In a rapidly growing organization, the expansion process itself may provide this opportunity. More generally, however, the maintenance of opportunity requires some measure of an up-or-out policy in the various sales grades and at various supervisory and managerial positions. This is not to suggest that men with years of service should be ruthlessly dumped but rather that manpower development should be programmed over the years so that weaker personnel are either strengthened or moved into positions in which they do not act as impediments to the advancement of those who are able and prepared for greater responsiblities. Where younger men are not performing adequately, it may, indeed, be a service to them to encourage them to find positions more in line with their capabilities and attitudes rather than leaving them in a position with poor prospects for advancement. For older men, transfers of duties or even early retirement may sometimes be required. What is clear is that under modern competitive conditions few firms can afford the luxury of an ineffective sales organization developed through seniority and aggravated by the loss of the better men.

The career path concept has been offered as one solution to the problem of inducing growth and maintaining promotion opportunity. Under the career path concept a definite minimum and maximum time is established for each grade. To avoid "lockstepping" a wide spread is provided between these two limits. For example, the range for junior salesmen might be six months to three years. Thus the most able and best performing juniors can be considered for promotion as early as six months after they begin work; those who have not been promoted at the end of their third year are counseled to seek careers more in line with their capabilities and dispositions either within or outside the firm.

If the growth path leads from regular salesman to a senior

[3] Olof Henell, *Some Science in Personal Selling* (Stockholm: Esselte Reklam AB, 1961), p. 43.

salesman position entailing additional responsibilities, the career path might establish the time-in-service limits for regular salesmen as two to six years. A recruit knowing the career path can see the types of opportunities which are open to him and the times required to reach various points.

A well-designed career path provides for the elimination of the poorer performers through the exit requirements and, in additon, provides an opportunity for the most able performers to move ahead as rapidly as their progress permits.[4]

When applied to an entire sales organization, the career path idea may be embodied in a series of two or more paths which branch out according to the men's abilities and interests. In this way a professional sales career path with appropriate recognition and rewards can be provided for those whose interests or abilities are more aligned with accomplishing things themselves than through others. Many fine salesmen do not necessarily make good managers, nor in some cases would they wish to become managers at all. They should, nevertheless, be offered opportunities to advance in their own field, including the opportunity to earn more than some sales managers if their performance warrants.

The use of rapid advancement to encourage the better men is not restricted to firms which employ formal career paths. It does, however, generally require some affirmative top management emphasis on manpower development. For example, management may make it clear that it expects selective rather than "en bloc" advancement of men during the first few years of their service. The importance of manpower development can also be made clear to supervisors by evaluating their performance in terms of the professional progress attained by the men supervised—that is, more emphasis on the long-term promotion records of a supervisor's men and less emphasis on their current sales records.

Personnel development planning requires procedures to identify men with good potential for promotion or reassignment. These will not necessarily be the men with the best performance in their present jobs. An average salesman may have managerial capabilities superior to those of a top performing one. Some companies develop promotability rankings or otherwise seek in an organized way to identify men with promotion potential.

A drug manufacturer requires that regional sales directors submit to headquarters, twice a year, the names of men who should be considered for promotion.

[4] For a description of the career path concept and an example of its application, see Andrall E. Pearson, "Sales Power Through Planned Careers," *Harvard Business Review*, January–February 1966, pp. 105–116.

An industrial products company tries to give personnel at all levels the opportunity to accept next-level responsibilities under supervision. In this way the company believes that it can identify men with promotion potential without disrupting their effectivenss in their present position.[5]

TOOLS FOR LONG-TERM DEVELOPMENT

Manpower development requires more than unblocking opportunities and encouraging men to grow. It must provide the means through which this growth can take place. Among these means, formal training in the salesman's *present* job has already been discussed (Chapters 7, 8). For those to be given new responsibilities, additional training in the nature of these responsibilities and the means to deal with them is generally called for.

Training for Growth

Training for new responsibilities must be recognized as a *different* activity than training to maintain or improve competence in a man's present assignment. Moreover, the timing must be relevant. So-called management training given when the trainees can be spared from other duties and without regard to the individual man's status in respect to promotion is likely to lack relevance. If new knowledge and understanding is, nevertheless, achieved, it may be quickly lost if not found applicable to the job which the man is currently performing. Hence, training for new responsibilities should be scheduled when men are at least reasonably close to consideration for promotion or immediately after such promotion.[6]

Many firms are notoriously weak in providing managerial training for new field sales managers, apparently believing that successful sales experience is sufficient to equip a man for managerial duties. Some firms, however, recognize the problem and provide management seminars and similar training programs designed especially for the newly appointed district or regional manager.

Training for managerial responsibilities should, if at all possible, take place before, rather than after, a man is placed in a managerial position. One authority suggests that each salesman who might have managerial potential be given the opportunity to train himself for managerial responsibility, but that the alternative of remaining a field salesman and achieving advancement in that area should also be made clear to him. The salesman may thus choose the road which he

[5] Morgan B. MacDonald, Jr. and Earl L. Bailey, *The Firstline Sales Supervisor* (New York: National Industrial Conference Board, 1968) (Experiences in Marketing Management, No. 17), pp. 11–12, 14.
[6] Saul W. Gellerman, *Management by Motivation*, p. 105.

prefers, with his supervisor offering guidance but not directing choice. If the management training program is carefully structured—for example, through home study and student self-development projects—each man can proceed at his own pace. Some will decide that managerial duties are less to their liking than sales work, thus providing a self-selection device devoid of any stigma of being passed over. More importantly, the able salesman who, after examining the nature of a junior managerial position, opts to remain in selling is unlikely to be unhappy when others are selected for managerial assignments.

An additional advantage of preassignment managerial training is that it can provide a pool of men who have qualified for managerial duties which can be drawn upon as vacancies occur. Thus, filling managerial posts is less likely to be opportunistic or to rest on the happenstance of availability at a particular moment.[7]

Providing a Growth-Inducing Environment

If professional managers and professional salesmen are grown, not born, any nurturing of the growth process must recognize that the process is a continuous one and that most of it will occur outside of the context of formal training programs. In terms of Gellerman's analogy to a tree, "competence grows when it is systematically nourished, pruned of its errors, and transplanted, as it grows larger, to new ground on which it has ample ground to flourish."[8] Gellerman holds that a growth-inducing environment includes at least the factors of strotohing, feedback, coaching, and career management.

Stretching involves giving a man responsibilities a bit beyond those for which the man himself or his superiors believe he is ready. Stretching accelerates the growth of competence. The assignment not only provides motivation, but its successful attainment provides a reinforcing reward which acts to motivate further achievements.

Performance feedback—how a man is doing in his present job—is now commonplace as an accepted part of performance evaluation. Also important for professional growth is feedback from superiors about a man's standing with the firm and his prospects for promotion. Periodic career counseling can fill an important need in letting men know where they stand.

---

[7] See William J. E. Crissy, Gary A. Marple, and Earle Conant, "Field Assignments for Individual Managerial Development," *Business Topics,* Winter, 1963, pp. 49–63, for an exposition of the preassignment, self-development idea and an excellent example of its use in one company. Reproduced in Wotruba and Olsen, *Sales Management: Concepts and Viewpoints, A Book of Readings* (New York: Holt, Rinehart and Winston, Inc., 1971).

[8] Gellerman, *Management by Motivation,* p. 107.

Coaching is a major supervisory responsibility and a teaching tool for upgrading men and assisting them in personal growth.[9]

Career management involves corporate dedication to the professional growth of its people. In application, career management will often intrude into traditional management prerogatives. To prevent sacrifice of career management policies to the needs of short-term problem solution, a career management program requires an administrator with a voice of sufficient power in the organization to override divisional and functional managers seeking to secure shorter term goals.

For the most part, and despite the extensive formal training and retraining activities of many firms, professional growth must be the accomplishment of the man himself. The bulk of the task of executing any manpower development program thus rests with those who work most closely with the individual salesman—his supervisors in the field.

> The critical role of supervision is suggested by the findings in one study of salesmen who had attained managerial status. Ninety per cent of these managers attributed their growth and development to the adept way their superiors directed subordinates and the understanding relationships thereby developed.[10]

Long-term development of salesmen and sales managerial personnel rests in a significant way on the effectiveness with which day-to-day (short term) individual salesman development activities are carried out.

SHORT-TERM DEVELOPMENT OF THE INDIVIDUAL SALESMAN

The fundamental man-development problem in the short term is to bring the goals of the salesman and of the firm into a sufficiently compatible relationship so that efforts to reach these goals will be mutually supportive. Short-term development of the individual salesman is basically a matter of developing and operating a supervisory system to accomplish this.

SUPERVISORY RELATIONSHIPS

Supervision refers to the relationship between a manager and his subordinates. Some view this relationship as basically a means

[9] Gellerman believes this to be such an important activity in management development that he proposes a separate staff managerial coaching activity to provide coaching over and above that provided by line superiors who are, by virtue of their present positions, primarily interested in getting present jobs done. (*Management by Motivation,* pp. 113–115).

[10] John J. McCarthy, "Establishing a Climate for Sales Force Success," *Sales Management,* XCLIII: No. 10, May 15, 1967, Part 1, pp. 73–80.

through which managers get things done through people. Thus Phelps holds that "Supervision is the means by which a company induces its salesmen to cultivate the market along effective lines."[11]

Such a view accords with a "top down" theory of management. It conceives of the supervisory process as largely one of executing plans and decisions made at higher levels and assuring conformance to those plans. The role of upward communication, in this view of the supervisory process, is largely one of providing feedback on the results of activity and processing incoming information.

However, as McGregor has pointed out, "The success of any form of social influence or control depends ultimately upon altering the ability of others to achieve their goals or satisfy their needs."[12] This seriously questions the traditional view for its failure to accord adequate weight to the role of the salesman in the execution process. In an earlier chapter, objection was raised to views of the sales process in which the customer is seen as a passive object while the salesman is considered as sole actor. In the same way, too narrow a view of the process of supervision sees the salesman as a passive object being "supervised" to carry out mandates provided by others, rather than as an active goal seeker.

A broader view of supervision must recognize the community of interest in compatible goals which can be developed among the members of a selling organization in much the same way as successful sales relationships are developed through the generation of such a community of interest between salesmen and their customers. "Supervision is an influence process. The manager is trying to influence salesman behavior, just as the salesman is trying to influence customer behavior. The overriding purpose of supervision is to influence the salesman to behave in a manner consistent with the company's policies and objectives."[13]

In this broader context,

Supervision involves the development and maintenance of a system of formal and informal relationships among various echelons within a sales organization, such that the goals of the various members are made compatible and the means of attaining these goals are made consistent and mutually supporting among the various individuals involved.

[11] D. M. Phelps, *Sales Management* (Homewood, Ill.: Richard D. Irwin, Inc. 1951), p. 663.
[12] Douglas McGregor, *The Human Side of Enterprise* (New York: McGraw-Hill, Inc., 1960), p. 20.
[13] Kenneth R. Davis and Frederick E. Webster Jr., *Sales Force Management* (New York: The Ronald Press Company, 1968), p. 570. Sentence sequence altered.

The supervisory process is thus participative; both the supervisors and those supervised are active participants in the process. Each group provides inputs in the way of personal goals and perspectives on organizational goals. Each provides its perspectives on desirable or acceptable means of attaining the goals. Each group receives outputs from the process, in the form of comparative perspectives which must be reconciled with its own attitudes.

Supervisory relationships are established in part by the formal structure of the sales organization. However, although the designated authority of formal organizational relationships provides the official right to manage, actual influence may be exercised very largely through the informal or de facto set of leader-follower relationships.

Leadership is the ability of an individual to influence others in their perception and behavior. Essentially, the leader is able to convince the follower to accept as desirable a particular or general goal, and to elicit his cooperative participation in attainment of it. Acceptance of the goal is induced by determination of it according to a common value system which reconciles interacting priority inputs of each. Participation in attainment is secured by ensuring that such endeavor will be suitably rewarded. Ultimately, however, leadership derives from the action of the follower—that is, from his willingness to be led. It is thus quite distinct from formal authority. Members of any group may look upon their formally designated superior as the sole leader or they may regard some member of the peer group or another individual as the person they will follow. The occupant of a supervisory position in the formal organization has, thus, only the opportunity to exercise leadership. Whether he will lead will depend on whether he is able to secure the followership necessary to make him a leader in fact. If a supervisor is to be a leader, he must so reconcile his interests and the company's with those of the salesmen that the men will regard following his leadership as the most efficacious way of achieving their own goals.

The practice of leadership is an important part of supervision. Hence leadership capability is an important attribute of the successful supervisor. Like other human skills, leadership capabilities can be developed.

The effective leader must enjoy the respect and confidence of his followers. Generally, this means that they must respect his knowledge and judgement as well as have confidence in the consistency of his practices with their own goals. This does not mean, however, that the leader should be "one of the boys." Quite the contrary, the results of several studies consistently indicate that leaders who in their own minds are psychologically distant from their groups have more effective groups than do leaders who are more closely related to (feel greater connection with) their groups. Stated differently, the leader who feels that he is, in reality, part of a "happy family" has been found to be consistently less effective than the leader who sees himself as being aloof and apart from his group.[14]

The essence of any supervisory system is two-way communication. Supervisors communicate with their subordinates through messages, written and oral, and by their actions. Subordinates communicate in these same ways with their supervisors. In a larger context, supervisory levels are merely way-stations in the communication of messages between the sales force and higher echelons of management. Each supervisor is thus both a recipient of messages from "above" and "below" and a provider of messages to both these groups.

An effective communications network must be both procedurally and substantively efficient. It must be procedurally efficient in the sense that the messages in the system provide a maximum of information with a minimum of distortion and noise. It must be substantively efficient in the sense that the content of the messages works to further the goals of the persons in the system and of the organization for whose benefit the system exists. Messages, of course, are not transmitted for their own sake. An effective supervisory system is one in which the messages passed through the system affect the conduct of the various parties in ways which best serve the system as a whole.

GOALS OF THE SUPERVISION SYSTEM

The supervisory system of a firm has the broad task of nurturing compatible interrelationships within the sales organization, and between members of the sales organization and other individuals within the firm. In particular, it should seek to provide a favorable work environment, to develop manpower, to strengthen morale and induce commitment to the firm, to interpret and enforce company policy, and to provide channels for the flow of intelligence from and to the field organization.

Creating a Favorable Work Environment

A prime responsibility of any supervisor is to create and maintain a work environment conducive to a high level of performance.[15] This entails the establishment and maintenance not only of working conditions suitable for sales work but of interpersonal relationships among the salesmen themselves and between salesmen and others in the firm so as to encourage a high level of work performance. The

[14] Philip B. Applewhite, *Organizational Behavior* (Englewood Cliffs, N.J.: Prentice-Hall, Inc., 1965), pp. 119–120.
[15] Davis and Webster, p. 564.

salesmen need to know more than simply the rules of the game, including their responsibilities, their authority, and the basis on which they will be evaluated. They must also be confident that the tools which they need and the supporting activities upon which they depend for the performance of their work will be appropriate, adequate, and timely.

Developing Manpower

Supervision has often been described as a continuation of training, in that the supervisory system is expected to maintain and to extend the skills and knowledge of those supervised. In addition to providing resources for such upgrading, supervision must provide the incentive for men to attain defined aspiration levels and, ultimately, impel them to raise the aspiration levels themselves—that is, to make men want to better their performance. At all levels of supervision, manpower development is a major responsibility. One important information systems organization, in evaluation of its field management personnel, considers a supervisor's development of his men second only to his current sales level. In this respect, supervisory systems which merely implement current operating policies and training programs which merely extend knowledge and skills appropriate for the man's present responsibilities are likely to fall far short of full development of human resources.

Strengthening Morale and Inducing Commitment to the Firm

The development and maintenance of morale is a major responsibility of the supervisor. Many morale problems are symptomatic of inadequate communication within the organization. For example, some men may not understand clearly the rationale for managerial actions, or they may not fully realize what is ordinarily expected of them. Others may feel that management either does not understand their problems or the particular problems of their jobs or is indifferent to seeking remedies for them. Such morale difficulties reflect underlying communication deficiencies within the supervisory system.

The orientation of the communications system itself may contribute less than it could to higher morale and commitment. Commonly, the supervisor is treated as the nexus of the communications system. Messages flow to him for dissemination to the sales force; intelligence and results of field operations flow to him from the field for processing and forwarding to higher echelons of management. This orientation results generally from top-down theories of management. The supervisors represent the junior officers and noncoms who transmit instructions to the troops, report on the results of execution, and forward filtered intelligence from the field to the decision makers at headquarters.

A more market-oriented approach would suggest that the critical interaction for an organization is its interaction with its market. Thus the salesman should become the nexus of a communications system which involves customer personnel on the one hand and individuals playing a variety of roles—for example, marketing management, product managers, designers, production and distribution planners, marketing researchers—at different levels in the selling firm on the other. The role of the supervisor here is to develop and improve the communications network through which the salesman exchanges information and influences with various groups within his own firm. By thus conceiving of the salesman as the center of the marketing communications network, the salesman's morale is strengthened because the system is now conceived as centering on him. This accords with the general principle that morale is positively related to the centrality of an individual's position in a communicative network.[16]

Interpreting and Enforcing Company Policy

Supervisors are charged with interpreting company policy to men in the field, securing compliance, and adapting policies to local conditions. In some circumstances, the latter may require securing the approval of higher authority for deviations or suggesting modifications in the policies themselves. In this role the supervisor becomes the salesman's advocate.

Providing Channels for Intelligence Flow

One of the salesman's primary responsibilities is the collection of information and the initial stages of its processing into intelligence.[17] Here supervisors have a normal responsibility to ensure performance of such activity and, in addition, have intelligence-processing responsibilities of their own—screening, evaluating, supplementing, and forwarding intelligence to other echelons and activities. Supervisors should review their mental and documentary files for information which bears usefully on the particular item of information obtained from the salesman. For example, Salesman F reports several inquiries about a tool from his customers; his supervisor knows of other situations encountered by other salesmen in the solution of their customer problems which might well be resolved by a similar tool. These bits of information need to be brought together if the best intelligence is to be furnished to those responsible for the development of the product line. Information which is insufficiently transmitted (blocked) or improperly interpreted can have serious reper-

[16] Applewhite, p. 105.

[17] The role of the salesman as an information source is examined in Chapter 9.

cussions on the morale of the salesmen who furnish the information and on the intelligence base upon which higher echelons must rest their decisions.

TECHNIQUES FOR EFFECTIVE SUPERVISION

The central task of supervision is to develop salesmen in their capabilities for customer service, information handling, and working relationships in the company. To accomplish this, the supervisor must encourage the salesman to accept responsibility and to deal with the problems such responsibilities involve. He must avoid thrusting a crutch into the salesman's hand at the critical moment. Like the child learning to ride a bicycle, the salesman must develop a capability to solve his own problems; he cannot do so if the instructor (parent) refuses to let him solo and to learn to deal with any crises involved.

This is not to suggest that demonstration sales and coaching on the job are undesirable. On the contrary, they can be a useful part of the training process. Where the sales supervisor steps into a selling situation, however, the purpose should be clearly instructional—that is, to demonstrate and not to salvage an unfortunate situation. To be sure, there will be situations in which managerial personnel will find it necessary to intrude themselves into a sales situation because of larger considerations. It should be recognized, however, that each case in which the manager has for the moment reverted to salesman represents in some sense a failure of sales supervision.

Much of the supervisor's work, like much of that of the salesman, is to promote change. In overcoming resistance to change, human perceptions are critical. Success in modifying the salesman's behavior may be more a function of how the change is offered than of the nature of the change itself.

An understanding of the broad fundamentals of human behavior is indispensable to effective interaction. It can rarely be acquired solely through observation and experience because behavioral bases are internalized. The sales manager may be well advised to accept a premise found useful by many behavioral researchers—that everyone's behavior is reasonably logical to himself. Thus to understand a man's actions, we must see the situation as he sees it; whether his view is "right" or "wrong" is at this point irrelevant.[18] A few key behavioral concepts are outlined in the appendix to this chapter.[19]

In a society in which many of the lower-order needs have been

[18] Gellerman, p. 17.
[19] The reader unfamiliar with the behavioral sciences should read the chapter appendix before proceeding.

reasonably well met, the salesman's esteem and self-actualization needs are likely to play significant roles—witness the growing concern of young men for jobs which represent a socially useful contribution.

In seeking to understand each man, the supervisor must guard himself against convenient blindness and oversimplifications; he must deliberately avoid both substitution of his own values for those of his salesmen, and the blanket assignment of presumed value scales based on stereotypes. The supervisor must continually be on the alert for clues to the needs of each man. Failure to understand which needs apply to each man, and to what degree, can easily lead to fruitless appeals to needs that have been adequately satisfied, or at the other extreme, to those which have not yet emerged. The emphasis must be on those needs which are relevant. A man with unfulfilled safety needs is unlikely to be strongly motivated by appeals to his aesthetic needs; while a man with well-gratified lower needs may derive maximum motivation from inducements aimed at his self-actualization needs.

Positive Supervision

The first task of the supervisor is to maintain a continuing understanding of the need status of each man. Personal discussions and observation of what may "turn on" the salesman are the principal sources from which the supervisor must derive this information. The supervisor must be engaged in a continual learning process himself, lest his understanding of his men become obsolete as the men develop. In this perspective, telephone and written communications and even meetings in the supervisor's office are, despite their economy in time and travel, incomplete substitutes for face-to-face interaction in the *salesman's*—not the supervisor's—environment. Group communications, through sales meetings in which the salesmen actively participate, provide additional sources of information, chiefly about peer-group goals and standards but also about individuals and their needs and goals. The manager's job in both cases is to be a good listener, a competent observer, and an astute perceiver.

Based upon an understanding of the salesman's needs, positive supervision should demonstrate the congruence of company and salesman goals and should provide the salesman with the capability for goal attainment. The supervisor's task is to demonstrate to each man that his needs—whatever they may be currently—are best met by performing in the desired way. For some of the more advanced types of sales work (categories 1 through 4 in Chapter 2) this may entail showing the salesman how his, say, self-actualization needs are met by artful and successful development of customer relations and solutions to customer problems.

In many types of sales work the salesman may set certain immediate objectives, the attainment of which will aid his reaching his long-term goals. Supervision here is necessarily supportive rather than directive.

The supervisor seeks through counseling to assist and encourage the salesmen to set worthwhile goals for themselves and to cultivate the means to attain them.

> A manufacturer of chemicals to remove pollutants considers all salesmen to be territory managers. It extends the management-by-objectives concept to them. Salesmen set their own goals and prepare call plans to attain them. If the supervisor believes these goals are too high or too low, or that the salesman's plans are not adequate to attain them, counseling will be employed. Managers do not, however, direct changes either in the salesman's goals or in his work plans.
>
> Managers do seek to monitor the salesman's conformance to his own plans. If filed itineraries or call reports indicate departure from plans, the appropriate manager will inquire of the reasons for divergence. Some departures from planned itineraries occur because of customer calls for help. While in some cases, such a call requires an immediate visit, the company has found that in many situations the customer merely wants assurance that the salesman will call reasonably soon—say, within the next ten days. Through counseling, managers assist the salesman to learn how to evaluate the customer's call for service.

If the salesman has previously learned that his long-term needs are best met by establishing and attaining short-term goals which are in both his and the firm's interest, he can provide his own motivation not only to perform well but to use his human capacities to devise better methods of achievement. Thus the whole man, not just the legs and mouth of the salesman, is enlisted in the effort.

If a man's full potential for self-development is to be nurtured and released, supervision must use all its communications skills toward that end. Working with men in the field, the supervisor must encourage his salesmen to set goals which are worthwhile both in meeting their individual needs and in meeting those of the company. Suggestions on methods of attainment must be offered in the context of supporting the salesman's achievement of his goals rather than through reference to the guidelines or rules of an authoritarian system.

Incentive devices (for example, contests, promotional meetings, and incentive compensation) are widely used to stimulate salesmen to greater effort. The principal rationale for such stimulatory devices lies in the belief that the monetary or other rewards will motivate the salesman by meeting his desires for greater material income. Another rationale is that they serve as short-run attention-focusing devices which preempt the other goals the men seek. Some incentive programs also seek to meet esteem or other needs. Although there is generally a dearth of proof from carefully designed experiments, many practicing sales managers believe that such devices play a significant role in stimulating salesmen to better performance.[20]

One hazard in incentive devices is that they may aim too low in the salesman's need hierarchy. Furthermore, by setting at a low level what it believes the salesman's needs to be, the company may convey to the salesman the impression that company executives believe that his interest is solely in meeting those lower-level needs. If this premise is in fact correct, the device may provide powerful incentive. But a material reward can hardly be expected to assist in the realization of the salesman's esteem or self-actualization needs and indeed may detract from their attainment.

Programs which stress recognition rather than, or in addition to, tangible reward may overcome this defect. However, all stimulatory devices may divert the salesman from the development of long-term customer relationships to the attainment of short-term rewards. In addition, they may distort the sales job by placing emphasis on activities being rewarded at the moment. This very factor makes such devices extremely useful in focusing attention on particular activities to which management wishes attention devoted for a given short period. However, side effects may make such devices quite undesirable for extended usage or for the attainment of longer-term objectives. Sound administration of incentive programs requires regular checking of the consistency of short-run program objectives with longer-range goals.

Minimizing the Negative Factors in Supervisory Relationships

The supervisor is a formally identified leader. His job is to keep the organizational machine tuned up so that each individual in it is motivated toward organizational goals. Hence, he is responsible for providing initial direction of sales endeavor, and for redirecting the efforts of individuals as feedback may indicate or in response to changed customer needs.

Various problems will occur: conflicts of objectives will arise; goals will not always be achieved; other departments of the firm will not always perform in a manner which the individual salesman be-

---

[20] For design criteria and examples of incentive devices, see D. M. Phelps and J. H. Westing, *Marketing Management* (3rd. ed.) (Homewood, Ill.: Richard D. Irwin, Inc., 1968), Chapter 29.

lieves is best. Moreover, problems of equity will occur in evaluating and rewarding performance within the group. Salesmen may feel, perhaps correctly, that certain responsibilities which they are asked to assume or certain duties which they are expected to perform are inappropriate. Communications will not always be fully understood and their full and intended impact throughly perceived.

In addition, frustrations and the rigors of sales work may disappoint or even disillusion the salesman so that his confidence in the possibilities of goal attainment is shaken and his motivation lags. The supervisor must assist the salesman to overcome these difficulties and where possible must minimize the impact of the human problems which may be encountered.

The foregoing suggests the many areas of potential friction between salesmen and other elements of the firm, supervisors in particular. The able supervisor will operate so as to eliminate or minimize many of these problems and to deal effectively with those that do arise.

Guidelines aid the supervisor in minimizing the conflicts in the various relationships so that positive supervision can have its greatest impact. Among them may be the following:

1. Understand an individual's motivation before seeking to offer incentives to him. Appealing to a high-order need when the man has an unmet, severe low-order need is likely only to mark the supervisor as a man who does not understand.

2. Work periodically in the field with each salesman in order to observe his motivations and methods, to exchange views on aspirations and goals, and to provide guidance.

3. Make each man feel individually important. Use praise and recognition whenever warranted—but honestly.

4. Encourage men to bring problems and grievances to sales executives.

5. Encourage the acceptance of responsibility by individual salesmen. Do not impair it by stepping into sales situations.

6. Maintain open, two-way communications flows with each man. One thoughtful executive suggests the following as important elements in maintaining such a flow:

   a. Don't refrain from communicating performance information to a salesman because you think "he doesn't need it." Everyone needs it—good or bad.

   b. Beware of "voltage drop," that is, loss of meaning as a message travels through communications channels.

     c.   Check to be sure your messages are properly under-
stood. Get feedback.

     d.   Acknowledge communications from your salesmen;
send those warranting it up, follow up on them, and
keep the salesman informed.

     e.   Let your salesman know *first.*

     f.   Be honest with your men. Never lie for any reason—
this destroys the essential element of trust.

     g.   Listen.[21]

7.   Seek to minimize any possible effects of the administrative system (for example, expense accounts, routing,
reporting, scheduling, vacations, sales meetings) which
may be adverse to the motivation of the salesman. This
involves regarding such activities, insofar as possible,
as support activities for the salesman and making clear
to the salesman just how they support him. Such activities
should be "consumer oriented"—that is, the salesman
should be used as a source of what should be provided.
Activities which, *in the salesman's eyes,* are not supportive of his work should be carefully reviewed on a
regular basis to determine if they are necessary and
appropriate in their current form. The reporting system,
in particular, should be treated insofar as possible as a
service to the salesman.

8.   Ensure that the salesmen are clearly aware of the ultimate
objectives of the instructions, policies, or duties with
which they are expected to conform. Where the purpose
is obscure or ambiguous, advice may be necessary. In
some instances, revision or rewrite of policy may be
needed.

SUPERVISORY EFFECTS OF OTHER ACTIVITIES OF SALES MANAGEMENT

The relationship between a manager and his subordinates
and the ability of that manager to influence the behavior and direct
the activities of subordinates is affected by other sales management
activities. In particular, the evaluation and compensation systems
and administrative arrangements play a role in the behavior of the
salesman. At times, such activities provide added thrust to what the
sales supervisor is seeking to accomplish; at other times, these influences work at cross purposes.

[21] J. Porter Henry, Jr., "The Ten Biggest Mistakes Field Sales Managers Make:
#1—Flubbing the Communications Task," in *Sales Management,* Vol. XCI,
No. 1 (July 5, 1963), pp. 42–47.

Directive Effects of Evaluation Methods

If salesmen believe (correctly or not) that they will be evaluated on the basis of certain particular activities or that their performance will be judged largely on the basis of those activities, their efforts will normally be directed to those activities rather than to any suggested by the supervisor. This is a not uncommon problem. For example, a supervisor may stress the cultivation of markets and the development of long-term relationships with prospective accounts; at the same time the salesman may expect that he will be evaluated on the basis of number of accounts opened or the dollar value of orders written during the current period.

As most evaluation methods do not measure progress toward attainment of long-term company or salesman goals, the hazards are real that such measures will work against the programs of supervision. Sales managers need to assure themselves that the evaluation plan is not indirectly discouraging the kind of behavior which the supervisor is trying to develop.

Directive Effects of Compensation Plans

A similar problem exists with respect to compensation plans. Many compensation plans, especially so-called incentive plans, place a very heavy—often a sole—emphasis on a single or very small number of "results," generally those which are most easily measured, such as current sales. An understandable effect is to direct the salesmen's interests and efforts to those activities which produce such "results." The compensation plan may thus influence behavior in a manner counter to that which the supervisor is trying to induce.

Directive Effects of Administration Practices

Administrative practices such as those dealing with work required for routine reports and their timing, the scheduling of meetings, and the reimbursement of expenses may have adverse, if unintended, effects on the goals the supervisor is attempting to reach.

Report preparation may preempt time that might otherwise be used for call preparation. Sales staff meetings may lead to less effective routing and scheduling of sales calls than might otherwise be possible—for example, a two-hour Monday morning meeting which results in salesmen traveling during hours when customers could be seeing them instead of traveling on Sunday evening, thus resulting in a loss of much of a business day. A liberal mileage allowance may encourage returning home each night especially if reimbursement for overnight costs is either cumbersome or niggardly.

In addition to being reviewed for their own efficacy,[22] adminis-

---

[22] See Chapter 11.

trative routines should be appraised in terms of their side effects, including their tendencies to influence the behavior of the salesmen in their daily work.

EVALUATION OF SUPERVISION

Supervision may be evaluated from three perspectives.

In terms of its output, one may ask, "How well are the objectives of supervision being attained?"

In terms of the application of inputs, one might inquire, "How properly are the supervisory inputs being applied?"

Finally, in terms of resource allocation, the question may be posed, "Is the right amount of supervision being employed?"

Evaluating Attainment of Supervisory Objectives

Measures of the performance of supervisors in developing their men are, at best, indirect. The evaluation process is thus largely one of informal appraisal using such indirect measures as attainment of sales objectives or the promotion records of subordinates trained.

The results of many facets of the supervisory process are observable only indirectly through the examination of pathological conditions which supervision should, in the ideal case, forestall. A number of these pathological conditions will come to the attention of executives in the normal course of operations. This is likely to be especially true of so-called personnel problems—those associated with low morale and disgruntled or unhappy personnel. Other malfunctions of the supervisory process can be isolated only through alert perception of pathological indicators, or, in some cases, only by specific field studies to determine the existing state of affairs. Hence, malignant conditions may persist for extended periods until they are identified and steps taken to correct them.

A few of the more common problem areas may be examined at this point. In each case, the means by which the problem can be identified by management and the nature of the supervisory weaknesses which it suggests are noted briefly.

LOW MORALE

Low morale, or a general pattern of unfavorable attitudes toward the job and job relationships, is most likely to come to the attention of management when specific problem cases arise. Disputes among salesmen or between salesmen and supervisors, complaints outside the established chain of communication, threats to resign, and an excessive number of resignations are indicative of morale problems. It may also be manifest as a condition of general departmental apathy. Although morale problems can arise from a number of factors, their chief source is the failure of supervision to control adequately the negative factors in supervisory relationships.

EXCESSIVE TURNOVER OF DESIRABLE PERSONNEL

Total turnover of sales personnel can be readily derived from records. In itself, however, such a figure is of little worth since it does not reveal which men are being lost, nor why. A degree of turnover is acceptable, even desirable: some of the men selected probably will prove ill suited for sales work, or incorrectly placed in their assigned jobs. In addition, age, health, and personal factors will bring about some separations. Moreover, an organization which virtually no one ever leaves and from which no one is ever discharged is likely to be one in which standards are lax and discipline lacking.[23] Hence the manager should seek not the lowest possible total turnover but rather should seek to minimize the loss of *good* men from *preventable* causes. While a high total turnover figure suggests that some good men are being lost, and a low figure that too many weak men are being retained, an awareness of the nature of the turnover (*which* men are being lost) and the reasons for personnel losses is necessary for a full understanding of the significance of turnover data. If better men are being lost from causes which are or should be under the company's control, there may exist serious supervisory deficiencies, such as weakness in developing manpower, or a failure to create a favorable work environment, or inadequate control of negative factors. On the other hand, such probing may disclose that nonsupervisory factors (for example, compensation out of line with the market) are at fault. In any event, the management which fails to probe the causes of turnover (through termination interviews and by other means) foregoes an opportunity to secure an insight not only into the causes of turnover but into the effectiveness of the supervision process itself.[24]

FAILURE TO FOLLOW COMPANY POLICIES

Some instances of the failure of salesmen to follow established company policies can be detected by examination of data provided

[23] It is recognized that such an organization is almost an impossibility. Medical problems would still affect it, and lax standards and lack of discipline would inevitably mean limited and constantly deteriorating success, with poor compensation and diminishing prospects of survival. Nonetheless, over the *short term* such organizations do exist: a business with rampant nepotism; a trade association supported by taxes (called dues) on a productive industry, but itself not subject to any real performance test; military garrison troops; and individuals at an educational institution (not all of them students).

An extraordinarily low turnover rate may also indicate that an organization is exceptionally good, its opportunities and rewards excellent—especially in conjunction with a good selection system.

[24] Discriminant analysis may be useful in isolating factors contributing significantly to turnover.

through the internal reporting system. For example, do the accounting records show that orders written conform to established policies in respect to customer classification? In respect to special orders? To terms of sale? To prices and discounts? Do call reports show that the salesmen are servicing accounts as prescribed by policies?

Other evidence of nonconformance to policy may come from customers, either in complaints or as a result of field investigation involving customer interviews.

Significant evidence of noncompliance with company policies suggests that the supervisory function of enforcing, interpreting, and securing modification of policies is not being well performed. Commonly, the fault lies in inadequate communication to the sales force of policies and their relevance, and the importance of observance. In some cases, however, the difficulty may lie in the failure of supervisors to perform their adaptation and modification responsibilities adequately. As a result, the salesman, believing modification or approval of an exception to be unlikely, simply violates the policy in what he deems to be both the company's and his own best interests.

NONCOMPLIANCE WITH ADMINISTRATIVE ROUTINES

Noncompliance with administrative routines may be revealed through the operation of the routines themselves (for example, failure to provide full product, delivery, or terms on orders; failure to furnish complete expense report information; failure to communicate with office at designated times). Other types of noncompliance (for example, failure to follow routing plan, failure to report change of itinerary, or improper use of company vehicle) may go undetected until a system malfunction or other unexpected event reveals them.

Noncompliance with routines, like nonconformance with company policies, suggests supervisory weaknesses in discharge of communication and enforcement responsibilities.

POOR CUSTOMER SERVICE

Poor customer service by salesmen is most apparent when customers complain. These complaints may concern the work of the salesman himself—for example, he made promises which he could not or did not keep. Often, however, customer complaints which are not specifically directed at the salesman may reveal that the account is not being serviced well. For example, a customer may express dissatisfaction with the performance of a product, the true cause of which is the failure of the salesman to diagnose properly the customer's problem and to prescribe the correct product. Similarly, a service complaint may indicate that the salesman failed to make clear to the customer the delivery, installation, maintenance, or repair services which would be provided. On the other hand, such complaints may be traced to other activities (for example, manufacturing, inspection, quality control, shipping, billing) or to faulty communications between such activities and the salesman (for example, failure to furnish accurate information to the salesman).

Many problems of customer misunderstanding are reflections of a failure at the salesman-customer interface and, in turn, may reflect the salesman's failure to service the account in an able and proper way. Other problems result from faulty communication within the salesman's firm. Because supervision is responsible both for manpower development, including keeping the men in tune with the market, and for the internal communications system as well, it shares at least a portion of the responsibility for such communications breakdowns.

Waiting until customer complaints or lost accounts reach the attention of the manager may be a quite unsatisfactory means of ascertaining deficiencies in sales service. Some firms supplement this information source with field studies which interview personnel in buying organizations to determine their appraisal of the sales personnel who call on them and, in particular, of the quality of sales service which they receive. Such a survey may reveal, for example, that buyers regard the company's salesmen as less reliable than competitors' men for, say, information. Such a finding would indicate some rethinking about sales training and especially about maintaining the product and applications competence of the sales force.

POOR PERFORMANCE OF INDIVIDUAL MEN

Although poor performance of individual men may be noted from review of each man's current records,[25] it is sometimes fruitful to compare the performance of individual men within a supervisor's responsibility. The persistence of wide differences over long periods suggests either that the men differ very greatly in ability or that supervision has been unsuccessful in determining the reasons for the success of the better men and then using that information to strengthen the performance of the weaker personnel.

Where a number of salesmen are not doing well, the ultimate cause of poor performance may be poor selection, the failure to maintain an encouraging work environment (including motivation), ineffectiveness of training, a lack of success in building morale, or an ineffective two-way communications system. Further probing is thus necessary to isolate the problem.

NONGROWTH OF INDIVIDUAL MEN

Static performance, especially in expanding markets, suggests possible deficiencies in manpower growth and development by super-

[25] Evaluation of salesmen's performance is examined in Chapter 13.

visors. The issue here is not whether sales "beat last year's" but rather whether the salesman's additional years of service are reflected in professional growth. Has his ability to serve customers improved? Has he assumed greater responsibilities in the course of time? A situation in which all of the men working under a particular supervisor generally have static performance and seem to present little promotion potential suggests that the supervisor is not discharging well his responsibility for manpower development.

POOR AREA PERFORMANCE

Poor performance by individual district managers or other supervisors is most evident when wide differences in performance are noted—as among various territories—which cannot be explained by external factors. A widely varying range of performance according to any standard implies that, unless the standards are manifestly incorrect, some territorial managers are employing techniques which are more effective than those employed in other districts. Hence, improvement in some districts through the application of methods used elsewhere may be suggested. If wide differences persist, local management is suspect and a review of the supervision process in the weak districts is called for.

Evaluating Supervisors' Work

In evaluating the manner in which supervisors are performing their jobs, the analyst may be concerned with such questions as: (1) Are supervisors devoting the necessary proportion of their time to managing, that is, getting work done through working with others, as opposed to doing subordinates' tasks for them? (2) Have administrative routines been adequately delegated—for example, to office or customer service managers—or so routinized that the manager does not devote excessive time to them? (3) Did the supervisor's expenditures of effort conform closely to agreed-upon plans?

The Right Amount of Supervision

The "right" amount of supervision is dependent on the individual being supervised. Whether an individual is being oversupervised or undersupervised can be adjudged only in terms of the resulting relationships and performance.

For a sales organization as a whole, however, the relationship between amount of supervision and organizational performance is likely to be curvilinear, as in Figure 12-1. For a sales force of a given size, additional supervisors—that is, fewer salesmen per supervisor—can be expected to increase organization output up to a point, after which no additional benefits accrue and, eventually, a negative effect results.

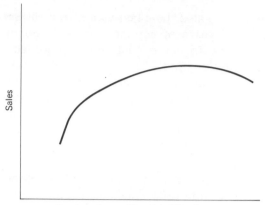

Number of supervisors per 100 salesmen

Figure 12-1
RELATIONSHIP BETWEEN AMOUNT
OF SUPERVISION AND ORGANIZA-
TIONAL PERFORMANCE

An oil company created a number of new territories within its marketing area, thus reducing the area for which a district manager was responsible. No increase in sales resulted—that is the return from the presumably closer attention to the territory was zero.

SUMMARY

Professional growth of individual salesmen requires deliberate programs to bring it about. Failure to provide the conditions and means for such growth is likely to lead to (1) chronic shortages of both able salesmen and sales executive material, (2) failure of the men to grow with their jobs and adapt to changes in them, and (3) difficulties in maintaining motivation as men mature.

Programs for professional growth must both encourage personal development of each man and provide the means through which that development can take place. The provision of a growth-inducing environment entails stretching, feedback, coaching, and career management. Training must go beyond that required for the man's present job and embrace new responsibilities which men must be induced to seek.

Supervision plays a major role both in the long-term development of men and in resolving the many short-term problems of making the salesman's and the firm's goals compatible so that they will be mutually supportive.

Supervision of the sales process is not, or should not be, the authoritative direction of subordinates in the rigid implementation of inflexible company policy. The sales supervisor is an intermediate in the system, the indispensable link between vision and realization. On his shoulders rest grave responsibilities to the firm, for successful execution of its policies, and to the salesmen, for their success and welfare. These responsibilities are not separate and rival, but rather are complementary—the success of both depends on the fulfillment by each. Failure of either will severely impair operation of both.

Generally, chances of success are increased when it is made clear to both salesmen and firm that they share (at least to some degree) certain common goals, particularly over the long term. Given such mutual objectives, salesmen will be disposed to work toward achievement of them, ordinarily by any particular activity the company may desire. If long-term goals are very compatible, and means of attaining them consistent and mutually supporting, it may be expected that all factors involved will exert every effort to achieve them—even to the point of, on occasion, cheerful subordination of particular short-term objectives.

A primary responsibility of the sales supervisor is to intermediate between administration and his field sales force, in order to ensure that the perspectives of both groups are reconciled so that goals, and means of attainment, are established and pursued on a reasonably consistent basis. Thereafter he must labor to ensure that this happy state persists.

The supervisor's most important tool in effective operation is communication. A good two-way communications system is perhaps the most vital element in the total structure; without it, nothing can function. All message "inputs" must be clear and meaningful. All must be received by those to whom directed. Otherwise, confusion, inefficiency, and ultimately breakdown of the system will result. So long as the communications system does function in both directions, suspicious pathological tendencies can be discovered and corrected before they become malignant, and the normally operating system can be periodically scrutinized, tested, and modified for better results. These positive measures devolve squarely on the shoulders of the supervisor.

Positive supervision may be regarded as the cardinal attribute of the successful supervisor. To such a man, each subordinate is unique and can best be influenced in his own particular way. The manager will determine as best he can the needs which activate each individual, will remain alert for changes in these need structures, and will base his efforts to influence each man on the incentive calculated to appeal most. He will ensure that he himself is the principal buffer between his men and the upper administration, both to minimize any adverse factors which may develop and to reinforce the favorable. While he may champion his men against the administration, however, he cannot do so in the market; and in fact here he must guard carefully against interfering *unless absolutely necessary* in order to train and develop the salesmen. He cannot do their work or make their sales.

In short, the manager must create and maintain a favorable work environment; he must interpret and enforce company policy; he must sustain each man's morale and strengthen his commitment to the firm; and he must make every effort to develop the men he directs in their particular and general capabilities for personal and company achievement. Successful discharge of these responsibilities of necessity rests on the establishment and maintenance of a substantively and procedurally efficient two-way communications system.

APPENDIX TO CHAPTER 12
Some Behavioral Concepts Relevant to Supervision

One cannot observe another's rationale; one can at best perceive only its outward manifestation in behavior. One may make inferences about the rationale and motivations which perhaps produced the observed behavior. But such inferences are likely to be little more than the observer's interpretation of the behavior, necessarily in the observer's terms and conceived in his frame of reference. They are not in fact the subject's rationale.

Since sales managers and salesmen occupy different roles in the firm, their perspectives will differ. Hence it is not only possible, but likely, that managerial inferences about salesman behavior may contain substantial error. Such error can be extremely costly since failure to understand the salesman's value and goal structures and how they are modified can easily lead to unwise managerial policies or supervisory tactics. In these circumstances the sales manager is well advised to acquaint himself with current views concerning motivation and behavior, especially those views which appear to be supported by evidence.[26] A few key concepts will be reviewed here.

[26] Experimental evidence on motivation in sales-type situations is rare. The reader is referred to literature on motivation and organizational relationships such as: R. F. Bales, *Interaction Process Analysis: A Method for the Study of Small Groups* (Reading, Mass.: Addison-Wesley Publishing Company, Inc., 1950); B. Berelson and G. A. Steiner, *Human Behavior: An Inventory of Scientific Findings* (New York: Harcourt, Brace & World, Inc., 1964); D. Cartwright and A. Zander (eds.), *Group Dynamics: Research and Theory* (2d ed.) (Evanston, Ill.: Row, Peterson & Co., 1962); K. Davis and W. G. Scott, *Human Relations and Organizational Behavior: Readings and Comments* (2d ed.) (New York: McGraw-Hill, Inc., 1969); R. L. Kahn, *et al., Organizational Stress: Studies in Role Conflict and Ambiguity* (New York: John Wiley & Sons, 1964); M. S. Olmstead, *The Small Group* (New York: Random House, Inc., 1959);

Probabilistic Nature of Human Behavior

Because man has a free will, no behavioral science technique can predict with certainty what any given individual or group will do when faced with a particular set of circumstances. But a sound set of tested theories can be useful in the prediction of what will be done and the attachment of subjective probabilities to various possible sets of behavior.[27]

Motivation

Motivation refers to an underlying psychological state that impels or causes behavior. . . . Strictly speaking a manager does not "motivate" his subordinates. The motive exists within the "motivated" individual. . . . Rather, the manager provides incentives for his subordinates. . . . An incentive can motivate behavior if the individual perceives that the reward will help him to fulfill a need, want, or desire.[28]

Thus it is incumbent on the supervisor to make every effort to discover what needs, desires, and other determinants of behavior may impel his subordinates, and how best they can be capitalized on to motivate suitable behavior.

The Hierarchy of Needs

A foward-looking theory of motivation is propounded by one prominent psychological "realist" Dr. Abraham H. Maslow, who elaborated the Jungian concept of "self-actualization." The term is defined as "a basic tendency toward the end of making actual what is potential in the self, toward maximal realization of one's potentialities." The natural course of normal human development is viewed as a gradual unfolding and gratification of certain essential needs and attributes of human nature, in sequential stages of progressive development from "lower" to "higher" motives and organization.[29]

Maslow asserts five classes of basic needs in a hierarchy of prepotency. These are: *physiological* (food, water, sleep, sex), *safety* (protection from hazards in the physical, economic, and political environment), *belongingness and love* (affectionate and loving relations with others), *esteem* (for oneself, from oneself and from others), and ultimately, *self-actualization.* The arrangement in a hierarchy of pre-

Rensis Likert, "A Motivational Approach to a Modified Theory of Organization and Management," in Mason Haire (ed.), *Modern Organization Theory: A Symposium of the Foundation for Research on Human Behavior,* Chapter VIII (New York: John Wiley & Sons, 1959), pp. 184–217.

[27] Applewhite, p. 2.

[28] Davis & Webster, *Sales Force Management,* p. 559.

[29] This discussion is abstracted from A. Maslow, *Motivation and Personality* (New York: Harper & Row, Inc., 1954), particularly Chapters 4, 5, and 6.

potency means that some are usually manifested earlier in the developmental process, and that a "lower" need must be adequately (not entirely) gratified before the next higher need can fully emerge. Thus normal psychological growth is in a succession of need "waves," in which the relative salience and potency of the different needs gradually shift. Once a man has graduated from lower needs through their adequate gratification, the needs simply come to assume a less important place in the whole motivational structure. Though a lower set may again become temporarily salient, it is never as obsessive and overpowering for the individual as initially. Of course, the fixity of needs in the hierarchy is not absolute, and the general sequence may be altered in various ways—a person may even become permanently fixated on fulfillment of one basic need set.

In addition to these basic needs, Maslow asserts other closely related personality essentials which are preconditions for the basic need satisfactions ("a set of adjustive tools, which have, among other functions, that of satisfaction of basic needs"). These are: *the desire to know, the desire to understand,* and the *aesthetic need* (which may not appear predictably). While these are vital "preconditions," they too emerge eventually as a distinct system of needs *per se.*

One must bear in mind here that Maslow is theorizing about *motivations to action* in terms of needs or desires. He is not talking about *behavior.* "The person will *want* the more basic of two needs when deprived in both. There is no necessary implication here that he will act upon his desires. . . . There are many determinants of behavior other than needs and desires." Some behavior is heavily influenced by stimuli in the environment so that underlying needs have only modest impact.

It is significant that particular needs are not generally exclusive or single determinants of behavior. In fact, most behavior is multimotivated. Each act serves to meet many needs—a meal satisfies more than just the need for nutrients; sex may gratify much more than the simple desire for sexual release.

The strength of a given motivation depends in an important way on the level of the need which generates the motivation, and its degree of fulfillment. It is particularly important to note that the current status of need gratification naturally colors the view of past and future—for the sake of a higher need one may allow himself to be thwarted in a lower need (though prolonged privation will eventually force a revaluation). Maslow explains this in terms of tolerance developed through habituation and through early (and solid) gratification of prepotent needs.

Clearly a need which has been largely satisfied will not generate significant motivation; and a need which, because lower-order needs still press heavily, is below the threshold of significance in the individual is likely to have little motivating effect. In short, the inducements offered to effect motivation must be in terms significant to the person one seeks to activate. *Within limits,* the relative motivational pull of any given need will differ with every salesman, and hence effective inducements must differ.

Relationship of Job Satisfaction to Performance

Studies in a number of industrial situations indicate that the factors which lead to job satisfaction are different from those which produce job dissatisfaction. The basic satisfiers are related to the *job itself.* The principal ones appear to be recognition, achievement, advancement, responsibility, and the work itself. These are closely related to the fulfillment of esteem and, perhaps, self-actualization needs. In contrast, the principal sources of job dissatisfaction are associated with *conditions which surround the job*—company policy, working conditions, supervision, interpersonal realtionships, and, to a certain extent, compensation. While improvement in conditions surrounding the job, if perceived by the salesman to be improvements, can remove sources of dissatisfaction and thus reduce turnover, such does not increase satisfactions. The latter requires that the job itself fulfill self-actualization or, at least, esteem needs in order that motivators will operate.[30]

Important as it is, however, it must be remembered that job satisfaction does not per se lead to superior work performance. It is only when the worker's own needs are met by the performance itself or if his tensions are reduced by that performance that job satisfaction and improved performance will necessarily be found together.[31] Moreover, performance which satisfies the salesman's goals may or may not provide the outcome the firm desires.

[30] Frederick Herzberg, *Work and the Nature of Man* (Cleveland: the World Publishing Co., 1966) Chapter 6. A number of recent studies suggest that Herzberg's two-factor theory may be an oversimplification. See *Annual Review of Psychology* Vol. 19 (1968), pp. 468–477.

[31] Applewhite, p. 26. In a study of 63 full-time appliance salesmen in a retail chain, Cotham found little evidence of statistical association between various satisfaction measures and sales performance. (James C. Cotham, III, "Job Attitudes and Sales Performance of Major Appliance Salesmen," *Journal of Marketing Research,* Vol. V (Nov. 1968), 370–375.) For a review of other studies see Timothy W. Costello and Sheldon S. Zalkind, *Psychology in Administration: A Research Orientation* (Englewood Cliffs, N.J.: Prentice-Hall, Inc., 1963), Chapter 6.

Effects of Goals on Performance

Clear knowledge of goals tends to improve performance.[32] In the case of groups, individual members become more involved in working toward goals of the group if those goals are clearly percceived.[33]

Moreover, performance tends to be positively related to the height of salesman's and manager's goals.

> Likert, in comparing forty independent sales units in a large company, found that in the high producing units both the salesmen and their managers had high goals.[34]

Care must be taken to ensure, however, that goals are not perceived to be so high that they are impossible to attain. The limited reported research in this area does not deal with sales personnel but is believed to apply to them. It suggests that challenging goals are more likely to produce maximum performance than goals which are either too easy or are thought to be so high that there exists only remote chances of attainment.[35]

Effects of Goal Attainment and Group Aspirations on Future Goals

It is generally true that successful attainment of a goal tends to lead to a higher level of future aspiration, while failure to attain a goal is likely to lead to maintenance, lowering, or abandonment of the goal itself.[36] In addition, there is another set of factors which influences an individual's level of aspiration—the norms considered acceptable by his reference group. Thus a salesman's own level of aspiration may be affected by the aspiration levels of his peer group.[37]

[32] A. R. Cohen, "Situational Structure, Self-Esteem and Threat-Oriented Reactions to Power" in D. Cartwright (ed.) *Studies in Social Power* (Ann Arbor: University of Michigan Institute for Social Research, 1959).

[33] B. H. Raven and J. Rietsema, "The Effects of Varied Clarity of Group Goal and Group Path upon the Individual and his Reaction to his Group," *Human Relations,* X (1957), 29–44.

[34] Rensis Likert, "New Patterns in Sales Management" in Martin Warshaw (ed.), *Changing Patterns in Marketing Management* (Ann Arbor: University of Michigan, 1962) (Michigan Business Papers, No. 37).

[35] For a review of the limited studies of the effect of goal difficulty on performance see Andrew C. Stedry and Emanuel Kay, *The Effects of Goal Difficulty on Performance: A Field Experiment* (Pittsburgh: Carnegie Institute of Technology, 1964) (O.N.R. Research Memo #135). None of the reported studies deals with sales personnel.

[36] Kurt Lewin, "The Psychology of Success and Failure," in *Occupations,* XIV (1936), pp. 926–30. Reprinted in Harold J. Leavitt and Louis R. Pondy (eds.), *Readings in Managerial Psychology* (Chicago: University of Chicago Press, 1964), pp. 25–31.

[37] Forrest W. Fryer, *An Evaluation of Level of Aspiration as a Training Procedure* (Englewood Cliffs, N.J.: Prentice-Hall, Inc., 1964), p. 7.

The Principle of Supportive Relationships

Likert also found that high-producing sales units were those in which group-oriented procedures had been used to analyze problems and encourage individual performance. He then advanced the principle of supportive relationships:

> The leadership and other processes of the organization must be such as to ensure a maximum of probability that in all interactions and all relationships with the organization each member will, in the light of his background, values, and expectations, view the experience as supportive and one which builds and maintains his sense of personal worth and importance.[38]

The concern both in Likert and here is with *ideal* relationship or structure. In actual fact, there doubtless are and will continue to be any number of cases wherein an individual remains with a company for purely personal reasons. There may be no community of interest and it may be infeasible to develop one, yet the man continues to do an adequate or better job. It is generally true to say that a person may be fundamentally self-seeking and yet will have some fealty, however superficial or transitory, to his company. He has, after all, become a part of it because he believes that he best serves his own interests by serving its interests. Even in cases where there may appear to be direct conflicts, provided they are neither too grave nor too frequent nor perpetually enduring, the salesman may subordinate his personal goal (at least his current short-term goal) in order to serve the company, insofar as he is convinced that to do so efficaciously advances his long-term goals.

Such casual relationships may be more common than one thinks; and they are not necessarily undesirable. As long as the salesman recognizes that, although *precise* short-term and intermediate goals and interests may be disparate, general long-term goals are efficiently served by continuing the present relationship, and as long as he discharges his own responsibilities to the firm in a satisfactory or better manner; then it is mutually beneficial to maintain the employment relationship.

This is probably the actual nature of a good portion (even the majority) of relationships. The contention here is that the task of the supervisor is to endeavor to transform the actual into ideal relationships. It may be necessary almost to transubstantiate the company in the salesman's eyes, to alter utterly his perspective, but as long as no deliberately false commitments are made, the resultant benefits to company and to the salesman could be substantial.

[38] R. Likert, *New Patterns of Management* (New York: McGraw-Hill, Inc., 1961), p. 103.

SELECTED READINGS

Bales, R. F., *Interaction Process Analysis: A Method for the Study of Small Groups.* Reading, Mass.: Addison-Wesley, 1950. The development of task, social, and emotional leadership; kinds of leadership in groups; and emergence of informal leaders to meet needs not provided by the appointed leader.

Bavelas, Alex, "Leadership: Man and Function" *Administrative Science Quarterly,* Vol. 4, No. 4 (March 1960), pp. 491–498. The changing nature of leadership. Possible consequences of more participative leadership arrangements.

Gellerman, Saul W., *Management by Motivation.* New York: American Management Association, 1963. Use of motivators for manpower development.

Herzberg, Frederick, *Work and the Nature of Man.* Cleveland: The World Publishing Co., 1966. Chapter 6. Herzberg's two-factor theory.

National Industrial Conference Board, *Behavioral Science: Concepts and Management Application* (Studies in Personnel Policy No. 216). New York: National Industrial Conference Board, 1969. Reviews contributions of McGregor, Maslow, Herzberg, Likert, Argyris, and Blake. Examines new approaches to learning. Reviews company interests and applications of behavioral science concepts to the work situation. Includes ten case studies.

National Industrial Conference Board, *Managing by—and with—Objectives* (Studies in Personnel Policy, No. 212). New York: National Industrial Conference Board, 1968). Nature and appraisal of the management-by-objectives concept. Includes five case studies.

Smith, Patricia Cain, and C. J. Cranny, "Psychology of Men at Work" in *Annual Review of Psychology,* pp. 468–496, Vol. 19 (1968), especially section entitled "Job Attitudes and Performance," pp. 468–477. Herzberg's two-factor theory and a summary of studies questioning its generality.

13 Evaluation of Salesman Performance

Feedback is an essential element in management. Much of the information needed to deal with sales management problems is derived from appraisal of how various strategies, tactics, programs, and procedures have affected sales response.

Of particular importance is information on how the sales force as a whole and the individuals within it perform their functions and the extent to which they attain specified goals. The evaluation of performance both of individual salesmen and of the sales force as a whole provides a major source of data for day-to-day implementation of sales management policies. It is also useful in evaluation of the consequences of the policies themselves.

THE NEED FOR PERFORMANCE EVALUATION

Evaluation of the performance of the individual salesman is required for such routine activities as the determination of compensation, the selection of personnel for reassignment or promotion, and the detection of performance weaknesses which require the attention of supervisors or trainers. In addition, knowledge that performance will be observed and evaluated serves as a form of motivation to the sales person, not only in the narrow "carrot and stick" sense but in the larger context of knowledge that superior performance will be recognized and appreciated. Because of the importance of knowledge of results in motivating individuals, both the results of periodic performance appraisals and day-to-day evaluations of current work should be communicated to the salesman as fully and promptly as possible.

At the policy level, evaluation of performance may suggest the strategies and tactics which are, and are not, feasible with a particular sales force. For example, deficiencies in performance on technical matters uncovered in the evaluation process may suggest that a plan to improve customer goodwill through a salesman-conducted technical assistance program would have a poor chance of success.

The evaluation of the performance of salesmen is also required as critical feedback about the consequences of sales-force policies and their implementation. A few of the many kinds of questions for which the evaluation of performance data for a number of salesmen or the entire force is relevant are:

Are changes in training called for? If so, what changes? Evaluation of performance in the field may reveal that the salesmen are performing some tasks well and others poorly or not at all. If such conditions are widespread, this suggests that training or supervision, rather than the salesman himself, is at fault.

Should efforts be reallocated among market segments, customer groups, or geographic areas? Evaluation of performance may reveal that the customer-response functions envisaged when present programs were established were erroneous or inaccurate; or perhaps they no longer apply. On the other hand, notable effectiveness in certain areas may suggest more intensive cultivation in those markets, thus calling for more resource inputs at those points.

Does the compensation plan now in use operate adversely to the goals of management or in support of them? Evaluation may reveal that salesmen are emphasizing present sales to the neglect of prospecting and account development because the compensation plans base rewards on current sales volume alone.

Which of various training programs produced the best salesmen? Which personnel sources? Which selection criteria? The test of training programs, personnel sources, and selection criteria commonly rests on the ways in which they affect salesman performance. If these procedures are to be evaluated, it is first necessary to identify the more successful, marginally successful, and less successful products ("graduates") of these procedures.

THE NATURE OF PERFORMANCE EVALUATION

Although the essence of performance evaluation is measurement, it is critical that the measurement concepts reflect *relevant* criteria. It is tempting to employ a readily available measure such as sales volume, percentage of potential attained, or market share as a criterion of performance. Yet such measures may bear little, if any, relationship to the sales task as conceived. Consider, for example, the salesman of a new kind of technology whose principal function is to establish sufficient *intercommunication* with prospective using industries so that the ensuing dialogue between personnel of his company and those of the prospective users leads, over a period of time, to the development of common interests, the redesign of both applications and products, and eventually, the establishment of buyer-seller relationships. Or consider the salesman whose job is to place a number of demonstration machines in various industries for testing and evaluation by possible users in order to provide guidance for the salesman's company in directing both its development effort and its marketing strategy. A more common example is that of the salesman dealing with an established account whose task is to "keep them happy" and to relay intelligence information to persons within his firm. Another is that of the detail man or architectural representative who seeks to inform the physicians or architects on whom he calls about the problem-solving capabilities of his products so that they will prescribe his drug or specify his product when an appropriate application presents itself. One need only refer back to the discussion of the nature of personal sales activities in Chapter 2 to appreciate that the establishment and nurturing of intercommunicative relationships is not easily evaluated by such short-term consequences as present sales.

What then do we wish to evaluate? If we accept the premise that the salesman's overall task is the development of communicative relationships, with messages flowing in both directions, it follows that evaluation of performance must measure how the salesman has, in fact, *affected the buyer-seller relationship.* Similarly, the evaluation of competence, or capacity to perform, rests on the salesman's capability for favorably affecting buyer-seller relationships.

MEASUREMENT CONCEPTS

Ideally, we should like to measure all those changes in buyer-seller relationships which are the result of the activity of the salesman whose performance is being evaluated. Some of these changes are readily measurable; others are not. In this context, *changes* refers not to differences from a prior time period but to differences from the *condition which would exist* if the salesman had no relationships with the buyer. Nor does "change" necessarily imply that the buyer has changed his source of supply. A change in relationships has occurred, for example, if the buyer, say, because of increased confidence in the supplier, more fully routinizes his purchases of an item and does less testing of the market even though the supplier remains the same. Salesmen's efforts which reinforce relationships which are presently producing orders are, in this broad sense, changing those relationships.

The term *buyer* embraces not only persons bearing that title but all persons in the buying unit, whether it be a large corporation, a public agency, or a household, who influence the buying process in any way. Moreover, the term *buyer* embraces prospects and other segments of potential within the salesman's defined area of responsibility whether he in fact calls on them or not. The failure of a prospect to learn about the company's offer or the decay of a previously established image because the salesman failed to call are as much a result of the salesman's work as a change from the position of a second-source supplier to that of a primary source or the establishment of a good working relationship with a new customer. In short, we want to compare what actually occurred, both good and bad, with the salesman present with what would have occurred without him.

A buyer-seller relationship is a continuous phenomenon. It is a *state* which exists at every point in time and a *process* over time. It includes the attitudes, dispositions, and images which each party holds of the other—for example, seller X is a good source of supply for meat but is high on canned goods; Y is knowledgeable about certain problems; Z's engineers are especially competent in field F, but not field G; buyer B seeks our advice and technical aid but places his orders with our lower-priced, less technically able competitor. Relationships are continually modified over time as a consequence of the communication process, broadly conceived. This process embraces not only oral and written language communications among buyers, users, salesmen, engineers, receiving room personnel, and so on, but the myriad of messages received in the processes of mutual problem solving including, especially, the purchase and use of products.

Events are discrete phenomena. Events such as purchases, sales, deliveries, and service calls result from relationships and, in turn, lead to modifications of those relationships.

Unfortunately it is impossible to measure accurately all of the nuances of information, attitudes and disposition which comprise a buyer's conception of a seller and his offerings or a seller's conception of a buyer and his problems. Perhaps some day we shall be able to measure perceptions with sufficient accuracy to be useful as an evaluation tool. For the present, however, we must usually settle for measures not of the changes in relationships themselves but of *observable consequences* of the changes in those relationships. The consequences most easily observed are clearly discernible events such as the signing of a new contract, a switch in a buyer's source of supply, the receipt of purchase orders from a firm not previously a customer, the loss of an account, an observed increase in source loyalty, or changes in the volume of a customer's purchases. Less discernible, although often of greater import in the long run, are changes in the attitudes, knowledge states, perceptions, and predispositions of customers and prospects.

Although feasibility generally dictates that we content ourselves with measures of observable consequences, this should not blind us to the fact that such consequences are a step removed from what we should really like to measure—the changes in relationships brought about by the salesman's efforts.

While it is easiest to measure the results of salesmen's activities in terms of current time periods, such as the period used for budgeting sales and expenses, many of the activities of the salesmen produce effects over extended periods, sometimes with little or no effect on present revenues. Work designed to impart knowledge of a firm's capabilities, improve image, develop and maintain goodwill, seek out new types of accounts, or secure trials or tests of company products are examples of efforts of this sort. They require effort and often expense in the present but produce revenues only in later, possibly distant periods. A salesman who is evaluated largely or solely on current "results" has an incentive to produce immediate results. Consequently, he may push for immediate sales in a way that constitutes "mining" a market. In such operations, concern is focused entirely on the immediate sale with little interest in long-term customer benefit or the feedback from satisfied customer usage. The effects of such efforts can easily be to undermine or destroy the future prospects of the company in such markets, although measures of present sales would suggest successful operations.

Ideally, we should like to measure the effects of the salesman's work in terms of its contribution to the long-term relationships which a company has with its market. This well might take the form of the discounted value—that is, present value—of future profits resulting from the salesman's work—again measured as a differential from what they would be in the absence of his work. Because of the uncertainties involved in forecasting future outcomes as well as the difficulties of attributing cause-effect relationships when long time periods are involved, the evaluator must generally settle for measures which reckon the future only at heavy discounts or which embody very large subjective elements, for example, "We expect to have this contract for at least five years and to have a preferred position thereafter."

Table 13-1 summarizes the concepts presented in this section.

Table 13-1

SELECTED MEASURES OF SALESMAN ACCOMPLISHMENT

Time Period	Condition Measured	
	Changes in relationships	Consequences of changes in relationships
	(states)	(events)
Measurement period (period covered by evaluation)	Changes in present relationships including changes in perceptions and attitudes.	Changes in sales. Changes in business arrangements. Changes in behavior.
Longer period (future)	Changes in long-term relationships as a result of changes in knowledge, perceptions, or attitudes during the measurement period.	Changes in discounted expected value of future profits

In the next section, several of the tools used for sales force evaluation will be examined.

MEASURES OF SALESMAN PERFORMANCE

Four different levels of measurement of salesman and sales force performance may be distinguished:

  I.   measures of the changes in relationships brought about by sales force activity;
 II.   measures of one or more observable consequences of changes in such relationships;
III.   measures of the activities of sales personnel;
 IV.   measures of the competence of sales personnel.

Level I and Level II measures deal with the *accomplishment* of the sales personnel. This is the output of salesman activity. Level III measures are concerned with what the salesman does. They are thus measures of the *inputs* of sales activity. Level IV measures are concerned with the capability of the salesmen rather than what they do or what they accomplish. Measures at each of the levels may be appropriate as feedback elements in the sales management process.

In evaluating sales force accomplishment, we should prefer Level I measures where they are feasible. Commonly, however, the sales manager is forced to rely largely on Level II measures as indicative of what his salesmen have accomplished. For many facets of the salesmen's work, at only Level III measures may be available at tolerable cost. Level IV measures are only remotely related to what the salesman does. They may be useful in indicating the state of development of the individual salesmen and thus provide guidance for training and personnel development activities. Greater competence *should* result in better accomplishments, although it does not necessarily do so.

Level I—Measures of the Changes in Relationships Brought about by Sales Force Activity

The changes in relationships brought about by the activities of the sales force may be evaluated by measuring the state of the various relationships among personnel in the buying and supplying organizations before and after sales calls and other salesman activity has taken place. For example, one might compare the awareness, knowledge states, beliefs, or attitudes of the various buying influences in a purchasing organization at two time periods. Differences, above those which occur in appropriate control groups, may thus be attributed to the work of the salesmen. In situations in which inward information flow is an important salesman responsibility, the corresponding step might be to compare the awareness, knowledge states and beliefs about customers and their problems which are held at two points in time by members of the salesman's firm who are dependent upon him for information about customers.

Both observational and experimental studies may be used to measure changes in relationships. An observational study could, for example, seek to determine how the opinions held by buying influences about various possible suppliers and their capabilities change over time. If the effects of changes in environmentals and other marketing variables can be neutralized through a control group or appropriate statistical treatment, the effects of the salesman can be derived.

An observational study need not be confined to examining changes in attitudes or opinions if changes in relationships can be observed in a more direct way. Thus the evaluator might seek to determine how the buying influences conceive their relationship with the salesman's firm. Do they consider their personnel to be the best source of certain kinds of assistance? Is the firm their preferred source of supply for a range of needs? Only for certain items? Is it merely a source of last resort?

Experiments may also be used. One experiment to measure the effect of specific sales calls was conducted by G. David Hughes. First, he determined the awareness and attitudes of prospects for adding machines. A scale was developed to measure awareness and attitudes towards each of fifty-four items in four categories: (1) the prospect's evaluation of his need for this equipment, (2) his evaluation of adding machine features, (3) his image of four leading adding machine companies, and (4) his image of adding machine salesmen in general. Initial measurements were taken in two cities in order to make allowance for the fact that the ambient state in each territory is likely to be unique. The respondents were then divided randomly into an experimental group and a control group. The experimental group received two sales calls. The first call sought to estimate the buyer's need, left literature with the buyer, and sought to make an appointment for the second call. The second call attempted to make a demonstration. A second set of measurements of awareness and attitudes was then taken. The observed differences were attributed to the work of the salesman.[1]

The interpretation of observed changes is not always straightforward. Attitudes on some factors may move in the favorable direction while others move in the reverse one, not necessarily because the salesman produces an adverse effect, but in some instances because the buyer, as a result of cognitive dissonance, readjusts his appraisal of some factors when new knowledge modifies others. Hughes observed that respondents who increased their rating of the importance of the feature "adding fractions" tended to downgrade some other factor such as salesman's pleasantness or heaviness of load on present equipment.[2]

By seeking to evaluate specific results of salesman activity, experiments such as those conducted by Hughes are capable of providing guidance as to what the salesman should do. Specifically, by determining the effects of different presentations on awareness and attitudes and the interrelationships of changes in attitudes, efforts can be diverted from product features and sales approaches which have minimal effect to those which are more likely to influence buyer behavior.

To the extent that sound linkages between awareness and attitudes, on the one hand, and behavior, on the other, can be established, before-and-after measurements of awareness and attitude afford promise of measurement of the effects of the salesman's work on relation-

[1] G. David Hughes, "A New Tool for Sales Managers," *Journal of Marketing Research,* May 1964, pp. 32–38.
[2] Hughes, pp. 32–38.

ships between his firm and those upon whom he calls, including, in appropriate cases, its effect on sales.

Level II — Measures of Observable Consequences of Changes in Relationships

The development and use of direct measures of the effect which the salesman has had on the relationships between his company and his accounts is difficult and costly. Therefore, regular evaluation of salesman's performance is almost invariably limited to measurement of some of the results of the relationship changes which the salesman has helped to bring about. The most easily observable measure is current sales. However, other types of results can be measured.

MEASURES OF SALES VOLUME OR PROFIT CONTRIBUTION DURING THE EVALUATION PERIOD

Current sales represent a readily available, easily understandable measure of salesman's performance. The criteria used for evaluation may consist of total sales volume, or of sales volume related to some standard, or of the extent to which sales conform to particular sales management goals, such as the sale of the more profitable items.

Sales volume measures proceed from the premise that current salesman's work bears fruit in present sales in a precise one-to-one relationship. Such a premise, while sometimes useful as an approximation, is of limited appropriateness for a number of reasons.

Many of the salesman's tasks produce results only over long periods — the cultivating of a valued prospect, the nurturing of goodwill for his company, the generation of confidence in his own competence, judgment and recommendations, for example. Often much of the salesman's time and many of his responsibilities are directed precisely to the attainment of goals such as these.

Sales results in any territory are the outcome of many factors other than the work of the salesman. The ambient expected sales volume — the result that would occur if the salesman were not involved — will depend on many diverse factors. These include market potential and its distribution, historical market penetration of the firm, competitive conditions, physical makeup of territory, aid provided by advertising, direct mail, company technical personnel and other marketing inputs, and such windfalls as drastic changes in the quantities or types of goods suitable to customer's needs. Although some of these difficulties can be avoided by developing a standard, others cannot.

TOTAL SALES OR PROFIT CONTRIBUTION   Total sales or profit contribution provides a crude measure of performance. Where the primary interest of the firm is in immediate sales rather than in the development of long-term relationships and where other factors have limited influence on sales volume, total sales may provide a suitable, if rough, yardstick of performance. It is most applicable to one-shot sales situations and where sales represent such a small proportion of potential that the latter does not act as a constraint.

Total dollars of gross margin or total contribution to profit which can be attributed to the salesman may be preferable to sales. Such measures are closer to the firm's goal than sales volume per se.

Gross margin criteria, popular in the 1930s, may be especially relevant in sales situations in which the salesman has pricing discretion. Evaluation, and possibly even compensation, on the basis of total gross margin contributed serves to discourage price shading as well as encouraging the salesman to devote more efforts to the higher gross margin items in the line. A major objection to the use of a gross margin basis is its dependence on the dubious premise that high gross margin items are necessarily more profitable to the firm. While this premise is sometimes justified, often it is not. It is not unusual for high margin items to be among the least profitable items—for example, where they represent items in only limited demand, accomodation items, items which are costly to sell, deliver, or service, or are produced for special orders.

To avoid this difficulty, net contribution (to overhead and profit) or net profit from the territory may be used. The use of net profit proceeds on the rarely justified premise that the salesman has control over and thus should be responsible for, all the elements which determine profitability—for example, cost of expedited delivery resulting from production delays. It violates the general principle that a man should be evaluated only on those factors over which he exercises control. Where most of the costs which are associated with a salesman's coverage of his territory and those involved in filling the orders thus secured are direct, assignable costs, net contribution to overhead and profit may be a useful means of evaluating performance. Use of net profit per territory is open to the more serious objection that such profits rest, often in an important way, on allocation rules and procedures which are not only beyond the control of the salesman but are in their very nature open to challenge as to logical validity. Thus they introduce ambiguities into the evaluation process and can easily become a source of endless controversy.

SALES RELATED TO SOME STANDARD   Sales results are commonly compared to some standard. Perhaps the oldest and crudest form of standard is to relate sales in a department or territory to sales for the previous year. Despite its crudeness, comparisons with last year are still employed to evaluate departmental operations in many retailing firms. Similarly, manufacturing organizations compare current results in individual territories with those of last year. Some firms use longer periods: a drug firm uses the most recent three-year's sales in setting standards for territorial performance evaluation. The use of the previous year's results as a standard presupposes that last year's performance was in some respects ideal. If it was less than ideal, any deficiencies in it will be perpetuated by its use in future evaluation and planning activities. For example, suppose that a company exerted little effort in the previous year to reach certain types of accounts with the result that no sales were made. In the following year substantial efforts were undertaken in this market and a few sales were achieved. Although penetration of the market during the second year may have been exceedingly poor, it can to made to look good by comparison with the even poorer initial year.

Current-day managers are more likely to relate sales to sales or market potential—the opportunity which is believed to exist in each territory. By expressing each salesman's sales as a percentage of the territorial market potential, differences in the demand variables from territory to territory are taken into account. To the extent that accurate and up-to-date measures of potential are developed, one source of misinterpretation of the significance of sales totals is thus eliminated.

It would, of course, be possible to eliminate the effects of differences in potential entirely by creating territories of equal potential. For reasons which have been examined in the chapter on territories, such a practice can lead to poor resource allocation. Moreover, the other sources of misinterpretation of the significance of sales totals would remain. Differences in the extent and quality of competition in each territory, physical makeup of the territory, propensity of different types of accounts to shift suppliers, windfall events in each territory, and the effects of the application of other marketing inputs are some of the factors that are independent of the salesman but affect the level of total sales.

In order to overcome the first of these difficulties the manager may use company sales potential rather than market potential as a yardstick. As company sales potential has presumably made allowance for the effects of competition, this source of distortion has been removed.

Is this desirable?

If the company sales potential is obtained by applying a historical market-share relationship to market potentials in each territory, an additional source of error is introduced; its importance depends largely on whether the company's real opportunity to modify its share is subject to significant change over short periods. If it is, the essentially backward-looking perspective of the company potential figures makes them less desirable to use than might otherwise be the case.

Quotas or other performance standards employed in directing the sales force are also useful in evaluating performance.

While sales in relation to some standard such as market or sales potential or quota represent a somewhat more meaningful measure of salesman's performance than the use of raw sales data alone, it presumes that sales would have been zero without the salesman. In some direct canvassing situations involving one-shot sales, this may be literally true. Often, in industrial sales work, however, sales will continue at the established level for a period of weeks or months after the salesman's calls cease. Before long, however, decay of prior sales work sets in. Often it proceeds sharply. At the other extreme, where personal selling is used in conjunction with other marketing efforts such as consumer advertising, point-of-sale, and distribution policies to secure wide exposure, some level of sales will continue even without the personal sales effort. In such circumstances, the entire result cannot properly be attributed to the salesman's efforts.

A somewhat more sophisticated method of relating sales to potential is to compare actual sales with a forecast representing the sales volume which would be expected to occur in a territory if it were covered by an "average" salesman delivering an "average" performance.

One method of measuring performance in this way proceeds from the premise that observed differences in the actual sales among territories are the combined result of: (1) territorial characteristic effects, (2) salesman attribute effects (what the salesman is), and (3) performance effects (what the salesman does).[3]

In the simplest case all territories are assumed to possess identical characteristics including demand variables, competitive intensity, and working conditions such as the distance between accounts and terrain. Thus, all differences in sales are attributed to the salesman.

In the more realistic case, allowance can be made for the ter-

---

[3] For a detailed explanation of the method see Patrick J. Robinson and Bent Stidsen, *Personal Selling in a Modern Perspective* (Boston: Allyn & Bacon, Inc., 1967), pp. 59–61.

ritorial effects by preparing sales forecasts for each territory based on territorial characteristics alone. To the extent that such forecasts account for all interterritorial differences other than those associated with the salesman and his efforts, all differences of actual sales from such forecasts represent the effects of salesman attributes and salesman performance.

Stated differently, we may start with a crude forecast that all territories would have "average" sales if they were not affected by territorial characteristics, by salesman attributes, or by the activities of the salesman. The variance of actual sales from such forecasts may be said to reflect some combination of territorial effects, salesman attribute effects, and salesman performance effects. We then prepare a set of forecasts, say, by regression analysis, which take due account of territorial characteristics, for example, potential, competitive strength, difficulties of coverage, but not the other factors. The differences between this forcast for each territory and the original one represent the effects of the territorial characteristics. The deviations of actual sales from the new forecast will be smaller than the deviations from the original forecast because we have through our new forecasting equation accounted for some portion of the deviation as being due to territorial factors.

Some of the remaining deviations of actual from forecast or expected sales reflect imperfections in the forecasting procedure. If the forecasting data and procedures are reasonably good, however, most of the residuals represent the effects of salesman characteristics and performance.

If the company has data upon which to measure the effects of salesman's characteristics on sales—for example, studies showing the relationship between salesman attributes and attained sales—a new set of forecasts can be prepared reflecting this source of causation as well. To the extent that sound forecasts can measure fully the effects of territorial and personal characteristics, they provide a measure of what would occur if *only* those factors were operating. To the extent that actual sales deviate from such forecasts, they are attributed to other factors—that is, what the salesman *does*. Thus we can evaluate the salesman's performance in each territory against the norm which would occur if the salesman had produced no deviation from the "normal" performance which the territorial and human attribute effects would produce. This difference can be portrayed as a percentage of the forecast:

$$\frac{\text{Actual Sales} - \text{Forecast Sales}}{\text{Forecast Sales}} \times 100$$

Robinson and Stidsen cite the case of a company which, following this procedure, determined that 30 percent of the observed differences among territories was associated with differences in territorial characteristics, and 36 percent was associated with the characerisitics of the salesmen. The remaining 34 percent was attributed to what the salesman does, although some portion of this is no doubt due to the imperfections in the forecasting equations for the other two factors. Salesmen were then evaluated by predicting what a territory's sales would be if only territorial and salesman attribute effects existed. The differences between these predictions and actual sales —that is, the residuals—represent the salesmen performance effect. They are expressed as positive or negative percentages of the predicted sales for each territory.

Prediction and forecast as used here refer to values of territorial sales which would exist if the territory performed in accordance with the forecasting equation and no other influences were operative. Such predictions (forecasts) do not need to refer to future time periods. The analyst might, for example, reason that "if territory A behaved like the average, sales in territory A last year would have been $x. As sales in territory A were actually $y, it follows that other factors have caused a difference of y-x in territory A sales."

SALES RELATED TO PARTICULAR SALES MANAGEMENT GOALS
As supplementary methods of evaluation, sales may be related to particular management goals, such as the expense-sales ratio or the distribution of sales among products, customer types or order sizes.

Salesmen are sometimes compared in terms of their sales-to-expense ratios. Even if only expenses controllable by the individual salesman are considered, such a criterion has little merit. It suggests that a low *average* expense rate is desirable and thus tends to discourage pursuing sales volume which would raise the mean expense ratio even though such volume would be profitable in terms of the marginal inputs involved.

Some companies go so far as to evaluate the salesman on the basis of the profit generated in his territory. Such a practice proceeds from the rarely justified premise that the salesman has control over, and thus should be responsible for, all the elements which determine profitability. On the other hand, to the extent that the salesman has control over conformity to an expense budget, he may appropriately be judged on his conformance to expense, as well as to revenue, expectations.

Some companies evaluate salesmen at least in part by the average gross profit earned by the salesman (that is, the gross profit to sales ratio). Along the same lines, others examine the proportion of total sales which is made up of high-margin items. The inference behind both of these forms of appraisal is that the sale of a large proportion of higher margin items indicates superior salesman performance. It derives from the notion that low margin items are "easy" to sell and that the salesman should be recognized for selling the more difficult-to-sell items. The flaw in this logic is that higher margins may reflect many things besides difficulty of personal selling. Some products may have high margins because they are expensive to handle or are produced on a special order basis or because they embody unique features of value to customers, all factors which are quite unrelated to difficulty to sell. If in fact such items are more difficult to sell, why is this so? If it is because they are of less value for customers, is it really in the firm's interest to encourage the salesman to push them? Moreover, does the difficult-to-sell-item require so much additional salesman time that the extra margin is in fact lost in the extra sales time consumed? The concept of rewards for the sales of higher margin items avoids the questions of the reasons for the high margin. A salesman's performance in selling more profitable items may be an appropriate measure of success only if all relevant costs have been taken into account. This is sometimes overlooked when profit margins are emphasized.

> A case in point is offered by the manufacturer who offered rather substantial quantity discounts for bulk orders but complained to the author that his salesmen were not bringing in a sufficient proportion of small orders with the result that his average gross margin was below "normal." He wanted the salesmen to bring in more high gross margin (small) orders so that the firm's average gross margin would be increased.

Measures which evaluate sales work on the basis of which items are sold should be used only with due regard for the fact that they may tend to subvert the salesman's responsibility to serve the customer's best interest. The same type of objection may be raised to so-called balanced selling criteria. They proceed from the premise that the salesman should sell the mix which best suits the producer rather than those products which best fit customer needs.

Other ratios which are sometimes used in evaluation are the order/call ratio, the number of customers to potential customers, and the proportions of orders of various sizes written by a salesman. The order/call ratio indicates the proportion of sales calls which were "successful" in the sense of procuring an order. It is useful primarily in direct-sale situations in which the salesman's task is to "get an order" as opposed to establishing a relationship in which the customer places his orders with the supplier through his purchasing routine when his needs arise. Even then, it is an equitable measure only if the groups called on have a propensity to buy which is consistent among sales territories and over time. The percentage of potential customers who are customers provides a measure of the success of the salesman in securing at least a token order from each account. While somewhat more comprehensive than the order/call ratio, it reveals little about how successful the salesman is in establishing himself as the account's regular or preferred source of supply.

These ratios are often useful in helping supervision to identify strong and weak spots in the salesman's overall performance, but their use as regular forms of evaluation can backfire.

> A large oil company evaluated its salesmen at least in part on their order/call ratio. Knowing this to be the practice, some salesmen upon entering a customer service station and finding that the operator needed a particular item would write up that item only and avoid the sales of other items. In this way, the salesman obtained credit for an order on this call and left behind a higher probability of an order on the next call than if he had attempted to ascertain and supply all the dealer's needs on a single order. When a study revealed this situation the company ceased using the order/call criterion.

At the opposite extreme, it is argued that sales per call or the proportion of orders in various size brackets will indicate the extent to which the salesman is concentrating on the larger accounts and is encouraging smaller accounts to accumulate large orders instead of placing numerous small ones. The latter practice is often a serious problem in sales to the trade where small dealers, especially in lines with low and irregular turnover such as drugs, tend to order frequently in quantities which are unprofitable for suppliers to handle. However, the mere tabulation of a salesman's sales by order size does not explain the order-size pattern. A large number of small orders *may* indicate that the salesman is not effective in securing the business of the larger accounts in his territory or that he has failed to get his small trade accounts to accumulate their needs. On the other hand, a large number of small orders may reflect circumstances quite beyond the salesman's influence, such as the size of customers' requirements and the nature of customers' emergency needs. Like many other types of sales analysis, the examination of sales by order size or by annual volume of purchases per account may provide a useful starting point for isolating trouble spots. But it provides a basis for evaluating salesman's performance only when it is coupled with appropriate investigation of the causes of the size distribution and the extent to which these causes are in turn controllable by the individual salesman.

Overall, we may observe that ratios are more useful in spotting areas for detailed investigation than they are for measuring the performance of salesmen per se.

MEASURES OF OTHER CONSEQUENCES OF CHANGES IN RELATIONSHIPS

Especially in industrial selling and in sales to the trade, much of the salesman's work is devoted to the development of relationships rather than the consummation of particular sales transactions. In addition to sales volume, the evaluator will therefore wish to examine other kinds of events which are likely to be consequences of changes in relationships which the salesman has contributed to bringing about. Which events are likely to be important will depend on the responsibilities of the particular sales job. A few examples will suggest the kinds of measures which may be developed to evaluate the salesman's performance of particular functions.

CHANGES IN ACCOUNT STATUS   The number of new accounts gained, either in an absolute sense or in relation to the number of potential buyers in the territory who are not accounts, provides a measure of the extent of new-account development work and its success in converting nonaccounts into accounts. The number of accounts upgraded from using the firm as an incidental or secondary source to using it as a primary supplier of the item in question provides some measure of the extent to which the salesman has nurtured relationships. The converse measures, loss of accounts and downgrading of the firm as a customer's primary source of supply represent comparable negative factors.

CHANGES IN COMMUNICATIONS EFFECTIVENESS   An important function of many salesmen is to forestall complaints, including complaints which are never disclosed to the supplier. Another is the prompt and amicable resolution of those problems which do arise (troubleshooting). Fewer complaints from customers ascribable in whole or in part to the work of the salesman (for example, incorrect recommendation of proper product, unwarranted promise of delivery date, incorrect statement of terms or credit policies, failure of salesmen to follow proper procedure to insure customer satisfaction) suggests improved salesman performance. Similarly, the degree to which complaints are well resolved suggests how well the salesman is performing his trouble-shooting function.

For the most part it is difficult to measure how well the salesman has communicated information to his customers and how well the salesman has furnished sound intelligence to his superiors. Formal studies are generally required to evaluate performance in this area, although subjective evaluations of the coverage provided by a salesman and his credibility can be made both by his superiors and by his customers.

Subjective evaluations of communications effectiveness are likely to be unduly influenced by the most recent events. The likelihood of recall of more remote events may depend on the extent to which they were memorable—perhaps even on whether they were atypical. When asked to rate the communications performance of salesmen, raters, whether supervisors or customers, are, hence, quite *unlikely* to be evaluating on the basis of equal weight for all events over the entire rating period. These difficulties can be partially ameliorated by having supervisors record comment-worthy events as they occur and by requiring that considerable weight be given to such recorded data when ratings are made.[4]

All of the measures of accomplishment which have been suggested must be used with due regard for the fact that factors other than the salesman play a greater or lesser role in affecting the events being measured. These external factors can be controlled through properly designed experiments. Unfortunately, such experiments are inappropriate for regular evaluation of the entire sales force. Hence, the manager needs to rely on "results" of sales work which are observable from regularly collected data or subjective evaluation by those with whom the salesman interacts.

Evaluation procedures of the types suggested do not, however, need to be taken on blind faith. In most cases, the hypothesis that the cause of the changed relationship was the salesman can be tested by one-time or periodic experiments. Following such a test, the evaluator can proceed in his daily work on the premise that the hypothesis has remained valid and that the observed changes are the result of what the salesman has done. However, this premise should be reexamined from time to time through experiments of limited scope.

Level III—Measures of Activities

Even complex measures of the consequences of the salesman's work of the type set forth in the previous section do not measure all relevant facets of the salesman's performance. Hence, sales managers often supplement attempts to measure the *results* of the salesman's work with measures of his *activities*—that is, what he does with his time. Such activity measures may reveal directly whether the salesman is applying his efforts in the desired manner. They can indicate

---

[4] To reduce bias, evaluations based solely on comment-worthy events recorded at the time of occurrence could be obtained by having the evaluations made by an independent party relying solely on such recorded notations.

whether the salesman is really working a full day, if he is performing all of the different duties expected of him, and whether he is allocating his time in the proportions which management believes to be most effective. In this way, activity measures provide important information to the supervisory system.

Various types of activity reports are employed to record how the salesman spends his time, how many calls he makes, how many demonstrations he performs, how many calls were made on nonaccounts, how far he traveled, how many hours he worked, how much of his time was spent in talking with customers as opposed to time between calls, or how much of the time was employed in diverse activities. Much activity data is provided by the salesman himself. Other data, such as number of orders written, is obtained from accounting records. Still other data is generated by having supervisors rate their men on the performance of various activities. Because such ratings are subjective perceptions of the rater, it is considered good practice to have multiple ratings where feasible. Information from activity reports can be supplemented by time and duty studies which attempt to obtain more detailed information in these same areas. Some of the data from activity and time and duty reports may be expressed as ratios (for example, proportion of total time spent in promotion or in interviews) or in activity rates (for example, number of calls per week, number of demonstrations per day).

To be of maximum value to management, activity data needs to be related to some standard or base. In more routine types of selling, performance standards may be developed from time and duty studies or, more commonly, from historical experience. In less routine types, it is often necessary to make special studies to determine reasonable levels of activity.

It is imperative when using measures of activity to keep in mind that such measures are basically measures of *inputs* rather than outputs. Unless these inputs yield well-established, known results, the use of an activity measure can mislead management into believing that the salesman is achieving goal-related outputs. Like the military report of the number of shells fired or the number of bombs dropped, activity reports tell nothing about what, if anything, has been accomplished by the activity.

Level IV—Measures of Competence

In addition to, and sometimes in lieu of, measuring salesman's accomplishments, many firms seek to evaluate a salesman's competence. This is commonly achieved not by measurement in the usual sense but by having supervisors or other superiors rate the salesman on factors which are believed to represent salesman competence. The forms commonly used for such evaluations include such things as product knowledge, ability to plan, personal appearance, and such personal attributes as judgment, attitudes, initiative, and ingenuity. Often rating forms include subjective evaluations of competence factors along with subjective evaluations of activity performance.

Subjective evaluation of competence factors may have direct utility in evaluating the success of a recruitment or training program designed to develop particular types of competence. It should be clear, however, that measures of competence to perform effectively in the field are quite different from measures of that performance itself.[5]

COMBINATION OF MEASURES INTO A SINGLE RATING

There are a few instances when an overall measure is needed, although for many purposes—for example, promotion, reassignment, retraining, the development of training programs, the isolation of difficulties for correction through supervision, and the determination of the extent to which particular sales force goals are being attained —individual measures of specific facets of sales-force performance are directly relevant. Compensation is a notable example in which a composite measure of performance is desired.

> A steel company evaluates its branch manager-salesmen on three criteria: (1) Sales quota attainment by product, adjusted for factors beyond the salesman's control (for example, failure of a customer to secure a large contract, thus substantially reducing the quantities of steel to be purchased from the company); (2) Attainment of call quota on key accounts; and (3) Administrative performance.

Not infrequently, composites incorporate a number of measures of accomplishment, activity, and competence.

Often, in practice, sales managers avoid the issue of multiple measures and their relative weights by using a single yardstick such as one of those which has been suggested, and then "allowing" for "intangibles" in a subjective and unstructured way. In other firms, a single objective measure of performance, such as sales volume, is "balanced off" by a formal rating system of salesman evaluation by supervisors or other line executives. Such ratings often embrace a review of activity reports (Level III measures), appraisals of competence factors (for example, product knowledge) and the rater's opin-

[5] For a discussion of the concept of salesman competence and its measurement, see Patrick J. Robinson and Bent Stidsen, *Personal Selling in a Modern Perspective.*

ions of the salesman's attainments in the field which have not been subject to Level I or Level II performance measures. One drug company rating form provides for supervisor evaluation on such diverse matters as:

Customers' responsiveness Reception by M.D. and office personnel Performance in hospital selling	Accomplishment measures
Use of physician card reference file Maintenance of list of hospital personnel Maintenance of list of products purchased by physicians Follows routine efficiently Drug store stock checking	Activity measures
Attitude towards work Attitude towards company Judgment Personal appearance Resourcefulness[6]	Competence measures

As suggested earlier, the greatest value of rating forms is generally in the information they yield on particular accomplishment, activity, or competence factors. If, in addition, they are to be used to obtain a composite score, ratings must be numerically scaled and weights assigned. A final point score can then be derived.

The rater himself is a major problem in all subjective rating arrangements. In discussing the interview in the treatment of selection (Chapter 6), it was noted that the interviewer may tend to compare the candidate with himself or with *his* perception of what the man specification should be. Similarly, in rating performance, and especially, competence, the rater finds it difficult to divorce his standards from those prescribed by the rating system. This difficulty can be partially overcome by having ratings by two or more independent individuals.

Another problem arises from the vagueness of standards. What is "excellent" product knowledge? How does it differ from "good" product knowledge? What is a "satisfactory" relationship with customers? How does one identify a "good" rating on initiative?

Grading standards may differ. Using a 4.0 scale, one rater may consider 3.0 to be a good rating and 3.5 to be an excellent one. Another rater in the same company scores most of his men 3.9 or 4.0 and considers a 3.7 as a form of damning with faint praise. How does a third party interpret the scores, given these uncertainties?

[6] Selected from items listed on a drug company rating form in D. M. Phelps and J. H. Westing, *Marketing Management* (rev. ed.), pp. 756–757.

One device is to attach a word definition to each grade, or at least to each group of grades. Thus a glass company rating form includes the following item:[7]

3. Thoroughness and accuracy of reports and records of calls.	Reliable and complete records of work done.	Usually accurate and complete records.	Inferior reports and records.	Careless and incomplete records.
	10 9 8	7 6 5	4 3	2 1 0

Another device seeks to avoid the standards problem by asking the rater to compare the performance or competence of the individual being rated with his peers. For example:

Exceptional: Not more than one man in 100 is this good.
Excellent: In the upper third of all men whom I have rated.
Good: In the middle third of all men whom I have rated.
Fair: In the lower third of men whom I have rated, but not unsatisfactory.
Poor: Unsatisfactory.

A system which seeks to combine both types of approaches is sometimes used in which word descriptions are used for the guidance of the rater as to what is expected but, in addition, the rater is asked, at least in respect to his overall evaluations; *"Of all the persons whom you have rated in this rating period how many have you placed in each of the categories?"*

Devices of this type are especially appropriate in situations in which the rater is evaluating a number of individuals at the same time and in which the completed rating forms are likely to be dispersed into the employment records of the various persons evaluated.

Regardless of the method used to secure uniformity of standards in rating activities, whether the raters actually distribute their evaluations in accord with the assigned scales can be determined only by ex-post tabulations of ratings assigned.

Still another device is suggested by Allan Easton. He proposes that each rating be in terms of a previously defined ideal level of performance for each item. Scores are then assigned on a scale in terms of distance from the ideal score of, say, 100 points.[8]

Scores derived from rating a number of factors, whether they be performance factors, activity factors, or competence factors, can be averaged or summed to provide a composite score. Not infrequently,

[7] Phelps and Westing, p. 760.
[8] Allan Easton, "A Forward Step in Performance Evaluation," *Journal of Marketing,* July, 1966, pp. 26–32.

measures of all three types of factors are combined, although the logic of so doing may be questioned.

Commonly, composite scores are obtained by assigning a value on a numerical scale for each factor rated. The numerical point scores can then be summed. Weights can be assigned directly as multipliers of the various scores or indirectly by providing a longer scale for factors considered to be more important. Thus a scale of 0–15 might be assigned for product knowledge while only a 0–5 scale is provided for personal appearance. The averaging method is usually either a single point total or an arithmetic mean of the several assigned scores.

Any of the various averaging methods may be used wherever a number of factors are to be combined into a single score. The executive must recognize, in any case, that the apparent precision of the result may be illusory, given the subjective nature of both the scoring and weight-assignment processes.

EVALUATION OF THE EVALUATION SYSTEM

The evaluation system, like any other managerial practice, should itself be subject to a critical examination from time to time in order to determine if it is performing its function adequately and properly. In appraising an evaluation system, the analyst is appropriately concerned with whether relevant criteria are being employed, whether the measures being used are valid and reliable ones, and whether the operation of the system supports company goals or contains significant dysfunctional elements.

Review of Evaluation Criteria

Of primary concern in appraising the evaluation system is whether the criteria employed in evaluating salesmen are themselves the most relevant ones. In particular, do the criteria conform to the goals which have been established for the field sales force? If, as is usually the case, there are a number of diverse goals for salesman activity at any particular time, do the evaluation criteria appropriately reflect the *relative importance* of each of these goals?

It is not surprising to find that evaluation systems tend to evolve so as to give heavier weight to the more easily measured factors rather than to those which may in fact be more significant. Indeed, it is easier to measure sales in a territory during a quarter than to measure the accretion to or diminution of goodwill in a territory in a quarter. Thus measurement considerations can easily lead to questionable emphases in the evaluation scheme.

Another significant concern is whether the criteria chosen are relevant to the responsibilities assigned the salesman and to the authority which they possess. A criterion which reflects activities beyond the control of the person being evaluated is not only weak on this ground but may encourage dysfunctional activity. In the case of field salesmen, such criteria as net profit for a territory, bad debt experience, percentage of merchandise rejected by buyers, and sales growth rate over the previous year, are examples of criteria which are likely to be inappropriate except in the rare situation in which these factors are entirely within the assigned responsibility of the individual salesman. To the extent that other individuals within the organization (for example, production personnel, credit department) or environmental factors (for example, quantities consumed by the buying firms) are beyond the salesman's control, they should not be used for evaluation of his work.

Review of Measurement Devices

Measurement devices should be reviewed for their information content. Appropriate criteria may have been selected but the measuring devices used may yield inadequate or misleading information on the extent of conformance to particular criteria.

The analyst will wish to concern himself with whether the various measures used are *valid.* Do they measure what they purport to measure? This would not be the case, for example, if an activity measure (say, number of calls) were treated as an accomplishment measure (say, consequences of calls on buyer disposition and future behavior). Nor would it be true if a competence measure (for example, product knowledge) were interpreted as if it were an activity measure (for example, information furnished to buyers) or a measure of accomplishment (for example, changes in buyers' information state). Conversely, an accomplishment measure (say, sales) may be improperly treated as an activity measure (say, how hard the man has worked). In some cases, the analyst may discover that one facet of performance is being measured but viewed as a measure of some other aspect of performance. An example of the latter situation would be the use of a change in sales volume as a measure of the extent to which goodwill or customer understanding had been developed. None of the measures suggested are in themselves undesirable. The analyst's concern, rather, is whether the measures being used do, in fact, measure what the sales manager believes is being measured.

An additional concern is whether the measurements are *reliable.* Stated differently, are the measures sufficiently accurate portrayals of the measurement being taken so that we have reasonable confidence that repetition of the measurement would yield the same result? In statistical terms, reliability asks whether the sample of observations or reports is large enough and sufficiently free of biases to be representative of all the events which it purports to measure.

A training manager might well ask, "Does a written product-knowledge test accurately measure the range of product-knowledge of the examinee?" Most students can recall instances in which an examination seemed, to them at least, to ask for an inadequate or perhaps poorly selected sample of their knowledge or understanding of a particular topic.

Subjective evaluation processes, such as rating systems, are particularly subject to biases which impair their reliability. Is the sales manager judging customer relations performance by the two complaints which he received or by a review of a sample of the relationships between the salesman and his entire customer and prospect group? Is his evaluation based heavily on evidence mentioned by a customer in the course of a golf game? In sales work where the supervisor can rarely observe the salesman at work, he is often forced to rely on information provided by those with whom the salesman comes into contact in the course of his daily work. Unfortunately, the representativeness of the contacts which enter into the raters' evaluations is at best unknown. In fact, as a consequence of the widespread use of management-by-exception principles in business, the sample of cases which come to the attention of a supervisor or company executive are, on the contrary, quite likely to be the atypical ones. Hence, persons in such positions may obtain very distorted views of the state of affairs in the field. Formal studies involving samples of respondents or observations selected to secure representativeness are sometimes needed in order to overcome the inherent deficiencies in perspective which grow out of the use of management by exception. The analyst, in reviewing the system for evaluating salesmen, will want to satisfy himself that the measures used are derived from representative samples of the work being evaluated.

Moreover, the measures which a supervisor or other evaluator states, or perhaps even believes, he is using, de jure, may not, de facto, be the bases on which overall evaluations are made and/or rewards assigned.

Regional managers in a large industrial sales organization were asked to indicate the criteria which they used in evaluating district managers. A staff analyst then matched the district managers' scores on these criteria with the merit raises and bonuses given these district managers by the same regional managers. *None* of the stated criteria had a significant relationship with the rewards given. The analyst then tested three other factors for possible association with rewards using data covering a three-year period.

a. *Tenure:* No significant correlation with rewards
b. *Frequency of regional manager's visit to district:* Significant negative correlation. (Hypothesis: Regional managers "go where the problems are.")

c. *Distance in miles between district office and regional office:* Significant *direct* correlation. That is, the further a district manager is from the regional manager who evaluates him, the greater his rewards for performance. Moreover, the inverse was observed for assistant district managers; for them rewards were smaller as distance increased. The company has not been able to explain these phenomena.

The results of the analyst's work left the company with the unresolved question, "What are the regional managers (and thus the company) really rewarding?"

The same company has district managers prepare an evaluation form annually for each salesman. Comparison of these evaluations with compensation rewards revealed significant associations, with a correlation coefficient, $r = .55$. As this yields an r^2 of only .30, this leaves 70 percent of the differences in pay unexplained. Trial of other factors such as tenure revealed no significant relationships. Thus the question "What are we really rewarding?" may be raised with respect to the salesmen as well.

Review of the Operation of the Evaluation System

It was noted earlier that the evaluation process serves as one means for the motivation and direction of the sales force. The knowledge that certain criteria are used to evaluate performance influences the attitudes salesmen hold toward their various duties and the manner in which they allocate their time and efforts. These influences are not automatically favorable ones. The analyst will generally wish to determine if the operation of the evaluation system tends to encourage activities which are undesirable in the larger context of the firm's goals, operating policies and programs, and the system of human interactions which it seeks to cultivate.

An elementary question along these lines is whether the evaluation system tends to reinforce or oppose conformity to company policies. Of particular concern here is whether evaluation criteria which are heavily weighted in favor of current sales may lead to not only the neglect of activities in the company's long-term interest, but even to a push for immediate sales without regard to true customer interest. More generally, do the various evaluation measures encourage the salesmen to conform to the various company policies, such as those involved in account solicitation, avoidance of customer loading, cultivation of territories, equitable treatment of accounts, and delivery and credit terms; or do they provide incentive to short-cut or ignore policies? Along these same lines, do evaluation practices support supervisory activities and the drive toward established goals or do they motivate the salesman to operate at variance with these goals and operating systems?

Even if it does not encourage contravention of company policies or supervisory or firm goals, an evaluation system may have a dysfunctional effect through its influence on the activities in which the salesmen engage and how they allocate their time. In short, it may encourage some types of work at the expense of other types, not by administrative design but as an unintended by-product of the evaluation system.

Finally, one may inquire whether the evaluation system used in a firm is compatible with valid concepts of the relationships among the various members of the firm such as salesmen, supervisors, regional managers, and home office personnel. For example, is the system as free as is feasible from elements which are likely to be considered arbitrary by those being evaluated? If the underlying sales management philosophy follows McGregor's Theory Y seeking to draw on the salesman's inner interests and desire for personal accomplishment, is the evaluation system so wedded to a Theory X type reward-punishment philosophy that it works against the larger managerial goal?

SUMMARY

The evaluation of performance of both individual salesmen and the sales force as a whole is essential both for the day-to-day implementation of sales-management decisions and policies and to provide feedback on the operation of the policies themselves.

A major problem in the establishment of an evaluation system is to establish criteria which are relevant to the salesman's job and responsibilities.

In principle, the most desirable measure of a salesman's accomplishment is a comparison of the relationship between the firm and its customers with the salesman in the field and what it would be without him. Such measurements require well-planned observational or experimental studies. Thus they do not meet the need for regular evaluation of the salesman's performance.

As a proxy for changes in relationships brought about by the salesman's work, the manager must generally rely on measuring observable consequences of the salesman's work such as sales volume, contributions to profit margins, or customers gained or lost. The major problems in the use of such observable measures lie in the need to establish standards of performance for each consequence being measured and isolating the salesman's causal role in the results observed. In addition, although some observable consequences themselves are easily measured (for example, sales, new accounts) others are more elusive (for example, changes in communications effectiveness).

For many purposes such as supervision, training, and the analysis of effort-result relationships, the sales manager needs to know what the salesman is *doing*. These needs are met by activity measures. Data for such measures may come from internal records or from the salesman's reports themselves.

In determining training, and especially retraining needs and for some personnel assignment decisions (for example, transfer, advancement), the manager may be interested primarily in the salesman's competence. Measures of competence are largely subjective.

Although perhaps less useful than measures of accomplishment, activity or competence, taken alone, composite measures which embrace all three are sometimes used to determine the overall performance of the salesman.

Evaluation systems should be reviewed regularly to insure that the criteria used remain the most relevant ones, that the measurement devices used are both valid and reliable, and that the operation of the evaluation system does not in itself induce dysfunctional behavior.

SELECTED READINGS

Meyer, Herbert H., Emanuel Kay, and John R. P. French, Jr., "Split Roles for Performance Appraisal," *Harvard Business Review,* XLIII, No. 1 (January–February 1965), pp. 123–129. A critical evaluation of the performance appraisal interview as a motivational technique. Based on studies at the General Electric Company.

National Industrial Conference Board, *Measuring Salesmen's Performance* (Studies in Business Policy, No. 114). New York: National Industrial Conference Board, 1965. Performance measurement and appraisal practices of a number of companies. Includes forms used.

Phelps, D. Maynard, and J. Howard Westing, *Marketing Management* 3d. ed. Homewood, Ill. Richard D. Irwin, Inc., 1968, Chapter 31. Review of appraisal techniques.

Robinson, Patrick J., and Bent Stidsen, *Personal Selling in a Modern Perspective.* Boston: Allyn & Bacon, Inc., 1967, Chapters IV, XIV. Chapter IV deals with measuring the effects of the salesman on buyer response. Chapter XIV suggests an approach to measuring salesman competance.

14 Compensation

Sales managers seek compensation arrangements which will attract able men and induce them to carry out their tasks in a way which best advances the company's progress. Probably no other area in sales-force management has witnessed so much fluidity due to managers seeking to attain these goals. This concern has made compensation a frequent topic of articles over the past forty years, as each new crop of writers has come forth with its "perfect plan" for sales compensation.

Much of the dissatisfaction with compensation plans and the perennial search for a perfect plan spring from a failure to concede the multiple functions of compensation. Too frequently, perhaps, the manipulation of monetary compensation is seen as the sole means of direction and motivation. It is expected to do the job more properly performed by supervision. In extreme cases, it is even regarded as a substitute for training and the development of skills: "Provide strong incentive compensation," we are told, "and the salesman will accomplish." It is as if baseball batters would achieve a home run every time at bat, if only they were compensated each day by a straight commission on total bases! No need for batting practice; incentive is the thing!

FUNCTION OF THE COMPENSATION SYSTEM

Intrinsically, the function of a compensation system is to *compensate the salesman for his performance.* As part of a system of rewards, compensation arrangements are inevitably based on a presumed ability to evaluate the performance being rewarded. In many plans, this performance-reward relationship is mechanistically formalized, as, for example, when men are paid on the basis of a commission on orders obtained during a particular period. In other plans, different evaluation criteria are introduced into the reward system, for example, through adjustments of a man's base salary to reflect aspects of his performance believed by management to be significant. Because the measurement of performance is fraught with so many difficulties (Chapter 13), a compensation plan which rewards in proportion to performance can at best represent an attractive goal. Attainment will necessarily be limited by the extent to which available surrogates fail to measure performance fully and accurately.

As a reward system, compensation serves to *induce* as well as to pay. The argument for so-called incentive compensation rests largely on the directional and motivational benefits which such schemes allegedly provide. It is argued that the salesman is motivated to work harder and that through the judicious manipulation of commission rates, a manager can induce the salesman to allocate his time in a desired way and to sell the particular combination of products which the management finds most desirable. Straight salary plans, on the other hand, may provide inducement in different directions (for example, to work certain hours) or make it easier for management to make other means of directing the sales organization (for example, supervision) more effective.

A third function of compensation is to secure and maintain the commitment of the salesman to the company. Although social constraints in the United States do not yet place as much responsibility on the employer as in some Asiatic and European countries, it is clear that an employer takes on certain obligations to salesmen and other employees quite unrelated to their performance. Market conditions, considerations of need, equity and justice, and recognition of long-run effects of current pay scales all require that sales trainees be provided a "living wage," often on a scale far above their current contribution, in exchange for their commitment to the company even for a short period. In the same way, combinations of market and social pressures require firms to make provision not only for the disabled and the superannuated but also for those who are not now producing commensurate value but who have been committed to the firm for a number of years.[1] Even a plan of compensation which directs sales activity well and rewards salesmen for their performance, well may fail to attract or hold able men if it does not provide an appropriate level of compensation for commitment.

MULTIPLE EFFECTS OF COMPENSATION PLANS

The perennial debate over "incentive" compensation obscures the fact that every compensation plan has three types of effects: (a) directive effects, (b) personnel management effects, and (c) customer effects.

Directive Effects

Every plan serves in some way to influence how the salesmen will spend their time and the means which they will employ in achieving personal and company goals. The ideal plan will provide incentive not only to keep the salesman fully active in the discharge of his responsibilities, but also to adhere to managerial policies and procedures in the performance of duties and the allocation of effort

Incentive plans characteristically encourage the salesman to do the *particular* things which carry rewards under the plan. Indeed, this is precisely what the incentives are designed to do. So-called nonincentive plans influence the salesman by encouraging other kinds of activities and, perhaps, by placing him in a somewhat closer relationship with his supervisors.

Personnel Management Effects

Among the personnel management effects of any compensation plan are its capability of securing and holding able salesmen and its effects on their morale and attitudes toward the organization, toward training, and toward the various facets of performance of their jobs.

From a personnel management perspective, an ideal compensation plan should be objective, perfectly sensitive to changes in the

[1] Laws vesting rights in employees in some Asiatic countries approach an automatic tenure system for workers who have been with the firm even a few years. Thus such employees must be paid a socially or union-determined scale until they reach the retirement age, without regard to their contribution to the firm's output. Perhaps a closer analogy to the sales situation is the statutory protection which manufacturers' representatives possess in France. If the services of such a representative are terminated by the manufacturer, the representative is entitled to liquidated damages equal to the full gross commissions (that is, without reduction for his operating expenses) for the next three years, based on those of the most recent year.

salesman's performance, and, at the same time, insulate the salesman from the effects of factors over which he has no control. While these goals can never be fully achieved in practice, they can be approached by arrangements which reduce the risk of arbitrary pay determination, and avoid rewarding or penalizing the salesman on the basis of environmental factors which he is unable to affect.

Failure to insulate the salesman against the effect of environmental factors may lead to overpayment in times of favorable business activity and underpayment when adverse conditions exist. The obvious inequity of the latter may in practice be so disruptive of satisfactory personnel relations that firms may find it necessary to supplement the inadequate compensation of salesmen in slack times.

As the salesman has little or no control over other functional activities of the firm, it would appear inappropriate to base the pay of salesmen on the results of those activities. Compensation based on net profit is particularly objectionable in this respect because so many of the elements which enter into net profit are beyond the control of the salesmen. Among such elements are production efficiency, labor disputes, raw material costs, advertising effectiveness, financing activities, credit standards, product quality control, service department performance, and local taxes.

Personnel management considerations also require mutual understanding of the pay system and agreement as to its equity. Thus, unnecessary complexity is to be avoided. Moreover, the system must not only treat salesmen fairly in fact; they must *believe* that they are being treated fairly.

Customer Effects

The method of compensation has indirect effects on the salesman-customer interaction through the directive effects already noted. In addition, the method of compensation may directly influence the type of relationship which the salesman has with the customer. The ideal compensation plan will encourage the salesman to take the long-term perspective and to develop the kinds of community of interest with prospects and customers which will enhance future relationships. A significant flaw in some incentive schemes is that they may induce the salesman to take an adversary rather than cooperative stance in dealing with the prospective buyer. Such abuses of the marketing-service concept as dealer loading and high pressure tactics are likely to be associated with compensation schemes which place very high value on immediate sales and little or no value on longer-term benefits. Although not inherent in them, plans to encourage so-called balanced selling or the sale of those items which are most profitable to the seller may produce similar conflicts of interest. Other arrangements may produce other types of influences on salesman-customer relationships and thus produce corresponding customer effects. The growing customer orientation of the market place is likely to require increased attention to customer effects.

DEVELOPMENT AND OPERATION OF COMPENSATION SYSTEMS

The activities involved in developing a sound compensation system and maintaining its viability are illustrated in Figure 14-1.

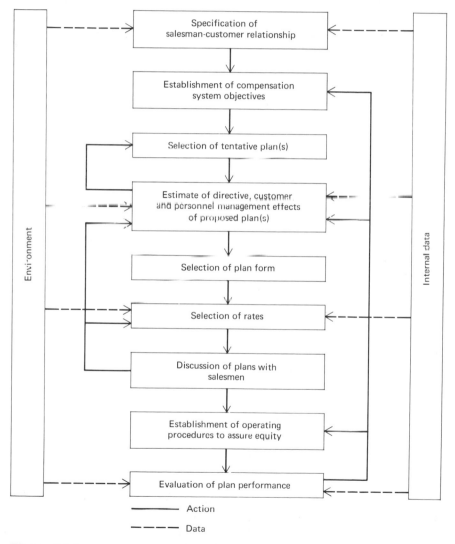

Figure 14-1
DEVELOPMENT AND OPERATION OF A COMPENSATION SYSTEM

The development of a sound compensation plan entails a sequence of activities: specification of the desired salesman-customer relationship; establishment of specific objectives for the compensation system; selection of one or more plans for detailed evaluation; estimation of the probable directive, customer, and personnel management effects of each plan being considered; and the final selection of plan forms and rates.

The operation and maintenance of compensation arrangements involves satisfactory interaction with the salesmen to assure their acceptance of the plan, the establishment of procedures to assure equity in administration, and the development of an evaluation system to provide for periodic, if not continual, appraisal of compensation system performance. This appraisal must be fed back into the system so that the system may be modified in the light of actual outcomes as well as to reflect new factors in the environment.

Specification of the Salesman-Customer Relationship

As the salesman-customer interaction provides the rationale for the entire sales management process, it must serve as a starting point for plan development. In large part, the nature of this relationship will determine the extent to which concern with customer effects must be paramount. The need at this point is to make the nature of the intended relationship explicit so that the functions of the sales force, the kinds of interactions envisaged with various personnel in the buying unit, and the duties of the men can be derived from it. The specific objectives of the compensation plan can then be related directly to these functions and responsibilities.

Establishment of Compensation System Objectives

Given the desired salesman-customer interaction, what role toward its attainment should be played by the compensation plan?

The answer to this question rests in part on the extent to which other managerial resources are available to direct and induce motivation of the sales force. To the extent that such other resources are limited or unavailable, the reward system may need to assume greater directive burdens. Where other managerial tools are available and effective, compensation may be more directly related to its primary role, provided only that it reinforce, rather than offset, the work of trainers, supervisors, and other managers.

Definition of the role of the compensation plan in achieving overall sales-management objectives will depend on the answers to such questions as: What is the relative importance of immediate sales as opposed to long-run customer and market development? How broad is the scope of the salesman's duties? How well is the performance of various duties reflected in immediate sales? How much influence over activities should be provided directly through supervision, rather than indirectly through money incentive? How will the maintenance of competence be accomplished? Is compensation being relied on as the sole means of inducing the salesman to apply himself?

Selection of Specific Plans for Consideration

Answers to questions such as the foregoing will indicate the general nature of the compensation plans appropriate in a particular situation. Moreover, if some type of combination plan is indicated it should reveal the relative importance of the various elements in it. The manager can then select those plans which appear to be appropriate for further detailed examination.

Evaluation of Specific Proposals

The selection process should go beyond identification of a plan which the manager believes will properly blend the desired elements so as to achieve his objectives. A number of alternative plans should be subjected to careful scrutiny, and perhaps eventually to formal research to provide answers to three critical questions:

1. What will be the directive effects of the proposed plan?
2. What will be the effects of the proposed plan on customers?
3. What will be the personnel-management effects of the plan and what personnel-management problems are likely to arise?

Examination of the latter question should include effects on salesmen's earnings and standing in their peer group.

The answers to these questions may suggest revisions of the proposed plans in order to make them more effective for the management of the particular sales force. In any event, unless these questions can be answered with at least some degree of confidence, the manager has no sound basis for *any* compensation-plan decision.

Some maintain that every proposed compensation plan should be field tested before adoption.[2] In a large organization it may be possible to test a new plan in selected areas, to observe the effects on salesmen and their performance, and to modify the plan before final adoption. However, many organizations are too small to be able to operate a test area insulated from the rest of the sales organization.

[2] See Kenneth R. Davis and Frederick F. Webster, Jr., *Sales Force Management* (New York: The Ronald Press Company, 1968), p. 645.

For others, the delay involved in awaiting test results and the difficulties involved in evaluation argue against delaying a compensation plan improvement to conduct tests.

Plan Selection and Implementation

Based on compensation plan objectives and the estimates of the directive, customer, and personnel management effects of each alternative considered, management must select both a compensation plan (for example, salary with bonus for attainment of quota) and a set of rates (for example, salary scales or rates of commission). Operating procedures must also be formulated to assure equity in administration. For example, the circumstances under which a commission will be paid to particular salesmen must be spelled out.

The successful implementation of even an ongoing compensation plan requires understanding communications between management and sales personnel. Salesmen must understand the plan and its rationale and must *believe* that it is equitable and fair. To this end, management must not only explain, but must be sympathetic listeners so that misunderstandings may be avoided and problems resolved in their incipiency.

When changes are under consideration, participation of the salesmen, at least to the extent of securing their views, is essential. Suggestions and comments from the field may reveal aspects of the proposal which had not been fully recognized or fully allowed for by management. If a new plan is adopted, it is imperative that both the plan and its rationale be discussed with the salesman prior to implementation and while changes are still possible. Management must be able to explain the plan and respond constructively to criticisms of it. That is, it must convince the salesmen as knowledgeable buyers that the plan is in the best interest of both salesman and firm. Compensation is such a vital matter to the salesmen that acceptance of any plan by the men is a necessary condition for its success.

Continuing Review of Compensation

Changes in the sales job, changes in the environment, and changes in conditions in the labor market may call for modifications of the compensation system. Even were such changes not present, the directive, customer, and personnel management effects of any compensation plan in use may differ substantially from those envisaged at the time the plan was adopted. For these reasons, every compensation plan should be subjected to regular review.

In addition, a number of pathological conditions in the sales force may suggest that a reexamination of the compensation plan may be in order. Among these conditions are high turnover of the better men, unsatisfactory performance of some duties which appears attributable to dysfunctional consequences of some element in the compensation plan (for example, excessive numbers of small orders associated with a reward system based on number of orders obtained), salary adjustments on a "squeaky wheel" basis, and evidence that the compensation plan is directing men in a manner opposite to that which supervision is seeking.

In a sense, every compensation system should be viewed both as an operating system and as the subject of an observational study. Results of every plan, including "successful" plans, should be carefully analyzed so that its effects are known and alterations can be made.

ELEMENTS OF COMPENSATION PLANS

One way in which compensation plans seek to achieve the diverse functions which have been suggested is to build plans of several elements. This requires *more than merely combining desirable features of different elements while seeking to avoid their pitfalls.* The total plan must reflect the directive, personnel management, and customer effects which it will produce. Different plans may be needed when a company has sales forces with different duties—for example, calling on chain buyers versus field work in stores; calling on specifiers versus installers; working with OEM accounts versus customers buying for use in their internal operations.

Fixed Elements

Fixed elements are paid on a time basis, without regard for the performance of the salesman during the pay period. A basic salary is the most common fixed element, although guarantees and drawing accounts on which overdraws need not be repaid provide the same features. Salary and other fixed elements are only fixed for the particular pay period; they may be adjusted from time to time based on performance or other considerations, but such adjustments apply to future rather than past periods.

Elements Which Vary with Some Measure Which Is Believed to Represent Performance

Commissions and so-called bonuses which depend on the work of the salesman or of a group of which the salesman is a part, represent variable elements. A difficulty with variable elements is that the causes of variation in the performance measure are not precisely known or may not be causally related in a one-to-one manner to the work of particular salesmen. An increase in purchases by a customer may be the result of the salesman's efforts, or it may merely reflect changes in the level of the customer's needs. Securing a number of new accounts *may* be a direct consequence of the efforts of the salesman, or it may merely reflect that some customers of competitors have become dissatisfied with their old source of supply. Failure to retain an established account *may* be the result of poor work by the salesman in charge, or it may reflect the fact that the proposal prepared by the firm's technical staff was inferior to that submitted by a competitor. Often a combination of factors brings about the observed result. In short, we do not always know the proportion of the observed variation which is the result of the work of the individual salesman.

Fringe Elements

Two types of fringe elements are employed in sales work. One type of fringe is the benefit such as a special vacation, choice of a territory, or a reward which is dependent in some way on the salesman's performance. A second and more important type consists of employee benefits which are largely or totally independent of the work of the salesman during any particular period. Such fringes are generally either uniform for all employees of a given class (say, salesman's car), or even for all employees of the firm (say, hospitalization, access to company recreational facilities), or are provided in some fixed relationship to salary or other compensation elements (say, group life insurance, retirement benefits, profit-sharing bonus).

Fringe elements have increased markedly in importance since the 1930s for a number of reasons: the increased desire for security which has developed among all elements in society; the institutionalization of employment with the growing role of the corporate business and the professional manager; high levels of employment for the better part of three decades so that often men select employers rather than merely taking any job offered. With institutionalization, the fringe benefits available to other kinds of employees tend to become company-wide. Moreover, the prospective recruit can see in the package of fringe benefits evidence of what the firm will do for him that is somewhat more tangible than discussions of opportunities for advancement or of the excellence of the men with whom he will be working. Some fringe benefits, such as profit sharing, are alleged to develop company esprit and thus make the salesman more likely to "commit" himself to the firm and align his personal goals with those of the firm. Finally, the tax structure with its heavy emphasis on cash income provides a strong inducement for compensation in forms which are tax free to employer and employee alike—for example, recreational facilities, insurance, medical care, meals, use of company facilities.

Intangible Rewards

A portion of the compensation in virtually all jobs is intangible in form. Managements generally tend to overrate the importance of monetary rewards and to underestimate the significance and power of intangible ones.[3]

Perhaps the most important intangible reward is the satisfaction which comes from a job well done or from knowledge that one's work has made a contribution to the well-being of others. A related reward is the commendation or appreciation expressed by others—for example, recognition of one's work. If one were to accept McGregor's Theory *Y* as the sole explanation of human behavior, these intangible returns for human effort could themselves be the sole compensation. For many types of "volunteer" activities such intangible rewards do serve as the sole means of compensation. However, both market factors (demand for workers) and the economic need of the worker to obtain tangible income require that tangible, monetary compensation also be provided for most jobs. This fact should not blind us to the fact that, particularly in mental work such as that performed by salesmen, the intangibles represent an important, if unmeasured, portion of the compensation received. With increased affluence and the breakdown of the social and educational barriers which restrict occupational choice, the social desirability of an occupation may be expected to weigh more heavily and the paycheck less heavily in the years to come. In this situation, the salesman's sense of accomplishment and of contribution are likely to become a larger factor in the total compensation complex.

LEVEL OF COMPENSATION

In terms of its effect on the ability to attract and hold able men, the level of compensation is more important than how pay is calculated. Proper levels of sales compensation have become increasingly important as selling has become a higher level job with greater responsibilities and demanding more able men. The less reliance that recruiters can place on a residual labor supply, the greater the need for a fully competitive pay level.

A *base level* for a sales force is the amount which the firm must pay to secure and retain men of the desired caliber. This is the amount which the average salesman will earn. The variance around the base level suggests the range of total compensation which is provided to men of varying performance and ability within a sales force. In establishing compensation levels, the manager must consider both

[3] This tendency is noted by L. G. Lindahl, "What Makes a Good Job?" *Personnel*, XXV, No. 4 (January 1949), pp. 263–266.

the base level and the range of variance around it. Levels of compensation which are too low for the men involved impair both recruiting and the ability to hold able men. Levels which are too high may result in excessive sales costs.

How would you determine pay levels for salesmen to be hired by two MBAs to sell a new business system for small business?

Over the long term, sales compensation levels are very largely determined by market forces. With able sales candidates finding themselves in a seller's market for their service, a sales manager's offer which fails to reflect the going rate will not attract or retain the needed numbers of qualified men.

The need to meet the going market rate is most evident for recruits and for less specialized sales jobs in which sales skills and information are highly transferable between companies and industries. Market conditions play a somewhat smaller role in the case of salesmen who are so highly specialized that their opportunity costs are lower. These salesmen are similar to executives in that they tend to be tied somewhat more closely to the firm than less skilled salesmen and workers. However, their constant contact with the outside world and often limited cohesiveness with others in the firm limit some of the frictional force which keeps many white collar workers and executives tied to a particular firm. Thus, even specialized salesmen derive some protection against underpayment from a market which is open to them.

The important role played by market forces does not relieve the management of the problems of determining appropriate compensation levels. What is the market level for a certain type of work entailing certain kinds of skills and experience? Some clues may be provided by published reports of trade associations and from surveys (for example, National Industrial Conference Board, Dartnell Corporation), by observing the compensation obtained by candidates pursued but not secured, by offers received by existing salesmen, and by inquiry of firms whose sales tasks are similar to that of the sales force under consideration. But because each sales force's relationship with its market is in some sense unique, these clues can at best provide only rough guidelines.

Determination of the proper level of sales-force compensation depends on accurate job analyses and the development of relevant man-specifications. It should also reflect peer-group values as to fair compensation for an individual.

Some would even suggest that salesmen's compensation levels should be tied to that of other employees of the firm—that is, that the job should be graded in the same manner as blue collar and other white collar jobs and the pay level established accordingly. Such a procedure would substantially ignore the influence of market forces, which tend to be greater for sales than for many other types of personnel. The able salesman has skills and knowledge of a type which are often widely demanded. If the compensation which he can earn for a given company or in a given industry is less than those skills command elsewhere, the firm or industry will be unable to attract and hold adequate numbers of able people. The mobility of able salesmen thus provides a market floor which protects the salesmen against serious underpayment and is quite independent of going rates for other employees of the firm. As a consequence, internally determined compensation levels which primarily reflect internal wage-level consistency are likely to be out of line with market realities, particularly in the short run.

Nevertheless, some consideration may need to be given to the relative entry-pay levels of sales and other employees with similar entry backgrounds. In determining pay levels, the primary uses of the job description and man specification are, however, in the determination of the appropriate market rates to examine. That is, which outside jobs are the relevant ones for comparison? At times these may be similar jobs in the same industry; often similarities are more apparent than real and the relevant market lies outside.

The maintenance of the proper compensation level over time is a continuing problem. Initially, compensation levels may have been set incorrectly because of inaccurate understanding of the nature and responsibilities of the job, inappropriate ties to other jobs in the firm, or misjudgment as to the market rate for salesmen of a particular type and skill. Even if the original levels are established correctly, they may quickly become obsolete because of changes in the nature of the sales job—for example, as relationships with buyers evolve over the life cycle of a product or industry. Moreover, market conditions, especially for recruits, change rapidly so that a starting level appropriate at one time may within a year become either excessive or inadequate.

The need for general compensation-level adjustments is not always conspicuous. Unlike a product which is priced out of line, inadequate sales compensation may not result in an immediate loss of personnel or drying up of the supply of recruits. It may persist for some time in the form of an inadequately remunerated force and a below-average body of recruits. If a chronic condition is permitted to develop undetected, the caliber of the sales force will decay.

Some companies pay their salesmen in excess of the market rate. In some cases this is a conscious policy which seeks to obtain the best and may be predicated on the premise that high compensation levels, like high wage rates, need not result in high selling costs if, by employing superior men, the firm is able to achieve higher than average productivity.

> A parts manufacturer attempts to pay above the market to attract and hold the best men available. In a few cases, salesmen have earned more than the men to whom they report.

In other situations, an excessively high compensation level results not from conscious plan but as a result of uncertainty of the value of salesmen, management lethargy, or a fear that particular salesmen have become indispensable and control their accounts.

METHODS OF COMPENSATION

A compensation method, or compensation plan, refers to the manner in which compensation for particular men for specific pay periods is determined. Most compensation plans embrace two or more of the compensation elements discussed earlier.

This section will first examine the nature, merits and weaknesses of straight commission and straight salary plans. Not only are these plans important in their own right, but an understanding of the directive, personnel management, and customer effects of each is essential if a soundly based multi-element plan is to be employed.

Commission Plans

Commission compensation is tied *directly* to a measure of performance. A wide variety of commission plans are used. The *basis* on which a commission is calculated is commonly dollar or unit sales or such sales, adjusted for allowances, write-offs, or special charges.

COMMISSION RATE BASES

Usually, the same commission terms apply to all territories, although some companies pay different rates of commission in different areas. This situation is most likely to apply where the salesman must pay all expenses out of his commission and there are substantial differences in the cost of covering different territories or where territorial problems necessitate higher compensation and there is no fixed element in the compensation plan through which allowance for these conditions can be made.

Commission rates can be tailored to take goals other than gross sales volume into account. As the firm's goal is not sales, but profits, it is argued that salesmen should be paid on the profit earned by their work. To emphasize the importance of profitability, gross margin dollars rather than sales dollars may be used as the commission basis.

Alternatively, commission rates may be varied with items sold, higher rates being paid on those items which management, for any reason, wishes the salesman to push. Higher rates may be paid to encourage emphasis on new additions to the product line or on items which are more profitable to the firm (not necessarily those carrying the highest gross margin). Different rates may be paid on sales to different classes of accounts (users paying list prices versus distributors entitled to functional discounts), or sales on different terms (cash versus extended credit), or at different prices (sales at posted prices versus those involving price concessions).

The rationale behind many varying commissions is that compensation should reflect the profitability of the business secured in order to induce the salesman to pursue more profit, rather than merely more sales—a view that is particularly pertinent if the salesman is viewed as a "territory manager." The overall merit of such contentions should be judged with regard to the customer and personnel-management effects of the arrangements as well as their immediate directive effects.

For example, if a salesman can allocate his time among buyers of more or less profitable items, rewards which encourage his attention to the buyers of the more profitable item raise no customer-effect problems. A similar situation exists if the salesman has a choice in selecting among alternative items to be shown to a customer, *when the alternatives are equally good for the customer.* Differential rewards do, however, raise the danger of encouraging an adversary relationship between salesman and customer. That is, the salesman may be tempted to push the item with the greatest commission *even when that item is not in the best interest of the customer* and thus of the long-term interest of the seller.

> Some retailers, for example, use PMs (push money) to get salesmen to push private or less-known brands which, because of favorable store buys, can provide the customer with a good value while at the same time providing the store with a larger margin than some other lines. Such an inducement creates no adversary interest.
>
> Other retailers use PMs to get salesmen to sell overpriced, shopworn, or market-rejected items because they find that a small PM (say, $1) may be as effective as a much larger markdown (say, $3) in moving obsolete merchandise or "buyers' mistakes." In such operations, differential commission rates may be used to switch customers from good to poorer values.

Commissions based on profit are open to the additional objection that profits are affected by many factors beyond the salesman's control. The salesman may be penalized because of production or financial developments unrelated to his own work. In most situations, too many activities beyond the salesman's control affect net profit so that profits are an inappropriate basis for compensation. There are exceptions, such as in some types of job order work.

> An acoustical tile contractor's salesmen take responsibility for the total job—developing and following leads, estimating, checking the work, follow-up and even collection of the receivable. In this situation, compensation on the basis of job profit is quite appropriate.

Despite their apparent attractiveness, prudence suggests that possible arrangements which seek to direct the salesman's efforts among products in the line should give careful consideration to possible customer and personnel-management consequences.

FIXED VERSUS SLIDING SCALE RATES

The commission rate may be fixed for all sales of an item or it may vary with the size of individual orders or with the amount sold by a salesman during a particular period.

For some large-unit, customer-specified industrial and construction products, the commission rate may be varied with the size of the individual order. The salesman's task in such cases is often to secure the specification of his firm's product. It is argued that the effort required is not proportional to the size of the customer's purchase and, moreover, that the salesman, though influencing the *fact of* purchase, has little influence over the *amount* purchased. Thus a firm might pay 3 percent on the first $50,000 of the contract amount, 2 percent of the next $100,000 and only 1 percent on the contract amount in excess of $150,000.

Commission rates are sometimes varied with the total volume achieved by the salesman during a period. Most commonly, the commission rate is progressive. After the salesman attains some desired level such as quota or an amount which brings his total salary and expense ratio down to some predetermined goal level, the rate is increased. The rationale for such an approach is that the incremental sales achieved after this point is reached are more profitable to the company, basic sales costs having been recovered. So the company can afford to share the extra profit with the salesman and should do so to induce further effort.

At the other extreme, some firms have regressive structures. Lower commission rates apply to additional volume increments. It is argued that this practice limits the extent to which the salesman can benefit from windfalls and reduces the likelihood that a salesman will earn more than the sales manager or company president.

COMMISSION PLANS WITH GUARANTEES

A guaranteed floor under commission earnings is sometimes provided in the form of a nonreturnable drawing account which the salesman can use for minimum living expenses until commissions are earned and received. Alternatively, a small salary is provided, with commissions starting either with the first sale or at a higher level, presumably after the "salary" has been earned. Such plans also serve to provide a training salary for recruits until they move into the commission range.

Although called salary-and-commission or combination plans such plans are generally de facto commission plans inasmuch as it is not anticipated that salesmen who fail to reach the commission range will remain with the sales force. The premises underlying such plans and their directive, customer, and personnel management effects are generally similar to those for other commission arrangements.

PREMISES UNDERLYING COMMISSION PLANS

The underlying premise of all commission plans is that the efforts put forth by the salesman produce results *of the type used as the commission basis in direct proportion to those efforts.* Based on this premise, proponents of straight commission compensation contend that this plan pays each salesman precisely in accordance with his efforts. The tenuous nature of this premise is obvious from the many problems noted in the previous chapter. It is rarely true that the success of a salesman on a particular call is *solely* the result of what the salesman does.

Differences in opportunities, buyers' situations, and effects of other elements in the marketing mix may normally be expected to lead to different results in different sales areas at any particular time. Factors outside of the salesman's control exert some influence in all sales situations. To the extent that they are important, they invalidate the basic premise underlying commission compensation.

A secondary premise underlying commission plans is that the selected commission base fully reflects all sales objectives. While this may be true in one-shot sales situations (for example, residential real estate, retirement homesites; door-to-door vacuum cleaner sales), the shifting emphasis toward the salesman as a builder of long-term relationships often makes it inappropriate to evaluate and compensate him on the basis that "today's sale is the thing."

A growing recognition of the inapplicability of the basic premises of commission compensation to many types of today's selling has undoubtedly played a role in the decline of straight commission forms of compensation. The quest for greater security, and the more complex selling tasks have also played a role.

DIRECTIVE EFFECTS OF COMMISSION COMPENSATION

Commission compensation is the ultimate in the use of the "carrot" to induce a salesman to perform as management desires. The extensive consideration often given to manipulating commission rates for the purpose of inducing salesmen to sell particular items or to behave in particular ways attests to the widespread feeling among sales managers that commission compensation serves as a very significant force for motivating the salesmen to maximize effort and for directing salesmen along particular lines.

Straight commission provides maximum incentive for immediate sales. It is alleged further that straight commission encourages the salesman to try harder and to utilize his time fully and wisely. However, its heavy emphasis on immediate returns may or may not be consistent with the long-term goals of sales-force and company management. It can easily lead to neglect of missionary and other development work, skimming the cream from markets and "rutmanship"—taking the route of least effort in terms of both customers called on and items suggested to them.

A more subtle directive effect is the lesser control which supervisors have over salesmen compensated on commission. Men whose pay is based entirely on a particular type of result may well resist suggestions, or even instructions and policies, which they believe to be of little or no help in achieving their goals. Thus the very independence which provides the motivation—the fact that the salesman is his own man to prosper or fail—leads to more limited control by management in the direction of the salesman's work.

CUSTOMER EFFECTS OF COMMISSION COMPENSATION

Because it rewards closing sales rather than service, the customer effects of commission compensation may be less favorable than those which management would prefer. The likelihood that an adversary rather than a cooperative relationship with customers will be created is substantially increased. Dealer loading, high-pressure selling, and an emphasis on those products which most reward the salesman rather than those which would best serve the customer are possible, although by no means inevitable, effects of commission compensation. To the extent that customers recognize that the salesman is rewarded directly for sales made to them, the credibility and integrity of the information and assistance provided by the salesman may be impaired.

Undesirable customer effects are not inevitable under commission compensation. Indeed, where the salesman recognizes that he must prosper largely on the repeat business of satisfied accounts, the problem is likely to be minimal. Such a situation exists, for example, in some types of sales to the trade where the salesman's only long-term means of success is through helping his trade customers develop volume in their own operations. Nevertheless, because commission compensation creates a presumption of an adversary relationship, the sales manager has a stronger need for other means to encourage relationship development between his salesmen and their accounts.

PERSONNEL MANAGEMENT EFFECTS OF COMMISSION COMPENSATION

It is generally believed that commission compensation tends to attract the type of man who is willing to forego the assurance of an income for the opportunity to earn a greater one and that such men constitute a superior group of salesmen. It thus serves as a desirable recruiting aid. The validity of this contention does not appear to have been tested by careful research. A contrary position seems to be indicated by the experience of those firms which have either abandoned recruiting at colleges because commission compensation was unable to attract college men or have moved away from straight commission in order to make their offer more attractive to them.

A significant advantage of the commission plan is that it makes reductions in pay level more palatable as they occur as a result of lower accomplishment by the salesman. Even if lower sales were largely the result of external factors, the resulting lower commissions do not appear arbitrary and hence are less likely to create personnel problems than would a corresponding reduction in salary. This advantage is tempered somewhat by the fact that a large reduction in pay due to circumstances beyond the salesman's control is likely to lead to demands for a guarantee of some sort.

The commission plan weeds out misfits and those whose immediate sales performance is unsatisfactory more promptly and with less need for managerial action than other plans. It thus seems to avoid the need for many separation decisions. This very fact may, however, serve to conceal deficiencies in selection, training, and supervision with which management ought to concern itself. In fact, the presence of an "automatic dump" procedure may serve to discourage appropriate managerial attention to proper selection and training. Aside from the cost to the firm in money and customer goodwill of a "sink or swim" posture, there are important social questions involved. Is a firm acting in a socially responsible way or is it seeking to transfer to the individual salesman responsibilities which it should assume?

Although incentive compensation should lead the salesman to use his time fully, it does not automatically do so. The extent to which commission salesmen will "satisfice" remains a largely unexplored area. To the extent that the salesman is "in business for himself," he well might be expected to consider whether additional activity is worth the effort once a satisfactory level of earnings has been achieved. To the extent this occurs, the incentive has become inoperative, although the weakened capability of supervision remains.

> An extreme case in the author's experience was the case of a group of older salesmen for a dry goods wholesaler. An analysis of the orders sent in by salesmen raised doubts as to whether some men were in the field more than two or three days per week. As management had relied on the commission incentive to keep the men fully active, it did not obtain activity reports from them. Because this practice was long established, they were unwilling to institute such a system of reports. Thus the salesmen were in fact independent agents. As their income needs were modest, they were under no compulsion to work more than a few days per week.

Nor does a good incentive insure that a salesman will use his time wisely. This is largely a matter of training and the development and maintenance of desirable work habits (Chapter 7).

As noted in Chapter 8, the maintenance of salesman competence is becoming an increasingly grave problem in a world of rapidly changing technology and accelerated change in consumer wants, product applications, and marketing arrangements. Activities to maintain and restore the salesman's competence to deal with these changes are essentially overhead in character. They do not produce commissions. Hence incentive compensation provides a reward system which works against retraining. To offset this, retraining programs may need to be packaged with heavy layers of entertainment or other inducements.

Commission plans also entail administrative problems which, unless satisfactorily resolved, may have adverse effects on the relationships between the salesman and the company.

ADMINISTRATIVE PROBLEMS WITH COMMISSION PLANS

Most of the administrative problems with commission plans arise because the underlying premises upon which the plan is based do not fully hold. Because factors in the environment change, circumstances beyond the control of the salesmen will affect the dependent variable (that is, sales) which is being used as the commission base. A recession may result in a sharp decline in sales. Customers may make changes (up or down) in their spending plans. Major users move into or out of a particular salesman's territory. New directions in the space program, in defense, in housing, or in dealing with urban problems bring sharp expansion in some industries and decline in others. A defense emergency leads to a windfall of orders. Changing distribution patterns wipe out opportunities. The result of such events may be that the commission salesman reaps the greatest reward when he does the least work and suffers the lowest return when market conditions are adverse and he must work the hardest.

In an attempt to offset the differences in territorial potential, or in the difficulties of covering a territory (for example, metropolitan areas densely populated with large buyers versus nonmetropolitan areas sparsely populated with smaller accounts), or to compensate for differences in living or operating costs within different territories, different commission rates may be applied in different territories. While understandable in principle, it is difficult both to establish rates which properly reflect different conditions and to modify the rates over time to reflect changes in conditions without having such modifications appear arbitrary or inequitable to one or more salesmen. Hence, the use of different rates is likely to be most feasible where distinct classes of accounts or servicing situations exist and are not likely to undergo radical change (for example, sales calls on "country" versus "city" drug stores). The use of different commission rates to reflect differences in living or operating costs is hard to justify. Such costs are not likely to vary with sales volume. Hence, if differential pay is necessary, it would appear more appropriate as a fixed element than as a factor in variable compensation.

Some administrative protection can be afforded the salesman through a drawing account or income guarantee. This does not, of course, protect the company against overpayment for windfalls. Not only is such an overpayment costly, but it may lead the salesman to place an excessive value on his own performance and lead to problems when more normal conditions return. Alternatively, commission rates can be adjusted to reflect changes in environmental conditions. But this raises substantial problems of fairness and equity, especially if rates are lowered just as the salesman feels that he is about to benefit.

Another set of problems arises where different members of the sales force, or even persons charged with other functions, have roles in the sales process or influence the accomplishment measure. One such problem arises where the service to the customer is best provided by having the salesman call in other salesmen or technical personnel to secure their ideas and expertise. Another set of problems arises when the individuals participating in the buying and use process come under the responsibility of different salesmen.

The simplest case of the latter is that in which sales are made to a buying activity for a multiplant firm. Actual purchases will come from the buying office, but much of the sales work to secure adoption may have taken place at the various using activities. Which salesman should receive the commission? If it is to be divided, on what basis should the division be made?

A similar situation exists in sales to chain stores. Actual purchases may come from the buying office, but much sales work is involved in activities at the store level to secure shelf-space and local promotion and to see that the store is properly serviced so that stock-outs do not occur. Different salesmen are generally involved. In fact, in some cases company sales personnel will deal with the central office while sales tasks at the local level are performed by manufacturers' representatives (called "brokers" in the food industry) or distributors' sales personnel.

Another type of arrangement exists in selling to some large food and variety chains. In many of these organizations store managers have substantial discretion in items to be carried but are restricted to those items which central office buyers have approved —that is, are "in the catalogue" or "on the list." The sales task is twofold: to secure inclusion of the item on the approved list prepared by the central buying activity and to convince individuul store and department managers to stock, display, and promote the item. A satisfactory volume of sales is likely to result only if both of these jobs are done well. How should the credit for success or blame for failure be allotted? To whom should commission be paid or how should it be divided?

A more difficult case arises where promotional activity must be directed to a number of firms at different levels in the buying process in order to achieve a single sale.

In much construction work, specifications are prepared by architects and engineers for various materials and components. These specifications may demand a single proprietary product. Such an arrangement is generally considered quite costly, however, as it leaves the buyer of the material facing a monopoly situation in his solicitation of bids and subject to unacceptable delays if the chosen source cannot meet the schedule. Hence, the usual practice is to provide either that any one of several brands may be used or that a proprietary product "or equal" be used.

The contractor who purchases and installs the material will have his own preferences. Since he will be responsible for the performance of the structure, he will tend to prefer products which he believes will perform in a satisfactory manner. Moreover, as construction involves bringing together literally thousands of different products and scheduling their assembly into the structure, the contractor-buyer is concerned with the kind of supply service which he will obtain. Hence, he prefers the lines which are available from sources whose performance is known and upon which he has found he can rely.

Given this situation, the manufacturer of a specified construction product must exert promotional efforts both at the architect-engineer-specifier level and at the buyer-installer level. Unless this is satisfactorily accomplished, success in securing a specification may be negated by the substitution of an "equal" product preferred by the actual buyer, either for its own sake or because it is the line carried by his regular source of supply. Similarly, success in convincing the actual buyer of the merit of a product will be of little effect if the product is not acceptable to the architect or engineer. Often, however, the architect will be located in a different area than the construction site so that different sales territories are involved. Even if they are in the same geographic area, they may be called on by different salesmen because of differences in the nature of the sales work involved. To whom shall the credit for the sales be given? Should one of the salesmen suffer a loss of income where he performed his job well but no sale resulted because the other did not?

An even more difficult problem arises if the salesman is responsible for service after the sale. Perhaps even a different territory is involved. The following example, although it applies to manufacturers' representatives rather than company salesmen illustrates the problem.

A marble producer provides the material used in the interior walls of large office buildings. Typically, the specifications are drawn by New York or Chicago architectural firms who must be convinced to use marble rather than some other form of wall material in lobbies, corridors, or other spaces. Construction may take place anywhere in the United States. If it is a large building, it may be undertaken by one of the large construction firms such as McCloskey, Fuller, McShain or similar organizations whose base of operations is not likely to be in the city in which the building is to be erected. Relationships with these firms must be maintained both in order to insure that they do not seek to convince the architect to substitute a less costly material so that they can keep within the overall contracted amount and also to reduce the likelihood that they will obtain their marble from another marble company. Another purpose of such contacts is to obtain orders for jobs in which the original specifier may have had a competitive marble supplier in mind.

Finally, some work is required at the building site itself. The local representative may need to secure replacement of missing or broken pieces or to expedite shipment of pieces needed because of modification of the building plans. Moreover, after the building is in use the owner may need to buy a few pieces to replace breakage. Over the years, small quantities may be needed in connection with interior alterations of the building. These orders must be serviced by the local sales representative although they are so small that the commission thereon at regular rates would not make it worth his while to handle them. If the local man is to be compensated for his service work, it must come from a share of the revenue generated by the original sale. How should the commission be divided among the man calling on the architect (New York), the man calling on the contractor (Philadelphia), and the man in whose territory the building is to be erected (Tulsa, Oklahoma)? The marble company uses an arbitrary percentage to divide the commission among these parties.

Salary Plans

Salary plans involve weekly or monthly payments of a fixed amount. The salesman's performance is reflected through periodic adjustments in salary rather than through determining his current pay.

PREMISES UNDERLYING SALARY PLANS

The underlying premise for a salary is that the firm is compensating the salesman for the commitment of his time and services to the company. The salesman is being paid for his commitment during the pay period rather than for some "results" of his work. Because the salaried salesman is clearly an employee of the company, the salesman is more obligated to conform to the wishes of the management than in the case of a commissioned salesman who may feel that his time is his own to do with as he best sees fit.

DIRECTIVE EFFECTS OF SALARY COMPENSATION

Salary compensation does not in itself provide any direction or incentive to the sales force but it provides the milieu in which the other directional tools of management can play their roles without interference from the monetary reward system.

CUSTOMER EFFECTS OF SALARY COMPENSATION

Because it does not emphasize present sales, salary plans reduce the likelihood of an adversary relationship developing between the salesman and the customer.

PERSONNEL-MANAGEMENT EFFECTS OF SALARY COMPENSATION

Straight salary plans minimize the conflicts of goals between salesmen and management. Such conflicts can develop under incentive plans geared to immediate sales when management concerns are aimed at longer-term objectives and market relationships. In the same way, salary compensation avoids conflicts when management wishes the salesman to devote time and efforts to cultivating new types of markets, to increasing his competence or proficiency in some area, or to engaging in other activities which do not yield immediate sales results.

Inequities can develop in straight salary plans if they fail to reflect differences in work load, required activities, or the performance of different men, or if they are not adjusted to reflect changes in these factors, or are adjusted in a manner which the men believe to be arbitrary or inequitable. These difficulties are not so much a result of the use of a salary plan but of the administration of it. Sound administration of a salary plan demands that it reflect both a man's commitment and a periodic adjustment based on accurate evaluation of all facets of a man's performance. Unless accurate evaluations are made, so-called merit increases may be little more than awards for tenure. Under these circumstances, the individuals of real merit tend to be underrewarded relatively, and often absolutely as well. The poor performers may tend to be overpaid and, more seriously, may accept the vote of confidence which the merit increase implies. Some firms have found it embarassing to have to discharge a poor performer only a short time after his having been granted a "merit" increase.

Straight salary plans avoid many of the personnel-management problems of commission plans such as the split commission problems arising from multiple efforts and divided responsibilities, and somewhat reduce the problems of equity which appear when different salesmen enjoy territories with different potential or at different stages of development.

ADMINISTRATIVE PROBLEMS WITH SALARY PLANS

Sound administration requires that a man's salary reflect both his commitment and his performance over time. Thus it demands periodic salary review based on a sound evaluation of each man's work (Chapter 13). Through such reviews, salaries can be made responsive to as many facets of performance as are embraced in the evaluation system. If men know that they will be evaluated and their salaries reviewed regularly on the basis of the evaluation, salary plans can provide incentive. Although a man is not rewarded in the present for some particular event, he can expect that he will be rewarded in the foreseeable future based on his current performance.

The effectiveness of salary plans as incentive devices depends on the validity of the evaluation system used in connection with salary review and the confidence which the salesmen have in its objectivity and equity. If it is known that current sales volume is virtually the sole criterion of performance for salary review purposes, a salary plan will soon be burdened with all of the single-purposedness handicaps of straight commission but without its benefits. At the other extreme, if salary review is nothing more than the unstructured opinion of supervisors as to which man is doing a "well-rounded" job, rewards may go to the apple polishers and those whose good works happen to come to the attention of the rater. Sound salary administration requires periodic review and readjustment based on evaluation of each man's work which is both accurate and believed by the men to be accurate and fair. These activities are the sales managers' responsibility.

Salary-Plus-Incentive Plans

In salary-plus-incentive plans, hereafter called "incentive plans" or "bonus plans," the salary is the principal element of compensation. Such plans differ in outlook from salary-plus-commission plans in which the salary serves chiefly as a guarantee against inadequacy of commissions but is not intended to be the main basis of compensation.

Salary-plus-incentive programs have been growing in importance. A study by the National Industrial Conference Board in 1966 found that 67 percent of some 665 manufacturers were using some combination of salary and incentives in paying salesmen in 1965; this contrasts with 48 percent in 1946.[4] More specifically, of 191 manufacturers who changed sales compensation in the period 1955-1965 the clear trend was toward combination plans (Table 14-1).

A common form of salary plus incentive program is the salary-quota-bonus system in which the salesman receives a bonus for attaining quota (or some specified percentage, say, 90 percent of quota), with the bonus increasing for further attainments.

A steel company which pays salesmen on straight salary, adds a bonus if quota is reached. In fairness to the salesman, quotas need to be adjusted in the case of major volume losses not the fault of the salesman (for example, cutback in consumption by a major customer).

The directors of a manufacturer of components allots funds to a bonus pool each year, the amount being based on business conditions. Salesman's participation in the pool may vary from 10 percent to 25 percent of his annual salary depending on his performance relative to various product-line and overall quotas. Quotas are adjusted to reflect orders rejected for manufacturing operations reasons (for example, lack of capacity to produce a particular item at the time required).

[4] National Industrial Conference Board, Inc., *Compensating Field Sales Representatives,* Studies in Personnel Policy, No. 202, (New York: National Industrial Conference Board, 1966). Data includes all types of combination plans, a broader scope than the salary-plus-incentive plans discussed here.

Table 14-1

SALES COMPENSATION PLANS
USED BY 191 MANUFACTURING
COMPANIES CHANGING PLANS
BETWEEN 1955 AND 1965

	Percent of Companies	
Type of Plan	Prior Plan	1965 Plan
Straight commission	15%	3%
Straight salary	47%	14%
Salary plus incentives*	38%	83%

*Includes all types of combination plans.

SOURCE: National Industrial Conference Board *Compensation Field Sales Representatives,* Studies in Personnel Policy, No. 202.

A drug manufacturer bases salesmen's bonuses on quotas derived from 3-year historical sales.

Bonus plans fit nicely with the idea of multiple, rather than single, short-term goals for sales work. The bonus can be based on a number of elements instead of, or in addition to, quota.

A food manufacturer considers such factors as shelf-space assigned relative to competitors and to market share of products; conformity of store prices to list prices; extent of stock-outs and speed of correction; and number of promotions placed, as well as percentage of quota attained.

A home appliance manufacturer includes expense control performance in its bonus formula.

A building products manufacturer assigns extra bonus credits for sales of specific profitable items over their respective item quotas.[5]

A different building products manufacturer supplements salaries with a bonus based on gross margins.

Bonus programs also work well with management-by-objectives philosophies. Salesmen and managers can develop diverse objectives for a number of factors; attainment can enter bonus calculations.

[5] National Industrial Conference Board, Inc., *Incentive Plans for Salesmen,* Studies in Personnel Policy, No. 217, (New York: National Industrial Conference Board, 1970), pp. 48–52.

In establishing the incentive portion of a salary-plus-incentive system, the particular activities or salesman-induced events which are to be rewarded need to be identified. Priorities must be established as among alternative goals which might be rewarded. Then suitable measures must be selected—for example, exceeding a sales quota, securing an above-normal number of new accounts, reducing expenses a certain percentage below budget.

Rewards for performance may be expressed directly—for example, $50 for each new distributor secured. Alternatively, points are assigned for various levels of goal attainment on each criterion. Point totals are then translated into either absolute dollar bonuses or bonuses expressed as a percentage of the salesman's salary.[6]

In the aggregate, bonuses paid to salesmen averaged 10 to 15 percent of salary in 100 plans examined in a 1968 National Industrial Conference Board Study. The better men, of course, enjoyed higher increments.[7]

PREMISES UNDERLYING BONUS PLANS

Bonus plans seek to secure the basic benefits of a salaried sales force and at the same time provide inducement for extra effort either in general or, more commonly, *along designated lines.* A basic premise is that a salesman's normal living costs will be covered by his salary and that such salary compensates him for normal performance.

DIRECTIVE EFFECTS OF BONUS PLANS

Bonus plans are generally established to encourage specific behaviors other than, or in addition to, those intended to increase immediate sales. For example, the firm may reward the development of a new application by a sales engineer, a shift of sales time to more profitable lines, or the expenditure of greater effort in prospecting even though the immediate payoff may be low. To avoid loss of motivation for any activity, the total number of factors used should be limited. Diffusion over more than three or, at the most, four factors may seriously weaken directive effects.

CUSTOMER EFFECTS OF BONUS PLANS

Because the salesman's principal earnings come from his salary, bonus plans tend to involve a somewhat lesser hazard of

---

[6] For an examination of the development and operation of salary-plus-incentive plans in 100 organizations, see *Incentive Plans for Salesmen.*
[7] *Incentive Plans for Salesmen,* Chapter 8.

adversary relationships with accounts. Moreover, bonus points can be provided for various services to customers including those which may not have immediate payoffs in sales.

PERSONNEL MANAGEMENT EFFECTS OF BONUS PLANS

Bonus plans offer a number of personnel management benefits. In fact, some are instituted to overcome salesman dissatisfaction with salary plans which are insufficiently sensitive to performance or to overcome personnel management or administrative problems in the use of commission plans.

A bonus plan may be useful to relieve "salary compression" brought about by tight recruiting situations. The salaries sometimes necessary to interest some recruits—for example, technical and professional graduates—in selling careers may be extremely high in relation to their production and to the salaries of senior men. A bonus plan provides a way of providing improved differentials for the productive men without permanently adding to fixed salary overhead.

An important advantage of bonus plans is that the behaviors to be rewarded can be modified from year to year without altering the basic compensation plan. Commission plans lack this flexibility.

ADMINISTRATIVE PROBLEMS WITH BONUS PLANS

Incentive plans which reward performance over quota, or some percentage of quota, are, of course, subject to all of the problems involved in setting quotas which are meaningful and perceived as equitable by the men.

Bonus plans are often designed to encourage a repertoire of behaviors leading to achievement of a number of goals. In such cases, a major administrative problem is to mold the bonus plan to fit corporate priorities and to modify the plan as new priorities emerge. As the incentive plan is one way in which priorities are communicated to the salesman, poor plan design can mislead the salesman as to *priorities* even though there is common agreement as to overall *goals*.

The president, concerned with payback period and return on investment in a new product and with financial and production officers expressing their concerns, may assign top priority to dollar volume of the new product sold *this year.* The marketing vice president, trying desperately to place enough of the new product on the shelves to block out the largest possible area from potential competition, considers the number of distributors which take on the new product as of considerably greater significance. In such circumstances, a compromise may be reached in which first-year volume and distributors secured both accrue bonus credits. This leaves the choice of priorities to each salesman. The incentive plan that is supposed to direct his efforts does not push him one way or the other. It fails to indicate the true priorities of the company's management. As a result, some salesmen may concentrate on getting maximum orders from their biggest accounts. Perhaps others will seek to secure distributors. In any case, the results are likely to be spotty so that neither goal is realized.[8]

SUMMARY

Compensation fulfills three functions: (a) It pays the salesman for his performance (which presumes some ability to measure performance); (b) It induces the salesman to align his goals with those of the company, and as a result, to behave in a manner tending to mutual benefit; and (c) It recompenses the salesman for his commitment to the firm—that is, the price paid for the use of a social resource.

Every compensation plan has (a) directive effects, (b) personnel management effects, and (c) customer effects.

Sound compensation plans must be developed in the context of intended salesman-customer relationships. A plan appropriate for one type of relationship can be most inappropriate for another.

Evaluation of compensation plans is largely a matter of estimating the prospective directive, personnel management, and customer effects of alternative plans. Growing customer orientation of markets suggests that the latter will increase in importance in evaluating compensation plans.

SELECTED READINGS

Day, Ralph L. and Peter D. Bennett, "Should Salesman's Compensation Be Geared to Profits?," *Journal of Marketing,* XXVI, No. 4 (October 1962), pp. 6–9. Gross margin and net contribution as bases for compensation

National Industrial Conference Board, Inc., *Incentive Plans for Salesmen.* Studies in Personnel Policy, No. 217. New York: National Industrial Conference Board, Inc., 1970. Use of incentive bonus plans

Tosdal, Harry R. and Waller Carson, Jr. *Salesman's Compensation,* Vols. I–II. Boston: Division of Research, Graduate School of Business Administration, Harvard University, 1953. The definitive reference on compensation

---

[8] Adapted from *Incentive Plans for Salesmen,* pp. 53–54.

Postscript

15 The Sales Force of The Future

Is there a social role for the salesman in an age of mass media, electronic communication, and automated data processing and goods handling? Does personal selling have a future? If so, what will that future be? How will personal selling change? What implications do prospective changes in the nature and role of personal selling have for the practice of sales-force management?

This chapter deals with these questions by (1) examining the changing environment as it affects the nature and role of personal selling, (2) forecasting changes in the role of personal selling in the economy, and (3) suggesting the implications which these changes and new managerial tools and capabilities will have for sales force management.

In speculating about the future, it is tempting to dwell on the managerial tools and electronic marvels which will make it *possible* to do things differently. The more fundamental changes, however, are likely to reflect that which is *desirable* in terms of overall system effectiveness. In terms of the future of personal selling and sales management, the more basic influences are those which are changing the relationships among people and between people and goods. It is these relationships which underlie the economic function of personal selling. Hence, attention will first be devoted to the question of what is likely to happen to the needs for interactive personal communication.

ENVIRONMENTAL CHANGES OF SIGNIFICANCE TO THE ROLE OF THE SALES FORCE

Five types of environmental change are likely to continue to exert important influence on the character and role of personal selling: (a) changes in user problems in the marketplace; (b) changes in users' abilities to deal with these problems; (c) changes in the resources and methods available to the salesman for his work and to the sales manager as inputs to the management process; (d) increased business size and responsibility; and (e) acceleration of the process of change.

Changes in User Problems

As societies become more affluent, people gain a wider choice over the needs which they can satisfy. In terms of Maslow's hierarchy, as more basic needs such as food become at least partially satisfied, other needs such as those for self-esteem, for the esteem of others, and for esthetic pleasures emerge and become prepotent.[1]

Moreover, a larger economy provides a wider choice of means for the satisfaction of a given type of need. The only form of economic security in some societies is in the ownership of arable land. In others, artifacts, silverware, or coin provide additional forms with the added element of transportability. In more developed cultures, the development of professional or technical skills may provide yet another form of meeting needs for economic security. To take another example, esteem needs may be met through physical or sexual prowess or self-adornment in most societies. In more developed ones, though, clothing, automobiles, homes, or travel experiences may be employed to meet these same needs. The point is not that groups differ in their ways of meeting different needs, but that the more affluent economy affords its members a broader selection of the means which each individual can employ to meet a particular need.

The size of markets in the more affluent economies also makes possible a wider selection of goods from which to choose within any

---

[1] The concept of a hierarchy of needs is examined in the Appendix to Chapter 12 with reference to the motivation of the salesman. Here, the same hierarchical principles are noted for their context in understanding consumer values at different income levels and in societies at different stages of development.

given general category. As markets grow, it becomes possible to offer a wider choice and thus to more nearly provide the product and service attributes which individual customers would consider optimal. The diseconomies of small scale production and distribution require that the variety of offerings be sharply limited in smaller markets. This is most notable in the case of goods which are susceptible to substantial production economies from long runs, such as is likely to characterize economies in the mass production stage of development. Consumers in such economies find that many classes of goods are available to them but that selection within a class is likely to be quite limited; the classic example is perhaps the famous Model T, which was available "in any color of the customer's choice provided it is black." Industries and economies break out of the mass production of identical products when their markets attain considerable size and become diverse enough and possess the economic power to demand more individualized treatment. In the U.S. this stage was reached in automobiles in the 1930s, appliances and housing in the late 1950s and early 1960s, and is now permeating many industries. On the production side, such tailoring to the diverse wants of individuals and groups becomes economically feasible with the development of mass-produced components so that a supplier can provide more or less unique, or at least customerized, assemblies from mass-produced components. Automated production processes which substantially reduce set-up costs promise to accelerate this tendency rapidly. The combined effects of widespread economic growth and automated technology in both production and communication indicate that the variety of products from which consumers can make their choices will continue to expand.

This breadth of choice extends to the services of supply as well as to the physical products used by consumers. Thus one may choose not only among means of transportation and makes and models of cars or trucks but whether one wishes to own, lease on a long-term basis, rent on an "as required" basis with or without drivers, or purchase the service from an independent contractor. Moreover, within even these choices one may select from among alternative methods of financing, for the arrangement of maintenance and operating services, and so on.

Not only does the industrial or household consumer have a wider variety of products and services from which to choose, the products themselves have become more complex. Many formerly nontechnical products are acquiring a technical content. The technology of others is becoming more complex as various features (for example, automatic controls) are added to improve performance in one or more applications. As a consequence, the user's problems of choice are, for most products, far more complex than in a simpler era. Not only is there more to go wrong with a complex product, there is more risk of not making the wisest choice because of insufficient understanding of the relative *performance consequences* of particular product attributes and attribute combinations. Which kind of paint is best for a particular type of application? Which textile is the most suitable in the light of particular application or use hazards (for example, exposure to strong sunlight, heavy traffic, particular kinds of soil or abuse)? The user is confronted with significant and often difficult problems of finding the best match of product to his particular need. As noted earlier, product attributes which are highly desirable in some applications may have little value or may even be undesirable in others. Thus, the user is confronted with a significant and often difficult problem of finding the best match of product to application.

The rapid pace of product development and technological change in both user needs and supplier offerings also adds to user problems. By the time he has had learning experience with an item, it has been supplanted by a new version. Even if the model purchased earlier and found satisfactory is still available (for example, a 1957 automatic washer) the buyer understandably prefers more recent models with additional features and improvements in serviceability or maintenance characteristics. As noted in Chapter 8, the pace of technological change is quickening. It promises to quicken even further as new competitors penetrate the innovational industries and as the consequences of these developments spread throughout the economy.

The overall result of wider consumer choices, greater complexity of the products from which choices are made, and accelerated rates of technological change is to make the buyer's selection problem more, rather than less, difficult. Thus, despite the growing role of unidirectional communication of all types (advertising, shelf markers, instruction tags, and so on), a substantial gap is likely to remain between what the buyer already knows from previous learning and what the buyer feels is necessary in making decisions.

Changes in Users' Ability to Deal with Buying and Consumption Problems

Consumers too have been changing. The level of education among buyers is rising everywhere. Consumers are more knowledgeable not only in the sense of formal education but through greater consumer mobility, expanded exposure to mass media, social and occupational contacts over a wider social and geographic area, and more extensive learning through purchase and/or use experience.

Consumers are becoming increasingly sophisticated in the understanding of products and product performance. Coupled with rising expectations as to performance, they are becoming more demanding in the quality of performance of products and those who supply them. One aspect of this increasing demand is the new strength recently evident in the forty-year-old consumer movement. As a result, the burden of both prescription and performance is being increasingly thrust on the supplier. This is most obvious in demands for increased government participation in consumer protection activities. Less obvious, but perhaps of greater overall significance, is the increased ability and willingness of consumers to shift sources of supply in response to shortcomings or perceived shortcomings in suppliers' services—including their advisory responsibility of providing and recommending appropriate products. The expanded number and, perhaps more importantly, growing variety of supply sources for most products has strengthened the market position of users of all types, household as well as industrial. Rising living standards, increased diversity of supplier types, increased mobility of consumers, and increased educational and experience levels are likely to make users even less willing to settle for a barely satisfactory product or a marginally tolerable supplier.

At least in the more advanced countries in which consumers enjoy some reasonable measure of sovereignty, neither "take it or leave it" products nor "take it or leave it" services are likely to survive for long. Consumers expect and will increasingly require that the level of performance (as to both products and services) of suppliers be raised. In particular, greater consumer information needs and greater consumer ability to enforce informative service behavior on suppliers will demand a much higher standard of system performance in providing consumers with information of decision value to them. This not only requires that unidirectional messages be more relevant and useful to the decision processes (for example, more informative advertising, labels, and tags) but that interactive communications (personal selling) must be improved in terms of its benefits to buyers.

Environmental Changes in Resources Available to Sales Management

Environmental changes affect the provision of sales-force service as well as the demands made upon it. A major factor in structuring the sales force of the future will be the growing cost of the use of people rather than machines. These rising costs have two types of effects. On the one hand, they make it desirable to shift to less costly means those activities which can suitably be shifted. This is a manifestation of the familiar substitution of capital for labor with rising labor costs and of fixed for variable costs with rising volumes of output. Thus we may expect continuation of the trend to substitute unidirectional for interactive communications media whenever unidirectional messages can meet the communications needs. This trend is already well advanced in persuading consumers to try many types of products including new types of durables, new forms of food and new types of recreation, and to accept or prefer new features in virtually every consumer product. Unidirectional communications have also made substantial headway in communicating new ideas to industry and to the trade. Because of technological advances, costs for unidirectional media tend to rise much more slowly than human personnel costs. This suggests further shifts of duties away from salespersons and toward unidirectional media for much, though by no means all, of the work historically performed by salesmen of type 4 (educators), type 5 (oral catalogue machines) and especially type 6 (routers or human signposts.)[2]

Improved data processing and communications technology will make these transformations increasingly feasible. The computer opens up the possibility of rapid, or even real-time, analysis and synthesis of inputs. Thus sales management can be informed more quickly and more thoroughly on the state of environmental factors, including those affecting opportunity or relevant to the deployment of effort. Automated feedback systems can and will provide vastly improved understanding of responses to sales efforts. Today's primitive and largely conjectural models of customer behavior will be replaced by models more carefully grounded in tested hypotheses. The result will be that the sales manager will be operating in an environment which, though more demanding on him, will provide him with somewhat better and more up-to-date readings on the environment in which he is working and the probable outcomes of various actions which might be taken.

Increased Business Size and Responsibility

Tendencies toward increased economic and social roles for large organizations will continue.

Several factors suggest that large organizations will increase their role in the economy. In addition to scale advantages, such organizations offer some advantages to consumers as people become more mobile. As many travelers can testify, consumer risk is reduced if the traveler, visitor, or new resident can select a familiar brand name or patronize a chain or franchised outlet (for example, McDonald's, Burger-King) with which he has some familiarity.

The privity doctrine is dying. Society increasingly expects the ultimate suppliers upon whom the consumer relies (for example, brand-name owners; franchisers) to accept responsibility to consum-

---

[2] For classifications of types of salesmen see Chapter 2.

ers and society for the activities of those who market their products. The discharge of these responsibilities will entail more concentration of authority in these organizations.

Demands for greater business responsibility to consumers, for the societal consequences of their activities (for example, pollution), and for dealing with larger areas of social concern (for example, overcoming the problems of poverty, minority groups) all favor the larger organization.

Finally, long-term survival and growth are generally important goals of corporate enterprise. Such firms are far more likely than family enterprises to view both business and social issues in their larger and longer-term perspectives.[3]

Acceleration of the Process of Change

The growing role of change as a social process in its own right has important ramifications for both personal selling and sales management. For selling, more rapid change thrusts an even larger burden on the salesman as change agent and as aide to the buyer faced with the need to solve his problems in a changing world in which his own learning rapidly becomes obsolete.

For sales management, acceleration of the process of change requires that adjusting to change will be a growing problem.

The future role of personal selling and of sales management will be conditioned largely by environmental changes affecting buyers and similar changes that affect the conditions under which sales forces must operate. Wider choices, more complex products, and more rapid change all tend to make both industrial and consumer buying problems more difficult. Fortunately for buyers, their ability to deal with these problems will continue to improve through more and better education, greater sophistication in the marketplace, and a social environment which places greater responsibilities on suppliers.

These conditions will place increasingly greater responsibilities on suppliers to aid buyers in their choices in the marketplace and to provide leadership for constructive change. The character of personal selling will change in response to these factors. The next section examines the role of personal selling in the society of the future.

---

[3] Long-term survival and growth, while generally important goals of corporate enterprise, are much less significant in family enterprise. The greater market orientation of modern business may thus be due, in part, to the major role of corporate capitalism and the relative decline of family capitalism. In less developed economies in which family capitalism still dominates, sellers, especially in the trades, are much more likely to view the system as a disposal-for-profit, rather than a supply-for-consumer, system.

PERSONAL SELLING IN THE SOCIETY OF THE FUTURE

The strong environmental forces at work will further strengthen the power of the consumer, not only in individual dealings in the marketplace but as director of what the economy will produce. Personal selling, like other marketing institutions, will increasingly become a service to consumers rather than a disposal system for producers.

This is not to say that sellers will not seek to use the most sophisticated tools available to "manage" sales forces so as to further long-term profit-seeking goals. Rather those goals must be viewed in the broader social context in which profits serve as the lubricant which makes the system run for the benefit of consumers rather than as the ultimate goal of a producer-directed economy. The pace of change may well be open to question. But the direction seems clear. Our affluent economy has the technical capability to produce wide varieties of goods and services. It is subject to continual adjustment, largely— but by no means solely—through market forces. It well may be closer than societies have yet been to the kind of social good through private goal seeking to which Adam Smith referred nearly two hundred years ago in arguing that an "invisible hand" would convert actions of individuals taken in self-love into the common good.

This optimistic view does not propose that charlatans and seekers of the fast buck will suddenly disappear. To the contrary, regulatory and other social forces will be required to keep such practices in check as in the past. But recent history makes clear that in selling, as in other facets of business, honesty and service to the market are the most profitable—possibly the only—courses of action for the business which wishes to survive and grow. Such firms are rapidly displacing market mining operations; there is no reason to suspect that this tendency will be reversed.

Continued Decline of Heavily Unidirectional Personal Selling Activities

The use of personal salesmen for the delivery of unidirectional messages is hard to justify even today. With continued development of print, and especially electronic, media the use of personal salesmen to deliver messages which can be provided in identical form to many buyers seems destined to decline further. Persuasion to inform and promote change in these circumstances hardly warrants one-to-one human contact. The salesman with the standard pitch thus seems likely to decline for the same reason that self-selection has displaced the salesman in the buyer goods collecting process wherever a standard message, label, or sign would meet buyer needs.

The use of salesmen merely to indicate what is available (as oral catalogue machines) and primarily to route buyers to goods (as human signposts) seems likely to disappear while their use as educators is likely to decline for less technical products. Salesmen performing this type of duty, if they are to survive, will need to shift toward an interactive service *of value to the buyer.* Where the buyer needs no such personalized guidance or assistance, the decline and eventual demise of the personal salesman seems indicated.

Greater Importance of Salesmen as Interactive Change Agents

An abundant economy provides a wider selection of goods so that each user can more precisely meet his needs. A rapidly changing set of offerings presents users with increased difficulties in making optimal choices. As a consequence, the number of situations in which the buyer can benefit from informed assistance in the selection process will grow.

INDUSTRIAL AND INSTITUTIONAL MARKETS

Personal selling will grow most rapidly in serving industrial and institutional markets. Operating in the vanguard of rapid change, participation in problem discovery, assistance in problem solving, and advising on applications will be the principal growth areas. Even in so-called commodity-type products, the development of product variants bearing attributes of particular value to particular kinds of users is increasing rapidly. Often these attributes are variants in the products themselves; at other times they come in the form of tailored packaging, technical aid, integrated scheduling of supplier and user operations, or other services which add value for the buyer. The industrial salesman will play a growing role as such quality-service factors become increasingly important as the basis of buyers' supplier selection decisions. To perform these tasks well, the industrial salesman will necessarily be more of a learner about the customer's business than a teller about his own products and firm.

SALES TO THE TRADE

Sales to resellers will be heavily interactive and in the context of helping the customer to be a more effective and responsible merchant. In the words of one wholesaler: *"The salesman who has only merchandise has nothing to sell."*

This is hardly new. Practices such as "loading the merchant" have been on the decline for at least four decades. Salesmen to the trade have remained important as educators (showing new lines) and as catalogue machines (indicating what is available). These two roles seem destined to be limited as improved and less costly transport enable successively smaller merchants to attend trade shows or to shop in major supply markets. Moreover, as the importance of the one-man shop declines, so does the need for the merchant to do as much buying as possible without leaving the shop.

Despite the growth of massive retail organizations, much small scale retailing will remain, especially in innovative lines, in specialty categories, and in situations particularly suited to small or local retailing (for example, certain closely knit communities). Salesmen will still provide a major supply service to these retailers.

Much of the informational work now performed by travelers will be provided by electronic means or print media. The survival of the traveler of the future will depend on his ability to provide *services to buyers* which cannot be routinized by these or similar means and which require human interactions for the best results. The store advisors now provided by voluntary chain wholesalers in lieu of salesmen suggest the kind of role which suppliers' salesmen will perform for smaller and moderate sized retailers. They will be an essential part of the *internal* communication structure of the independent supplier-retailer consumer support system as that system competes with other systems for consumer patronage. Such salesmen will need to become expert in the operation of customer businesses if they are to offer meaningful assistance in this activity.

The role of salesmen calling on large retail organizations is also becoming more demanding. The salesman may need to convince increasingly sophisticated headquarters personnel of the merits of the products and deals which he is offering and that their common interest is best served by providing a maximum of shelf space for his product. Generally this is in a context of intensive competition with rivals for the same positions on the shelf or participation in promotional activities. Increasingly sophisticated headquarters personnel and store managers will require that the salesman calling on them be able to demonstrate that the sales, inventory management, and control effects of his proposals will serve the store's goals more effectively than those of competitors. Moreover, if he misleads or misinforms, the buyer's information feedbacks will in all likelihood find him out so that the long-term effects of a "successful" sale well may be adverse.

RETAIL SELLING

The consumer also is faced with more difficult problems of choice. Open displays, labels and tags, and print and electronic media provide the buyer with a plethora of data about what is available. Competitive forces, social pressures, and governmental activity will insure that even more such data will be provided in the future. The consumer's problem is thus likely to be one of choosing which is best for his particular needs. It is at this point that the buyer can benefit from assistance.

In some lines such as insurance counseling, investment advising, and interior decoration, distinctive occupations have already developed to meet consumers' needs for guidance. For most products, however, the buyer relies upon the informed salesman for assistance in choosing that which best fits his particular needs and intended usage. Retail selling has been moving in this direction for some time. In the future, however, we may expect that the old-time retail sales opening "May I help you?" will be taken literally by consumers; it will no longer be a convenient opener for a stock sales line. In this context, the role of the salesman as a receiver and interpreter of information from customers becomes more significant.

E. B. Weiss has argued that "retail salesmen can't be trained; and shouldn't be". The argument appears to rest on a view of the retail salesman as a mere clerical goods deliverer, a type of activity which we have excluded from the definition of salesman. As stated in the previous section, the salesperson who does nothing *for the buyer* will occupy a tenuous role at best. The use of sales persons in retail stores is thus likely to be concentrated in those situations in which the buyer is likely to need selection assistance or information of a type which cannot be portrayed by tags, labels, or other print or electronic media. Such salesmen will need considerable training if they are to achieve competence in understanding buyers' needs and interpreting cues obtained from them. The continuing interest of retailers in sales training and in securing manufacturer help to increase the competence of retail salespersons attests to this need.

If the future of personal selling at retail is to lie largely in consumer advisory activity, both the training and the organization of personal selling in retail stores will need to be changed. The salesman-advisor will, in many lines, need substantial proficiency in technical matters, especially the performance characteristics of alternative products under various use conditions. Such proficiency is found in few retail sales persons today. It probably could not be developed in the majority of retail sales personnel, even if stores could afford it, which they cannot. This suggests that the division of labor in stores must be carried further. Specifically, the three functions usually performed by retail sales persons will need to be separated. The *transactional* function can be performed mechanically or by a clerk trained only in transactional routines. The *reference* function (Where is it? Do you have it? Does it come in green? Is it machine washable?) is largely a matter of providing simple attribute information. Much of this can be provided by signs, displays, and tags. Sales persons performing this function require knowledge only of the line carried, its basic attributes, and its location. The *advisory* function entails buyer assistance in product selection for particular use situations. A major problem in retail stores today is that the salespersons are expected to be multifunctional and are, as a consequence, trained to do none of the jobs well. The task which is growing in importance in a consumeristic society is performed the least well!

If the advisory function is recognized as a distinct job, persons could be trained as specialists in providing that advice on particular product lines in much the same way as technical specialists function in industrial markets. Large retail organizations could afford such specialists in consumer aid as their numbers would not need to be large if their work was confined to their respective fields of expertise. A department store with several branches, for example, might require only one carpet advisor on duty in its main store. Customers desiring to interact with a technically knowledgeable person would be referred to this individual. Branch stores could secure access to him through closed circuit audio-visual systems or, where appropriate, the customer could be referred to the main store. In short, instead of having many multipurpose salesmen throughout the store system, none of whom are fully qualified to assist the consumer with application problems, a single purpose, centrally located advisor might assume this role.[4]

Small specialty stores well might develop on the basis of the knowledgeable advice which they can provide a particular customer group.

The common thread in all three types of markets—industrial, trade, and consumer—requires that the salesman of the future will be even more of a *learner* and less of a talker than has been the case until quite recently. His competence in understanding the other party's situation will increasingly dominate the need for mere presentation skills.

Growing Role of the Intelligence Function

In all fields, the role of the salesman as an intelligence gatherer will grow. As the economy becomes more and more directed by buyers and users rather than by producers, the intelligence function assumes paramount importance in the selling organization. While much intelligence can, and undoubtedly will, be obtained through marketing research activities, much can only come through the salesman's day-to-day contact with the market if it is to be relevant and timely. The

---

[4] Interior decorators have had similar relationships to the sales organization in some department stores for at least a quarter century.

salesman of the future will thus be a major factor in changing *his company* as well as a force in changing *his customers*.

IMPLICATIONS FOR SALES-FORCE MANAGEMENT

Changes in the environment, in the nature of the personal selling job and in the tools which modern management technology provides for the sales manager will affect virtually every facet of the sales management process. Some of the more significant directions in which sales management will change will be noted briefly.

Greater Precision in Defining the Role of the Salesman

The high costs, both of acquiring and keeping the salesman in the field and in terms of lost opportunities, demand that the job of the salesman in a particular situation be much more precisely defined than has been customary. Long lists of duties which now constitute the job description of many salesmen are likely to be superceded by a careful determination of the ways and conditions under which personal interaction is meaningful in terms of the *buying system's* frame of reference. With this understanding, those activities which involve primarily unidirectional communication can be transferred to appropriate media. At the same time, order filling and raw data-providing activities will be routinized and mechanized. A major management responsibility will be to remove from the personal selling responsibility those functions which are no longer appropriate and continually to redefine the nature and scope of the duties of particular sales forces. As noted earlier (Chapter 3), these duties change with the development and maturity not only of products but of relationships between buying and selling systems.

The changing role of the salesman will lead eventually to an upward change in the status of the salesman in the community.

Greater Attention to Communications Needs in Sales-Force Organization

Overcoming *geographic* distance is becoming less costly, as nearly any location can be reached without loss of a business day, and with the decline of telephone tolls. At the same time, overcoming *conceptual* distance becomes more difficult as a result of product and service proliferation and the increased specialization of tasks, skills, and abilities in using as well as supplying organizations. Moreover "Zook's Law" ("Everything is more complicated than it seems") is getting ever-widening applicability. As a consequence, territories will increasingly be defined in terms of market segments which have similar problems in their buyer-seller relationships rather than on the basis of geographic space. At the very least, individual salesmen can thus develop the needed expertise to deal with market segments with more or less common buying problems and interactive needs rather than attempting to be all knowledgeable to a variety of buyers whose only common feature is where they are located on a map.

Expansion of Real-Time Information Systems

Market development of voice-to-computer and facsimile transmissions already in existence and imminent improvements in information handling technology and capability suggest that much of the communication between salesmen and their offices will be on a real-time basis. Thus a salesman will be able to obtain current information both of a briefing type and in response to his queries on an instantaneous basis. Much present report preparation will be transferred to machines without loss of its currency.

Improved Abilities to Measure Opportunities and Response Functions

Better data, improved means for data collection and processing into intelligence, and better understanding of relationships through more extensive and formalized hypothesis testing will provide the salesman and the sales manager with a better understanding and measurement of opportunities and their constituents than we have today. Moreover, increased sophistication will lead to greater appreciation of the effects of "treatments."

In particular, wider use of both observational and experimental studies will provide sales managers with a more objective understanding of response functions of various groups so that effort may be deployed more effectively. At the same time, a greater understanding of the interactive nature of personal selling, as opposed to the view of the salesman as doer and the prospect as passive responder, will hopefully temper any tendency to depersonalize personal selling to the application of successful formulae. Interaction will remain an art.

Improved Selection Procedures

Selection procedures in many companies do not fully utilize available techniques for measuring individual differences and relating them to job performance. Both societal and competitive pressures will require improvements in both selection and assignment. In addition to wider application of what is presently known, new knowledge secured from directly relevant studies should lead to further improvements.

Increased Use of Quantitative Tools for the Deployment of Effort and Salesman Support

Quantitative tools are particularly suitable for such effort-deployment problems as the development of optimal routes and schedules and the allocation of time among various activities. They are also useful for the improvement of paper and material flows and other salesman-support activities. Wider use of quantitative tools for those portions of the salesman's work which are not human-interactive seems certain.

Reorientation of Training Activities Toward the New Role of the Salesman

Training will move away from heavy reliance on product knowledge and toward increased attention to users' problems. This is necessary not only so that the salesman can be competent to deal with the customers' problems but also so that he can communicate with them. Viable communication generally requires a common language which in turn requires at least some measure of common experience. Thus the salesman must understand the buyer's position not only to help with his problems but just to communicate effectively.

Salesmen's training will also need to help the salesman develop an ability to grasp the consequences of an everchanging environment. It will thus take on more the character of a liberal education to enable him to better understand and deal with the world around him.

Training emphasis on methods of presenting ideas and information to buyers will be gradually replaced with an emphasis on the perceptual and diagnostic needs required for salesman competence. In personal selling, "How to understand what the man is trying to tell us," will inevitably displace "How to tell the man about our wonderful products." Although the development of persuasive skills will remain a part of the salesman's need, the development of his perceptual skills must eventually dominate.

Training practices themselves will be substantially improved. Among the factors which will lead to this improvement are increased knowledge of the learning processes and the diffusion of that knowledge, new pedagogical techniques, and more widespread validation of training programs through measurement of their effects on trainees' job behavior.

Enlarged Role for Competence-Maintenance Activities

The changing role of the salesman and the pervasive effects of accelerated technological and environmental change will require much more extensive competence maintenance activity than is currently popular. Regular retraining for competence maintenance will become an important activity of sales management. Despite more effective communication methods (for example, casettes) the average salesman is likely to spend a greater proportion of his working year in maintaining his competence than is currently the case.

Less Hierarchical Supervision

Major breakthroughs in the behavioral sciences are likely to have widespread effects on the supervisory process. Even the limited understanding which we have today suggests that salesman-supervisor relationships will become more participative and interactive and less hierarchical.

Increased Role of Intangible Personal Goals

In a society characterized by affluence and occupational mobility, physiological and safety needs become less dominant. Higher level goals (in terms of Maslow's hierarchy) such as esteem, esthetic, and self-actualization needs become more prepotent. As a result, money rewards have less significance. Supervisors will need to appeal increasingly to esteem, knowledge, and self-actualization goals.

Recruiting will place less stress on potential income and more on job challenge and helping solve individual and societal problems. In compensation, money will be somewhat less important and sense of accomplishment of worthwhile things more significant.

Increased Attention to Manpower Development

Manpower development for tomorrow will supplant sales volume for today as the central responsibility of many supervisors. Individual differences in abilities and interests will be increasingly recognized. In many firms this will include provision for increased levels of account responsibility, based upon competence and performance, for those who are not appropriately moved into managerial positions. As the differences between the work of field salesmen and managers grow wider, the need to properly reward each type of work on its own merit will increase. Career path concepts are useful in dealing with this problem.

More Sophisticated Evaluation Tools

A more general understanding of the role of the salesman in developing and maintaining relationships will spur the search for more relevent evaluation methods. Improved data processing capability and sharper concepts should at the same time enable managers to develop more meaningful yardsticks for evaluating and rewarding performance. Adjustments of compensation on the basis of overall performance will become feasible for a larger number of firms. Straight commission and other compensation plans based on mechanistic formulae are likely to decline. This decline is likely to be furthered by the changing role of the salesman himself, with the sharpest growth in personal selling being in the types of work not readily amenable to measurements confined to immediate payoffs.

Greater Objectivity in the Management Process

In sales management, as in other facets of marketing, progress will be made in replacing rule of thumb decisions based on untested hypotheses with more formal decision processes and more objective determinations of association and of causation. This does not mean that management will become a mechanistic process. On the contrary, many inputs to the management process will necessarily remain subjective. In addition, one must remember that human behavior is probabilistic rather than deterministic. People will still be people. They will forget, make mistakes, and have personal likes and dislikes toward people and things.

Increased Emphasis on the Monitoring of Change

With accelerated change and the competitive need for high performance, managements will find it necessary to devote more efforts to monitoring change and attempting to understand its implications. As the trend toward market orientation expands, the need to watch the changing needs of various individual, business, and social groups will become even more critical.

Internal records will have to be more thoroughly analyzed for use as early warning systems. Changes in response functions to different offers or to the use of different approaches by the salesmen may provide the clues to changes in the buying processes which are needed if the selling organization is to keep aligned with changes in what buyers need from the interactive process.

In general, relatively more effort will have to be devoted to the process of adjusting the sales organization to a changing world and relatively less to operating the system in the (ever-shortening) "present" situation.

SUMMARY

The changing environment is eliminating the need for personal selling where only unidirectional messages of information and persuasion are needed. High personnel costs are reinforcing this trend. At the same time, environmental forces are strengthening the need for personal salesmen to assist consumers and industrial buyers in choosing among an increasingly specialized array of offerings. A result is that the salesman of the future will be much more a provider of advisory service to buyers than a pusher of products for his employer.

This role implies that the salesman will be more independent in his actions in the field, and at the same time more closely tied to the firm's communication system of which system he will be both a major information user, and a major information provider.

These changes have many implications for sales management. It will be mandatory to define the salesman's role more precisely when the cost of keeping him in the field is high and he enjoys substantial independence of operation, being tied to his employer largely by common goals. Developing manpower and maintaining its competence will become even more important sales management responsibilities. Much of present day supervision may be superceded by self-management by the salesmen themselves; other more routine duties can be programmed and handled mechanically or electronically.

Improved managerial tools will provide better data on opportunities and response functions and will permit more effective deployment in the field. More sophisticated evaluation measures and more objective managerial tools will improve performance of both salesmen and managers.

Human interaction fills an important need in the consumer support system of a user-directed economy. Personal selling must fill that need. Sales management must develop and orient the selling function toward that end.

Index

A